A History of Russia
and Its Empire

A History of Russia and Its Empire

From Mikhail Romanov to Vladimir Putin

Kees Boterbloem

ROWMAN & LITTLEFIELD PUBLISHERS, INC.

Lanham • Boulder • New York • Toronto • Plymouth, UK

Published by Rowman & Littlefield
4501 Forbes Boulevard, Suite 200, Lanham, Maryland 20706
www.rowman.com

10 Thornbury Road, Plymouth PL6 7PP, United Kingdom

British Library Cataloguing in Publication Information Available

Library of Congress Cataloging-in-Publication Data

Boterbloem, Kees, 1962– author.
  A history of Russia and its empire : from Mikhail Romanov to Vladimir Putin / Kees Boterbloem.
    pages ; cm
  Includes bibliographical references and index.
  ISBN 978-0-7425-6838-9 (cloth : alk. paper) — ISBN 978-0-7425-6839-6 (pbk. : alk. paper) — ISBN 978-0-7425-6840-2 (electronic) 1. Russia—History. 2. Soviet Union—History. 3. Russia (Federation)—History—1991– I. Title.
  DK40.B596 2014
  947.08—dc23
                                                                    2013013853

♾️™ The paper used in this publication meets the minimum requirements of American National Standard for Information Sciences—Permanence of Paper for Printed Library Materials, ANSI/NISO Z39.48-1992.

Printed in the United States of America

Contents

Preface

A textbook can never do proper justice to the past of a country as vast and complex as Russia in its various incarnations since 1613. Then again, no work of history has ever been able to present a truly comprehensive or exhaustive depiction of the past (and some may say that works of literature, such as Joyce's *Ulysses* or Proust's *In Search of Lost Time*, have been more successful at doing this than any history book). Given the limits to this volume's size, I can merely touch on certain things and will omit vast parts of Russian history, let alone Ukrainian, Kazakh, or Georgian history. But I have tried to include something of the history of the predominantly non-Russian parts of the former Russian Empire and Soviet Union; the manner through which these parts were incorporated into Russia; and the relationship between the Russian center with the non-Russian periphery thereafter. For, before 1991, it can be argued that this was the last of the great "multinational" empires, a country in which almost two hundred distinct ethnocultural groups lived, rather than a nation-state.

And I have placed a fair amount of emphasis on the fact that this empire was continually faced with challenges from other polities on its borders and far away from them. Russia may be seen as a "civilization" sui generis, as Marshall Poe recently suggested, or a distinct "intelligible field of study" for the historian, as Arnold Toynbee much longer ago proposed (Toynbee added the other Eastern European Orthodox countries to this "field"), but its history cannot be understood in isolation. The relevance of this history becomes more evident to the reader if it is embedded in a broader discussion of world history. Again, a discerning reader will undoubtedly be disappointed in this respect, for my outlining of the international cross-cultural contacts that left an imprint on Russian and Soviet history merely skims the surface.

Inevitably, more attention has been given to nineteenth- and especially twentieth-century developments. This is partly the consequence of the greater amount of writing from and about these centuries. Furthermore, more recent developments will be of greater interest to most readers. It is particularly from approximately 1812 onward, too, that Russian history acquired a greater-than-regional significance that goes beyond the history of eastern (or northern) Europe and northern Asia. Obviously, this importance dramatically increased from 1917 onward. Because of its global significance, Soviet history takes up a large part of this book. Meanwhile, the more than twenty years that have passed since the implosion of 1991 have begun to allow historians to place the Soviet experiment somewhat more clearly within the general historical development of Russian history, as I have tried to do in the following pages.

Political developments provide the narrative framework of this book, which may be appropriate for an empire in which politics took such a priority, especially in recent times. But I am sure that this emphasis will not please all readers. Perhaps less obvious in the following pages will be my conviction that one of the few constants in Russian history is the absence of the rule of law. In tsarist times, the autocrat stood above the law and ruled in a wholly arbitrary manner. Tsar and subjects alike equally ignored the law. In Soviet times, too, despite an elaborate codex, the regime systematically ignored its own laws and, in response, so did its subjects. And since 1991, arbitrary rule has once again gained ground, not just in Russia, but also in most of the other states that have succeeded the Soviet Union.

Irrespective of the book's political emphasis and my view about the perpetual absence of a Kantian Rechtsstaat in Russia, and despite the omissions and the somewhat greater weight given to more recent history, it is nonetheless my aim to have the reader come away from studying this book with a basic (albeit undoubtedly colored by my interest and selection) understanding of the last four hundred years of history of the people who populate the vast territory from St. Petersburg to Vladivostok and from Arkhangel'sk to Baku today. The text is intended as an introduction to Russian history, and not as the final word on it. I nonetheless hope that the reader will be sufficiently intrigued after perusing the following pages to pursue the study of all or parts of Russian history in greater depth.

The text has been organized in ten fairly sizable chapters, so that it can be used in almost any one-term college-level survey of Russian and Soviet history, regardless of the length of the term. If the book is used as a course textbook, instructors might have their students read some fiction, as well as watch films, listen to music, and so on, for such cultural products often bring the past much more quickly to life than any textbook can. Bountiful material in this regard (including many more excellent maps) is available and easily accessible on the Internet these days, and I have suggested some websites. Likewise, many fine collections of primary sources (translated from the original Russian) are available in English for both the Imperial and Soviet periods. Some primary sources (in English) are suggested at the end of each chapter, but almost all Russian-language sources available in print or online have been excluded, as most of the book's readers are presumed to have no reading knowledge of Russian. The reader is encouraged to further explore Russian history by my listing of some key scholarly works available in English (especially recent ones), as well as some Russian-language films (some of which are downloadable from the Internet for a fee, whereas others are, alas, difficult to find and a few remain without English subtitles). And in order to help readers find their way through the text, I have included at the end a chronology of the most important developments and events. I have not had the temerity to suggest any music, in which Russian culture is especially rich (from Ukrainian choirs and Pussy Riot, Nautilus Pompilius, and Vladimir Vysotskii to Glinka and Schnittke), ballet, or opera.

Acknowledgments

This book would never have been produced without the initiative of my two good friends, Ben Whisenhunt and Steven Usitalo. The project was kept alive through the enthusiasm of my editor at Rowman & Littlefield, Susan McEachern, who kept faith in its completion despite all sorts of delays. Thanks as well to Carolyn Broadwell-Tkach, Jehanne Schweitzer, and Naomi Burns at Rowman & Littlefield for all their aid in seeing this through. In Tampa, Derek van der Velde and Ben Sperduto were extremely helpful with the maps.

Almost a quarter century of teaching Russian history to students at McGill University, Nipissing University, and the University of South Florida informs the text. Several of my teachers (some of whom have passed away since) deserve thanks for their role in inspiring this book and contributing to my career as a historian, of whom Jan-Willem Bezemer and Willem Roobol in Amsterdam, Valentin Boss in Montreal, Philip Longworth in London, and Andrei Nikolaevich Sakharov in Moscow deserve special mention. Of those colleagues I met later, I am particularly grateful to Daniel Kaiser, David Schimmelpenninck van der Oye, Erik van Ree, Marc Jansen, Bruno Naarden, Jeffrey Veidlinger, Hiroaki Kuromiya, Norman Pereira, Paul Robinson, Steven High, Barbara Lorenzkowski, Anne Clendenning, Victor Peppard, Golfo Alexopoulos, Michael Decker, Bill Cummings, Jack Tunstall, John Belohlavek, Carola Tischler, Jan Foitzik, and Marshall Poe. This book would never have been completed were it not for the constant love and support of Susan, Duncan, and Saskia Mooney.

Note on Transcription

The transcription of Russian words and names largely follows that of the Library of Congress with the following exceptions: I have replaced the *ё* with a *yo*, as this letter is pronounced (therefore, "Semyon" rather than "Semen" or "Semën"). Names starting with *E* are rendered *Ye* (thus, "Yezhov" rather than "Ezhov"). "Iurii" has become "Yuri" in the case of Piatakov and Andropov. And Russian names that are well known in one version in English I have rendered as such (for example, "Tchaikovsky" or "Dostoyevsky").

Boundary marker between Europe and Asia (Prokudin-Gorskii Collection, Library of Congress)

1

The Rise of Russia in the Seventeenth Century, 1613–1689

Between 1598 and 1613, Russia was torn asunder by a civil war usually known as the "Time of Troubles" in English. The strife calmed down fairly quickly, once Mikhail Romanov was elected tsar. The first Romanovs not only restored a semblance of order in Muscovy but also made Russia into the preeminent state in northeastern Europe by 1700. This chapter discusses how they did that and what sort of state and society the first Romanov tsars ruled.

THE ROMANOV DYNASTY: MIKHAIL

In 1613, Mikhail Romanov (1596–1645) was chosen to be the tsar of Muscovy, a remote monarchy in existential danger on the outskirts of Asia and Europe. Muscovy, which only around that time began to be called Russia by Western Europeans—who knew very little about it—was populated primarily by Christians who pledged allegiance to Eastern Orthodoxy. They spoke an Eastern Slavic language, called Russian.

Their country, which had been a sparsely populated, albeit large, regional power on the Eastern European Plain during the sixteenth century, had done without a ruler for three years. Russia's plight was so dire that the Polish king Sigismund Wasa (1566–1632) and his son Wladyslaw (1595–1648) claimed the tsar's throne, while their soldiers occupied Moscow. The starving Poles were ousted after a siege by an army of Russians and Cossacks in 1612, inspired largely by a call from the Russian Orthodox Church's Patriarch Germogen (ca. 1530–1612), who had soon thereafter died in confinement in a monastery. The head of the Russian Church succeeded in rallying the believers where others had failed in the previous fifteen years. During this spell (often called the Time of Troubles, or Smuta), the country had been ruined because of armed conflict regarding the legitimacy of a series of claimants to the throne, a devastating

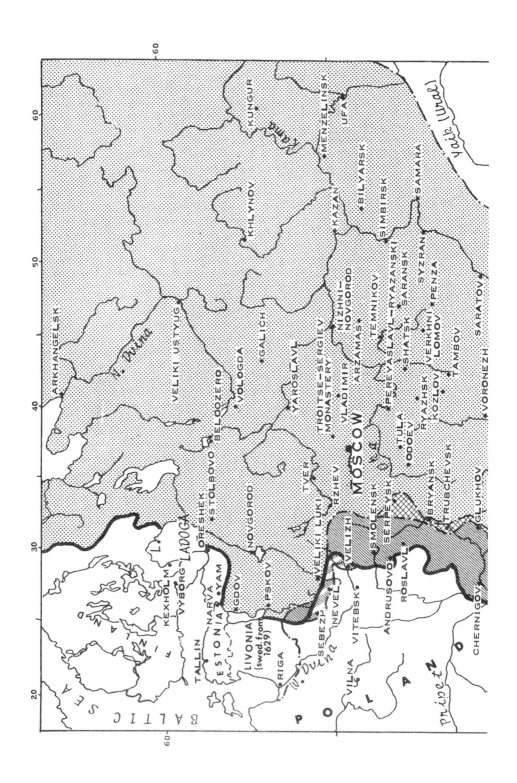

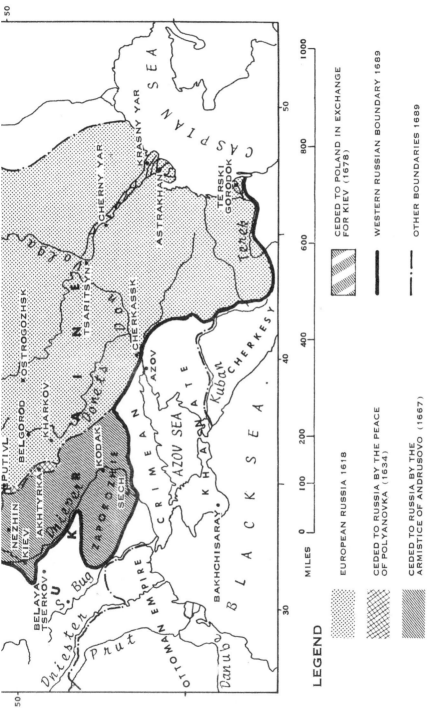

Map 1.1. European Russia, 1618–1689 (From Allen F. Chew, *An Atlas of Russian History*, New Haven, CT: Yale University Press, 1967. Used by permission.)

LEGEND

MILES

EUROPEAN RUSSIA 1618

CEDED TO RUSSIA BY THE PEACE OF POLYANOVKA (1634)

CEDED TO RUSSIA BY THE ARMISTICE OF ANDRUSOVO (1667)

CEDED TO POLAND IN EXCHANGE FOR KIEV (1678)

WESTERN RUSSIAN BOUNDARY 1689

OTHER BOUNDARIES 1689

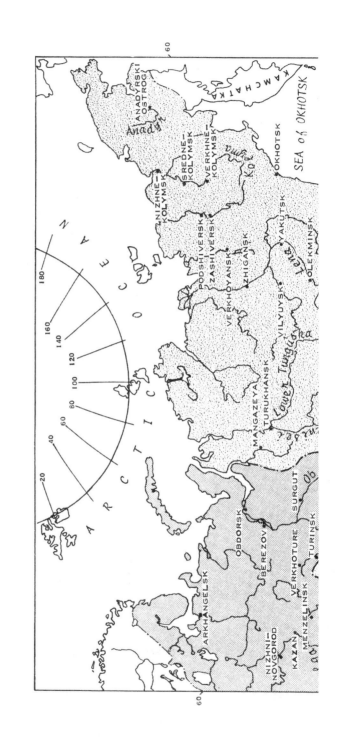

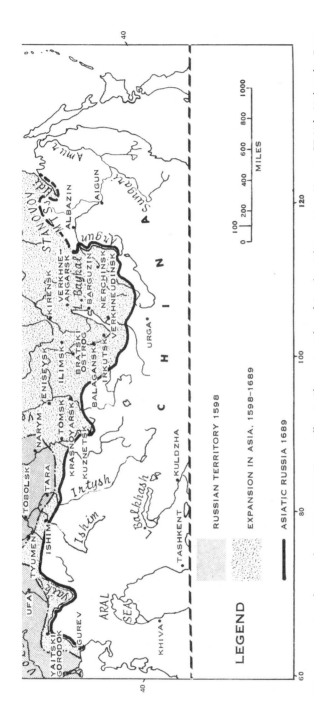

Map 1.2. Eastward expansion, 1598–1689 (From Allen F. Chew, *An Atlas of Russian History*, New Haven, CT: Yale University Press, 1967. Used by permission.)

famine, and various foreign invasions. Many proclaimed themselves to be tsar, but no one was recognized by all who mattered (especially the nobility, as it served as the country's military), until the patriarch called for the ouster of the Polish Catholic heretics who had defiled Russia's most sacred places in Moscow's Kremlin.

That it was Mikhail Romanov who was chosen to be tsar was the consequence of several considerations among Muscovy's political and religious leaders. In the first place, his great-aunt was the first wife (Anastasia, 1530–1560) of the last tsar whose rule had been uncontested, Ivan IV (1530–1584, ruled 1547–1584). Second, despite belonging to a prominent family, Mikhail was not associated with any particular faction in the civil war that had laid waste to Muscovy, because he was a mere teenager. His father, the Boyar (high nobleman) Fyodor Nikitich Romanov (1553–1633), had been forced by Tsar Boris Godunov (1552–1605) to take the tonsure (become a monk) and divorce Mikhail's mother (Kseniia Shestova, d. 1631), who was coerced to become a nun.

When he entered the monastery in 1601, Fyodor Nikitich had assumed the name Filaret. Filaret returned to prominence after the ouster of the Godunovs. In 1605, Filaret was made metropolitan of Rostov by one of Godunov's short-lived successors. This made Filaret the second-highest-ranking prelate in the Russian Orthodox Church. Filaret had fallen into Polish captivity in 1610 but remained a highly respected and authoritative figure in Muscovite political life. When his son was elected tsar, the patriarchal seat was left open to await Filaret's return, which occurred only after the conclusion of the Truce of Deulino of 1619 with Poland. Filaret was then duly installed as patriarch and was to rule Russia together with Mikhail.

Without his father's counsel, however, Mikhail needed to rely on others at the court. He could ill afford to banish all those from court who had been tainted by their previous collaboration with the disgraced regimes that had preceded his own. Few outside the "liberation army," which had been led by nobles of lesser rank and even some commoners, had clean hands in this respect. Indeed, since war with Sweden (with which peace was signed only in 1617), Poland-Lithuania, and a variety of pretenders to the throne was ongoing in 1613, settling scores with collaborators was not a wise strategy. The young tsar met fairly regularly during the 1610s with an advisory council (Zemskii Sobor or "Assembly of the Land"), in which representatives of all those who were not serfs (peasants tied to their lord's land) gathered to discuss matters of state with the monarch.

Mikhail met more regularly with an inner council, often called the Boyar Duma by historians, in which only the boyars had a seat, as well as some of the church leaders and top bureaucrats, a few dozen men in total. In this council could be found Mikhail's key advisors, such as Prince (Kniaz)[1] Ivan Borisovich Cherkasskii (ca. 1580–1642) and Prince Aleksei Mikhailovich L'vov (ca. 1580–ca. 1653), as well as, eventually, his father.

Mikhail's rule was geared primarily toward consolidation, but Muscovy recovered surprisingly quickly. Buoyed by this revival, an impatient and vengeful Filaret persuaded his son to declare war on Poland in 1632 in order to recover the border town of Smolensk.

The campaign failed, but the fact that it could be mounted at all speaks to a remarkable turnaround. Further indicative of this newfound strength was the Russian ability to deploy thousands of expensive foreign mercenaries in this war (1632–1634). And it was in Mikhail's reign that Russian explorers reached the Pacific Sea, confirming Russia's rule over the vast territory of Siberia.

THE ROMANOV DYNASTY: ALEKSEI

Mikhail's son Aleksei (1629–1676) was the same age as his father when he succeeded in 1645. All was not well in his realm, for he was faced with a series of rebellions, including in Moscow, in the first years of his reign. The revolts seem to have been the expression of an accumulation of grievances that had been festering for some years. Although Muscovy had recovered from the Time of Troubles under Mikhail, the government had stretched the country's resources to the limit in the lean circumstances of the onset of the Little Ice Age (1550–1650). The tsar's advisors especially became the target of popular wrath (some were slaughtered by a crowd in Moscow in 1648), but the causes of the unrest should be sought beyond poor advice. Whereas

Figure 1.1.   Smolensk's fortifications, seventeenth century (Library of Congress)

the adverse climate continually imperiled the harvests, a variety of mounting social and economic problems confronted the young tsar.

Taxes were paid by peasants and townsfolk, and their high level placed a strain on these groups. Although nobles and church were exempt from taxes, the traditional backbone of the army, the lesser nobility, had ever greater difficulty in honoring its obligation to serve in the cavalry. Their serfs could not produce enough of a surplus to equip them for war, while many nobles had been allotted too few serfs to sustain their expenses in the first place. In addition, the nobles resented the hiring of military experts and the reorganization of the army following Western European models. The traditional cavalry's role in battle was diminished, and nobles were deployed with foreigners and peasants, to which they strongly objected.

Aleksei managed to placate his nobles by prohibiting peasants' departure from their villages in search of better labor conditions or work elsewhere, tying them and their progeny as serfs forever to the land. The tsar did this in consultation with one of the last of the Zemskii Sobors. The decree was part of a law code (Ulozhenie) issued in 1649 that until the 1830s remained in force as the fundamental set of laws through which Russia was ruled. Apart from this code, Aleksei responded to the urban unrest by dismissing some of his key advisors, raising the wages of riotous musketeers (*strel'tsy*), who formed another traditional force of army specialists, and halting the collections of some of the taxes owing.

Aleksei then did what every self-respecting medieval or early modern Christian monarch was wont to do: go to war. But he was a cautious man by inclination and made sure that he could field an army that matched that of his enemies. For several years, over the objections of nobles and *strel'tsy*, foreign mercenary officers provided intensive training of noble and peasant cavalry

Figure 1.2. Aleksei, traditional contemporary image

and infantry according to the lessons of the Thirty Years' War (1618–1648), which had just concluded in Central Europe. Aleksei carefully consulted with another Zemskii Sobor to guarantee sustained support from the home front for his campaigns. And he found a cause that was far greater than the mere glory of his dynasty or the expansion of his country: religion. Ukrainian Cossacks, led by Ataman Bohdan Khmelnitskii (1596–1657), had risen against the Polish government's attempts to curtail their freedom and its support to efforts to convert Ukrainians to Catholicism. The war with Poland-Lithuania could thus be cloaked in the guise of a religious war.

The decision to attack Poland-Lithuania was made easier as well because the area promised to be the weakest of potential foes. Sweden, controlling much of the Baltic shores, had the reputation of having the strongest army of Europe. Meanwhile, Muscovy might have acquired by the 1650s the capability to defend against the Turkish-Tatar alliance that controlled the lands to its south, but it was still far from able to launch an offensive war against this Muslim behemoth.

The first Russian campaigns of the Thirteen Years' War (1654–1667) were highly successful, and Russia not only recovered Smolensk but also occupied virtually all of what is now eastern Ukraine, Belarus, and even took the traditional Lithuanian capital of Vilnius. Poland seemed on the verge of total collapse (the period is known in Polish history as that of the "Deluge," or Potop). Its debacle against Russia led to Swedish and Turkish incursions into Polish territory. Preferring a weak Poland to a strong Sweden and Turkey at his western border, Aleksei became sufficiently alarmed by this to conclude a truce with Poland in 1656 and turn against Sweden (1656–1658). Although Russian armies besieged the key port of Riga, the Swedes proved to be too formidable as opponents in this conflict. After an armistice of three years, in 1661 Sweden and Russia concluded the Treaty of Kardis, which changed little on the map. Meanwhile, the Poles recovered and managed to push back the Swedes, concluding a peace with them in 1660.

Concomitantly, in 1659 and 1660, the Poles recouped territory that had been in Russian hands. Afterward, military success alternated between the two sides, with neither gaining a definitive advantage. The Poles were handicapped by internal dissent and the outbreak of a civil war between various noble factions. This allowed the Muscovite negotiators to see a substantial amount of their demands accepted by the Poles in the Truce of Andrusovo of 1667, which gave the tsar title to Smolensk, eastern Ukraine, and Kyiv. Initially, the Ukrainian capital was to be ruled by Russia for only twenty years. When negotiators for both sides reconvened in 1686, however, Poland was embroiled in a conflict with Turks and ripped asunder by internal disagreement. The Polish king Jan III Sobieski (1629–1696) then gave up Kyiv permanently in the "Eternal Peace" that was concluded between Russia and Poland.

Aleksei thus added a crucial stretch of land to Muscovy. The acquisition of eastern Ukraine in 1667 had repercussions that are still felt in our own time. In the nineteenth century, Russians were to claim that Ukraine (then labeled "Little Russia" by them) was an integral part of the Romanov empire, claiming that Ukrainian was no more than a Russian peasant dialect. In the cities of Ukraine, Russian was the language of administration and much of the population. This was all the more so in eastern Ukraine, where industrialization led to an influx of Russian factory workers and miners in the second half of the nineteenth century. But Ukrainian nationalists were not to accept such Russian paternalism. Ukrainian nationalism as a movement, however, was to be much stronger in western Ukraine, which remained Polish until the late eighteenth century (and its fringes were eventually Austrian ruled), than in the east, acquired in 1667.

The further development of Ukrainian-Russian relations will be discussed later on, but it is nonetheless worthwhile remembering that even today the population of eastern Ukraine, a region much longer part of the Romanov empire than western Ukraine, is far less nationalist and far more pro-Russian. This is reflected in the hotly contested presidential elections in Ukraine, where pro- and anti-Russian candidates face off. The roots of this conflict can be traced to Tsar Aleksei Mikhailovich's victory of 1667.

The year 1667 was undoubtedly one of triumph for Aleksei. Not only had he defeated the Polish enemies who had held Russia in check for two centuries, but he also showed who was boss in the Russian Orthodox Church. Indeed, he felt confident enough to impose higher tariffs on Western European import-and-export trade with Russia and made a move to intensify economic ties with Safavid Iran. This was potentially lucrative, as the Persians were a key source for raw silk that was in high demand in Western Europe. Aleksei's attempts to reroute this trade away from the overland caravan route that ended at Turkish-held Mediterranean ports did not succeed in the end because he was confronted with the Razin rebellion in 1670–1671. This uprising caused the Russians to abandon the plans for a naval patrol to protect merchants interested in traversing the Caspian Sea and Volga with their goods.

Aleksei was pondering a new major war at the time of his sudden death in early 1676. He was tempted by Western European governments to resume hostilities with Sweden but may have been more interested in fighting the Turks and Tatars in alliance with Poland-Lithuania. This, at least, is what the regency council that took the reins after his death decided to do. That war proved once again that Russia could not yet be too overambitious: when the fighting ended in 1681, Russia had gained nothing for itself, its Polish allies, or its western Ukrainian Cossack allies. For the first Romanovs, great powers of the age such as Sweden and the Ottoman Empire were still too powerful to challenge successfully.

INTERLUDE

Aleksei's death was followed by an interlude in which regents held the reins of power for most of the period 1676–1689. Court rivalries between the clans of Aleksei's first and second wives and their relatives hallmarked the period, with one particular ferocious moment of reckoning in May 1682. Throughout, it was the Miloslavskii clan (relatives of Aleksei's first spouse) that held the upper hand over the Naryshkins (the family of Aleksei's second wife), but its efforts were always hindered by the absence of a credible male candidate for the throne. Fyodor III (1661–1682) was, besides young, in poor physical health, while his brother Ivan V (co-ruled 1682–1696) was physically ailing as well as mentally afflicted.

In addition, through some of their rash actions, the Miloslavskiis lost the potential support of those who liked to be convinced by the wisdom of the faction that was in the ascendance. In 1682, for instance, they encouraged disaffected *strel'tsy* to run riot in Moscow to browbeat the Naryshkins. The musketeers murdered some of the leading Naryshkin men as well as other boyars who had little to do with the Naryshkins. But they stopped short of dispatching the Naryshkin heir Peter (1672–1725) and his mother.

After 1682, the Miloslavskii faction was led ever more emphatically by Sofia Alekseevna (1657–1704) in the name of the official tsars, her brother Ivan, and her half brother Peter (who had been proclaimed as co-rulers in 1682). Sofia and her key advisor Vasilii Golitsyn (1643–1714), however, may have underestimated the smoldering misogyny of the Russian elite. More crucial was their decision to mount two campaigns (in 1687 and 1689) against the Crimean Tatars. These were costly affairs in terms of money and human lives, and neither ever came close to reaching the Crimean peninsula, or even engaging the Tatars in a significant battle. When Sofia appeared to try to underline her status as regent of Russia in 1689, most of her supporters switched sides to Peter, who had fled Moscow to escape possible assassination. Instead of Sofia, it was Peter who became the uncontested Russian ruler in the summer of 1689. The teenage tsar was fond enough of his half brother to maintain the fiction of co-rule until Ivan's death in 1696.

THE RULING SYSTEM

Although Muscovy had existed as an independent state in the borderlands of Asia and Europe for more than a century, and while it encompassed as much territory as Poland-Lithuania (the largest European state in terms of size), it collapsed quickly after its ruling dynasty became extinct in 1598. This shows, on the one hand, how much states' survival in the early modern world depended on the physical health of their rulers and the availability of legitimate adult successors when they died; on the other hand, it also displays how most states were very loosely organized polities that easily fell apart.

Thus, although the Russian central bureaucracy in Moscow was large by European standards after Mikhail Romanov came to power, it did not consist of more than a few hundred administrators before the eighteenth century. Many of these servants did not receive regular wages but lived off the proceeds from land or nonrecurring bonuses awarded to them by the government, and off the fees they charged from those seeking the government's aid. The main occupation of this government apparatus was maintaining the armed forces, but if they were comprehensively defeated, as happened in 1605 or 1610, the Russian state imploded with them.

But the bureaucratic tradition proved resilient. It was strong enough to restore a reasonably well-functioning government after Mikhail Romanov was crowned tsar. Indeed, some of the servants managed to survive in office throughout the Time of Troubles, despite all of the regime changes from 1598 to 1613.[2] They thus preserved certain bureaucratic methods and techniques through which the country could be ruled in a reasonably efficient manner, once order was restored by military means.

The new Romanov dynasty and the bureaucracy behind it relied on the support of the warrior class (the higher nobility of boyars and gentry class of *dvoriane*) and the clergy of the Russian Orthodox Church (at all levels of its hierarchy) for their survival. Tsar, boyars, civil servants, priests, and monks jointly maintained, and gradually increased, their government's power at home and abroad. A tacit agreement was struck in 1613 that Russia was once again to display itself as an autocracy, a country ruled by one all-powerful and all-seeing man, as it had always been. In exchange for maintaining this facade, the noble elite and bureaucracy were allowed to lord it over the rest of the population, with the church advocating meek obedience of the worldly government as the path to salvation for the faithful. This pact was enshrined by the Ulozhenie of 1649, which confirmed the unfree status of most of the tsar's subjects. The system worked so well by 1725 that it easily survived a series of succession crises in the eighteenth century. Already earlier (in 1682 and 1689), when disputes erupted about which member of the family was to rule, it appeared as if the collapse of Romanov rule as such had become a remote possibility.

It was only after Tsaritsa Catherine the Great's death in 1796 that the monarch's legitimacy began to be questioned by his subjects on the basis of rather different premises than in the early 1600s. By 1900, most of the leading lights of a complex mass society composed of 130 million individuals no longer considered one-person rule as the government best suited to Russia. But even then many peasants still worshipped their Tsar-Batiushka ("Tsar Little Father") as God's representative on earth. This highlights how ideas of accountable government or of political systems of checks and balances are a rather late development in human history: few people knew about them—and then only in an abstract manner (as through the example of classical Athenian democracy)—in most of the world around 1600 or 1700.

RUSSIA'S ECONOMY, SOCIETY, AND CULTURE

The means to run this empire and field its army came from two sources: peasants working the land and trade, especially in rare goods that were gathered in its vast lands and could be exported. In the latter case, Romanov Russia was lucky in finding great riches in rare animal furs (such as ermine, sable, fox, or mink) that were in high demand everywhere in the seventeenth century, especially in Western Europe. Under the first Romanovs, the fur trade may have provided the government with 10 percent of its income. Other goods, such as naval stores (wood, hemp, and tar) and saltpeter (essential to make gunpowder) or potash (important for dyeing clothes), too, were in high demand in Europe. The government also levied taxes on sales of goods and on wares imported from abroad.

But many segments of the Russian economy did not use money in the seventeenth century: the peasants produced foodstuffs for themselves and for their lords, who had been assigned peasant villages that were to provide for their livelihood. The noble lords either consumed or exchanged (mostly in kind, sometimes in cash) their share of this yield for arms and equipment needed for battle (their task in life) as well as their other expenses. Peasants, in addition, paid taxes (usually in kind as well) to the state. The state used this income to pay its soldiers during military campaigns (often enough in goods such as grain rather than money). It also used taxation revenue for other expenditures, such as the purchase of arms and ordnance at home and abroad. After 1649, only a minority of peasants were legally free. Most were serfs, bound to the land (and thus the landlord). Either they worked part of their time (often at least half a week) on their lord's land or they had to surrender a considerable amount of what they produced to their lords. The height of these burdens made farming even more a backbreaking sort of occupation than it already was in early modern Russia.

For, apart from the exorbitant burden placed on the peasants through serfdom and taxation, Russia's climate was (and is) inhospitable to farming. The growing season for crops ran in most places from early May to late September, leading to frantic stints of plowing, sowing, haying, and harvesting within that short period. The diet of all groups of Muscovite society was highly deficient until the elite developed a greater refinement of its menu, when it began to emulate Western European examples (thus various seventeenth-century visitors to Moscow observed how Russian nobles began to consume lettuce and other fresh vegetables). Traditionally, fresh vegetables were seldom eaten (not even in summer), and fresh fruit was only seasonally enjoyed. Russian peasants were highly skilled at canning cabbage and mushrooms or making preserves from fruit (especially berries), and they also made mildly alcoholic drinks from honey (*myod*) and rye (*kvas*). Meat, game, or poultry were rarely eaten by the serfs, but they did add to their table's variety by fishing in the innumerable lakes, rivers, and creeks throughout the country. The main staple remained rye, a hardy grain that can be grown at high latitude. Whereas it may be difficult for the reader to imagine how people survived on such imbalanced nourishment, the Russian diet was no worse than that consumed in most places of the world in the seventeenth century. Little changed in this until the twentieth century, with the important exception of the introduction of the potato to the menu toward 1800.

By the seventeenth century, the drinking of distilled alcohol had become normal in most Orthodox households. Although Russians were portrayed by Western visitors as inveterate drinkers who drank themselves into a stupor whenever given the chance, the consumption of hard liquor did not reach the diseased proportions of the nineteenth and twentieth century. Inebriation levels were likely no different from those elsewhere in the contemporary Christian world. Western Europeans were more than anything astounded by the manner in which Russians celebrated their holidays, when they gave themselves over to what seemed total abandonment (especially notorious was Maslennitsa, the Russian version of Mardi Gras or carnival). That was not the way to party in Western Europe, where people tended to revel in a somewhat less ebullient manner. But the English addiction to gin in the eighteenth century was as bad as the Russian addiction to vodka.

The Muscovite government did occasionally feel obligated to curtail excessive drinking. Tsar Aleksei implemented a government monopoly on taverns, an action that lessened popular consumption of strong liquor, for at that time few peasants yet mastered the intricacies of distillation (unlike in the nineteenth century and afterward). Vodka had to be bought for fairly expensive prices, and few could afford to do so more than a handful of times in the year. Of course, many of the tsar's subjects were Muslims, descendants from the Mongolians and Turkic Tatars who had ruled European Russia for more than two centuries (roughly speaking, from the 1240s to the 1480s). They usually refrained from the consumption of alcohol.

The bone-chilling cold of winter was fought by building wooden houses centered on the stove, which doubled as an oven. Peasants slept on top of the furnace or in cavities set within its sidewall, and farm animals often slept in the same quarters in winter. Some stoves had no chimney, while ventilation was poor (as a good airflow would let too much heat out) in every hut. People and animals shared their living quarters with innumerable insects. Because in both towns and villages wood was the prime building material, fires were common, regularly destroying Russian domiciles and sometimes killing their occupants. Westerners observed how Moscow's population tore down houses when fire broke out in the city rather than trying to extinguish the flames with water. At the same time, artisans in the capital were extremely skilled at construction, able to rebuild many a house in a day. But deaths through fire were a common fact of Russian life. Stone buildings began to be erected in greater numbers only in the course of the seventeenth century. Wooden huts, though, were to remain the norm in the countryside until the twentieth century.

Since this was normal before 1800 elsewhere, too, the reader may not be surprised to learn that the health of most Russians was poor, that child mortality was high, and that epidemics were frequent visitors to peasant households. Many women did not survive childbearing age because of complications during childbirth or a pregnancy gone wrong. Although in Russia the plague may have sometimes hit with less intensity or with a lower frequency because of the cold weather, plague nonetheless raged with devastating consequences (for example, in 1654 and 1771 in Moscow); often, the countryside was spared because of the great distance between settlements and the very low level of urbanization. Seventeenth-century Moscow may have had around one hundred thousand inhabitants, but no other town had more than ten thousand people.

Figure 1.3. Peasant hut, early twentieth century (Library of Congress)

It is moot in how far wise women were able to stave off many ailments and afflictions.[3] Such women took on the role of midwives as well. Whereas their healing techniques or aid in childbirth were undoubtedly far inferior to those practiced by modern medicine, they were likely as effective as the formally trained doctors of the age. If the Romanov tsars themselves may serve as an example, it can be noted that their reliance on Western doctors was to very little avail. Mikhail and Aleksei died before they reached the age of fifty, and Fyodor III was barely in his twenties when he succumbed.

A final point regarding the marginal quality of the average peasant's existence in seventeenth-century Russia should be made. Whereas tobacco consumption (sniffing, chewing, or smoking) was prohibited from the 1630s to the 1690s, seventeenth-century visitors observed a fanatical desire among Russians to consume the weed. Certainly, once Peter the Great legalized tobacco just before 1700, both the import and domestic tillage of tobacco reached vast proportions. If Russians could spend so much time, effort, and even money on acquiring a wholly frivolous luxury product such as tobacco, the standard of living cannot have been that low (a similar argument can be made about vodka consumption). And other circumstantial evidence seems to support this idea: the Eastern Slavic population grew rapidly in the eighteenth and nineteenth centuries, even before health care improved substantially in the second half of the nineteenth century (especially through inoculation). In the eighteenth century alone, the population may have doubled.

Peasant life was determined by the seasons, not just because of the cold, but also because the workday was long during the lengthy summer days and short during winter, when little else was done than chopping wood, some hunting and (ice) fishing, and making or repairing tools and clothes. Activity ceased so much on the farms that still in 1900 the authoritative *British Medical Journal* reported that in Pskov province peasants spent the winter in almost full hibernation, waking once a day to eat a piece of bread and have a draft of water.

The peasants had an elaborate tradition of songs and storytelling but were almost universally illiterate. Only by 1900, a majority of Russian children received a measure of general education. Before 1800, indeed, literacy was a rare phenomenon among Russians in towns and in the countryside, but it is difficult to assess how many people could read. A great number of Russian primers were printed in the seventeenth century (when government and patriarchal printing presses issued thousands of books), which leads some scholars to infer that more people could read than was later suggested by antitsarist historians (especially those of the early Soviet Union), who tried to depict Romanov Russia as a bog of ignorance. Almost all who were part of the clergy could undoubtedly read, and the secular clergy (the married parish priests of the "white" clergy, as they sometimes were called because of their dress) certainly taught their own sons, and possibly daughters, as well as others, basic literacy. Similarly, merchants and tradesmen in the towns must have had a notion of numeracy, necessary to function as economic actors. Still, we even know of nobles who could not sign their names. Scribes hiring out their services to people who wanted to petition the government were found in every larger settlement.

But only very few Muscovites were literate enough to write literature, loosely defined. Some of the best works of the age are church sermons. A handful of individuals wrote works of more lasting interest (although primarily for historians), such as Archpriest Avvakum's (ca. 1620–1682) autobiography (its authorship is in doubt) or Grigorii Kotoshikhin's (ca. 1630–1667) description of the Russian government. By the 1680s the first institute of higher education was opened in the Slavo-Graeco-Latin Academy in Moscow, modeled after the Ukrainian metropolitan Petro Mohyla's (1596–1646) academy founded in 1630s Kyiv. The students at this institute, too, were far from numerous.

Among non-Russians, literacy was probably as low as among Russians, while its prevalence might also be differentiated according to people's economic role. In addition, most of the non-Russian population had no printing presses to supply them with textbooks and other reading material. Furthermore, in Islamic communities the formal religious language was Arabic, a tongue not spoken anywhere inside of the Russian Empire, which hindered the spread of reading among Muslims. Meanwhile, the Russians understood a little bit more about mass than their European counterparts in

Figure 1.4. Traditional wooden church in Siberia, early twentieth century (Library of Congress)

the Catholic Church, for the liturgical language of the Orthodox Church was Church Slavonic, an older version of Russian. It was gradually replaced by vernacular Russian.

The reforms of Patriarch Nikon (1605–1681) during the 1650s of some of the Orthodox rituals observed in the Russian Church probably changed little about popular religious customs. As their Christian counterparts in much of Europe (before the confessionalization wave of the seventeenth century), the Eastern Slavic Orthodox believers traditionally followed an eclectic mix of proper Christian rituals and pre-Christian habits (for example, to have a picnic on your ancestors' graves on Rodinitsa in spring) and beliefs (as that in spirits and demons). This has led some observers to suggest that Russia had a "dual faith" (*dvoeverie*), half Christian and half pagan.[4] Many pagan deities and holidays were absorbed by Russian Christianity, not unlike the Western acceptance of things such as Christmas trees and Easter eggs (also popular in Russia), of which there is no mention in the Bible. Nikon's reforms, however, were of a very different kind than those strengthening the Christian convictions of many other Europeans at about the same time. Nikon's changes primarily affected the outward manner in which the Orthodox worshipped and did little to nothing in terms of enforcing a uniform Christianity stripped of lingering pagan elements. Thus, Georgii Fedotov suggested that even by 1900 the beliefs of the great majority of Russians should be understood as a dual faith. It does not seem coincidental that any witch craze was absent in Russia, a fact that is indicative of the acceptance of wise women and "natural" healers in Russian society.

WOMEN AND MEN IN EARLY MODERN RUSSIA

More likely than not to die of childbirth, women's lot was as harsh in Russia as elsewhere in early modern societies. The realities of the farming season, meanwhile, prevented peasant work from being too strictly assigned according to gender (with women taking care of the children and the farm animals, while men toiled in the fields). Women worked as hard as men in the villages, even if socially they had an inferior status. Often worst off were newly married women, since in many Russian villages exogamy was practiced, which meant that girls married outside of their village. In their new community, they lacked the protection of their family and might be exposed to the tyranny and physical abuse not just of their husbands but also of their mothers-in-law. Nonetheless, exogamy was not a standard everywhere. And practices were obviously different in non-Russian communities: In Islamic regions polygamy was often practiced, although it was far from universal. The number of wives a Muslim man had depended on his economic well-being. Most were far too poor to have more than one wife.

Whereas in Christian Orthodox villages the seclusion of women was a practical impossibility, in the towns elite women were often secluded in separate quarters (*terem*) and barred from going out in public. This went back to a late Byzantine custom that had been transferred to Russia in the waning days of the Eastern Roman Empire during the fifteenth century. Although seclusion became the custom at court and for aristocratic women, in nonnoble circles this sort of habit was impossible to observe for practical reasons, with women being full-fledged economic actors.

Meanwhile, among the elite, women were gradually given somewhat greater freedom in the course of the seventeenth century. Aleksei's first wife Maria Miloslavskaia (1625–1669) played a significant role in organizing her household and the court's charitable activities, while his second wife Natalia Naryshkina (1651–1694) encouraged the tsar's curiosity about matters European, leading to the staging of the first theater play at the court in the 1670s. One of Maria's daughters, Sofia, served as Muscovy's regent from 1682 to 1689. She was bold enough to commission the production of an engraved portrait to underscore her claims to the throne, even if the print was never distributed as she lost out to her half brother Peter at the time it was made. But despite his quarrel with his sister, Peter strongly promoted women's appearance in public, inspired by what he had witnessed in Moscow's foreign suburb and seen on his trip to Western Europe in 1697–1698.

Notwithstanding the strong influence of some women at the court, in all layers of society women enjoyed only few rights. It was, however, true that noblewomen could lord it over their domestic servants and field hands. And likewise, mothers-in-law and even widows in some peasant households might be able to exert power over women with less agency. Altogether, though, throughout society women enjoyed little agency and, despite the eighteenth century being an age of female rule in Russia, little changed in this respect until the twentieth century.

THE GEOGRAPHICAL CHALLENGE

Premodern Russians' acquiescence in autocracy can be in part explained by the challenges their country's geography placed before the government. In the early modern age, Russia was an immense country with a very small population (for the 1670s, the estimate is that Russia had approximately ten million inhabitants, which is only half the size of contemporary France's population). Many people accepted autocracy without demurring because the tsar played at best a minute role in their lives, especially if they lived outside the Muscovite heartland populated mainly by Russians (that is, the territory around Moscow stretching from Tula and Voronezh in the south, to Nizhnii Novgorod in the east, via Yaroslavl' and Vologda to Arkhangel'sk in the north, and to Novgorod, Pskov, and Smolensk in the west).

The means of communication and transport were too primitive to enforce the monarch's rule consistently. Even in the heartland, mud made traveling almost impossible in spring and autumn, and long-distance traveling in winter, when routes were in good condition for sleighs and mounted riders to use, was only for the hardy types because of the intense cold. The Russians had inherited from the Mongolians a fairly efficient "postal" system that allowed government officials and others to travel expeditiously through the use of stations located along the major roads where fresh horses were kept, but those roads were few and the distances remained formidable. Apart from traversing semihardened highways or snow-and-ice roads in winter, a good deal of traveling went over water, through a deft use of the innumerable waterways of Russia and Siberia. Rivers allowed for the easiest transport of goods in bulk (such as grain), but this was not exactly a fast way of moving. Going against the current was, of course, especially slow. With the growth of the population, ever more barge haulers were employed, but their loads progressed up and down the rivers only as quickly as a human being can walk pulling something heavy. And from autumn to spring, rivers could not be used.

Uprisings were periodic, but those who rejected the tsar's rule or boyar and church exploitation (the Orthodox Church had innumerable serfs working for it) often opted for a more promising option than rebellion (which invariably ended in the massacre of the rebels): flight to remote areas. Runaway serfs were hunted and sometimes brought back to their lords, but restrictions on means and time meant that posses could be out searching only for so long.

Russia, then, was in theory an autocracy, a country in which one person, who spent most of his time in and around Moscow, decided everything of importance that affected his subjects. In practice, however, this was a country in which many went about their lives rarely directly affected by the tsar's rule. The Romanovs delegated power to nobles, chieftains, Cossacks (in Siberia), local clerks, monks, and priests. These aristocrats, officials, soldiers, and clerics across the empire maintained order for the tsars, collected taxes and labor dues, and dispensed justice. Whether the dues owed to the tsar were ever given to the government depended on these subordinates' will. And whether the latter succeeded in collecting the taxes and tribute due to the government depended on the desire of the local population to pay them. If they had no such inclination, it was not too difficult to disappear into the steppe (grasslands), the taiga (forest), or the barren tundra.

WITHIN AND WITHOUT RUSSIA

The Romanov empire was never an empire made up of Russian speakers, or ethnic (Great) Russians, alone. Its history, and that of the Soviet Union, was one determined by the constant interaction of different cultures and ethnicities, within its borders and beyond it. Borders, indeed, were almost anywhere in the world utterly fluid in the seventeenth century (in the Russian case sometimes until the twentieth century), in the absence of good maps or artificial markers on the ground and any meaningful patrol of immensely lengthy frontiers (in Soviet times, more than one million border guards were deployed to watch the Soviet borders).

Russia's southern and southeastern borders in particular had been porous before the seventeenth century. This was the zone through which nomads had periodically entered the Eastern European Plain, since at least from the age of the Hittites three thousand years earlier (the Huns, Magyars, Polovtsy, and Mongols had done so in more recent times). The seventeenth century marks an important watershed in world history in this respect. Precisely during the reigns of the first Romanovs, nomads in Eurasia were definitively placed on the defensive by states in which most of the population lived a settled existence (apart from Russia, Qing China also ended Mongolian, Kalmyk, and Tibetan raiding).

The Russian heartland was protected better than ever in the seventeenth century against invaders from the steppes to the south and southeast. The end of the invasions from Central Asia that had plagued Europe for millennia was in the first place a consequence of the Russian advance into Siberia (beginning in earnest during the early 1580s) and of the greater control Russia acquired along the Caspian Sea's shores (Astrakhan, at the Volga mouth, became Russian in 1556). This led to a sustained effort on the part of the Russians to shore up their borders in the south and southeast.

They used the terrain's natural obstacles (dense forests, hills, and rivers) together with wooden palisades to create a protective fence or wall that ended the periodic Tatar incursions that had plagued Muscovy previously (hundreds of thousands of Russians and Ukrainians were captured in the sixteenth and seventeenth centuries, bought back for ransom, or sold at the slave markets of the Ottoman Empire such as at Istanbul and Kaffa). This "Abatis line" was further garrisoned intensively, with sentries continuously on the lookout for raiding parties; eventually, this line expanded and stretched out all the way from southwest of Moscow to the lands beyond the Volga. It seemed to be a version of the Great Wall of China at the other side of the Eurasian continent and was reasonably effective. Slave raiding into Russia proper became increasingly rare toward 1700. Russia, too, made the first crucial steps to bring the lawless (or, perhaps, stateless) borderlands (Okraina, or Ukraine) beyond this frontier under control. This latter process was drawn out (1654–1783), but significant headway was made by 1667, when the tsar acquired the title to eastern Ukraine and (for all intents and purposes) Kyiv.

Nevertheless, like other early modern states in Europe and Asia, Russia experienced several huge rebellions, in which the growing power of Moscow's central government was challenged. Within its borders, insurrections of a smaller scale were endemic before the early eighteenth century. These uprisings were informed by economic, social, and religious grievances, while they often derived as well from a broader cultural clash with Russian rule. Although rebels desired greater independence or freedom from Moscow, these revolts did not resemble the risings that engulfed the Russian Empire in 1917, because they lacked a coherent political agenda. Few challenged the autocracy, even if they rose against the tsar's government. Usually, the tsar's advisors were blamed, or the tsar was said to be an impostor.

In the seventeenth century, the first Romanovs and their boyars faced foreign wars with Tatars, Turks, Poles, and Swedes; the Razin rebellion along the Volga; and urban revolts in Moscow and other towns, while violent conflict with Kalmyks and Central Asian Kazakhs periodically erupted. In Siberia, the welter of native groups was only with difficulty controlled. I have pointed out the uncertain quality of the tsar's power over his subjects. Similarly, Michael Khodarkovsky has argued that for most of the territory outside of the heartland, Russia's "rule" amounted to a compromise between the central government and its subjects, where both sides believed to benefit more from their agreement to collaborate rather than to fight each other. This was no

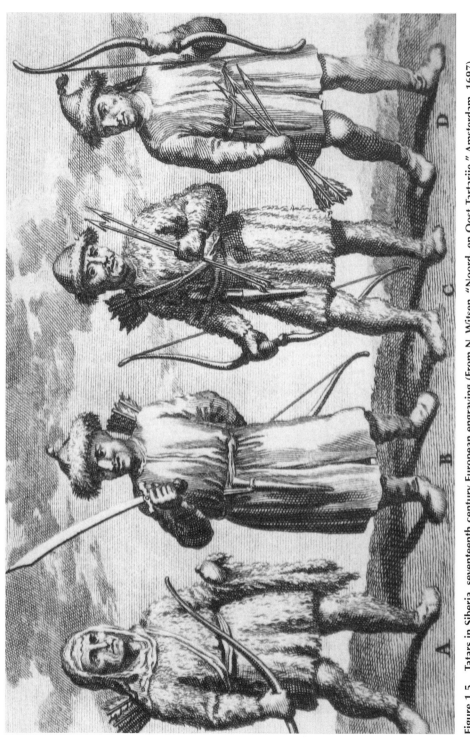

Figure 1.5.   Tatars in Siberia, seventeenth century European engraving (From N. Witsen, "Noord- en Oost-Tartarije," Amsterdam, 1697)

different from contemporary European empires in the Americas, where Spanish rule was tentative in South and Middle America and, as Richard White has suggested, when in North America European colonists and native American groups met on a "Middle Ground," with neither side imposing its will on the other.

Since Mongolian times the Muscovites were in the habit of co-opting the elite of subjugated peoples into their own nobility. The writer Vladimir Nabokov (1899–1977), who fled the Russian Revolution of 1917, thus suggested that he was a descendant of the Tatar Nabok family. A famous (and definitely nonfictional) example was that of the Cherkess princes. These chiefs of a northern Caucasian ethnic group became the princes Cherkasskii, redoubtable military commanders and senior advisors of the first Romanovs in the seventeenth century. Polish-Lithuanian nobles were equally welcomed into the fold of the Russian aristocracy (as in 1667, when those of eastern Ukraine were forced to choose between abandoning their possessions and moving westward or changing overlords and keeping their estates under tsarist rule). Such a strategy of integration aided the Russian cause handsomely. Once a community's elite was made part of Russia's ruling stratum, it proved much easier to control its rank and file. This was rather different from the manner in which the population of European overseas colonies was brought to heel.

Serfdom remained a phenomenon encountered primarily in Slavic areas or (later) in the Baltic region. In non-Slavic areas, society was differently organized. Groups such as Bashkirs, Nogais, or Kalmyks were allowed to maintain their traditional society and culture in exchange for their loyalty and little else. For a while, the Russians even paid local chiefs tribute in order to maintain good relations. Only very gradually were such nomadic groups incorporated into the tsar's empire in a more comprehensive manner by stripping away their autonomous rights. Siberian natives were sometimes bullied, as they lived in smaller communities and could easily be handled by Cossacks equipped with firearms. Cossacks held representatives from an ethnic group hostage in garrison fortresses to ensure their submission and the timely delivery of the customary tribute of furs.

COSSACKS

The Cossacks' history, in fact, is a good example of the slow and circuitous route taken by the Russian government to become the unchallenged sovereigns of an unruly set of previously autonomous communities located in peripheral regions. The Cossacks emerged somewhere in the course of the fifteenth century. Originally, they had been runaways from either Tatar or Turkish slavery or serfdom (their name is derived from the Turkic word "freeman"), who were soon joined by those fleeing Polish or Muscovite oppression. They spoke an Eastern Slavic dialect, varying from Ukrainian (along the Dnipro) to Russian, and were almost uniformly Orthodox believers (the Turks and Tatars traded extensively in Eastern Slavic slaves, and the Tatars were the Muscovite overlords until about 1480). They resided in fairly small, self-ruling communities, located in areas, such as at the

Dnipro rapids at Zaporizhzhia, that were difficult to penetrate for regular army units, whether Turkish, Polish, or Russian.

Cossacks lived off trade and plunder, and increasingly through serving as auxiliary troops in the Polish or Russian armies. During campaigning (or plundering) season, the men left their villages, while the women, elderly, and children tended to farms. Since they also engaged in piracy on the Black Sea and Caspian Sea, they somewhat bear a resemblance to contemporary pirates in the Mediterranean, the Caribbean, and elsewhere. Cossack communities originally were organized in a rather egalitarian manner (at least for the men). Male adults elected their chief (hetman) and made decisions collectively.

Cossack freedom was gradually curtailed by the Polish and Muscovite monarchs, who demanded the registration of Cossack membership in exchange for regular payments (often of grain and other goods in kind) to Cossack communities. They were to turn away new runaways who tried to escape serfdom by joining a Cossack community. This circumscribing of Cossack status gained in force in the seventeenth century, but it was not a smooth or irreversible process: the widespread revolt of Stenka Razin around 1670, which stretched from the mouth of the Volga to Simbirsk (Ul'ianovsk today) high up the river, found its origins in a conflict between "new" and "registered" Cossacks. Nor were all established Cossacks willing to give in to the tsar's demands and register on the monarch's lists.

Cossacks remained hard to control for long after, as is indicated by the Pugachev rebellion of the 1770s, which spread even farther than Razin's. Only after suppressing the Pugachev uprising was the Russian government successful in curtailing Cossack freedom, slowly taking away their autonomy. But in exchange, Cossacks enjoyed great privileges. They were well rewarded for their service in the Russian army and preferred as the armed muscle of Russia's colonial expansion into Siberia. Eventually, too, they became the tsarist regime's riot police, instilling fear into all of the population when deployed in an ever more restless country after 1861.

Cossacks also had a reputation of being ferocious anti-Semites, which went back to their resentment of Jews in the Polish-Lithuanian kingdom. Judaic and Orthodox believers often clashed because Polish nobles used Jews as the stewards of their estates in the early modern period. This made them the special object of resentment among Orthodox peasants (including those who joined the Cossacks). In addition, some Jews, who were barred from owning land while allowed to charge interest to Christians (which was not permitted to Christians according to canon law), served as moneylenders to impecunious Slavic peasants. Whereas only a small minority of Jews worked as bailiffs or lent money, all were blamed in times of social unrest, as in the Cossack revolt headed by Bohdan Khmelnitskii against the Polish king that began in 1648. In this rebellion (1648–1656), as many as one hundred thousand Jews may have been killed. This hatred of Jews persisted into the modern era, when Cossacks often spearheaded pogroms in late tsarist Russia (between 1881 and 1906), and the propaganda that rolled from the printing presses made anti-Semitism even worse.

Whereas Cossack traditions often sat uneasily with the tsars (for, despite all the concessions, Cossack communities retained certain traditions of liberty that defied

Russia's official autocracy), their Communist successors also clashed with Cossack communities. Most Cossacks chose the side of the anti-Bolshevik White armies in the Russian Civil War (1918–1921), and the Bolsheviks responded with massive persecution. Certain Cossack communities on the Don and Kuban Rivers became the first of many echelons of deported populations that punctuated Soviet history between 1919 and 1953. Collectivization translated to an even fiercer assault on the Cossacks, as most of them were identified as rich peasants (kulaks) and thus were subject to banishment at a minimum. After the collapse of the Soviet Union, Cossack communities were restored in many places, but evil tongues maintained that these self-styled Cossacks were impostors, for the true Cossacks had been wiped out by the Soviet regime.

RELIGION AND FOREIGNERS

Cultural contact with neighboring foreigners who eventually became incorporated into Russia also led the state to be religiously tolerant.[5] Islam existed peacefully alongside Russian Orthodoxy (and Kalmyk Buddhism and Siberian native religions were tolerated as well). But there was one peculiar quirk: other Christian religions were highly distrusted in the seventeenth century, especially Catholicism. Catholicism was associated with Russia's archenemy Poland-Lithuania, which had occupied Moscow in the 1610s and desecrated Russian Orthodoxy's most sacred shrines in the Kremlin. Jesuit conspiracies were suspected everywhere before Peter the Great's rule.

In a handful of designated places, Protestant worship was allowed, to accommodate the ever-increasing number of Western Europeans who resided in the Russian Empire after 1613. But even they were chased from living inside Moscow proper in 1654, when a wave of xenophobia steered by a religious reform movement combined with a plague epidemic and the outbreak of another war with Poland.

And this war was linked to a split within the Russian Orthodox Church. Russian Christianity's ways had diverted from the path of the other Eastern Orthodox churches because of Russia's remote location and cultural isolation under Mongolian rule in the Middle Ages. Inspired by Ukrainian clerics who had begun a theological counteroffensive against Jesuit attempts to convert Ukrainian Orthodox believers to Catholicism, from the 1640s Russian church leaders attempted to reform their church's rituals. They tried to align them with those of their more sophisticated and "Greek" Ukrainian colleagues. Tsar Aleksei actively supported this reform movement as it jibed with his political ambitions to rule Ukraine in place of the Polish king. It would be accepted more easily by the Ukrainians if he could be depicted as a champion of their oppressed faith.

As we saw, the Russian decision to go to war with Poland in 1654 was in part to liberate oppressed co-religionists (although the Ukrainian Cossacks who allied with Aleksei believed that the fight was to maintain their liberty as well). But in the course of the war, Aleksei fell out with the patriarch of the Russian Church, Nikon. Nikon had been Aleksei's choice for this office in 1652 and was trusted so much by the tsar that he headed the government in the tsar's absence when Aleksei personally

Figure 1.6.   Monks harvesting, early twentieth century (Library of Congress)

participated in the Polish campaigns (1654–1656). But Nikon soon exhibited signs of an unduly inflated sense of his own importance, posturing as a virtual equal to the tsar. His headstrong (or arrogant) nature had meanwhile led to mounting protest to his changes of the Russian Orthodox rituals (crossing oneself with three rather two fingers was one example), which Nikon had imposed to align Russia's church with that of Ukraine. Opponents of Nikon began to suspect that he was the devil's (or at least the pope's) tool, corrupting pure Russian Christianity.

Aleksei faced Nikon down, and the latter went into self-imposed exile at the lavish monastery he had built for himself near Moscow. Efforts by both sides to reconcile failed, and Aleksei decided to call a church synod at the end of the Polish War (it gathered in 1666). In the presence of two Eastern Orthodox patriarchs, Nikon was deposed, but his reforms were confirmed.

This confirmation caused traditionalists to leave the Russian Church. They were sometimes called the Staro-obriadtsy, or Old Believers, but more often condemned as schismatics, or Raskolniki, a word with which Fyodor Dostoyevsky was to play in his famous novel *Crime and Punishment* (even if its protagonist Raskolnikov separates himself from the morality of society at large). Different from European Protestants, Old Believers never took up arms against government agents who tried to apprehend them for heresy; instead, they often engaged in the practice of self-immolation. Communities locked themselves into their wooden churches and set them alight. This radical protest waned toward 1700, in part because Peter the Great was far less concerned with enforcing religious orthodoxy. Meanwhile, thanks to the Raskol (Schism), historians can make use of one of the most vivid pieces of personal writing of seventeenth-century Russia, the (alleged?) autobiography of a leading figure of the Old Believers, Avvakum.

Xenophobia forced Westerners to leave the city of Moscow in 1654 and settle in a townlet outside the city's walls, but the fear of contamination by foreigners was far from a consistent phenomenon in seventeenth-century Russia. Indeed, all Romanovs understood the necessity of calling in Western aid. Without it, Poles and Swedes might gain the upper hand on the battlefield, and Russia might be brought under the rule of a Catholic or Lutheran monarch. In addition, whereas the Orthodox mind-set was in principle a closed one, it could not wholly suppress innate curiosity. Aleksei was delighted to accept a Dutch-made globe, for example, at the height of the 1650s antiforeigner craze. In a more mundane sense, many among Russia's noble elite acquired a taste for German, French, and Spanish wines.

Most important, however, was the increasing reliance on Western expertise for warfare. A steady stream of mercenaries traveled to Moscow throughout the seventeenth century. They instructed Russian troops on the new manner of warfare with volley-firing infantry, dragoon soldiers, and so on, placing a much greater emphasis on training and discipline. Mikhail and Aleksei both sponsored the building of warships to sail the Caspian Sea, in both cases without success. But the idea inspired Peter the Great, with lasting consequences.

Besides Western Europeans training Russian troops and building ships, predominantly Dutch merchants brought vast quantities of arms to Russia, and Dutch entrepreneurs significantly expanded Russian armament manufacturing at Tula and Kashira. Some Dutch engineers helped the Russians build fortifications at exposed Russian towns along the frontier, but the Russians relied on their own experience in creating the long-fortified border several hundreds of miles south of Moscow.

NOTES

1. Those bearing the title of prince traced their ancestry to the first rulers of the Orthodox Eastern Slavs, the grand dukes of the house of Riurik (allegedly ruler in the ninth century).

2. Notorious among the servants who stayed in office was Ivan Gramotin (d. 1638).

3. Sometimes there were male shaman-like characters as well, not just in native Siberian communities but also in Russian villages in more remote territory.

4. Philosopher Georgii Fedotov (1886–1951) is the most famous of these observers.

5. These foreigners were called *inorodtsy*, rather than *inozemtsy*, the term used for expatriate Christian residents of Muscovy.

FURTHER READING

Translated Primary Sources

Olearius, Adam. *The Travels of Olearius in Seventeenth-Century Russia*. Translated and edited by S. H. Baron. Stanford, CA: Stanford University Press, 1967.

Petrovich, Avvakum. *Archpriest Avvakum: The Life Written by Himself*. Translated by K. N. Brostrom. Ann Arbor, MI: Michigan Slavic Publications, 1979.

Scholarly Literature

Boterbloem, Kees. *Moderniser of Russia: Andrei Vinius, 1641–1716*. New York: Palgrave Macmillan, 2013.

Davies, Brian. *Warfare, State and Society on the Black Sea Steppe, 1500–1700*. New York: Routledge, 2007.

Dunning, Chester. *Russia's First Civil War: The Time of Troubles and the Founding of the Romanov Dynasty*. University Park: Pennsylvania State University Press, 2001.

Etkind, Alexander. *Internal Colonization: Russia's Imperial Experience*. New York: Polity, 2011.

Hellie, Richard. *Enserfment and Military Change*. Chicago: University of Chicago Press, 1971.

Hittle, J. M. *The Service City: State and Townsmen in Russia, 1600–1800*. Cambridge, MA: Harvard University Press, 1979.

Hughes, L. A. J. *Russia and the West: The Life of a Seventeenth-Century Westernizer, Prince Vasily Vasil'evich Golitsyn (1643–1714)*. London: Oriental Research Partners, 1984.

Hughes, Lindsey. *Sophia, Regent of Russia: 1657–1704*. New Haven, CT: Yale University Press, 1990.

Khodarkovsky, Michael. *Russia's Steppe Frontier: The Making of a Colonial Empire, 1500–1800*. Bloomington: Indiana University Press, 2004.

Kivelson, Val. *Autocracy in the Provinces: The Muscovite Gentry and Political Culture in the Seventeenth Century*. Stanford, CA: Stanford University Press, 1996.

Kotilaine, Jarmo. *Russia's Foreign Trade and Economic Expansion: Windows on the World*. Leiden, Netherlands: Brill, 2005.

Longworth, Philip. *Alexis: Tsar of All the Russias*. London: F. Watts, 1984.

MacNeill, William H. *Europe's Steppe Frontier*. Chicago: University of Chicago Press, 2011.

Magocsi, Paul Robert. *History of Ukraine: The Land and Its Peoples*. Toronto: University of Toronto Press, 2010.

Michels, Georg B. *At War with the Church: Religious Dissent in Seventeenth-Century Russia*. Stanford, CA: Stanford University Press, 2000.

Perrie, Maureen, ed. *The Cambridge History of Russia*. Vol. 1. Cambridge: Cambridge University Press, 2006.

Poe, Marshall. *"A People Born to Slavery": Russia in Early Modern European Ethnography*. Ithaca, NY: Cornell University Press, 2001.

Romaniello, Matthew. *The Elusive Empire: Kazan and the Creation of Russia, 1552–1671*. Madison: University of Wisconsin Press, 2012.

Ryan, W. F. *The Bathhouse at Midnight: An Historical Survey of Magic and Divination in Russia*. University Park: Pennsylvania State University Press, 1999.

Shields Kollmann, Nancy. *By Honor Bound: State and Society in Early Modern Russia*. Ithaca, NY: Cornell University Press, 1999.

Slezkine, Yuri. *Arctic Mirrors: Russia and the Small Peoples of the North*. Ithaca, NY: Cornell University Press, 1996.

Smith, R. E. F., and David Christian. *Bread and Salt: A Social and Economic History of Food and Drink*. Cambridge: Cambridge University Press, 2008.

Stone, David R. *A Military History of Russia: From Ivan the Terrible to the War in Chechnya*. New York: Praeger, 2006.

Subtelny, Orest. *Ukraine: A History*. Toronto: University of Toronto Press, 2009.

WEBSITES

Benjamin Sher's site on all matters Russian: http://www.websher.net/inx/icdefault1.htm.
Russian and Russian-translated historical documents: http://www.vostlit.info.
Russian Orthodoxy: http://www.pravoslavie.ru/english.

FILMS

Boris Godunov. Directed by Sergei Bondarchuk. DVD. Soviet Union, 1986.

The Face of Russia. Directed by James Billington. VHS documentary. New York: Home Vision Entertainment, 2000.

Russian Empire. Vols. 1–2. DVD documentary. Directed by Leonid Parfenov. Russia, 2008.

1612. DVD. Directed by Vladimir Khotinenko. Port Washington, NY: E1 Entertainment, 2009.

Tsar. Directed by Pavel Lungin. DVD. Moscow: Nashe Kino, 2009.

2

Great Power, 1689–1796

In the eighteenth century, which may be said to begin with Peter I's takeover in 1689 and end with Catherine II's death in 1796, Russia consolidated its status as one of Europe's Great Powers. Its army was victorious in most battles, and significant territory was gained. Although in hindsight autocracy and serfdom appear to be backward principles of political and social organization, it can be argued that Russia experienced a (moderately) prosperous period during this era. Compared to that in other parts of the world during this age, the standard of living of Russia's population was fairly high and expressed itself in a decided natural growth of the population. Despite the palace coups that were regularly staged in St. Petersburg, much of Russia witnessed an unusual era of peace on the home front, rarely punctuated by the outbreak of an epidemic or a large-scale rising.

PETER'S SIGNIFICANCE

Rather more space is dedicated in this book to Tsar Peter the Great than to some of the other Romanov tsars who ruled Russia for more than three decades, because Peter's reign represents a pivotal moment in Russian history. Although one should be cautious about giving too much credit to individuals' ability to influence the historical process, in Russian history at least three political leaders had an indelible effect on the lives of millions of their subjects and their descendants: Peter, Lenin, and Stalin. Perhaps it is less surprising that those modern-day dictators exerted a strong influence on the lives of human beings, since they ruled when modern means of transport and communication were available to them. Remarkably, the consequences of Peter's rule were extraordinarily long lasting, even in the absence of such tools.

FINLAND

POLAND

TAMMERFORS
NYSTADT
ABO
VYBORG
KEXHOLM
KRONSTADT
ST. PETERSBURG
L. LADOGA
PETROVSKI
(PETROZAVODSK)
NARVA
DAGO IS.
OSEL IS.
TARTU/DERPT
PSKOV
RIGA
ALUKSNE
NOVGOROD
TVER
VILNA
GOLOVCHINO
SMOLENSK
DOBROE
LESNAYA
STARODUB
KIEV
MOSCOW
TROITSE-SERGIEV
YAROSLAVL
TULA
VORONEZH
KHARKOV
POLTAVA
TSARITSYN
KAMENNY ZATON
SECH
BRATSLAV
JASSY
KHLYNOV
VERKHOTURE
NIZHNE-TAGILSKI
VERKHNE-TAGILSKI
ALAPAEVSKI
EKATERINBURG
UFA
KAZAN
NIZHNI-NOVGOROD
SIMBIRSK
SYZRAN
SAMARA
YAITSKI GORODOK
SARATOV
CHERKASSK
KRASNY YAR

Tobol
Ural (Yaik)
Volga
N. Dvina
W. Dvina
Niemen
Pripet
S. Bug
Dniester
Prut
Don
Donets
Desna
Dnieper

20 30 40 50 60

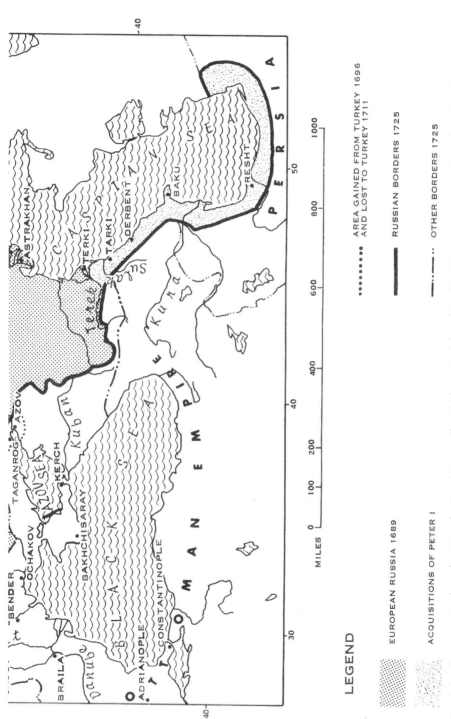

Map 2.1. European Russia under Peter the Great (From Allen F. Chew, *An Atlas of Russian History*, New Haven, CT: Yale University Press, 1967. Used by permission.)

LEGEND

EUROPEAN RUSSIA 1689

ACQUISITIONS OF PETER I

AREA GAINED FROM TURKEY 1696
AND LOST TO TURKEY 1711

RUSSIAN BORDERS 1725

OTHER BORDERS 1725

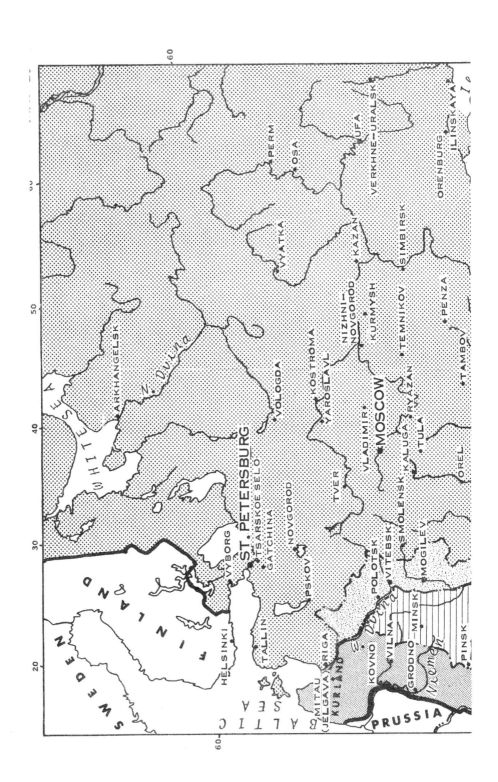

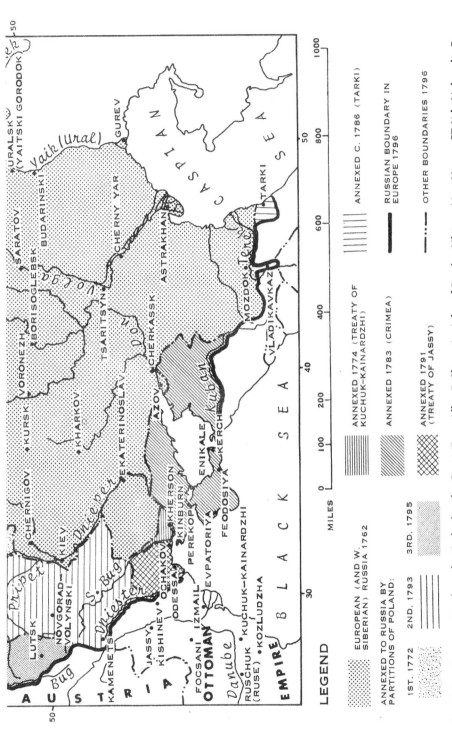

Map 2.2. European Russia under Catherine the Great (From Allen F. Chew, *An Atlas of Russian History*, New Haven, CT: Yale University Press, 1967. Used by permission.)

Figure 2.1. Engraving of Peter the Great, late seventeenth century (Library of Congress)

This was not so much because the tsar doubled at times as a dentist, shipwright, or barber, but because he made Russia into a permanent fixture on the European map, thanks to his military triumph over Sweden and his creation of a navy and port on the Baltic Sea. The transfer of the capital of Moscow to St. Petersburg underlines Peter's European ambition. And even though pulling teeth or cutting beards seem trivial in the greater scheme of things, he imposed a model of behavior on the Russian elite that was as significant as that enforced by the court of Louis XIV (1638–1715) in Paris and Versailles. King Louis made his nobles watch plays, operas, and ballets; he conveyed to his courtiers that they needed to have impeccable table manners and use a toilet when nature called, to distinguish themselves from the common folk and remain welcome at court. Women and men should interact as equal human beings, indeed, behave courteously to each other. This became recognized as the highest degree of "civilization," a standard for all to emulate, as the German historical sociologist Norbert Elias has argued. As Elias suggests, much of the way we behave to each other today goes back to the norms set by Louis's court. Similarly, much of the way the Russians behaved in the eighteenth and nineteenth centuries and beyond originated with Peter. One telling example (and sign of a somewhat different standard of "civilization" in Russia) was the enormous weight placed in Russia on science and education. This great appreciation of such pursuits goes back to Peter's own fascination with science and technology, and his creation of the Russian Academy of Sciences.

RUSSIA AND THE LAW; PETER AND THE NETWORKS

There is a constant in Russian history: although the country has known many law codes and vast amounts of legislation have been generated, in every period of Russian history the law has been systematically ignored or violated by individuals in all layers of Russian society and government, more often than not with impunity. The "rule of law," of obeying written rules, is an unknown phenomenon. Corruption was as rife in Romanov Russia as in the Soviet Union. It can be argued that graft was a universal phenomenon across Europe and beyond until the French Revolution and that Russia was no exception to this rule. But under the tsars or the Communist dictators and their successors, the law never firmly protected Russians and non-Russians from abuse of power and arbitrary rule. A few periods, such as the first decade of Tsar Aleksandr II's rule, stand out as times during which the law was more or less obeyed as well as equitably enforced, but they were all brief. Even then, however, the reigning political theory held that the tsar as autocrat was above the law. From 1866 onward, extralegal emergency laws overrode due process again.

To compensate for this absence of legal protection, people sought and found protection by participating in patron-client networks. In other words, it proved (and proves) far more important whom you knew than whatever your rights were. This may have been as true of Romanov Russia as it is today of Vladimir Putin's country. The height of lawlessness meanwhile can be identified in Stalin's time; then, even patron-client networks offered little protection.

A powerful, highly placed protector could make or break someone's career. Thus in the various palace coups and coup attempts between 1603 and 1801, the fall of a patron was accompanied by those of his clients, as would be the case with those high up in the government who were politically disgraced in the nineteenth and twentieth centuries and their followers. Between 1603 and 1801, meanwhile, the system of tsarist rule and aristocratic hegemony survived a succession crisis unchanged (for this was usually the moment court factions came to blows).

Thus, when Peter overcame his sister in 1689, he got rid of her immediate followers and ordered the execution of both the military chief of Sofia's faction, the head of the musketeers Fyodor Shaklovityi (ca. 1645–1689), and, eventually, her "ideological chief," the monk Sil'vester Medvedev (1641–1691). Her faithful companion Vasilii Golitsyn was exiled to a remote region, and Sofia herself was placed in a convent. But the Golitsyn family remained throughout the subsequent history of Imperial Russia one of the wealthiest and most influential clans. Thus, one of Peter's closest friends in the 1680s was another Golitsyn, Boris (1654–1713), who was a cousin of Vasilii's. Family clans were hardly ever destroyed root and branch, proof of the strength of the networks.

It is furthermore evident that marriage politics were important in gaining and maintaining influence. In the seventeenth century, several families rose to prominence in the tsar's entourage because one of their women married the tsar (such as the Streshnyovs, Miloslavskiis, and Naryshkins). Although the first Romanovs deliberately married women from families that did not belong to the leading boyar clans, the families of those whom they did wed were co-opted into this elite. The women themselves had little say in these matters, but certainly Aleksei's two wives were not without agency and saw to it that their daughters received a good education.

Wary of the power of these networks (and contrary to received wisdom), Peter moved rather cautiously toward the dramatic reforms that he would unleash on his country by 1700. In the first decade of his rule he undoubtedly listened more than his predecessors to Western European expatriates such as the French-Swiss Protestant François Lefort (1655–1699), the Catholic Scot Patrick Gordon (1635–1699), or the Calvinist Dutchman Frans Timmerman (1644–1702), but he was careful to acknowledge the scions of the most important boyar families, such as the Sheremetevs, Romodanovskiis, Prozorovskiis, Golitsyns, Golovins, Golovnins, and Dolgorukiis. Among the other key advisors he consulted were experienced bureaucrats such as Prokofii Voznitsyn (ca. 1640–ca. 1700), Emel'ian Ukraintsev (1641–1708), Nikita Zotov (1644–1717; his former tutor), and Andrei Vinius (1641–1716), whose careers had begun under Aleksei in the 1660s. All of them were part of extensive patronage networks.

Only gradually did lower-class individuals and foreigners who had begun their steep rise as genuine outsiders enter the inner sanctum of Peter's court, such as Aleksandr Menshikov (1673–1729), Cornelis Cruys (1655–1727), Iakov Brius (1669–1735), and Petr Shafirov (1670–1739). Judging by his judicious conduct in this regard during his early years in power, it is apparent that Peter very well understood how Russia was ruled. The tsar was careful in ensuring enough support on his side when he began to change his country and make it, in a sense, more European.

Peter, then, may have had an ulterior motive for his plan to transform Russia into a European Power. Ernest Zitser has argued that the tsar had been confronted from an early age with the check the traditional patronage networks placed on the tsar's power. He may have tried to undermine the traditional power of the boyars by creating a new nobility in which a significant place was given to upstarts, including commoners who had been promoted on the basis of their merit in the tsar's service. Eventually, this system of promotion was enshrined in the Table of Ranks (1722), which in theory made it possible for any free-born subject to achieve noble status.

Peter also routinely had his courtiers debase themselves in his All-Drunken Synod, a carnivalesque mock court, in which people other than the tsar himself played the role of rulers of matters temporal and spiritual. During the festivities, Peter dressed up as a Dutch sailor or even peasant, and high- and low-born caroused together (men and women) regardless of their social status. Once everyone awoke from their hangovers after thoroughly embarrassing themselves, it seems, they were all the more eager to obey their autocrat, to the detriment of their family's interests.

The outcome of this strategy was that, by the time of Peter's death, the monarch was far less constrained by the traditionally powerful boyar families than his ancestors had been. To maintain order in the land after 1613, autocracy had been in many ways upheld as a front behind which the tsar often had to maneuver delicately in tacit acknowledgment of his deal with the aristocrats who backed him. But by the time Peter died, Russia was far more truly an autocracy, in which the tsar could more than ever before draw his own plan, ignoring the higher nobles' wishes.

Still, even then the autocrat, it transpired, could not entirely behave as an arbitrary tyrant in St. Petersburg. Aristocratic networks remained powerful, as did the nobility as a class. If the tsar's behavior was too whimsical, he might find all of the highest circles aligned against him, with fatal consequences, as Peter III and Paul were to find out.

PETER THE GREAT: RUSSIA'S EUROPEANIZATION

The exact aims of Peter's reforms, meanwhile, were already a matter of debate when Peter was still alive (although increasing his country's military might was undoubtedly key). Even the tsar himself seems to have gone back and forth in considering his goals. To a degree, he seems to have tried to reshape his country in the image of the maritime Western European countries, as is betrayed, for example, in the layout of St. Petersburg (which began to be built in 1703), as well as in his stubborn persistence in creating a Russian navy. He was in some measure a devotee of the so-called Scientific Revolution that had spread across Europe, and he admired the findings of Newton and others. He tried to create an educational system in which European scientists in Russian service would set an example for Russian pupils to follow. While Peter immersed himself in such things as shipbuilding, he had other young (primarily noble) Russians apprentice in other military and nonmilitary trades across Europe. The study of military technology was exceptionally important to the tsar. Thus Europeanization (or Westernization) was paired with modernization, and whereas the two are not necessarily synonymous, they were hard to disentangle in Peter's project to reform his country.

It is likewise difficult to distinguish which European models most inspired Peter's reforms. In terms of administrative change, Sweden and various German states seem to have served as his templates. Technological advances adopted often originated in Britain, the Dutch Republic, or France (as in shipbuilding or weaponry). Mining techniques and miners were imported from the Holy Roman Empire. Scientists from Germany and France as well as England were recruited. Military and naval officers came from across Europe. A museum was established in St. Petersburg (the Kunstkamera) through purchasing several curiosity cabinets in the Dutch Republic.

One might identify an early phase, when Peter was mesmerized by all matters Dutch (1680s–1697), followed by an English phase (1698–1710s). A final period saw the tsar

Figure 2.2. The *botik*, on which Peter learned to sail, ca. 1690 (Library of Congress)

fall under the spell of German achievements and a fondness for French accomplishments. That Peter became suddenly enamored with France is perhaps most surprising, but the death of Louis XIV cleared Peter's path to visit France, which he did on his second visit to the West in 1717.[1] He appears to have liked much of what he saw, and Frenchmen were among the first members of the Academy of Sciences.

Paradoxically, the Grand Embassy (1697–1698), during which Peter lived for more than half a year in the Dutch Republic (primarily working on the wharves of the Dutch East India Company), cured him from his Dutch infatuation. He was perceptive enough to realize that the Dutch golden age had ended and that of England had dawned.

Thus Europeanization and modernization (as well as unlimited power as argued earlier) were key aims of Peter. Peter's Europeanization confronted the entrenched power of the Orthodox Church, with which he dealt ever more harshly. In 1689, he still needed the backing of the patriarch to oust his sister, but by 1700 he refused to allow the Russian Church to elect another patriarch. In 1700, underscoring his defiance, he ordered church bells to be confiscated to forge cannon from their bronze.

Even earlier he had rejected the church's long-standing prohibition on smoking tobacco, which Orthodox prelates saw as a sin worthy of the Antichrist. And he left the Old Believers alone, as long as they were willing to pay more taxes in exchange for their freedom of worship, while he happily cavorted with Western Protestants and Catholics. In 1721, he introduced a lay head of the church, the Oberprokuror, who replaced the patriarch as senior administrator of the church. So the Russian Church was led by laymen until the 1917 Revolution.

This is not to say that Peter was irreligious, or a sort of deist,[2] who by then were emerging among Western European intellectuals (for example, John Locke [1632–1704] and Isaac Newton [1643–1727] were both deists). Peter believed in a Christian God but in an eclectic fashion, selecting those parts of Orthodox tradition that suited him. To some degree, he seems to have fallen under the sway of contemporary pietism, a sort of individualistic Christianity especially popular in Protestant Germany around 1700.

Peter's reforms' crucial goal went beyond Westernization or absolutism for their own sake: he was determined to follow in his father's footsteps of expanding Russia and transforming his country into one of the Great Powers of the world. He needed Western inventions, technology, and expertise to achieve this goal. He believed that such a strategy could be rigorously enforced only if it was not watered down by people who were not as farsighted as he was. Therefore Peter's policies were constantly informed by military-strategic considerations. Like his father and grandfather, he faced formidable odds. Russia was surrounded by powerful empires. Peter was wise enough not to take on all comers, except for in one moment of hubris.

In 1696, Peter conquered the Tatar fortress of Azov, an achievement trumpeted far and abroad, and recognized by the Turkish overlords of the Tatars in 1700. But he foolishly decided to declare war on the Ottoman Empire in the midst of his war with Sweden (1700–1721). Peter did so when he had King Charles XII (1682–1718) on the ropes after the comprehensive defeat of the Swedish army at Poltava in 1709. Rather than knocking out the Swedes in the immediate aftermath of Poltava, he moved southward into Turkish domain. The Russian armies suffered a crushing defeat at the Battle of Pruth in 1711, and Peter barely escaped Ottoman capture. Azov, located where the Don River drains into the Sea of Azov, and therefore an excellent port to develop a Black Sea fleet, had to be given up. It took two generations before the Russians recovered the city. The defeat of 1711 against the Turks was also costly in another way, for it caused Russia to slow down its pursuit of the Swedes, and the Great Northern War was to last another decade.

The Turkish-Tatar repulse of the Russian offensive shows the strength of Russia's enemies, as does the longevity of Swedish resistance in the Great Northern War. But Sweden was defeated in the end, formally surrendering the territory on which St. Petersburg had been built since 1703, as well as territory that is Estonia and much of Latvia today.

And Peter was quite successful in crippling Poland-Lithuania. As Norman Davies has suggested, the so-called Silent Sejm (parliament) of 1717 was a watershed in the relationship between the two empires. There, Peter's emissaries made Polish representatives accept a sort of Russian protectorate over them (comparisons have been drawn with Poland's existence as a Soviet satellite state in the Cold War). By 1721, then, Poland-Lithuania and Sweden had made way for Russia as the Great Power of northeastern Europe. Meanwhile, another state had begun to flex its muscle. Recognized as Prussian king in 1700, the former elector of Brandenburg expanded his realm at the expense of crumbling Sweden and Poland. The repercussions of this development would still be deeply felt two hundred years later, not in the least by Russia.

From the perspective of today especially, it is noteworthy that Peter, after all the warfare in Europe, turned to the southeast and conquered much of the western and southern shore of the Caspian Sea from the Iranians. Most of these conquests were lost again during the 1730s, but Peter's campaign underscored that Russia was not necessarily halting its expansion at the northern foothills of the Caucasus mountain range. Subsequently, Russia often meddled in Persian affairs, eventually clashing with British interests. It was no coincidence that in 1943 Stalin chose Teheran as the meeting place for the first gathering of the Big Three in the Second World War. And even today, as much as any country it is Russia that often champions the interests of (a very isolated) Iran.

Peter's victorious campaign against Iran also signaled that Asia might be an easier target for Russian expansionism than Europe. In Asia, Russia's ever more modern military technology made it less challenging to subjugate local states. Indeed, thanks to their firearms, the Russians had already earlier acquired a crucial advantage in their conquest of Siberia.

PETER: MAN AND MYTH

Because he has become such a legendary figure, it would be amiss not to say something about Peter's personality. This is all the more relevant since his semimythical stature seems to go back to the wondrous impression he already made on others when he was alive. Taller than his father, being more than a foot above the average in those days of five-foot-five men, Peter stood out in a crowd. When he traveled to Holland in 1697, his efforts at staying under cover miserably failed because of his height. His facial expression was often disfigured by a tic, through which he had to grimace uncontrollably. He had a lively mind, and his inability to concentrate on any topic for very long suggests that he might have been diagnosed with ADHD (attention deficit hyperactivity disorder) had he lived in our age. Symptomatic was his inability to learn much of a foreign language (although his spoken Dutch was eventually decent enough). As an adult, he could not even write his own language very well. But he was quick in learning practical new skills and had a knack for artisanry, as his ability as a shipwright suggests.

He maintained a feverish pace when working and when partying. The All-Drunken Synod often reveled for days on end, perhaps in honor of the traditional

Russian habits of multiday celebrating. He could hold his drink better than almost anyone and seems to have been about the only one at the court who did not suffer from excruciating hangovers but went merrily back to work. Peter's sex life, too, was vigorous, and he probably liked both women and men. As was not unusual in his day (although a bit rarer among the aristocracy), he liked sleeping in the same bed with male friends as much as with female companions.

Whereas Peter's father had enjoyed two very companionable marriages, Peter much more resembled his counterparts elsewhere in Europe, such as the Polish king (and Peter's client) Augustus the Strong (1670–1733), whose nickname referred to his numerous offspring (and thus his supposed sexual stamina) rather than to his forceful rule. At first, Peter probably got along decently with his first wife Evdokiia Lopukhina (1669–1731), who bore him a son, Aleksei, in 1690, a year after their wedding. In the next few years she had two more sons, who died as infants, however. This was a common occurrence in the early modern era but not necessarily experienced as less of a tragedy than it is today. Whether through this traumatic experience or not, Peter became estranged from Evdokiia by the time he departed for Western Europe in 1697.

Because royal monogamy was so unusual, Peter's promiscuity was probably not the key cause of his eventual breach with Evdokiia (nor would she have been able to do much about it). She tried her hardest to remain married to Peter when the tsar became desperate to leave her. According to the Orthodox Church (which regulated people's lives in this respect), the sole manner in which he would be granted a divorce was by his wife entering a convent. After the tsar had returned from the Grand Embassy to Western Europe in 1698, she accepted only with the greatest reluctance Peter's demand to become a nun.

It appears that Peter's rejection of Evdokiia was rooted mainly in Peter's dislike of her adherence to the old-fashioned ways of Muscovy. Initially, he wanted to replace her with a woman of German-Baltic extraction from the foreigners' quarters near Moscow. He would, however, never marry this Anna Mons (1672–1714). Evdokiia, meanwhile, was permitted great freedom as a nun and did not observe celibacy. She was indeed not fond of the ever more radical reforms Peter began to impose on his country after 1698. In her resentment she was joined by her son Aleksei, who rebelled against his father by choosing to join the conservative opposition to the tsar, much of which was inspired by church prelates. Peter, in turn, grew more and more impatient and indeed contemptuous of his son and heir.

Although Aleksei studied for a while in German Saxony and married a German princess, he did not become greatly enamored of the West. And his character was the opposite of that of his extraverted father. Paradoxically, when Aleksei broke off relations with Peter in 1716, he fled to Vienna rather than hiding somewhere in Russia. The choice for Austria was facilitated because the Holy Roman Emperor was Aleksei's brother-in-law. Peter, still at war with Sweden, judged his son's defection as high treason. Assured through an alleged promise by his father that he would be forgiven for his flight, Aleksei returned to Russia in 1718. Rather than showing

Aleksei mercy, Peter had him tortured and confess to seditious plans aimed at taking power. Together with a number of other alleged plotters, Aleksei was executed. Even his mother Evdokiia was convicted of involvement in conspiring against her ex-husband. Peter was so much enraged by his son's treachery that he abolished primogeniture and decreed that henceforth each monarch was allowed to designate his (or her, as it soon turned out) own successor.

Aleksei's opposition was not just informed by Peter's infatuation with things European. He also seems to have had his doubts about his father's habit to promote commoners (or about Peter's undermining of the unwritten agreement by which boyar clans and tsars kept each other in check), such as Peter's favorite male companion, Aleksandr Menshikov. Menshikov was an arch-intriguer who had risen quickly through the ranks in the days when Peter as a teenager and young man had waged mock battles with military units. Menshikov had served as a soldier in one of Peter's favorite units-in-training. These Imperial Guards were wholly drilled and prepared for battle along Western European lines and, when they saw action for real, equipped with the most advanced weaponry.

After the death of Peter's favorite foreigners Lefort and Gordon in 1699, Menshikov became Peter's most trusted companion (and perhaps his lover). Menshikov introduced Peter to the woman who was to become his second wife, Marta Skavronskaia (1684–1727), in 1703. Since she was of low birth (and of foreign extraction, for she hailed from the Baltic area, too), Peter married Marta (baptized as Catherine in the Orthodox Church) in secret in 1707. Eventually, however, he forced Russia's elite to accept her as his legitimate wife, even if she had started life as a foreign commoner. Catherine gave birth to a dozen children, but only Elizabeth (1709–1762) and Anna (1708–1728) survived into adulthood. With Catherine, Peter almost had the sort of companionable marriage that his father had enjoyed with his wives. He so much relied on Catherine (who traveled with him on his second journey to Europe in 1716–1717) that she was ultimately made his co-ruler (not long before his death) and duly succeeded him (with Menshikov's support) in 1725.

Altogether, Peter had a tumultuous and highly tragic family life (and it should be remembered that as a ten-year-old in May 1682 he had seen some of his uncles murdered by *strel'tsy* in Moscow). His sexual habits, meanwhile, led to his contracting the common scourge of the day, syphilis. It would, at a minimum, hasten his death.

Peter was honored by his own Senate, an advisory council set up to replace the Boyar Duma, with the title of "emperor" and the moniker "the Great" in 1721, upon the conclusion of the Great Northern War. It is rare that monarchs during their lifetime are thus recognized. It shows how by that time Peter's authority knew no bounds. Dissenters had been exiled or executed, and the traditional restraints on the tsar's power exercised by the ranking noble families had been notably reduced. It also hints at Peter's fine understanding of the importance of what in a later age would be called propaganda. Already after his capture of Azov, he had a sort of Roman triumphal entry organized in Moscow, in a conscious emulation of the great emperors of antiquity.

And he had his assistants trumpet his accomplishments abroad. Europe duly took notice. A celebrated sign of the recognition of Peter's lasting greatness can be discerned in the biography of Peter the Great penned by the towering figure of the French Enlightenment, Voltaire (1694–1778), published around 1760. In Russia itself, it was Catherine the Great (1729–1796, ruled 1763–1796) in particular who inspired a cult of Peter, after which the empress consciously styled herself. St. Petersburg's Bronze Horseman, a sculpture "to Peter the First from Catherine the Second" is eloquent testimony to her fondness for her predecessor. Apart from those supportive of Peter (among whom we can count Stalin), he has had his bevy of detractors, from the nineteenth-century historian Nikolai Pogodin (1800–1875, who nevertheless admitted to the tsar's profound impact on the Russia of his day) and the Slavophiles (who believed that Russia had gone astray and lost her true essence because of Peter) to the early Bolsheviks (who despised the tsar's despotism) and the current historian Evgenii Anisimov (b. 1947, who has portrayed Peter as a sort of Soviet dictator before his time).

It remains difficult to come up with a definitive assessment of Peter, doing justice to the bad and good parts of his activities. He certainly did nothing to overcome the growing gap between a privileged (and now increasingly educated) wealthy elite and a downtrodden majority who eked out a marginal existence. But abolishing serfdom and human (or at least male) equality was not something any European monarch seriously considered before the second half of the eighteenth century. Peter was no different in his contempt for the peasants from Augustus the Strong or Charles XII.

It should also be noted that none of Russia's greatest waves of territorial expansion occurred under his rule; his father and Catherine the Great can take far more credit for this. Peter added only the coastal strip along the Baltic Sea northward from Riga to Viborg. Perhaps his conquest of the Caspian littoral should be added to this record, if it is ignored that the Russian advance here was ultimately rather short lived.

What can be suggested is that, thanks to his exceptional skill at self-propagation, as many (and especially Western) historians have underlined over the last generation, he may have received somewhat too much praise for transforming Russia. Peter did not upturn a virgin soil. His grandfather, father, and siblings had pointed the way. Certainly, Aleksei's undeniable victories against the Poles with the help of Western experts and arms stand out. Peter's rule provides less of a turning point than he liked to proclaim himself. Indeed, as I suggested earlier, the tsar would not have been able to reform his country so profoundly in certain respects if his country was not ready for it (or, more concretely, if many around him did not agree that Russia needed to change if it was to survive).

ROMANOV EXPANSION EASTWARD: SIBERIA'S CONQUEST

Over one of Russia's key conquests, Peter indeed exerted little influence: Siberia. The conquest had already begun in the sixteenth century, although the fate of the landmass hung as much in abeyance during the Time of Troubles as did that of the rest of Russia. But after Mikhail Romanov was crowned tsar, Russia's rule in Siberia was confirmed. Around 1640, the Cossack Semyon Dezhnyov (d. 1673) reached the Pacific's coast at the Sea of Okhotsk. Gradually, Siberia became more than an almost unknown territory dotted with a few Russian-held fortresses. Semyon Remezov (ca. 1640–ca. 1724) mapped the territory around 1700. At exactly the same time, the Dutchman Nicolaas Witsen (1641–1717) both produced a modern map following the Mercator projection and wrote a thousand-page description of this "North and East Tartary," the first of its kind, both of which he sent to Peter the Great. Kamchatka's peninsula was explored around 1700, and by 1725 Vitus Bering (1681–1741), a Danish-born explorer, departed St. Petersburg to find an answer to whether the continents of Asia and America were linked.

What was different under Peter, compared to his predecessors, was his great interest in exploring and mapping Siberia. To a degree, this change of attitude toward this vast territory may have been brought about because the yields from animal furs began to decline from overhunting (and possibly from a drop in demand in Western Europe). Under Peter, Siberia was investigated for its potential for trade (linking East and Central Asia with Europe overland) but even more so for mining purposes.

Peter was heavily influenced by the economic theories that held sway in Europe in his day, which argued that countries should limit imports from abroad as much as possible, as importing was a drain on the treasury. This could be done by substituting foreign-made wares with one's own products. Peter successfully supervised a significant economic transformation of Russia in this respect. During his rule, his empire became self-sufficient in terms of iron production and arms manufacturing. This, for a country that was almost permanently at war, was a great advantage. Much of the iron was mined in the Urals and western Siberia. It allowed Russia to be the world's leading iron producer until the early nineteenth century.

All of Russia's expansion in Siberia was accompanied by imperialist behavior of the kind practiced by Spain, Britain, France, or the Dutch Republic during this age. But there were some specific historical roots as well, for Russia was also the successor to Mongolian rule over Siberia. Scholars debate how deep a cultural and political imprint the Mongolians left on Russia. The habit practiced by the Russians in Siberia of taking hostages from native communities in exchange for their obedience and annual tribute had been a Mongolian practice. Indeed, when Muscovy was ruled by the Mongols (from approximately 1240 to 1480), it had often been forced to surrender its own hostages to the Tatar khans who were its overlords. In the seventeenth century, as we saw, native hostages were guarded in the Russian-garrisoned-and-fortified administrative centers, to ensure the reception of the fur tribute (*yasak*) imposed on the Siberian hunting-and-gathering communities. Once the fur quota was received, the hostages were released, but they were soon replaced with new ones to guarantee delivery of the next round of hides.

Little to no effort was made to interact otherwise with the Khantys, Tungus, Enets, Korchaks, or Chukchis before 1700. The Russian Orthodox Church was

Figure 2.3. Siberian fortifications, nineteenth century (Library of Congress)

not a proselytizing creed in the manner of the Catholic Church, lacking the sort of militant monastic orders such as the Jesuits. Some of the Finno-Ugrian peoples of European Russia and Siberia did eventually convert to Orthodoxy, but this was a process of very gradual assimilation, not one in which conversions were routinely enforced with a heavy hand.

As long as the Russian colonists stayed within the traditional parameters of their relationship with the native Siberian population, they faced little opposition.[3] Some communities may have moved farther away from the Russian towns to avoid contact, but there were few rebellions. The Russians followed the tradition of the Mongols, and even if the natives had succeeded in chasing them out, they would have likely been replaced by a new master, whether Central Asian or Chinese. Of course, there were many instances in which Cossacks or administrators misbehaved, abusing the local population or extorting too much tribute to line their own pockets.

During Peter's reign, the Russian manner of rule over Siberia began to change, and the Russian impact on the lives of the native peoples intensified. Very gradually a Russian immigration into Siberia commenced, helped along by a slowly increasing number of banished political and religious convicts. Once the fur wealth declined, the prospecting for metal ore began, leading to the opening of the mines and arms plants that aided Peter to wage his wars. The mines were worked by serfs who were ascribed to the mine owners, thus becoming virtual slaves.[4]

Meanwhile, Peter's lively curiosity was drawn by Siberia. He was interested in its fossils, skeletons of mammoths, shamanistic tools, and so on. He also wanted to establish whether or not Asia and America were linked over land. So he sponsored Bering's explorations, even if the tsar died long before the first expedition led by the Dane returned with news of the (Bering) straits that separated the two continents. In Bering's wake, scholars and scientists from the Academy of Sciences in St. Petersburg began to investigate the past and present of Siberia, engaging in archeological and ethnographic fieldwork. Many of their findings can still be found today in the Kunstkamera and the archives of the academy.

CULTURAL AND TECHNOLOGICAL TRANSFER: RUSSIA'S KEY TO SURVIVAL

What Peter writ large was something that has been a key component of Russia's longevity. He identified early on that his country would survive and prosper only if it adopted foreign innovations, technology, and even culture. In our globalized world, this is perhaps of little surprise, but at the time few realized the importance of such borrowings or adaptations. In the sixteenth century, Tsar Ivan IV had begun to hire foreign soldiers and doctors, and allowed English traders into his country. This added to the traditional cross-border or cross-cultural contacts Russia had enjoyed with East-Central Europe (Poland-Lithuania especially), southeastern Europe (first the Byzantine Empire and then the Ottoman Empire and the Orthodox prelates within it), the Caucasus, and Central Asia (the remnants of, and successors to, the Mongolian empire there). The first Romanovs realized that the most dynamic region of their age was to be found in Western Europe. They relied on Western European military expertise and imported Western European arms and artisans as well as novelty goods in ever greater amounts. It was Peter who concluded that in order to survive Russia should wholeheartedly partake in technological changes that were epochal. That this might change Russia's cultural traditions was not to be mourned, as long as Russia survived and thrived.

Ever since Peter, the more perceptive of Russia's rulers (and since 1990 or so most Russians) have followed in Peter's footsteps. Like Peter (despite professing otherwise), they usually combined Western-style modernization while preserving parts of Russian tradition. And it can be argued that their strategy worked: Russia remains the largest territorial state on earth, when all of the world's other great non-Western empires of the early modern era have been vanquished, victims of a combination of Western aggression and a failure to adopt Western innovations. Perhaps in this sense Peter's example may have had the longest lasting effect.

Peter gave Russia a new capital and a new navy, and he stimulated education, establishing, for all intents and purposes, the Academy of Sciences (and earlier navigational and military schools) in 1725. He obliged all sons of the elite to get an education. Many went abroad to sample the latest European inventions and techniques. Russians began to learn foreign languages, and in the course of the eighteenth century, French began to rival Russian as the aristocracy's preferred language. Western-style palaces, manor houses, and townhouses arose across the country. St. Petersburg was laid out according to rational principles of town planning, emulating both Venice and Amsterdam. Peter oversaw the building of a canal system that linked St. Petersburg to the Volga. He supervised the development of domestic manufacturing of arms on a massive scale as well as that of textiles (primarily for the military). Ship's wharves appeared in St. Petersburg.

Although it is not quite clear how far he was prepared to go with this, he tried to open up Russia's elite to those commoners who distinguished themselves. He appears to have realized that in England or Holland the most dynamic element in society was formed by newcomers or upstarts, who were given the opportunity to join society's elite if sufficiently meritorious. In Russia, such rewards for talented commoners did not exist before 1700. Peter's Russia was far from a meritocracy, and the elite closed ranks again not long after the Table of Ranks was introduced in 1722. Of course, serfs were in theory excluded from making any career at all. Still, remarkable careers for those with exceptional talents were possible ever after Peter's reign. The trickle of nonnoble Russians (such as Mikhail Lomonosov) who (literally) rose through the ranks became a steady stream even before serfdom was abolished in 1861.

FEMALE RULE

When Catherine the Great deposed her husband in 1762, a provincial official cried out about the empress's temerity in revolting against her husband's God-given dominion over her. Male dominance over women, he said, was the rule everywhere in the world, and he refused to swear allegiance to the new monarch. Nonetheless, a protest such as his was an isolated affair in eighteenth-century Russia: few others in 1762 expressed dismay with yet another female ruler. It is meanwhile intriguing that Russia was ruled primarily by women between 1725 and 1796 but that this made little difference to the subordinate role women played in all layers of the Russian and non-Russian societies that made up the tsaritsas' empire.

Scholars cannot fully explain this paradox. What may be noted is that, outside of European states in which the succession to the throne was followed the so-called Salic Law (which excluded women), female monarchs did sometimes reign in early modern Europe, as in Spain (Isabella of Castile, 1451–1504), England (Mary Tudor [r. 1553–1558], Elizabeth [r. 1558–1603], Anne [r. 1702–1714]), and Sweden (Christina [r. 1633–1654]), indicative that royal charisma might supersede gender (i.e., female monarchs thus basically lost their sex as public personae). Although (elite) women in the late Byzantine Empire had been secluded (a custom adopted by Muscovy), female empresses can be found in its history.[5] But there was Muscovy's tradition of seclusion, nonetheless, and then there was the Mongol legacy, which was one of resolute male authority, too.

It appears at least that the effect of more than a generation experiencing the presence of women in high places was of influence on the acquiescence of female rule from 1725 onward. Sofia, Peter's half sister, had been a trailblazer. While she overplayed her hand when she sought formal recognition of her status as co-ruler, she did pave the way for the acceptance of women as part of public life that occurred under Peter. Peter, then, managed to persuade the Russian elite that it should accept his second (and low-born!) wife as a figure of authority, who could replace him at the helm. At the same time, apart from one grandson, still a child, there were no male Romanovs alive in 1725 who were close relations of the tsar. Thus, also for pragmatic reasons, Catherine I was proclaimed empress upon her husband's death.

Scholars have sometimes hypothesized that the easy acceptance of female rule in Russia was linked to a primordial Slavic worship of the "earth mother." Despite all the misogyny ostentatiously running as deep as in other cultures, traces of the worship of women as creators of life (such as Mary the mother of Christ) permeated Russian culture (possibly another sign of dual faith). Because of this awe, Russians were unusually predisposed to the acceptance of women's rule over them. This theory is attractive but hard to prove. Whereas one may find in the works of the great nineteenth-century novelists Dostoyevsky, Turgenev, or Tolstoi a remarkable idealization of strong female characters, it is quite a jump to declare this as typical of Russians' veneration of women throughout the ages. After all, other sources suggest that Russian men were prone to beating women, a practice about which few blinked an eye, indicative of rabid misogyny.

Finally, it must be reiterated that Catherine I, Anna Ivanovna, Elizabeth, and Catherine II accomplished very little in terms of improving the lot of women in their empire. Nonetheless, they did not wholly ignore women's lives, of which the most celebrated example is Catherine II's encouragement of girls' education. Perhaps, too, eighteenth-century efforts to humanize Russian laws and their application benefitted women even more than men. And to their credit, the four women ruled without causing undue hardship on their subjects. Their empire's main areas of settlement remained at peace throughout their reigns, leading to greater prosperity, of which the strongest evidence is a remarkable population growth during the eighteenth century. In this time period, Russia fought wars but at its borders or beyond, not in or near the main areas of Russian settlement.

In the end, then, the empresses were accepted because they donned a masculine guise when ruling their country. Catherine the Great liked to wear the uniform of the Imperial Guards and even had herself portrayed in one (in which regard she consciously styled herself after Peter the Great). Since the monarch stood above the law and occupied a zone somewhere between her subjects and God, she was beyond gender. In practice, meanwhile, all four women encountered sometimes greater obstacles because of their sex than the men who preceded them or were to succeed them.

The role of favorites at the Russian court may have never been as strong as it was during the eighteenth century, even if their influence was exaggerated by contemporary observers and scholars who were contemptuous of women's talents as politicians. Still, the tsaritsas relied on an exclusively male bevy of advisors and assistants (Catherine II's friend Ekaterina Dashkova [1743–1810] excepted), and had to negotiate with them as if they were male rulers. And, except perhaps for Catherine II (who most self-consciously took on a male role), they seemed to have often used their main advisors as conduits who could execute their wishes rather than directly ordering people about. Being a woman did certainly not make it easier to be Russia's autocrat.

THE ACADEMY OF SCIENCES AND RUSSIAN CULTURE

Peter's successors remained loyal to his education program. Thus, in the months after his death, the Russian Academy of Sciences opened. At first this was a research institute in which foreign academics found employment together with Russians who had studied abroad, but gradually, especially after the creation of Moscow University in 1755, homegrown talent emerged. The eighteenth century is something of a cultural transition period for Russia, during which vestiges of a society with an intensely religious and inward-looking culture were only gradually replaced by a secular mindset. Peter's actions shook the elite awake from its slumber, but the emergence of a viable hybrid culture that combined both Russian traditions as well as non-Russian cultural influences (from within and outside the empire) was gradual. Increasingly, the Russian elite embraced an outward-looking and flexible mind-set, rooted in an inferiority complex. Before the wars with France that began in the 1790s, some nobles became so infatuated with French culture that they preferred to speak French rather than "uncivilized" Russian. This fashion faded only in response to the wars with France from the 1790s onward.

This extreme admiration for "Western civilization" may have lingered until the 1830s, if Pyotr Chaadaev's disparaging words about Russian cultural achievements were at all reflective of Russians' sense of their own country (see chapter 3). Indeed, neither eighteenth-century Russian literature nor Russian science had much to offer that has stood the test of time. Mikhail Lomonosov (1711–1765), Russia's first scientist, developed a number of provocative theories in the natural and social sciences, but none of them hit the mark. The writings by the poet Aleksandr Sumarokov (1717–1777) and the playwright Denis Fonvizin (1744–1792) are very dated and seem pale echoes of foreign models. Perhaps an exception can be made for the 1730s satires of Antiokh Kantemir (1708–1744). The 1790s essays of Nikolai Karamzin (1766–1826) appear to herald the beginning of a truly great literary Russian tradition, even if Karamzin is best known as a historian in defense of the autocracy. The historian Vasilii Tatishchev (1686–1750) deserves mention because he was Russia's first truly secular historian, but his history is not especially readable or full of valuable findings. Still, there is ample material available to gain a good insight into the mind-set of Russia's nobles in the eighteenth century, from Tatishchev's work to memoirs, correspondence, and forays into literature (even if the last is almost wholly derivative). A good example is *Chronicles of a Russian Family* by S. T. Aksakov (1791–1859). Such "ego documents" are virtually absent for the previous centuries. Of course, we know little about the mind-set of the serfs, as they remained on the whole illiterate. Court documents sometimes serve as useful sources in this regard, as do nineteenth-century memoirs (of which Aksakov's work is an example).

From extrapolating the evidence from a later period it seems obvious that beneath the upper layers of society, especially in the countryside among the peasants, very little changed in terms of culture. Life continued in its primordial manner, determined by the rhythm of the seasons. But it is not quite true that no changes occurred at all in peasant life. Peter the Great enforced tax collection by way of a "soul tax" on all adult men, which caused village communities to introduce new methods to cope with the increased demands by the government. They often decided to periodically redivide village land to ensure that all households could pay their dues. If at a new tax assessment more adult men were counted in a household, the family needed to cultivate more land to pay its dues. This, of course, represented a significant change for the peasants.

In addition, Peter the Great introduced a new recruitment system for the army in 1705, which demanded that every twenty households supplied a soldier when the government issued a call-up. The recruit was to serve for the rest of his life. And call-ups recurred almost annually. Obviously, conflict might arise about who might be chosen for this life sentence. The departure of the young man for the army was usually accompanied by his mock funeral, with the village community engaging in profound professions of grief. The system remained in place until the 1870s, when general conscription was introduced (the term of service was reduced to twenty-five years toward the end of Catherine the Great's reign).

Altogether, then, this was a transitional era in terms of elite culture, in which much from abroad (especially from the much-admired West) was absorbed by the Russians but often sat ill with Russian traditions. A hybrid or original culture had yet to emerge, and the balance between borrowing from "the West" and staying true to "Russian tradition" remained ever after a constant in the manner Russians thought about themselves, as is palpable in Russian art and literature of later periods. But this culture was capable of astounding feats in arts, literature, science, and scholarship, as soon became apparent after 1800. Among the mass of the population, fundamental cultural change occurred only once serfdom was abolished in 1861, followed by other key reforms, and the empire embarked on economic modernization around the same time. Gradually, a sort of trickle-down effect could be observed, with the small middle class of urban-based merchants and artisans adopting parts of elite culture (through education and emulation), followed by the industrial working class. The peasantry was most resistant to adopt modern ways, but it, too, changed its outlook eventually,[6] a development dramatically accelerated by the events between 1914 (when the First World War saw most adult males leave their villages to serve in the armed forces) and 1934 (when collectivization was more or less completed). Still, even during the 1960s, in wide swaths of the Soviet countryside (even near Moscow) villages lacked electricity and running water, making daily life a rather different proposition than in the cities.

ANNA'S AUTOCRACY

Peter's wife's rule was short (1725–1727), as was that of his grandson Peter II (1727–1730). The young tsar seems to have been led by those who desired some sort of return to the pre-Petrine era, but their attempts to restore Moscow as the capital was as short lived as his reign. The succession of the Duchess of Kurland, Anna Ivanovna (1693–1740), meant an irrevocable resumption of Peter's policies. Although she was a daughter of Peter's half brother, she had lived among the culturally German nobility of the Baltic region and had fully adopted European ways.[7] Her succession was orchestrated by some of the highest peers of the realm (whose ancestors had been boyars) in a sort of attempt to return to the first-among-equals early Romanov monarchy. The Golitsyn and Dolgorukii clans wanted to formally limit the tsaritsa's power and believed they could make her agree to a shared power arrangement. But once Anna and her coterie of Baltic nobles had established themselves in St. Petersburg, they understood that the old boyar clans could be subdued. They turned to those newcomers who had risen quickly to the top during Peter's rule, especially the Imperial Guards, who were distrustful of the high nobility. The guards stood to gain little from any power-sharing arrangement between the tsaritsa and the high noblemen. A sort of alliance between the guards, the gentry from which they primarily hailed, and the tsaritsa ensured the survival of the autocracy intact.

Anna's reign was the high point of German cultural influence at the Romanov court, as most of her advisors (such as Ernst Biron [1690–1772], Andrei Osterman [1686–1747], and Khristofor Minikh [1683–1767]) were of culturally German extraction. She took after her uncle in terms of her carousing, but she kept Russia out of most foreign engagements, thus continuing a peaceful intermezzo that brought relief to the empire after Peter the Great's incessant wars. But like her predecessors, she had no children who survived her, and she chose as her successor her sister's grandson, who was a baby when Anna died in 1740. Ivan VI's (1740–1764) succession found little support at the court, and he was quickly deposed in favor of Elizabeth (1709–1762), the only surviving daughter of Peter and Catherine I. As she had been born before her mother Catherine formally became empress, she had earlier been ignored for the succession, but by 1741 there were few candidates left besides her.

ELIZABETH

Elizabeth (Elizaveta Petrovna), like Anna, has not really been given much of a fair shake by historians (indeed, in the late twentieth century, Anisimov became the first Russian historian ever to write scholarly biographies in Russian of both Anna and Elizabeth). In part, this is because both ruled between the towering figures of Peter and Catherine the Great. But it is also due to certain images about them that have been perpetuated. They are usually seen as loose women, heavily dependent on male advisors and not really accomplishing very much throughout their reigns. Anna is condemned for her excessive reliance on "Germans," while Elizabeth is often reduced to Catherine the Great's evil stepmother.

But while we are awaiting really scholarly biographies about the two of them in English, what should at least be said about both is that they consolidated the new-found status of Russia as one of Europe's premier powers. Indeed, Elizabeth oversaw Russia's triumphant participation in the Seven Years' War (1756–1763), in which the Russian army put the hallowed Prussian army of Frederick the Great (r. 1740–1786) to flight. Afterward, the Russians occupied Berlin in 1760. Frederick might never have gone down in history as a "Great" had it not been for Elizabeth's death in early 1762. Her immediate successor was Peter III (1728–1762), her nephew, who was more a Protestant German than an Orthodox Russian and infatuated with the famous Prussian king, with whom he immediately entered peace negotiations. Frederick was miraculously spared a comprehensive defeat.

Elizabeth, too, was fond of parties and spent lavishly on all sorts of luxuries, but she built palaces as much or as little as her male contemporaries in Warsaw or Paris. She did oversee the foundation of Moscow University. And it should be reiterated that Russia knew an era of considerable prosperity between 1730 and 1762. If a government's competence can be measured at all in those days long before electoral accountability, the well-being of its subjects might be one decent criterion by which to judge it. And Anna's and Elizabeth's subjects seemed to be doing rather well, if their number increased by at least 50 percent between 1725 and 1762. Of course, they benefited from the absence of the virulent epidemics that had plagued Russia in previous centuries and from a fairly mild climatic age with decent harvests. But they should be given credit for not jeopardizing this prosperity and for fighting wars outside of the Russian borders, thus minimizing the debilitating effect of warfare on Russian soil.

CATHERINE THE GREAT'S SIGNIFICANCE

Under Catherine the Great, Russia did fight many wars and of considerable length. But she, too, unleashed campaigns fought outside Russian borders. In the process, she eliminated two of her country's perennial enemies, the Crimean Tatars and Poland-Lithuania. At Catherine's accession in 1762 the disappearance of both polities seemed a foregone conclusion, but her predecessors had refrained from administering the death blow to them. The Tatars were more and more propped up by their Ottoman overlords, but the Turks themselves were weakening, gradually losing their hegemony in western Asia and Eastern Europe in the course of the eighteenth century. Whereas the Turks still fought offensive wars in the late seventeenth century (of which the second siege of Vienna in 1683 is the most celebrated example), a hundred years later their focus had shifted to shoring up the sultan's defense by shortening the front lines. The Turks no longer had much control over peripheral regions and client states (as in North Africa, too), nor could they defend them very well if they were attacked. In the end, in 1774 at the Treaty of Kuchuk Kainarji (a settlement in today's Bulgaria), the Ottoman Turks surrendered their claims to the northern Black Sea coast and the Crimea to Russia. In 1783, the Crimean Tatar khanate was officially annexed by Russia. The last remnant of the Mongol Empire in Europe had disappeared.

Catherine meanwhile oversaw the absorption into her empire of a large slice of the once formidable Polish state. It had already since 1717 been dominated by Russia but had managed to survive primarily because the three Great Powers of eighteenth-century Eastern Europe could not agree on dividing the spoils. Neither Prussia nor Austria wanted Russia to take over all of Poland. But heavily steeped in the mind-set of the Enlightenment, Catherine, Frederick the Great of Prussia, Maria Theresa of Austria (1740–1780), and especially her son Joseph II (ruled in Austria 1780–1790) decided that Poland's survival was an affront to rational principles of good (absolutist) government. Strategically, too, the demolition of Poland made good sense to the Russians. The country still nominally ruled Belarus in the 1770s, protruding rather far eastward toward Moscow and outflanked in the south by the new territories Russia gained on the Tatars. Riga and Smolensk were still virtual Russian border towns.

By 1795, instead, Russia had moved a great deal westward on the map. She now included almost all Eastern Slavic Russians, Ukrainians, and Belarusyns. But she also included most of the Western Slavic Poles. In hindsight, the annexation of historical

Figure 2.4. Catherine partitions Poland, eighteenth-century British caricature (Library of Congress)

Figure 2.5.   Statue of a conquering Catherine the Great in Vilnius, nineteenth century (Library of Congress)

Poland was probably not one of Catherine's best moves.[8] Although initially only a minority of the Polish *szlachta* (the nobility) rejected Russian rule, in the course of the next generations Polish nationalism became a mass phenomenon. And Poles and Russians were in conflict in a most abject violent manner throughout much of the twentieth century (with especially bloody consequences for the Poles).

SOPHIE VON ANHALT-ZERBST: RUSSIA AND THE ENLIGHTENMENT

Catherine thus earned the moniker of "Great" because she added large stretches of territory to European Russia. Meanwhile, she also firmed up the Russian foothold in the Caucasus, accepting sovereignty over part of Georgia in 1783. But the German woman who became Russian empress in 1762 accomplished far less in other respects, despite her promises to change her country for the better. Circumstance prevented her from doing so, or so she often claimed. She once wrote the French intellectual giant Voltaire (1694–1778) that it was easy for him to suggest all sorts of reforms on paper but that she had to write on human skin. This betrays her genuine frustration with the lack of progress she made on the domestic front in remaking her country into a humane civilization populated by educated citizens. No matter how much it irked her, though, the fact remains that she accomplished very little in alleviating the plight of the serfs, creating a civil society, or developing a power-sharing arrangement that gave the country's elite some sort of means to hold the autocrat accountable (other than through assassination).

Catherine (born Sophie von Anhalt-Zerbst) grew up in northern Germany. She was spirited off to Russia as a fifteen-year-old in 1744, where she first converted from Lutheranism to Russian Orthodoxy (and took the name of Ekaterina, or Catherine) before marrying the designated heir to the throne, himself a German-raised prince, Peter of Holstein-Gottorp. Peter was the son of Peter the Great's other daughter who had (barely) reached adulthood, Anna (the sister of the reigning empress Elizabeth).

As wife to the heir presumptive, Catherine suffered through a long period in which she was subjected to growing humiliations on the part of her husband and of Elizabeth. While at first she seems to have gotten along well with her husband, the couple grew increasingly estranged, with both seeking solace in extramarital affairs. Thus we are unsure about the father of Catherine's only child who reached adulthood, Paul, who was born in 1754. Catherine herself suggested that his father was Count Sergei Saltykov (1726–1765) rather than Peter.

Catherine was a studious type and mastered not only Russian but also French.[9] She therefore became acquainted with many of the works of the heyday of the Enlightenment, such as those by Voltaire or Montesquieu (1689–1755), while work by the Italian legal thinker Cesare Beccaria (1738–1794) profoundly impressed her. In his key work *Of Crimes and Punishments* of 1764, Beccaria argued for the humanization of legal practice. This was an era in which judicial torture was still common practice across Europe, as was corporal punishment, and disproportionate sentences were handed out for minor crimes and misdemeanors. Beccaria was opposed to the death penalty and suggested that the punishment should fit the crime. Catherine likely read Voltaire's translation of Beccaria. She was to a degree successful in making Russian penal practice less draconian.

Apart from Beccaria's ideas about the law, Voltaire's advocacy of tolerance clearly influenced Catherine's religious policy. Besides a friendly attitude toward Islam in non-Russian regions, this broad-mindedness for a while benefited the Jewish population that suddenly became the tsaritsa's subjects in great number through the First Polish Partition. When even more Jews were added in the Second and Third Partition, Catherine introduced more stringent discriminatory policies toward the Jews. Many Russian clerics and nobles refused to deal with Jews and demanded their residential segregation. So in 1791 she introduced the Pale of Settlement. It mandated that her Jewish subjects could reside only in the former eastern Polish-Lithuanian Commonwealth, the lands of what is today western Ukraine, Belarus, eastern Poland, Lithuania, and Moldova. Only if they converted to Russian Orthodoxy were Jews free to settle elsewhere. Here, too, as with much else Catherine did, she struck a compromise between abstract ideals and the demands of Russian society, although decidedly favoring the latter.

While the influence of the Enlightenment on Catherine's actions can be further discerned in her attempts to develop New Russia and in her own copious writings, only in the field of education did Catherine introduce meaningful reform, and only in a rather limited fashion. Her main achievement in this respect was the introduction of formal education for (noble) girls at St. Petersburg's Smol'nyi Institute in 1764. Otherwise, her lofty ideas came to naught.

Although Catherine was very prolific in striking commissions that were to look into reforms, nothing much was produced by them that became policy. Most famous was her Instruction (Nakaz) for the Legislative Commission that gathered in 1767 and 1768. The discussions within this body, composed of representatives of all layers of Russian society, were to lead to a new Russian legal code that was to replace Tsar Aleksei's Ulozhenie of 1649. Nothing came of them after the empress became distracted by the war with Ottoman Turkey that broke out in 1768. When this war neared its victorious conclusion (as reflected by the 1774 Treaty of Kuchuk Kainarji), Emel'ian Pugachev's (ca. 1742–1775) rebellion broke out. Pugachev was a sort of second coming of Stenka Razin, bundling within his following a wide array of disaffected people, from Cossacks, Bashkirs, and other nomads who felt threatened by the creeping interference of the Russian state in their lives to serfs driven to desperation by their lords' exploitation. Ultimately, Pugachev was as unsuccessful as his predecessor had been a century earlier.

Confronted with this violent expression of the "popular will," a term that had been recently coined by Jean-Jacques Rousseau (1712–1778), Catherine became gun-shy. If she ever had any inclination to reconstitute Russia's government as one based on a "social contract" between people and sovereign, as Rousseau had advocated in his famous 1762 treatise, she now abandoned any such thoughts. Her disgust at the French Revolution and her alarm about the writings by Novikov and Radishchev (see the next chapter) were therefore the logical conclusion of a trajectory that saw her move from being a qualified adherent of progress to an inveterate political reactionary.

THE LIMITS OF CATHERINE'S POWER: FOREIGNER, WOMAN, MURDERESS, OR AN AUTOCRATIC FACADE?

Catherine's ultimate rejection of some of the most crucial Enlightenment ideals was born of conviction that their application was not very practical. In addition, however, she was also in a difficult position as empress. Although she was Russia's autocrat, her power was by no means unrestricted in practice. Her claims to the throne were rather dubious. Peter the Great had abandoned the principle of automatic inheritance of the throne by the oldest male child, and every succession until 1796 was chaotic as a consequence. Neither Catherine I nor Catherine II had any

Romanov blood in her veins. In 1762, Catherine had been crowned empress because no one wanted to return to the ruin of the Time of Troubles and she appeared the only sensible choice as her husband's successor. Any suggestion that her young son Paul might succeed was quickly dismissed.

Still, both Paul's presence and Catherine's complete lack of any hereditary right to the throne, as well as her complicity in her husband's deposing and murder, made her position shaky. Although apparently few in Russia ever raised the point, all knew that Catherine ruled by the grace of the high nobles and Imperial Guards who had engineered Peter III's fall. She felt obliged in exchange to leave their hegemony within Russian society unchallenged. Therefore, she confirmed her husband's decree that released nobles from obligatory state service in 1762. She eventually even went further by granting Russia's aristocracy inalienable privileges in the 1785 Charter of the Nobility, the only estate to enjoy such rights.

In a deeper sense, however, Catherine's evasion of facing the plight of the majority of her subjects was no more than following the rule book that had been tacitly agreed to by monarchs and the secular and religious elite at the end of the Time of Troubles. The tsar or tsaritsa could rule as an autocrat, if the nobles and clergy could lord it over the rest of the population, and live off the fruits of the labor of those worker bees. In other words, this was an autocracy only in theory. Despite the comparatively large Russian bureaucracy, both in St. Petersburg and in the towns, it was better staffed only when compared to its European contemporary counterparts. This was still government light, with a mere few thousand servants, rather than the hundreds of thousands deployed by Stalin in the twentieth century.[10] The autocrat had little to no control over the enforcement of her rule in any place that was more than a few hundred miles from St. Petersburg, in the absence of modern means of transport and communication. In 1775, Catherine tried to divest some of her power by administrative reorganization, dividing the country into the provinces (guberniia) that still today can be found on maps of the Russian Federation. But even they were far too large to bypass the crucial support lent by nobility and clergy in maintaining the traditional social hierarchy and enforcing the monarch's authority.

We have already pondered the question of whether Catherine's efforts toward reform were also handicapped by her gender, and concluded it was a hurdle she largely overcame successfully. Still, it also complicated her ability to launch any far-reaching initiatives toward political or social reform. There is no denying that Catherine met with an intensely misogynist press abroad. She was made into a Jezebel bereft of human traits in caricatures published in European publications, while a barrage of writings were diffused in which her allegedly voracious sexual appetite was outlined. This was the age in which pornography was born and cartoons became popular among a broadening reading public in Central and Western Europe, and Catherine seems to have been an ideal subject because of her sex and the country she ruled. Russia was depicted as a country populated by savages, by barbarians who had missed out on the great Western heritage of the classic age and Renaissance. This was not a new trope, but it became more refined in the Enlightenment. Russia was more and more portrayed as the non-West, or anti-West, in a sort of essentialist dichotomy. Even the fact that she was virtually the only country with female monarchs in the eighteenth century confirmed this otherness of Russia.

It has also been suggested that Catherine had to rule prudently because she was a "German." This, it seems, is an anachronistic construct invented by nineteenth-century historians. What counted was that she was a genuine Orthodox believer, and in 1762 she was for this reason preferred over her husband because Peter III clearly faked being faithful to Orthodoxy, remaining in truth a Lutheran. There is no denying that there were a few rumbles among the disaffected in the aristocratic ranks or in the clergy about her German background, but such xenophobes were rare.

Catherine otherwise did everything right, closely meeting the ideal image of the monarch of her day. Her armies were time and again victorious on the battlefield, and the standard of living in her empire was generally good, famine being largely absent from Russia during her reign. She was confronted with one particularly widespread plague epidemic in central Russia, especially Moscow, in 1771, but it proved to be the exception to the rule. She could have cashed in on this impressive record and done more to change her country into a more equitable society. Instead, Catherine seemed to some a relic of the past by the time of her death in 1796. This was caused primarily by the whirlwind of the French Revolution and its epochal consequences. Suddenly the political paradigm had changed.

POLAND PARTITIONED: NEW RUSSIA

The First Polish Partition was completed in 1773 without the Poles and their king Stanislaw Poniatowski (r. 1764–1795) being able to put up much of a resistance, as they had been exhausted by internal conflict. Poniatowski, in fact, had been Catherine's lover at one point,[11] but he could not capitalize on the continued good relationship he maintained with the empress. He proved to be a determined defender of his country, but to no avail. It was Frederick the Great of Prussia who played the role of "honest broker,"[12] preventing a war from breaking out between Russia and Austria over Poland. The Austrians believed they had been shortchanged in the course of the Russian victories over Ottoman Turkey, which yielded Catherine significant territorial gain. The Habsburgs received compensation in the form of Polish Galicia, while Frederick acquired the land that separated eastern from western Prussia (more or less what later became the Nazis' notorious Corridor). Catherine took primarily what is now eastern Belarus and southern Latvia, a fairly insignificant addition to her realm. But she kept the territory surrendered by the Turks, which at that point was of the foremost importance in her thinking.

In addition, after 1773 the remainder of independent Poland continued to be considered a Russian protectorate. This somewhat unresolved state of affairs lasted another twenty years. In 1793, alarmed by Polish moves toward a sort of broad-based representative government (inspired by the French Revolution's example), Catherine struck an agreement with the Prussian king Frederick William II (1786–1797) to further carve up Poland. Russian troops had already occupied Warsaw the previous year to ensure that the Poles would not object (some, indeed, fought the Russians but had little chance). In 1794, led in the field by a hero of the American Revolution, Tadeusz Kosciuzko (1746–1817), the Poles rose against the Russians, but this rebellion only hastened Poland's destruction. In 1795, Catherine, together with Emperor Franz II (1768–1835) of Austria and Frederick William divided up the remnants of Poland in three ways.

Ironically, Poland's partitions had begun because monarchs pursuing Enlightenment ideals decided that Poland's messy oligarchy had to make way for rational government, providing education, roads and bridges, hospitals, and the like. But the Poles in the end faced three despots who were frightened by the Polish efforts to reform their government based on Enlightenment ideals and the American and French revolutionaries' examples (who had adopted constitutions wholly based on the Enlightenment's political theories).

Russia gained vast amounts of European territory in the Second and Third Partitions. In 1793, she annexed much of western Belarus and western Ukraine. In 1795, Lithuania, southern Latvia, and parts of western Ukraine were added. At the end of the Napoleonic Wars as well in the reshuffling of the map at the Congress of Vienna (1814–1815), parts of Poland proper, including Warsaw, became Russian ruled. In the 1650s, Tsar Aleksei's armies had already occupied Vilnius. It had taken almost one and a half centuries before Russia was able to take the Lithuanian capital for good (or, at least, for another century plus). Catherine had succeeded in a way Peter had only dreamed about.

When Catherine attacked the Turks and Tatars in 1764, she dubbed the northern Black Sea shore "New Russia." It bespeaks her ambition, which was heavily influenced by her ideas about rational government. Russia would be developed here in a manner that was orderly and logical, and would become a beacon of prosperity that was to set an example for the rest of her empire to follow. She appointed Grigorii Potemkin (1739–1791), another of her lovers, as governor of this territory. He had the assignment to make New Russia work, once the war with the Turks concluded in 1774.

The project to develop New Russia does hint at Catherine's earnest desire to rule for the common good. She believed that she could lead her country out of its blighted present into a radiant future. And she justified her annexations to herself and others in this manner. Thus she took Joseph II on a tour of her new lands in the 1780s, showing off the supposed prosperity Russia's rule had brought to a region formerly merely known as "the borderlands" (Okraina, or Ukraine).

Potemkin, equally convinced of the eventual affluence the Russians would bring to Ukraine, was, however, on this occasion forced to turn to a sleight of hand to impress the Austrian visitor. Although recent research suggests that he refrained from erecting the eponymous "Potemkin villages," he did spruce up the settlements through which Catherine and Joseph traveled. For today's historian, it is difficult to assess whether

Russian rule in this newly acquired region constituted an improvement for its inhabitants. Certainly, an area that had been in a stage of warfare since perhaps primordial times was suddenly pacified when it was brought under the control of St. Petersburg's government. At last, people could go about their business without having to fear murderous and plundering raids by Turks, Tatars, Cossacks, and others.

But Catherine did not quite trust the local population to capitalize on this opportunity. The empress invited farmers from her native Holy Roman Empire to settle in Russia. In particular, Anabaptists (or Mennonites), never very popular in the German states because of their egalitarian convictions, moved to Ukraine and were given generous land allotments and other support. They succeeded in transforming their villages into fairly prosperous farming communities. But they were segregated from the surrounding population through language, religion, and culture. Most important, the Volga Germans (as they eventually came to be known, since many actually settled outside of Ukraine) were not enserfed. Their motivation and initiative were not thwarted by the conditions faced by Russian and Ukrainian peasants, who often had to work more than half the week on their lords' estates, or surrender half of their yields to their lords. Perhaps the abolition of serfdom would have been a more straightforward route toward the development of New Russia.

Catherine, too, invited foreign nobles (especially after the French Revolution broke out in 1789) to settle in New Russia, offering them not only land but also serfs. Oddly, the Russian authorities often described the territories of New Russia as "empty lands." They thus implied that these lands were devoid of inhabitants, ready to be settled and brought into cultivation. That people actually lived there and had survived until that time was of no apparent concern to the empress or her bureaucracy, even if they offered them to the new landowners. It reminds one of how North American colonists and governments spoke or thought similarly about the lands populated by Indian Americans. They were the "People without History," to use Eric Wolf's phrase, and thus remained without a voice in determining their fate.

Of course, when the Russians annexed this territory, Ukrainians (Cossack and non-Cossack), Jews, and others lived there. This denial of noteworthy human existence on the part of the Russian overlords in western Ukraine was symptomatic of the traditional contempt of "subalterns" among Europe's or Asia's rulers. Nonetheless, the influence of the inchoate ideas about various categories of human beings that emerged in the Enlightenment (influential works by J. F. Blumenbach and Carolus Linnaeus both ranked human beings in a sort of protoracist hierarchy) may also be discerned here. The local inhabitants were deemed inferior creatures, standing low on the ladder of human development.

NOTES

1. Whereas Russia and France never went to war during Peter's reign, the tsar was a fervid admirer of King Stadtholder William III (1650–1702), Louis XIV's greatest foe.

2. A deist is someone who believes that God has created the earth but then has no further interest in its subsequent development.

3. Most of the Russian colonists were in fact Cossacks, who in Siberia formed the armed muscle of Muscovite administration before 1700.

4. Serfs are usually distinguished from slaves because they cannot be removed from the land they and their ancestors have tilled; once serfs were forcibly ascribed to mines, they became almost indistinguishable from slaves.

5. Irene (752–803) and Zoe and Theodora in the eleventh century were female empresses.

6. Even by 1900, peasants were often reluctant to send their offspring to school, as it allegedly taught children useless and possibly sacrilegious things.

7. Kurland in the Baltic region was located in what is Latvia today.

8. Historical Poland is the territory inhabited primarily by Poles rather than Ukrainians or Belarusyns.

9. Catherine had received a thorough, private, early education in Germany.

10. The central Russian bureaucracy employed 623 people in the 1620s and approximately 2,700 around 1700. It had about 5,400 employees around 1750. By 1900, the number had ballooned to approximately half a million.

11. Catherine and Poniatowski were lovers before either of them ascended to their respective thrones.

12. "Honest broker" is an epithet given a century later to Otto von Bismarck (1815–1898) for his diplomatic maneuvers.

FURTHER READING

Translated Primary Sources

Aksakov, Sergei. *The Family Chronicle.* Translated by M. C. Beverley. New York: Praeger, 1985.
Catherine II. *The Memoirs of Catherine the Great.* Translated by Mark Cruse and Hilde Hoogenboom. New York: Modern Library Classics, 2006.
Tolstoi, Petr Andreevich. *The Travel Diary of Peter Tolstoi: A Muscovite in Early Modern Europe.* Translated by Max J. Okenfuss. DeKalb: Northern Illinois University Press, 1988.
Pososhkov, Ivan. *The Book of Poverty and Wealth.* Edited and translated by A. P. Vlasto and L. R. Lewitter. Stanford, CA: Stanford University Press, 1987.
Pushkin, A. S. *The History of Pugachev.* Translated by Earl Sampson. London: Weidenfeld and Nicholson, 2001.

Scholarly Literature

Alexander, John. *Bubonic Plague in Early Modern Russia: Public Health and Urban Disaster.* New York: Oxford University Press, 2002.
Anisimov, E. V. *Empress Elizabeth: Her Reign and Her Russia, 1741–1761.* Fort Walton, FL: Academic International Press, 1995.
Barrett, Thomas. *At the Edge of Empire: The Terek Cossacks and the North Caucasus Frontier, 1700–1800.* New York: Westview, 1999.
Boeck, Brian. *Imperial Boundaries: Cossack Communities and Empire Building in the Age of Peter the Great.* Cambridge: Cambridge University Press, 2009.

Bushkovitch, Paul. *Peter the Great: The Struggle for Power (1671–1725)*. Cambridge: Cambridge University Press, 2007.

Cracraft, James. *The Revolution of Peter the Great*. Cambridge, MA: Harvard University Press, 2006.

Davies, Norman. *God's Playground: A History of Poland*. 2 vols. New York: Columbia University Press, 2005.

Dixon, Simon. *Catherine the Great*. New York: Ecco, 2009.

———. *The Modernisation of Russia, 1676–1825*. Cambridge: Cambridge University Press, 1999.

Forsyth, James. *A History of the Peoples of Siberia: Russia's North Asian Colony, 1581–1990*. Cambridge: Cambridge University Press, 1994.

Frost, Robert I. *The Northern Wars: War, State and Society in Northeastern Europe, 1558–1721*. London: Longman, 2000.

Hartley, Janet. *A Social History of the Russian Empire, 1650–1825*. London: Longman, 1998.

Haywood, A. J. *Siberia: A Cultural History*. New York: Oxford University Press, 2010.

Hughes, Lindsey. *Peter the Great: A Biography*. New Haven, CT: Yale University Press, 2004.

Jones, W. G. *Nikolay Novikov, Enlightener of Russia*. Cambridge: Cambridge University Press, 1984.

Kahan, Arcadius. *The Plow, the Hammer and the Knout: An Economic History of Eighteenth-Century Russia*. Chicago: University of Chicago Press, 1985.

Kappeler, Andreas. *The Russian Empire: A Multi-Ethnic History*. London: Longman, 2001.

Kohut, Zenon. *Russian Centralism and Ukrainian Autonomy: Imperial Absorption of the Hetmanate, 1760s–1830s*. Cambridge, MA: Harvard University Press, 1989.

LeDonne, J. P. *Absolutism and Ruling Class: The Formation of the Russian Political Order, 1700–1825*. New York: Oxford University Press, 1991.

Lincoln, W. Bruce. *The Conquest of a Continent: Siberia and the Russians*. Ithaca, NY: Cornell University Press, 2007.

Madariaga, Isabel de. *Catherine the Great: A Short History*. New Haven, CT: Yale University Press, 2002.

———. *Russia in the Age of Catherine the Great*. London: Weidenfeld and Nicholson, 2002.

Marker, Gary. *Imperial Saint: The Cult of St. Catharine and the Dawn of Female Rule in Russia*. DeKalb: Northern Illinois University Press, 2011.

———. *Publishing, Printing and the Origins of Intellectual Life in Russia, 1700–1800*. Princeton, NJ: Princeton University Press, 1985.

Mironov, B. N. *A Social History of Imperial Russia*. Edited by Ben Eklof. 2 vols. Boulder, CO: Westview, 1999.

Montefiore, Simon. *Potemkin: Catherine the Great's Imperial Partner*. New York: Vintage, 2005.

Moon, David. *The Russian Peasantry, 1600–1930: The World the Peasants Made*. Boston: Addison-Wesley, 1999.

Plokhy, Serhii, ed. *Poltava 1709: The Battle and the Myth*. Cambridge, MA: Harvard University Press, 2012.

Riasanovsky, N. V. *The Image of Peter the Great in Russian History and Thought*. Oxford: Oxford University Press, 1992.

Schimmelpenninck van der Oye, David. *Russian Orientalism: Asia in the Russian Mind from Peter the Great to the Emigration*. New Haven, CT: Yale University Press, 2010.

Soloviev, S. M. *History of Russia*. Edited by G. Edward Orchard. 50 vols. Fort Walton, FL: Academic International Press, 1985–2005.

Sunderland, Willard. *Taming the Wild Field: Colonization and Empire on the Russian Steppe.* Ithaca, NY: Cornell University Press, 2006.

Wirtschafter, E. Kimerling. *Social Identity in Imperial Russia.* DeKalb: Northern Illinois University Press, 1997.

Wolff, Larry. *Inventing Eastern Europe: The Map of Civilization on the Mind of the Enlightenment.* Stanford, CA: Stanford University Press, 1994.

Wortman, Richard. *Scenarios of Power: Myth and Ceremony in the Russian Monarchy.* 2 vols. Princeton, NJ: Princeton University Press, 1995, 2000.

Zitser, Ernest A. *The Transfigured Kingdom: Sacred Parody and Charismatic Authority at the Court of Peter the Great.* Ithaca, NY: Cornell University Press, 2004.

WEBSITE

Alexander Palace, for the Romanov fans: http://www.alexanderpalace.org/palace

FILMS

Petr Pervyi. VHS. Directed by Vladimir Petrov. New York: Corinth Films, [1937] 1986.

Petr Pervyi: Zaveshanie. DVD [in Russian]. Directed by Vladimir Bortko. Spain: Divisa Home Video, 2011.

3

The Height and Decline of Imperial Russia, 1789–1855

At the moment the French Revolution erupted in 1789, Russia and Great Britain seemed the most powerful states in Europe and the world. Russia had acquired this status through a tremendous effort since 1613, toward which every Russian had been harnessed, as workers, warriors, clergy, or administrators. But Russia was a mighty preindustrial empire. The Russian rulers failed for more than half a century to perceive the crucial importance of the diffusion in industry of mechanized production processes that began in the United Kingdom around 1780. This led to Russia technologically and economically falling behind, which ultimately affected its military strength, as became apparent in the Crimean War (1853–1856). The failure before 1861 to respond to the challenge to the Old Regime as issued by the French Revolution through some sort of social modernization also had an impact on the fiasco of the Crimean War: the morale of the Russian serf-soldier was poor, no match for the opposing English and French troops who were better trained, armed, fed, and motivated. Any significant move toward a change of the Russian political system, meanwhile, was undertaken only in the early twentieth century, after the tsar was confronted with a revolution.

THE LIMITATIONS OF THE AUTOCRACY

Under Catherine the Great, the Russian autocracy reached its greatest flourishing, but the years of Catherine's reign increasingly highlighted as well the limitations of a personal dictatorship in a country with tens of millions of inhabitants. In practice, of course, for Peter I and Catherine II (as much as for Aleksei in the seventeenth century), autocracy was a fiction. Exerting meaningful control over subjects residing hundreds, or even thousands, of miles away from their capital was a practical impossibility for monarchs in preindustrial societies. The Russian rulers relied on the

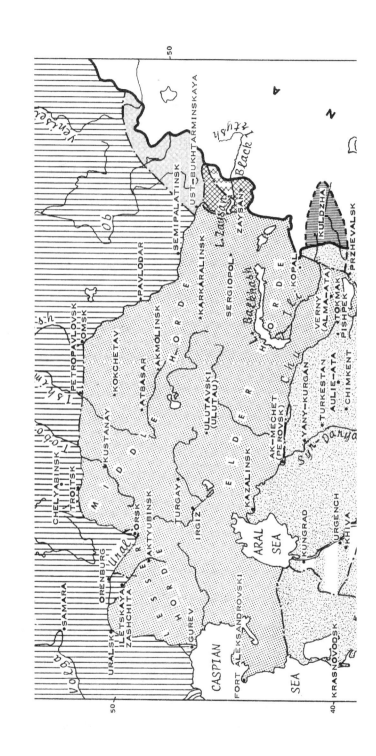

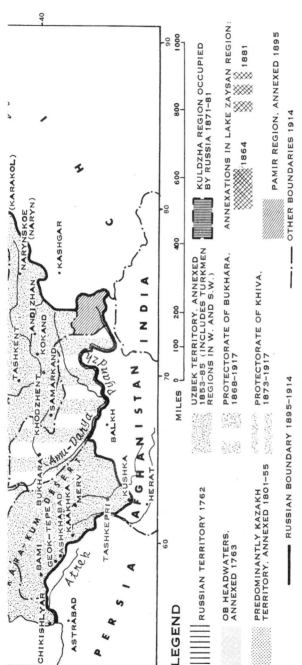

Map 3.1. Russian expansion in Central Asia (From Allen F. Chew, *An Atlas of Russian History*, New Haven, CT: Yale University Press, 1967. Used by permission.)

support of loyal servants who ruled in their name the empire's various subdivisions, which in themselves often covered hundreds of square miles.

The clergy inculcated obedience in their flock, and the majority of the tsar's subjects were (at least formally) Orthodox believers throughout the imperial period. From Peter the Great's reign onward, the Orthodox Church often resembled a government department concentrating on spiritual matters, led by a minister of religion, the Oberprokuror. Government proclamations were read by the priests in church. Peter even encouraged priests to denounce to the authorities those believers who confessed subversive ideas or activities, thus violating the time-honored principle of the secrecy of the confession. What minimal education the Russian peasant masses enjoyed was also delivered by the church and was primarily religiously oriented (as it was in Muslim communities along the Volga, on the Crimea, or in the Caucasus).

The monarchs relied not merely on nobles as senior administrators of peripheral areas in ruling their country and maintaining order. Aristocratic men continued the tradition of serving their country as army officers, even when the 1762 proclamation freed the nobility from obligatory state service. The understanding remained in force that it was the nobles' duty to enforce the tsar's or tsaritsa's rule in the villages that housed their serfs. While the aristocracy could do as it pleased with their serfs, it had no say in the autocrat's running of the central government. At the court, some of the traditional boyar families remained influential, even when they usually allowed the monarchs to select their assistants from outside their clans.[1] As a result, the tsar's inner circle was sometimes dominated by upstarts. Such new men might not be sufficiently sensitive to the wishes and desires of the traditional stakeholders, the boyars, and the senior clergy. Rumblings might then start that could lead to the formation of a genuine conspiracy, with tragic consequences for the autocrat.

Thus, resentment for Anna Ivanovna mounted when she seemed to particularly rely on German speakers such as Baron Khristofor Minikh and Count Andrei Osterman, but she avoided falling victim to a coup herself. Her designated successor, though, a defenseless baby, was quickly deposed by Peter's daughter Elizabeth and her backers. The German coterie that had been in the ascendance in St. Petersburg during the 1730s departed along with Ivan VI. In 1762, Peter III was assassinated as he alienated everyone within a few months. The Imperial Guards, in which young noblemen served as officers, were especially offended by the tsar's infatuation with Prussian ways.

Both Catherine II and Elizabeth relied for advice on favorites (sometimes their lovers) who did not belong to the real blue bloods but managed to play the various court factions well enough (and led the country to victory in war) to avoid being faced with seditious plots. But Paul (1754–1801), like his father, quickly riled everyone by being utterly insensitive to noble sensibility. He, too, was murdered. The overthrow of Ivan VI (who died in 1764 when Catherine decided that she could not risk letting him survive), and the murders of Peter III and Paul showed that there were checks on the monarch's power in practice, if not in theory.

Newfangled ideas nonetheless spread in Russia in the second half of the eighteenth century that went beyond seeking a remedy for the country's ills in the ousting of the monarch and replacing her or him with a new autocrat. Catherine the Great was intelligent enough to realize that she could not pick and choose those parts of the Enlightenment's new thinking about society and politics that she liked and ignore those in which she had no interest. But whereas she understood this in the abstract, she refused to accommodate critical voices that around 1790 began to ponder the wisdom of the continuation of the autocracy, or of serfdom. Perhaps she should not be judged too harshly for this. While it was the result of what may come across to us as an astoundingly patronizing attitude, it was common among Europe's aristocracy. Catherine was convinced that her subjects were not mature enough to function in a limited monarchy in which they were legally free. She appears to have allowed for such maturity to develop in the future. But that future was located somewhere after her death. For now, she treated almost all of her subjects as children.

The principle she and her offspring followed was that the autocrat knew best. Indeed, Catherine was appalled at the French revolutionaries. Their call for a society of equal and free men, ruled by a representative government chosen by the people, seemed to the empress the most outrageous temerity. And her trepidation regarding popular rule was vindicated when in France, after a relatively peaceful opening in 1789, the revolution devolved into an orgy of violence by 1793. The French, it appeared, had grossly overestimated their readiness for democratic government, proving Catherine's skepticism. For Catherine, the French Revolution confirmed how the Russians needed to obey their ruler unconditionally, both for the good of their country and for their personal well-being. She could find further comfort regarding her uncompromising viewpoint by pointing at Poland's ruin. Poland-Lithuania was evidently a country that had fallen victim to an unworkable sort of shared government between king and nobility, in which the king had eventually lost all authority.

To Catherine, the Parisian mobs of 1789 or 1792–1794 resembled Emel'ian Pugachev's hordes of the 1770s. In her view, these were inarticulate plebeians who were easy prey for unscrupulous demagogues. Instead, she believed that the ruler needed to bring her subjects very carefully to the light of reason. This was a process that would at a minimum take decades. She paid meticulous attention to the education of her two grandsons Aleksandr and Konstantin, for her defense of the autocracy had one Achilles' heel: the person of the autocrat. If a Peter or Catherine the Great sat on the throne, the country's prosperity and well-being was guaranteed. But if a Peter III or Paul ruled, things could go awry quickly and profoundly.

Of the six tsars who followed Catherine (and who all came to the throne with the autocracy wholly intact), none really fit the bill of the all-seeing and all-knowing monarch. Aleksandr II (r. 1855–1881) came closest to being a model ruler, but he was assassinated by restless subjects at precisely the time when he may have concluded that autocracy was an obsolete form of government for a modern mass society. And indeed, Catherine's idea about the autocracy was always a theoretical construct that in practice never worked in the way she liked to believe. In that sense, at least, Aleksandr II may again have been most realistic, or pragmatic, in pondering the imminent end of one-man rule in his country. Whereas his two predecessors (Aleksandr I and Nicholas I) at least at times appear to have admitted this possibility, Russia's tragedy was that the last two Romanovs (Aleksandr III and Nicholas II) were the least flexible of Catherine's successors in this respect.

Finally, it should not be forgotten that before 1840 Russia harbored more champions of the autocracy than detractors who yearned for its end. The first noteworthy Russian historian, Nikolai Karamzin (1766–1826), as well as the first generation of Slavophiles, were thus supportive of the one-man (one-woman) ruling system. When Catherine persecuted the publicist Nikolai Novikov (1744–1818) and the noble critic Aleksandr Radishchev (1749–1802) for subversive activities, few raised their voice in support of the duo (Karamzin was one of the few who came to Novikov's defense). In the case of Radishchev, that might have been impossible to do in the first place, for few were aware of his criticism of the regime. Catherine, in her guise as the empire's head censor, prevented his *Journey from St. Petersburg to Moscow* from being printed in 1790. Rather than a travel account, this text was a scathing indictment of serfdom. Radishchev was apprehended and sentenced to death; his sentence was commuted to banishment in Siberia, where he went mad.

Novikov's offenses were rather less severe, but Catherine seems to have concluded that this early example of a Russian *intelligent* had arrogated to himself a license to publish about matters that she considered to be the monarch's prerogative. She also began to suspect that allowing the publication of journals without her explicit involvement was a dicey proposition. Novikov's missteps were far less serious than the withering criticism Radishchev had leveled. Catherine's unduly harsh treatment of Novikov (he was ultimately sentenced to fifteen years of imprisonment in the Shlisselburg Prison in 1792) was in part reflective of the diminished tolerance of an elderly monarch. But some of it was motivated by a conscious desire to set an example: in this way, she warned anyone that works even remotely carrying the critical tone of the publications that had undermined the Old Regime in France were prohibited in Russia.

Under the pretext that she was going to bring order where anarchy existed before, Catherine also divided up what was left of Poland during the French Revolution. In part, however, this move seemed a cynical power play, as the eyes of much of Europe were on France rather than Eastern Europe. Catherine rejected as preposterous the claims made by Polish leaders and their king, Stanislaw Poniatowski, that they were in the process of introducing a more just government along French lines. While Catherine was appalled by the French revolutionaries, she happily capitalized on an opportunity that the French mayhem allowed her by commanding all of Europe's attention.

In conclusion, Catherine II began her reign as someone who was perhaps ahead of her time, who was more than almost any other European monarch in tune with the new ideas that came out of France. But by the end of her life, she had turned into Europe's leading reactionary, astounded not just by the radical turn Enlightenment thinkers took after 1762 but also by the French attempt from 1789 onward to apply some of the Enlightenment's ideas.[2]

The year 1789, then, when the French Revolution broke out, represents a crucial turning point for Russian history, too. For the next four generations, Russia's rulers fought a tenacious battle against those who called for the replacement of unlimited hereditary monarchy by a government accountable to its citizens, as advocated by the French revolutionaries of 1789. The last of the Romanov tsars comprehensively lost this struggle. From 1917 onward, Russia's new rulers tried to create a society based on an utterly radical interpretation of one of the foundational principles of the French Revolution, that of full human equality. This effort, too, failed.

PAUL AND SUVOROV

For various reasons, Paul hated his mother. Key among them was his suspicion that his mother had ordered the murder of his father (that is, Peter III). Paul, apparently, did not believe that his natural father had been Catherine's first lover, Sergei

Figure 3.1.   Generalissimus Aleksandr Suvorov, eighteenth-century portrait

Saltykov. What had spoiled a decent mother-child bond, too, was the fact that, as a newborn, Paul had been taken away from his mother by Tsaritsa Elizabeth. Paul was reunited with his mother in 1762, when the eight-year-old's presence at his mother's side aided her cause at the time of her coup. Toward the end of the 1760s, however, she increasingly began to shun Paul. She kept him away from the affairs of state at exactly the age he should have started his apprenticeship as a future monarch.

In the final decades of Catherine's reign, Paul lived with his second wife, Maria Fyodorovna (1759–1828), another German princess, in a sort of isolated existence in a large palace at Gatchina, not far from the capital. They had ten children. Not long after their birth, Catherine took away the oldest two boys, Aleksandr (1777–1825?[3]) and Konstantin (1779–1831), from their parents. Catherine had the Swiss philosophe Frédéric-César de La Harpe (1754–1838) tutor the boys according to Enlightenment ideals. It was an eerie echo of Elizabeth's kidnapping of Paul himself. It certainly worsened already severely strained relations between Tsaritsa Catherine and her designated heir.

Tsarevich Paul himself had no interest in the Enlightenment. Paul took after his supposed father Peter III in being a martinet, a man who fetishized things military. He spent extraordinary amounts of time on training in the Prussian style the regiments over which he had received command. Rather than conveying an image of military prowess to the outside world, Paul's fondness of Prussian drill bespoke an inferiority complex about Russian arms and ruffled Russian sensibilities among Catherine's courtiers. It, too, reminded them far too much of Peter III's worship of Frederick the Great and his Prussia.

When he came to the throne, Paul decided to change almost everything from the manner in which his mother had ruled. It speaks for him that he amnestied both Novikov and Radishchev. But the new tsar was oblivious to the Russian elite's great admiration for Catherine and her accomplishments. Catherine had made errors for which she was blamed by some of her subjects, but she was seen as one of the greatest autocrats ever to rule Russia. At the time of her death, she enjoyed great popularity among most who mattered, that is, the highest nobles, much of the provincial nobility, the Imperial Guards, and government officials. Paul seems to have been blind to this.

Thus within a few years the tsar antagonized almost anyone who counted. Paul closely resembles Peter III in his ability to offend anyone at the court and beyond. Like his father, he, too, managed to grab defeat from the jaws of victory. In its scope, Paul's failure to capitalize on Aleksandr Suvorov's (1729–1800) victories resembled Peter III's surrender to Frederick the Great out of sheer admiration.

Tsar Paul dispatched an army under Suvorov's command to Central Europe in 1798, under the terms of an alliance with the perennial foes of the French, Habsburg Austria,[4] and Britain. Although Paul disagreed with Catherine on almost every other matter, he shared with his mother an intense dislike of the French Revolution. The tsar's belligerent stance was also informed by a desire to come to the aid of the island of Malta in the Mediterranean. Paul had been elected protector of the Order of Maltese Knights in 1797. The next year, French troops had occupied Malta. They had been part of a French naval detachment on its way to Egypt, which transported General Napoleon Bonaparte (1769–1821) and his army. After they landed in Egypt, Bonaparte was to deploy his forces in an ill-fated attempt to conquer the Middle East and India.

The command over the Russian expeditionary force in 1798 was given to the renowned Generalissimus Suvorov, whose most recent feat had been the suppression of the Polish revolt of 1793–1794. Suvorov's armies proceeded to gain significant victories in Italy and Switzerland. Before 1812, such success was rare against the French forces. Rather than capitalizing on Suvorov's feats and forcing the French to sign a disadvantageous peace by having his general stand his ground, Paul made Suvorov lead his troops through a hazardous retreat across the Swiss Alps. The veteran managed as well as he could, but the Russian advantage was lost. The tsar had decided it was too complicated and costly to sustain the operation. Russia's involvement against the French therefore proved a colossal waste of resources and contributed to the tsar's growing unpopularity in St. Petersburg.

Victory over the French might have saved Paul. Instead, he had lost all meaningful support by 1801. Even his son and heir (Paul had restored the rule of primogeniture as soon as he had become tsar) Aleksandr turned against his father and condoned the plot that killed the tsar. Imperial Guards' officers dispatched Paul in March 1801. It was to be Romanov Russia's last palace coup. Future tsars were to die violent deaths for different reasons.

SPERANSKII

For a while, Europe and Russia fell under the spell of Bonaparte after he became French dictator in 1799. With the young general at the helm, the worst excesses of the French Revolution of the early 1790s were increasingly seen as an aberration. The new leader seemed a man of both military and political genius, resembling a classical hero such as Julius Caesar (and Bonaparte skillfully played on this identification). And Napoleon ruled an empire (in 1804, Napoleon I was proclaimed emperor of the French) that included much of continental Europe. It was a mistake to be contemptuous of so powerful a man, even if he was an upstart of obscure origin. Even Britain was at peace with France in 1802 and 1803.

Enlightenment ideas, while fading, still influenced most European monarchs around 1800, as was certainly the case with Tsar Aleksandr I. At the court in St. Petersburg, in certain noble circles, and among Polish aristocrats who pined for their lost country, expectations about the new Russian monarch were great. At the outset of his reign, Aleksandr, who relied on a small coterie of close friends for advice, began to ponder the idea of a gradual abolition of serfdom. He even gave a fleeting thought to the idea of limiting the autocracy. He also took seriously Polish wishes to restore independence, as championed by one of his intimates, Prince Adam Czartoryski (1770–1861), a high-born Polish nobleman.

For administrative and legal reform, Aleksandr turned early in his reign to Mikhail Speranskii (1772–1839), the brilliant son of a priest. After work as semi-

Figure 3.2.   Tsar Aleksandr I, early nineteenth century

nary teacher and as assistant to the Russian prosecutor general, Speranskii was promoted to the fourth administrative rank within the Table of Ranks in 1801, which automatically gave him a noble title. When in 1802 Aleksandr introduced eight ministries to replace the "colleges" that had administered the country since Peter the Great's days, Speranskii was appointed assistant to the minister of the interior, Count Viktor Pavlovich Kochubei (1768–1834), another of Aleksandr's boon companions. In this capacity, Speranskii began to develop plans that hinted at the limitation of Aleksandr's absolute monarchy. For as long as Russia remained largely outside of much of the warfare engulfing Europe (nonetheless, two defeats on the battlefield against the French were suffered in Central Europe, at Austerlitz in 1805 and Friedland in 1807), Aleksandr was at least tolerant of such suggestions. He did eventually move toward the emancipation of serfs in his empire, when he liberated enserfed peasants in the Baltic region, even if without land (which created a large landless population there).

But Aleksandr was a morose character who may have suffered from bipolar disorder. He grew up in a time when it became common to admit to one's mood swings.[5] Aleksandr never quite shook off a sense of guilt about his complicity in his father's assassination. On the brink of reform, then, he pulled back, choosing instead to remain faithful to autocracy and ultimately rejecting any far-reaching plan to abolish serfdom everywhere in his country.

In 1812, Speranskii was dismissed. He became governor of Siberia a few years later, significantly updating its administration and strengthening the role of the central government in this vast territory. Under Nicholas I, Speranskii was assigned to the task of compiling a comprehensive legal code that was to replace the 1649 Ulozhenie. In 1833, Speranskii completed his task, listing tens of thousands of decrees that formed the legal framework for the tsar's rule over Russia. These were tremendous accomplishments from a man who worked prodigiously hard. Had Aleksandr kept him on as his key advisor, Speranskii might have been able to develop a plan toward the introduction of limited government and personal freedom for all in Russia.

THE WAR OF 1812

Aleksandr seems to have decided to leave Russia as it was when he faced the French invasion of 1812. Napoleon intended for this invasion to be a punishment of the tsar for violating the terms of the treaty the two emperors had signed at Tilsit in 1807. According to this agreement, Russia was prohibited from trading with the United Kingdom. At first, Russian merchants tacitly ignored the treaty, but eventually the tsar openly backed their defiance. Aleksandr argued that his country could not do without goods made by Europe's workshop, a Great Britain in which industrialization was just gathering speed after 1800. The supply of cheap English goods was impossible to resist, particularly because England had been one of Russia's key trading partners for centuries.

Aleksandr, too, wanted to avoid the impression that he was Napoleon's client, as were the Austrian emperor or the Prussian king around 1810. Russia had lost significant territory at Tilsit, including much of historical Poland, which Napoleon restored as the Grand Duchy of Warsaw, a French satellite state. This added to the Russian irritation with the arrogant Frenchman. Thus, Aleksandr took the bold step of defying the French emperor by departing from the Continental System, the French-dominated economic union of continental Europe. Napoleon responded by organizing the largest army hitherto seen in human history. It not only consisted of French veterans but included Polish, German, Dutch, and Swiss soldiers as well, and numbered six hundred thousand troops.

But the French emperor grossly underestimated the difficulty of invading Russia and the particularly adverse conditions of its terrain and climate. Russia had few decent roads (indeed, although in Europe paved roads had improved during the seventeenth and eighteenth centuries, asphalt as road cover was developed only in the early 1800s), and none could be used throughout the year. Even without giving battle, marching six hundred thousand men across hundreds of miles toward Moscow seemed a dicey proposition. The Russians made the Napoleonic advance all the more difficult by following a strategy that became legendary, that of the "scorched earth." Constantly withdrawing, they burned down all their houses and fields before the French armies arrived (who invaded on 22 June 1812), depriving the enemy soldiers of necessary victuals and shelter. This was all the more damaging since Napoleon was in the habit of having his armies march without the cumbersome baggage trains that had impeded the progress of early modern armies. Precious few supplies accompanied the Napoleonic army into Russia. They moved swiftly, but the ranks thinned with every mile, as disease and desertion struck, and troops needed to be left behind to garrison strongholds along the way.

Few battles occurred before the French army reached Borodino, not far west of Moscow, in September.[6] The French numbers had already been sharply reduced by then, primarily because of exhaustion and disease. They still nonetheless enjoyed a numerical superiority over the Russian defenders, who were led by Mikhail Kutuzov (1745–1813), a onetime subordinate of Suvorov. One day of fighting at Borodino saw neither side gaining a clear advantage. Kutuzov then ordered his army to retreat east of Moscow, leaving the city undefended. In mid-September, the historic Russian capital was in French hands. Napoleon waited there for five weeks for a Russian approach requesting a truce. The French position in Moscow was made difficult because much of the city (still built of wood) burned down just after the French had moved in. Thus little food was available to replenish depleted French stocks, and there was insufficient shelter to house the soldiers during the fall and winter.

In the end, Napoleon was forced to recognize that his bluff had been called. He was stuck in the middle of Russia, far away from restless Paris, where all sorts of

Figure 3.3. Early twentieth-century photograph of the Borodino battlefield (Library of Congress)

plots were hatched that aimed at overthrowing him. His troop numbers diminished by the day, and the first frost was felt in October. Therefore he ordered a retreat. Miserable fall weather (rain alternated with snow, with the soil turning from mud to hard frozen and then to slush) confronted the French troops. They were now also harassed by Russian partisans, who sought out isolated French units and annihilated them. The crossing of the Berezina River cost thousands of French lives. Napoleon abandoned his army toward the end of the year, after receiving word that some of the conspiracies in Paris were reaching a critical stage. Historians estimate that a mere thirty thousand troops crossed back into the Grand Duchy of Warsaw. In other words, Napoleon's forces had been twice decimated on their Russian campaign.

It was now only a matter of time before Europe's potentates changed their allegiance and their armies under Russian and British lead defeated the French emperor. In the fall of 1813, the French armies were comprehensively beaten at the Battle of the Nations at Leipzig. In 1814, victorious Russian troops marched in the streets of Paris. Later, Napoleon made a comeback after being banished to the island of Elba off Italy, but his "Hundred Days" ended at Waterloo in 1815 (in which the Russian army played no role).

What has never quite been convincingly explained by historians is Napoleon's odd decision to have most of his army advance in the direction of Moscow. Moscow was not the Russian capital at the time; the tsar resided in St. Petersburg. Indeed, it probably would have been far easier to supply an army that marched northward along the Baltic littoral, even if the seas were policed by the British Royal Navy.[7] And from the Polish Grand Duchy's border, St. Petersburg was almost equidistant to Moscow. Cutting Russia off from the Baltic Sea, too, would have ended much of the British smuggling on the tsar's realm. Perhaps the direction of the main French advance was calibrated after the movement of the main Russian army, which retreated toward Moscow. Before anything else, Napoleon was intent on teaching the Russians and their tsar a military lesson. But his Russian campaign was hardly that of a genius strategist.

The defeat of the French became the stuff of myth in Russia. Dubbed the "Great Fatherland War" or, later, the "Great Patriotic War," the victory was used by Russian regimes as an example of their country coming together at a time of its greatest peril. Lev Tolstoi's depiction of the conflict in his novel *War and Peace* contributed to this mythologization. But just as important was that Russia had triumphed against an opponent boasting of an invincible reputation. The Russian military performance in later major wars (the Crimean War, the Russo-Turkish War, and the First World War) was far less impressive. Only after the Nazi-led invasion of 22 June 1941 did Russia once again seem to achieve such an astounding victory. It was not coincidental that Stalin encouraged the use of the term "Great Patriotic War" for his war against Hitler. Still today, the wars against Napoleon and Hitler are celebrated as foundational moments in Russian history.

THE CONGRESS OF VIENNA

Napoleon's fall made Aleksandr the foremost European monarch on the continent. But the tsar had to reckon with Britain's status as the world's dominant maritime and economic power. And despite their humiliation at the hands of the French, Prussia and Austria remained among Europe's five Great Powers, eager to leave their imprint on the fate of post-Napoleonic Europe. As an equal partner with the previous foursome, France, somewhat surprisingly, was invited to attend a congress at Vienna that aimed to determine the fate of Europe. Briefly interrupted by Napoleon's Hundred Days in the spring of 1815, the Great Powers decided Europe's new borders at the Congress of Vienna in 1814 and 1815.

By 1814, the tsar had fallen under the spell of religious mysticism. Little remained of the man who treasured certain enlightened ideals taught by his tutor. Aleksandr's conservative turn can be traced to the French attack on his country in 1812. In this year, he dismissed Speranskii for being excessively influenced by "French" ideas. After the French invasion had collapsed, the tsar stood once more for unlimited absolutism at home and abroad. But Aleksandr I did not fully reject all reforms. In the 1810s, he oversaw the opening of several universities, while he abolished serfdom in his Baltic territories. And at Vienna he agreed to a resurrection of Poland as a country governed on the basis of a constitution. But this concession was hedged by making the Russian tsar himself the Polish monarch. Whenever he chose to do so, the tsar could override Poland's autonomy.

At the Congress of Vienna, Tsar Aleksandr postured as the man whose calling it was to lead a Europe infused with a revivalist Christian spirit, in which benevolent monarchs once more decided what was good for their subjects. This full-bodied rejection of everything associated with the French Revolution soon was labeled "reactionary." The tsar concluded a Holy League with the Austrian emperor and the Prussian king at Vienna. Its key purpose was to suppress any revolutions across Europe. The governments of France and England, both limited monarchies by 1815, declined to join this team of zealots. In the later 1810s and early 1820s, liberal revolts in Naples, Piedmont, and Spain were put down with the help of armed contingents from the reactionary Eastern European powers.

Although Aleksandr was tempted, he refused in the end to throw his support behind a Greek rising against the Ottoman Turks. He convinced himself that aiding the Greek rebels would be in conflict with the principle of legitimacy. It meant adherence to hereditary rule (which in the eighteenth century had hardly been the rule for the succession to the Russian throne, of course!). In Aleksandr's mind and that of his peers, this principle had kept Europe stable before the French sabotaged it through their subversive Enlightenment writings and subsequent revolutionary deeds. Support for legitimacy called for observance of the political status quo, and the rejection of any rebellion against hereditary rulers, even if they were Muslims such as the Turkish sultan.

After 1812, Aleksandr followed a domestic policy that was intolerant of any dissenting opinion. The tsar let himself be more and more guided by the utterly conservative Count Aleksei Arakcheev (1769–1834). In 1816, Arakcheev masterminded an attempt to create an army reserve on the cheap by way of military-agricultural "colonies." In these communities, soldiers were to engage in agriculture in peacetime, albeit subject to military discipline and corporal punishment (which was normal in the military). All able-bodied men in these colonies could be quickly mobilized in wartime. Since the term of army service was twenty-five years, ascription to any of these settlements virtually meant a life sentence. Meanwhile, villages outside the colonies continued to be apportioned a certain quota of soldiers according to the number of their households, with recruits chosen by lot. While Arakcheev's system (as well as the lottery) was harsh if seen from today's perspective, life in the colonies was perhaps not much harsher than life for the peasants who stayed outside the military. One might propose that peasant soldiers at least saw something of the world, unlike most of their enserfed peers.

Altogether, Aleksandr's last years were little different from the notorious reign of his successor Nicholas I. Beneath the surface, something was nevertheless stirring. Army officers began to discuss ideas for a constitutional monarchy, inspired by what they had witnessed in Western Europe in the 1810s in pursuit of the French. Some even contemplated the foundation of a Russian republic, which would very much stand out in a Europe of monarchies. And the printing presses did churn out more and more publications, which had a fissiparous effect, even if censorship was strict. Authors and scholars now began to find a distinct Russian voice, as is evident from the works of Aleksandr Pushkin (1799–1837) and the historian Karamzin. Karamzin wrote a history of Russia in which he defended the autocracy as the best form of government for his country (a position he had defended before the tsar in a sort of policy paper in 1812). Pushkin's *Prisoner of the Caucasus* was an instant success in 1823 (and has a timeless plot, as the Russian film director Sergei Bodrov's version of the 1990s shows).

PERENNIAL BACKWARDNESS?

A trope about Russian history is that the country forever falls behind (the times, the West, technologically, economically, etc.) but then manages to catch up only to fall behind again. In 1931, the Soviet dictator Stalin (1878–1953) suggested that his Communist country was a century behind the capitalist world; in order to survive against the capitalist foe, it needed to catch up in less than ten years. Of course, this trope proves to be dubious when investigated more closely. Any concept about "history repeating itself" is dicey. It is at best of limited use in understanding Russia.

Nonetheless, one may discern a cyclical pattern if one considers Russia a primarily European power and measures Russia's might against that of other European polities. Three or four periods of growth and decline in military-political significance can then be distinguished from 1613 to 2013. The first is the longest, spanning the seventeenth and eighteenth centuries. It slowly made Russia from a remote backwater into the strongest empire on the European continent, as was confirmed in its preeminent role at Vienna during 1814–1815. Then stagnation and decline followed, capped by the defeat in the Crimean War. Russia had fallen far behind the United Kingdom and France, and it compared poorly in terms of economic growth and technological advance, as well as military strength, to Imperial Germany after it was founded in 1871. The second era saw Russia desperately trying to catch up with the more advanced powers from 1856 to the First World War. Late Imperial Russia never quite succeeded in this before 1914.

Another rapid collapse followed, the low point being reached around 1920. The third period of growth covers the subsequent half century. Soviet Russia began as a destitute polity on Europe's fringe but was one of the world's Big Three by 1945. The country reached the height of its geopolitical power (indeed, a "superpower") somewhere between 1945 and the early 1970s. Then a rapid decline set in, brought to a halt only by around 2000. In the last dozen years, a process of renewal might be discerned that appears to lead toward Russia's once again assuming the mantle of the mightiest power in Europe.

Of course, when Russia is seen as a Eurasian power (let alone an Asian one), the country's rise from 1613 onward seems inexorable before 1991 (the territorial losses suffered in the 1904–1905 war against Japan would then hallmark the only significant setback, but even they were recovered in 1945). From a somewhat similar perspective, Russia could be considered the European colonial ruler in Asia with the greatest longevity.

As we have seen, in the first of the four periods sketched above, the early Romanovs (the three generations ruling the country from 1613 to 1725) effectively modernized their country (especially in military terms), allowing Russia to become one of Europe's Great Powers by 1725. The eighteenth-century tsaritsas successfully continued on this path. By the time of Catherine the Great, Russia was one of the two leading continental powers in Europe as well as the greatest power, together with China, in Asia. This power appeared to be confirmed in the Napoleonic Wars.

But at that very same moment, in fact, the Russian Empire's preeminence was imperiled by the Industrial Revolution that had overtaken Great Britain. Russia (which had been the largest iron producer in the world in the eighteenth century, among other things) now began to fall behind rapidly in economic and technological terms. Contemporary economists like Adam Smith (1723–1790) and Karl Marx (1818–1883) suggested that economies based on free labor performed far better than those in which great numbers of the population were unfree. They argued that the initiative of slaves or serfs was thwarted by their lack of freedom, as they had no incentive to reach higher production levels through innovation. According to Smith or Marx, the ruling class of such societies, too, had little reason to take economic risks, as long as it received a decent livelihood from the fruits of others' labor. Imperial Russia seems a case in point.

Around 1800, merely a small segment of the Russian population was involved in business, mainly in trade or artisanry. There were free and, increasingly, unfree artisans, plying minor crafts, from masonry to carpentry and the like (*kustary*) in the countryside. Some serfs, especially in the inhospitable area north of the Black Earth zone, paid their lords quitrent, which they earned with their labor as itinerant artisans or as seasonal workers, away from their ancestral villages. But whereas some serfs accomplished remarkable feats (such as setting up the first Russian textile mills and astounding artistic accomplishments), the majority languished under the thumb of the Russian landowners.

After 1800, the number of those enjoying a solid education grew in Russia, but learning does not necessarily translate into entrepreneurship. And illiteracy remained very high compared to Europe (though not to Asia). Around 1850, few among the

Russian, Ukrainian, and Belarusyn peasant masses or the inhabitants of the Caucasus and Central Asia were capable of reading. Progress was made in this regard after 1856: by 1900, literacy levels were far higher than half a century earlier, and predictions were made that illiteracy would be stamped out by 1930.

In the absence of a large middle class, the government had to serve as the catalyst jump-starting industrialization. Before the 1880s, it failed to do this in a consistent manner. Once its efforts became more coordinated, government initiative was joined by a growing number of Russian and foreign entrepreneurs, and industrialization truly took off. Seen in the light of subsequent developments, their combined efforts came too late. They failed to develop Russia's economy sufficiently to near British, German, American, or even French industrialization levels on the eve of the First World War. This belated development not only hampered the Russian military performance against Germany and Austria-Hungary but also caused the country to be in the throngs of the dislocation caused in every society by the early stages of industrialization. Toward 1914, the cities of the tsar's empire were teeming with uprooted people who had abandoned the traditional lives of their ancestors in the village but had not yet settled into an urban way of life. Housing was dismal, nutrition poor, accidents common in the factories and mines, and illness frequent.

Life had been as short and brutish (or even more so, possibly) in the villages, but the discrepancy between rich and poor had not been so evident as it was in the towns, where the wealthy lived in "respectable" abodes not far from working-class slums. And whereas in the villages hatred of the landlords' oppression had sometimes burst out in orgies of violence on a small and a large scale (as it had in Pugachev's time), protest was inarticulate and badly organized. In the Russian cities of the early 1900s, however, socialist activists persuaded the downtrodden that their harsh fate was not inevitable and that they could find power in solidarity with their fellow proletarians. In late Imperial Russia, the cities' mood was volatile, and the anger was being harnessed.

What followed were the First World War, the 1917 Revolution, and the Civil War, in which socialists in the name of the working class proved victorious. If Russia had been behind the leading industrialized countries in 1914, it was much further behind by 1921. For once, we can agree with Stalin, when he suggested in 1931 that his country needed to catch up, even if the backwardness he lamented was not just the result of the Old Regime's fumbling alone. Again, at the expense of extraordinary human suffering, it did so between 1928 and 1953. But success again bred complacency: the defeat of Nazi Germany, the development of an atomic and hydrogen bomb, and the first satellite and man in space provided an illusion that Russia had finally and permanently caught up with the West. As in the first half of the nineteenth century, however, economic and technological initiative was not encouraged by a regime that excessively curtailed human freedom. Thus in 1991, when the Soviet Union collapsed, the post-Soviet states were once more in the same position as Soviet Russia had been in 1921, or tsarist Russia in 1613 or 1856.

STAGNATION: THE DECEMBRISTS
AND THE THIRD DEPARTMENT

It is not as if Tsar Nicholas I (1796–1855, r. 1825–1855) was unaware of the obsolescence of serfdom. The problem was that he did not know how to dismantle it. He feared that any move toward its abolition might endanger the very survival of Russia. He patronized his subjects as contemptuously as had his grandmother (and older brother). Nicholas's pedantic condescension toward his peoples is well illustrated by his personal censoring of Pushkin's writings. The tsar's conviction about his subjects' inability to decide what was good for them made the emancipation of the serfs a difficult proposition. Nicholas considered all his subjects, from his ministers to the humblest beggar on the streets of Astrakhan, his servants. The fate of each of them was in his hands.

That the monarch stood above the law was the underlying principle of autocracy. In practice, however, Russia's system of rule had been based on a compromise between tsar, nobility, and church. Since, after their release from obligatory state service in 1762 and the confirmation of their rights in the 1785 Charter of the Nobility, the nobles became ever more a superfluous class, the tsar often treated them with contempt.[8] Somewhere Russia missed a key move on the chessboard that would have invited the nobility and religious chiefs to participate in a more formal setting in the political process. Abruptly in France, and gradually in Britain, Prussia, or Austria, the elite became a constituent part of the government, but Russia held firm to its autocracy until 1905.

In hindsight, some sort of compromise granting political rights to the elite in exchange for releasing the serfs from their bondage might have prevented much of the tragedy that was to follow. And particularly Nicholas I's reign might have been the right period to end both autocracy and serfdom. Although Nicholas was at least considering a strategy to abolish serfdom, he never seems to have entertained the thought that autocracy might have had its day, too.

That the time had come to consider far-reaching reform of Russia's government and society might have been evident from a comparison between Russia and the larger states to its west. In 1848, Austria was the last among them to abolish what was left of serfdom there. This took place during a revolution that almost ended Habsburg rule altogether. In that same year, the sort of unlimited monarchy restored at the Congress of Vienna a generation earlier was challenged across Europe. Even if these revolutions of 1848 failed to establish liberal democracies, almost everywhere the electoral franchise was widened, while parliaments acquired some degree of oversight over royal rule. But this was not so in Russia, where all was quiet in 1848. Nicholas was so much assured of the loyalty of his subjects that he dispatched an army to Hungary to help the Habsburgs back in the saddle.

Of course, one might suggest that Russia's government and social organization should not be measured against that of European countries. If compared to late Qing China or the Ottoman Empire, where unfree labor of some sort was still widespread around 1850, Russia was not lagging. Such an argument, however, might become one in which Russia is grouped among "Oriental despotisms," essentialized as a sort of Asian type of regime (a caricature in itself, of course), in which the mass of the population will always be doomed to be no more than drones. Such a simplistic generalization belongs to the same sort of uninformed reasoning that holds that Russians like to be governed by dictators.[9] And Russia's frame of reference was Europe, not Asia.

Several reasons made Nicholas I into the archconservative that he was. Unlike his older brothers, he had not been educated by an enlightened type such as La Harpe. Indeed, he never knew his grandmother Catherine II, who died in the year he was born, and he hardly remembered his father Paul. By the time he was a teenager, the reaction against things French (and everything associated with them, such as personal freedom or human equality) had descended on Russia, and the country was preoccupied with military matters throughout his adolescence. It is no surprise that Nicholas resembled his father Paul and grandfather Peter III in his militaristic view of life.

Apart from this infatuation with the military style, he was further shaped by the events surrounding his succession in late 1825. We saw in the previous chapter how in the final years of Aleksandr's reign army officers began to plot. A first-class opportunity to attempt to introduce a limited monarchy in Russia seemed to present itself when Aleksandr died in the fall of 1825 in Taganrog, in the south of Russia. Unbeknownst to many even inside Russia's leading circles, the next in line to succeed, his brother Konstantin (1779–1831), who was the viceroy of Poland, had renounced his rights to the throne. The official reason was that his second wife, Zhanetta Grudzinskaia (Joanna Grudzinska, 1791–1831), was of low aristocratic birth, which disqualified Konstantin from the throne (as he was in what was called a "morganatic" marriage). This reason was somewhat spurious because many previous tsars (Peter the Great first and foremost) had married below their station.

Few were aware that Konstantin's younger brother Nicholas had replaced him as Aleksandr's successor. No public announcement had been made at the time of this change in 1823. The conspiring officers in 1825 believed that Konstantin, who had served as viceroy of the constitutional monarchy of Poland for a decade, might be inclined to grant concessions that would end the Russian autocracy after he became tsar. It was true that the Southern Society of rebellious officers, led by Pavel Pestel (1793–1826), called for the establishment of a republic, but those who organized the uprising in St. Petersburg preferred a constitutional monarchy, and Konstantin seemed a credible candidate to serve as a constitutional monarch.

Upon the news of Aleksandr's death, the officers set their plan in motion. When news from Warsaw reached the Russian capital that Konstantin had renounced his claims to the throne, the plotters drew up several thousands of troops on a square in central St. Petersburg. The troops allegedly shouted "*Konstantin i konstitutsiia*," believing that Konstitutsiia was Konstantin's wife rather than a constitution. Although the story may be apocryphal, it does convey the rank and file's puzzlement about their officers' actions. The officers themselves had no clear plan about how to proceed further after their show of strength. A confused standoff ensued. Nicholas ordered loyal troops to surround the rebels and eventually had them pummeled by cannon, which ended this Decembrist Uprising.

Five of the ringleaders of the Decembrists were condemned to death, while many of their coconspirators were sentenced to long sentences of Siberian exile. Tsar Nicholas himself personally conducted some of the interrogations. The bungled coup took away any doubt he may have had about the manner in which he was to rule Russia. He immediately ordered the organization within his personal chancellery of a secret police with the brief to root out any subversive activity: the Third Department, headed by Count Benckendorff (1783–1844). It began to monitor anyone suspected of opposition to the tsar's one-man rule.

THE BIRTH OF THE INTELLIGENTSIA

Despite their zealous efforts, the Third Department's agents failed to stop the growth of opposition to the tsar's autocracy. Apart from monitoring subversive elements, Nicholas tried to find a positive manner in which to rally his population behind him and his country. His minister of education, Sergei Uvarov (1786–1855), developed a three-pronged ideology behind which the Russians were to rally, that of unwavering support for orthodoxy (*pravoslavie*), autocracy (*samoderzhavie*), and nationality (*narodnost'*). In practice, this ideology meant little more than adherence to the status quo and failed to elicit much enthusiasm. In addition, it excluded non-Orthodox Slavs, an ever-growing part of Russia's population.

In its (awkward) attempt to instill a sort of national pride among the Eastern Slavs in their country, this official ideology was most cuttingly countered by an essay written by Pyotr Chaadaev (1794–1856). Chaadaev's *Philosophical Letter* of 1836 declared that Russia, albeit a large country, had historically never produced anything of lasting benefit for humanity (meaning, in particular, in the arts and sciences). He implied that Nicholas's ideology was composed of windy slogans devoid of content. Already at the time of his writing, Chaadaev's proposition about Russia's utter uselessness was undermined, albeit not by the tsar. Chaadaev was a contemporary of Pushkin, whose work continues to belong today to the finest specimens of world literature. Soon the world heard from other Russian writers, scholars, painters, composers, and scientists as well. Indeed, 1836 was the year of the premiere of Mikhail Glinka's (1804–1857) *Life for the Tsar*, the first great Russian opera.

The much-improved educational opportunities after 1800 led to the growth of an erudite and articulate citizenry. Many of those who enjoyed secondary or postsecondary education were noble, but nonnobles increasingly attended a lyceum or gymnasium, secondary schools styled after academically rigorous French and German models. After they graduated from such schools, commoners nonetheless faced barriers in attempting to join society's elite, since they lacked aristocratic status. While some nevertheless made careers in the army or the civilian administration by rising through the ranks, others became disaffected and began to question a society based on inherent privilege. And in a development not unknown elsewhere (many French nobles in 1789 supported the abolition of their privileges in the French Revolution) and already foreshadowed by the Decembrists' rebellion, some noblemen and noblewomen, too, began to doubt the justice of a system based on a premise of fundamental human inequality. Aristocratic disgruntlement was additionally nourished by the denial of any noble role in Russia's government.

To the end of the 1830s, then, the first signs can be traced of an erudite clandestine opposition to the regime. Isaiah Berlin has placed this "birth of the intelligentsia" during a "Marvelous Decade," beginning in 1838 and ending in 1848. In different guises, this intelligentsia (a Russian term derived from a European term) became a fixture in Russian society ever after. The first intellectuals who pondered a change in Russia's governance and social organization met in discussion circles, of which the pioneering one was organized by Nikolai Stankevich (1813–1840). Another early leading light was Mikhail Petrashevskii (1821–1866), a follower of the ideas of the French socialist Charles Fourier (1772–1837) and a materialist. The young *intelligenty* (few were older than thirty in 1840), indeed, debated not just social and political change but religion as well. Many were atheists, the first time ever that unbelievers had appeared in any number in Russia. Among the Petrashevtsy Circle was a young writer, Fyodor Dostoyevsky (1821–1881). Other *intelligenty* included Aleksandr Herzen (Gertsen; 1812–1870), who already in 1835 was arrested for reciting verse critical of the tsar and who was the first true Russian socialist; the Ukrainian poet Taras Shevchenko (1814–1861); the literary critic Vissarion Belinskii (1811–1848); and the feisty nobleman Mikhail Bakunin (1814–1876), who was to be the founder of anarchism as a political movement.

Whereas the members of the Stankevich and Petrashevtsy Circles agreed that Russia's path forward should be found in remaking Russia in the image of Western European countries (and thus were eventually called "Westernizers"), another group emerged that took a wholly opposite viewpoint. These were the Slavophiles, among whom Aleksei Khomiakov (1804–1860), Ivan (1806–1856) and Pyotr (1808–1856) Kireevskii, and Ivan (1823–1886) and Konstantin (1817–1860) Aksakov were the leaders. They were all devout Orthodox Christians who suggested that Russia had abandoned its destiny when it began to introduce reforms based on Western ideas and models. For the Slavophiles, the villain of the plot was Peter the Great. They called for a return to (a mythical) pre-Petrine society, which had allegedly been one of harmonious village communities led by a genuine Orthodox spirit. Like the Westernizers, the Slavophiles condemned serfdom, but they were less critical of the autocracy as such. For some, indeed, the "most silent" and devout Tsar Aleksei Mikhailovich had been an ideal leader of Russia. Much of the Slavophile views were based on such historical myth, but their ideological opponents were likewise guilty of distortions of Russia's past and present.

To some degree, all *intelligenty* had been captivated by the philosophy of the German G. W. F. Hegel (1770–1831), even if many subsequently abandoned his concepts of the dialectic mechanism underlying the course of history, or that history's essence is about the realization of the World Spirit. Nor did any of them ever care much for Hegel's idea that German Prussia was furthest advanced on the road to the culmination of history, with its state incarnating this World Spirit to the greatest degree. Hegel, nonetheless, was to have a profound influence on Russian history. In particular, his emphasis on the importance of the growing strength of the state in history became dogmatic for most nineteenth-century Russian historians, led by S. M. Solov'ev (1820–1879). Hegel's dialectic, by way of Karl Marx's historical materialism, was a fundamental component in the Communist worldview of Lenin and his comrades.

The Third Department monitored the Petrashevtsy and Stankevich Circles but held off from a crackdown on the intelligentsia until revolution broke out across Europe in 1848. The tsar then ordered the rounding up of all critics. Thus, Dostoyevsky was arrested in 1849 and sentenced to death, only to have his sentence commuted at the last moment. He was banished to hard labor (*katorga*) in Siberia, from which he was to return a changed man. Few, however, experienced a similar catharsis. The government persecution of the intelligentsia was successful only in the short term. The genie was out of the bottle: socialism, liberalism, atheism, and nationalism spread across the tsar's empire in Nicholas's later years and during the subsequent reign of his son Aleksandr II (1818–1881, r. 1855–1881).

Because of its momentous consequences, historians have sometimes been blinded by the growth of this opposition at the expense of everything else occurring in the 1850s. After all, three-quarters of a century later, the "grandchildren" of Herzen, Bakunin, or Belinskii fomented a revolution of almost unprecedented scope. As a result, they have sometimes ignored that, toward the end of Nicholas's reign, members of the highest circles of Russia often ached for reforms as well. The tsar was not enthusiastic about discussions on this issue even by these people (as he did not like any discussion that had not been started by him) but did not prohibit them, increasingly aware that serfdom had had its day. Among those advocating serfdom's abolition was the tsar's second son Konstantin (1827–1892) and the tsar's sister Elena (1807–1873). They were patrons of various high-ranking bureaucrats such as Nikolai Miliutin (1818–1872). Eventually, Tsar Nicholas struck several commissions that began to study the practical implementation of serfdom's abolition. Miliutin was to become the most influential advisor of Aleksandr II regarding the emancipation of the serfs and the subsequent reforms of the 1860s.

GREECE AND POLAND

When he came to the throne, Nicholas I was as adamant a supporter of the concept of legitimacy as his older brother had been after 1812. But the tsar soon abandoned his unwavering support for this principle. When in 1821 Greek nationalists had risen against Ottoman rule, Aleksandr had stayed outside the conflict. True to his principles, he considered it the Turkish sultan's internal affair. But when the Turks were on the verge of suppressing the rebellion in 1826, Nicholas, after consultation with France and Britain, decided to throw his weight behind the Greek cause.

Nicholas justified his actions because he now reverted to a role played by the Russian tsars for generations: that of champions of Eastern Orthodoxy. In the 1690s, Peter had tried to organize a crusade to liberate the city of the emperor, Tsargrad, the name the Russians often used for Istanbul. Catherine the Great had once dreamed of seeing her grandson Konstantin installed as a sort of second coming of Constantine the Great, with Istanbul named once again Constantinopolis. In the Greek rebellion, the strongly religious Nicholas saw a chance to wrest, at a minimum, some of his fellow Orthodox believers from the Muslim yoke. War was declared on Turkey, which suffered a crushing defeat at the naval battle of Navarino off the Peloponnesian coast in 1827. Although several more years of fighting ensued, the Turks eventually recognized the futility of continuing a war against the strongest military powers on earth. In 1832, Greece's independence was recognized (its territory, by the way, was rather smaller than it is today).

The concept of legitimacy was always a fiction. After all, if the five Great Powers at Vienna and the subsequent conferences at Aix-la-Chapelle (Aachen, 1818), Troppau (Opava, 1820), Laibach (Ljubljana, 1821), and Verona (1822) had been consistent in their logic, they should have restored Poland's king. The Polish monarchy was a prime example of a historical kingdom that without much justification had been wiped off the map in the revolutionary period. At the Congress of Vienna, Aleksandr had made a minor concession in this direction by allowing the creation of a "constitutional" kingdom of Poland (also known as Congress Poland). But since the tsar himself doubled as the Polish monarch, Aleksandr and his brother Konstantin, who served as viceroy of Poland, largely ignored the terms of the constitution introduced in 1815. In this way, they stood once again in a time-honored tradition that pervaded Russian society from top to bottom, that of ignoring the law. It was, of course, difficult for a ruler to behave in one part as a monarch subject to legal restrictions, if he enjoyed unlimited power as an autocrat in the rest of his realm.

Many Polish nobles had accepted the disappearance of their kingdom in the late eighteenth century because they were allowed to continue to lord it over their serfs and were co-opted into the Austrian, Russian, or Prussian aristocracy, but some pined for the days of independence. In the dying days of the kingdom around 1790, Polish patriots had begun to organize a network of schools that taught Poles their language and history. As a result, the belief in a restored Poland began to spread beyond a few aristocratic circles in subsequent decades.

In addition, Tsar Nicholas was less than subtle in his treatment of Polish and Lithuanian Catholicism, which drove people into the arms of the Polish independence movement. In November 1830, the Poles rebelled. In early 1831, the Polish parliament formally deposed the tsar as king of Poland. But the Polish revolutionary militia, even if led by army officers, stood no chance against a Russian army that had far greater numbers, better training, and superior weaponry. The Poles fought tenaciously but were forced to surrender by the end of the year. Nicholas now abolished most of the Polish autonomous rights that had previously existed at least on paper. The Poles rose again in 1863, only to face another defeat. Polish nationalism, however, could not be denied. Finally, in the turmoil accompanying the Russian Revolution of 1917 and the end of the First World War, the state of Poland was restored.

Nicholas I was the first Russian monarch confronted by (the early incarnation of) modern nationalism, both at home and abroad. He also played a role in the nationalist revolt that gave Belgium its independence, attempting to help out his sister Anna. Anna was the wife of the Dutch heir to the throne, and Nicholas sought to preserve her adopted country of the Netherlands intact. Here, however, Nicholas was faced with joint British-French opposition, which was a marked contrast to their alliance with Russia in support of Greek independence. Belgium's independence was recognized by the powers in 1839.

Nationalism was still in its developing stages in much of Europe, even if its formidable power had been on display in the French Revolution, when hundreds of thousands of Frenchmen joined the army in defense of a state in which they thought to have a proprietary interest. It was an ideology difficult to understand for an autocrat, who disdained the masses as unwashed plebeians who needed to be led because they were incapable of thinking for themselves. And it was true that in much of Europe before 1848 nationalist groups were predominantly composed of educated middle-class commoners and upper-class nobles, who arrogated to themselves the right to speak for all the disenfranchised. In truth, nationalism did not have a mass following anywhere in Europe during the first half of the nineteenth century. Thus Nicholas I surmised that the nationalist cause was a ploy for power-hungry and self-serving elements, who did not care about the fate of the masses in whose name they rebelled. Nationalists' attitude stood in sharp contrast to the tsar's fatherly and selfless concern about his subjects. The Russian monarch carefully and impartially considered the interests of all his subjects in making his decisions.

RUSSIAN COLONIALISM

Before 1800, St. Petersburg's colonial policy toward non-Russian ethnocultural groups along the Volga and eastward toward the Pacific had been inconsistent, dependent on local geographical conditions and historical developments. At least until Catherine the Great's reign, the Russian rulers had been forced to accommodate themselves to the local conditions and strike compromises with the local population to ensure a modicum of collaboration and avoid rebellions. Until the middle of the eighteenth century, many Bashkirs or Kalmyks (living in the steppe toward the Volga mouth and east of the river), Siberian Tatars, Tungus, or Kazakhs considered themselves allies, rather than subjects, of the tsar.

Russian government officials went to great length to avoid offending local sensibilities. The Russians occasionally undertook an effort to convert especially the

Figure 3.4.   A mosque in Vladikavkaz, early twentieth century (Library of Congress)

"animists" to Christianity, but this never became a sustained campaign.[10] Muslims were left alone, by and large. The sort of rule the Russians imposed over non-Russian groups rather resembled the "indirect rule" of the British in India. It left the elite of the various ethnic communities in its place. But the Russians went further than the British, for they allowed some members of these elites to join the Russian aristocracy; the traditional stipulation that they had to convert to Orthodoxy disappeared in the eighteenth century.

Russian colonial policy was sensible because the tsar, like his European counterparts in their overseas empires, could not afford to engage in a strenuous costly effort to Russify or Christianize his subjects. From the late sixteenth to the early nineteenth century, Russian rule was shaky in Siberia and along the northern shores of the Caspian Sea. It survived primarily since it had few competitors in these regions. Revolts were nonetheless periodic, and in some of the notorious "Cossack" uprisings before 1800, non-Russians desirous of throwing off the Russian-Christian yoke played a significant role.

The influence of the Enlightenment then caused a shift in the Russian attitude. As the German sociologist Norbert Elias has pointed out, it saw the spread of the idea that Western Europe's leading classes harbored a superior culture or "civilization," with regard both to those they lorded it over in their own country and to non-Europeans (or, as Larry Wolff has noted, Eastern Europeans). Catherine the Great was the first Russian ruler affected by this new mind-set. Whereas she dismissed efforts to convert the non-Slavs to Orthodoxy, she encouraged bringing "civilization" to her blighted subjects (who included the Slavs). But a shift began to become apparent in the government's attitude toward non-Russians. Significantly, Russian authorities replaced the word *inovertsy* ("those of a different faith") with *inorodtsy* ("those not of the [Russian] tribe") in describing colonial subjects. Before the middle of the nineteenth century, this implied sense of superiority did not develop into full-blown systematic racism, for it was rooted in an inchoate sense of cultural supremacy rather than a belief in innate ethnic advantage. But it was laying the groundwork for the racism that would underscore late tsarist imperialist policy, which was to have a curious echo in Stalin's time.

As the German historian Andreas Kappeler has pointed out, Russian colonization policy particularly entailed the "taming" of allegedly "primitive" hunters and gatherers (under which rubric many of the peoples of the Arctic and eastern Siberia were grouped) and nomads (who grazed their cattle on the steppe that stretched from the northern Caucasus to the Chinese border). The concept of (Western or European and, indeed, Russian) civilization maintained that sedentary agriculture represented a superior stage of human development over nomadism, itself being a higher stage from allegedly primitive hunting and gathering. Those who were tasked with civilizing the "savages" in this respect were Slavic settlers, who began to move from the Russian heartland toward the Caspian Sea and into Siberia in the course of the eighteenth century.

Catherine the Great was so convinced of the superior ways of the Europeans that she even invited German-speaking farmers from the Holy Roman Empire to come to Russia. Many of them were given land in the lower Volga area and Ukraine, where previously nomads had herded their animals. Apart from the generous offer of land and other sorts of support to start up their farms, the Germans were often enticed to come since they were religious dissenters who had been persecuted in Germany for their beliefs (a great number of Mennonites were among them). By the early twentieth century, hundreds of thousands of German-speaking farmers lived in the Russian Empire. Similarly, European Tatars were enlisted to teach fellow Muslim communities, such as that of the Kazakhs, about the benefits of sedentary agriculture (an effort that did not meet with much success). Catherine, too, curtailed the free-roaming (and therefore by definition somewhat barbaric) ways of the Cossacks, once she had wrested the last of their communities from Polish rule.

In the second half of the eighteenth century, then, a Russian civilizing mission began to take shape. This greater Russian colonialist assertiveness was met with resistance among the colonized. In the Pugachev rebellion of the 1770s, for example, Bashkirs played a prominent role. They took up arms in response to the greater Russian intrusion into their affairs that had confronted them in recent years. And just prior to this conflagration, most of the Buddhist Kalmyks, who had annually trekked back and forth with their herds across the Volga since the early seventeenth century (after moving westward from northwest China), packed up and left. They migrated back to Central Asia when they were like the Bashkirs confronted with an excessively meddlesome Russian government.

As Siberian governor around 1820, Mikhail Speranskii codified the different stages of civilization by which the Siberian natives were distinguished. But he did not try to enforce Russification on hunters and gatherers or nomads. In that sense, Russian colonial policy remained consistent from its earliest days in the fifteenth century, when Mari or Chuvash were subjugated, to the pacification of the Caucasus or the Fergana Valley in Central Asia, four hundred years later. Rarely ever did the Russian authorities systematically pursue a policy of full integration of subject peoples that in the process caused the destruction of their traditional cultures.

There was of course a great discrepancy between St. Petersburg's guidelines for its colonial policy and formal organization of the various territories peopled by non-Slavs and the actual ruling methods practiced by administrators, soldiers, and colonists in these regions. Russian abuse of non-Russian populations was common from the fifteenth century onward. More often than not, in instances of maltreatment, the colonial government's officials backed the Russians against the native population. It often appears as if bullying was constrained only because local authorities could not afford to provoke an outbreak of revolt against Russian rule.

Although Soviet colonial policy and practice differed markedly in its rhetoric, Soviet rule, formally based on the principle of a "friendship of equal peoples," was far more destructive of native cultures than tsarist rule had ever been. This was because in the USSR economic development always took priority over the less important area of native rights, and the Soviet state was incomparably more intrusive. Traditional hunting-and-gathering cultures, especially in Siberia and the European Arctic, fell victim to the march of modern life. This is no surprise, perhaps, in the light of Marx's analysis of history, which claimed that historical development inevitably led to an urban industrialized world. On the ground, as previously under the tsars, and despite official professions about Soviet humanitarianism, the central government hardly curtailed Soviet officials in their imperious behavior toward local peoples. Part of this Soviet imperialism was a shocking disregard for the environmental consequences of unrestricted economic development.

Russian territorial expansion did not resume only in a western direction under Catherine the Great. While various princes of what is Georgia today had already been vassals of the tsars in the seventeenth century, when they were living in exile in Moscow, the foremost Georgian monarch officially submitted to Catherine in 1783. Although Iran attempted to recover this territory, to which it had historical claims, Russian arms made the annexation of eastern Georgia definitive by 1801. During the next decade, the western Georgian principalities changed their allegiance from the Ottoman sultan to the tsar. The Georgian annexations were fairly smooth because the Georgians were predominantly Orthodox Christians and considered

Figure 3.5.   Sochi on the Black Sea in the early twentieth century (Library of Congress)

Russians their religious kin. It may be telling in this respect that one of the Russian commanders in the 1812 war was Prince Pyotr Bagration (1765–1812), a scion of one of the ruling dynasties of Georgia. At around the same time, the Russians laid claim to what is now Dagestan, an area along the western Caspian Sea coast. This was another region that had been previously ruled by Iran, with a predominantly Muslim population. Different from Georgia, Dagestan remained restless.

Iran protested the Russian annexations, and war broke out in 1804. The Persian Empire had fallen into a steep decline from its heyday under Shah Abbas the Great (1571–1629). Peter the Great had already occupied the southern shores of the Caspian Sea in the 1720s, although this territory had been recovered by the Iranians in the following decade. Whereas a Persian comeback had occurred in the course of the eighteenth century, toward 1800 Iran's military was no match for Russia's armies. More than anything else, it was the difficult terrain that prevented a swift Russian victory and made the hostilities drag out until 1813, when Iran gave up (northern) Azerbaijan, in addition to eastern Georgia and Dagestan. After another war, most of what is today independent Armenia (the bulk of historical Armenia remained under Turkish Ottoman rule) was added to the tsar's empire as well. To an extent, Russian expansion in this "Transcaucasian" region led to population migrations, with Armenian and Georgian Christians from Iran and the Ottoman Empire moving into Russia and Muslims moving to Turkey (especially Sunnis) or Iran (especially Shi'a). Most of the local population stayed put, however, as none of the three empires engaged in systematic religious persecution.

Although in the first decades of the nineteenth century the Turks and Iranians recognized Russia as the sole overlord of the Caucasus and Transcaucasian regions, such recognition was not as quickly forthcoming from various population groups inhabiting the Caucasian mountain range. Some of the Muslim communities refused to be ruled by an infidel sovereign. In the northern Caucasus a long-term guerrilla war broke out around 1830. It was brought to an end only by 1864, after the insurgent leader Imam Shamil (1797–1871) had surrendered to Russian forces. A Sunni Muslim who spoke a Turkic language, Shamil has been claimed by the Chechen independence fighters in the 1990s and 2000s as one of their predecessors. Shamil was more likely an Avar rather than a Chechen, however, even if he led a revolt that included Chechens.

Figure 3.6. Shamil's *aul* (village) in the Caucasus, early twentieth century (Library of Congress)

The last remnants of the rebels were expelled to the Turkish Empire in the 1860s, although many of them refused to submit to the Russians and decamped to the Ottoman Empire. Even if most of them left of their own volition, some historians have suggested that this is a first instance of ethnic cleansing, the brutal practice of population deportation that became a widespread feature during the twentieth century. Those who departed for the Ottoman Empire often joined the Turkish army (and were known in Turkey as "Cherkess," while the European press called them "Circassians," even if they included men from various ethnic groups). Ultimately, at least four hundred thousand people left the Caucasus in the early 1860s, but many were allowed back into Russia when they found Ottoman Turkey less than hospitable.

THE GREAT GAME

When Russian troops traversed the Caucasus in the early nineteenth century, the British government became alarmed. Once the Napoleonic Wars were over, only two European powers ruled significant territory outside of Europe (as Spain lost most of its colonies in the immediate aftermath of the Napoleonic Wars): Russia and the United Kingdom. Both set their sights on Asia, and in British public opinion Russia replaced France as Britain's great rival. In the first half of the nineteenth century, the "Great Game," the rivalry between the two countries in Asia, remained in its developing stages. A string of independent states formed a buffer between the two empires, from Ottoman Turkey through Iran and the Central Asian emirates to China. But it was ironically one of the rare occasions when Britain and Russia found themselves at opposite sides in war, the Crimean War, that made Russia divert its attention more fully from Europe to Asia, and Russian-British tension in Asia reached its height. This switch coincided with the moment the British formally ended Mughal rule in India (in the 1850s) and their humiliation of China in the Opium Wars (of the 1840s and 1850s). With Russia moving southward and Britain moving northward, a clash over the division of the Asian spoils loomed toward the end of the 1850s.

After Russian moves into Sinkiang (Xinjiang) province in western China as well as Mongolia were checked by an English advance into Tibet, Iran or Afghanistan seemed the likely battlegrounds. Russia cast covetous eyes on Korea and the northeastern Chinese seaboard, too. In this latter theater the British stayed at arm's length, preferring to have their Japanese clients or other European powers, such as France and Germany, prevail over Russia. By 1867, Russia was so concerned with the English threat (which had been underlined in the Crimean War, of course) that it sold its exhausted North American colony (where the returns of the fur hunt had long since diminished) of Alaska to the United States. The Russians wanted to prevent Britain from acquiring this land, situated across the Bering Straits from Russian Kamchatka, and have their British foes add it to their Canadian Dominion.

The Great Game was driven in part by a search for raw materials, which became ever more important to feed the factories of the United Kingdom and even those of

Figure 3.7. A dilapidated mosque in Bukhara, ca. 1900 (Library of Congress)

Russia. Equally important was the search for markets to which industrial and other products could be sold. Ironically, few in St. Petersburg or elsewhere had yet an inkling of the economic importance of oil, and even fewer foresaw the possibility of vast oil reserves that could be won in such a remote and inhospitable territory as Russian North America. At the time, the seven million dollars paid by President Andrew Johnson's administration for Alaska seemed a princely sum to the Russian government.

THE GREAT GAME IN CENTRAL ASIA

While it divested itself of Alaska, Russia did lay claim to a vast region to the south of Siberia. The Russian advance into Central (or Inner) Asia was not unlike the European conquest of the African interior, with adventurers staking claims on behalf of a government that had little notion of what they were up to. Different from the Stanleys and de Brazzas in Africa, however, the Russian explorers and colonizers were military officers leading large regular army detachments. Without such military muscle, the conquest of the Muslim states in Central Asia would have been impossible. Most of this expansion occurred in the reign of Tsar Aleksandr II (r. 1855–1881), despite this tsar's repeated caution to his generals not to provoke a British response. Since the British had much less of a presence (or interest) in the area than the Russians feared, the subjugation of the Emirate of Bukhara in 1868 (in modern-day Uzbekistan), the Khanate of Khiva (Khwarezm, also in Uzbekistan) in 1873, and the Khanate of Kokand (parts of Tajikistan, Uzbekistan, and Kyrgyzstan) in 1876 proceeded without great difficulties. To the west of this territory, Turkmenistan (Turkmenia) was swallowed up between 1869 and 1885, under the pretext that it engaged in widespread slave raiding. After conquering Merv and Kushka in 1884 and 1885, Russia had reached the borders of the kingdom of Afghanistan. The British then made it clear that they would not tolerate any further Russian advances in this region. By the early 1880s, meanwhile, the Swedish brothers Nobel found oil in Russia's Transcaspian territories.

The conquest of Central Asia was a fairly simple affair for the Russian military, since the local fighters proved no match for the technologically superior equipment of the Russian forces. Because the conquests appeared almost effortless, a reluctant Aleksandr II approved the victories won by Mikhail Cherniaev (1828–1898), Konstantin von Kaufman (1818–1882), and Mikhail Skobelev (1843–1882). Violence obviously accompanied the Russian conquest. Russia claimed (as did Aleksandr's

Figure 3.8.   Vereshchagin's depiction of Samarkand in 1869

foreign minister Aleksandr Gorchakov [1798–1883] most famously in 1864) that it brought civilization to the region, establishing order where there had been none before. The government argued that Russia's benevolent influence would end cross-border raiding and plundering, especially if the conquest meant that territory ruled by one civilized European colonial power now bordered that of another (as in British-controlled India bordering Russian-controlled Inner Asia). For the benefit of all mankind, the selfless powers had subjugated all uncouth natives in their path. In justifying their conquest, Russian rhetoric often referred to the dichotomy between uncivilized nomads and civilized sedentary cultures.

Apart from the dubious quality of its civilizing mission, however, Russia's strategy was dangerous as well, potentially jeopardizing any peaceful existence for the local population. Russia's advance might lead to a war between European powers over their colonies. Russia and Britain were on the brink of war after the Russian conquest of Turkmenistan brought Russia to the borders of Afghanistan. War was avoided only after tortuous negotiations, leaving Afghanistan as an independent state under British protection. Once the British ally Japan had given the Russians a hiding in 1904 and 1905, Britain and Russia decided to share the oversight over Iran; compromises were simultaneously struck regarding other potential areas of conflict in Asia, formally bringing the cold war of the Great Game to an end.

Russian claims made at the time of the conquest of the region about the benefits that Inner Asia derived from an end to slave raiding or the gradual introduction of a higher standard of living may be questioned. The slave trade probably continued under Russian rule for a while. Any improvement of Central Asians' living standards needs to be weighed against the immense environmental destruction the Soviet regime especially wrought in the region. Finally, in drawing up a balance sheet regarding the Russian presence here, account should be taken of the massacres in which Russian colonial troops engaged, either during the initial conquest or later, in maintaining colonial rule. For example, Skobelev's soldiers killed thousands of Turkic men, women, and children during and after the storming of Geoktepe in Turkmenistan in 1881. The Basmachi rebellion in the Fergana Valley that began in 1916 under the tsars was suppressed only by Soviet troops in 1924 at the cost of innumerable human lives.

Previously, the Russians had laid claim to what is Kazakhstan today in an extremely slow process. The nomadic Kazakhs (whom the Russians confusingly called Kirgiz), whose cattle herds roamed across large grasslands, were divided into three loosely organized polities ("Hordes") in the early eighteenth century. Each of these Hordes was gradually incorporated into the Russian Empire. The first Russian advance into Kazakh territory dated from the 1730s, when the western and middle Hordes swore allegiance to the tsar (from the Russian perspective), or became allied to Russia (as the Kazakhs saw it). Effective Russian territorial control over the Kazakhs came about only between 1822 and 1848. At first, little was altered in the Kazakhs' daily life when they became the tsar's subjects, but that changed once growing numbers of European Slavs began to settle on Kazakh pastures after serfdom's abolition in 1861.

Russian authorities favored the settlers over the nomads. To the detriment of the Kazakhs, this conflict was brutally resolved in the Soviet era.

Despite the discovery of oil, Central Asia at first contributed little to the Russian economy (in this, too, it was not unlike most European colonies in Africa around this time). Oil's value became apparent only when Russia's industrialization gathered pace in the 1880s. Oil rigs, however, were rarely encountered before the First World War in the Transcaspian territories. Inner Asia had once been the region through which the Silk Route (originating in China) had meandered, but silk was no longer a rare or highly prized commodity on the world market by 1850. For the longest while, the region appeared to offer little besides a decent cotton crop. Indeed, neither Imperial Russia nor the Soviet Union managed to gain a significant economic benefit from their rule over Central Asia. Although it is impossible to render a precise cost-benefit analysis in this regard, it surely cost the Russian and Soviet imperial governments far more to rule these territories than what they yielded them.

Of little economic value, therefore, the Imperial Russian authorities left the predominantly Turkic inhabitants of Central Asia largely alone. The residents were allowed to observe the ways of their traditional Islamic culture without much interference. Muslims were exempted from service in the tsarist army (when this exemption was withdrawn in 1916, a widespread revolt broke out in the Fergana Valley).

THE AGE OF PUSHKIN, GOGOL, AND LERMONTOV

In the decade before the intelligentsia burst onto the scene, Russian literature suddenly discovered an authentic voice that found expression in the creation of works that matched anything literary ever written in other languages. This blossoming had been long in preparation. It is remarkable that so little of Russian eighteenth-century literature is memorable, while so much produced in the nineteenth century has stood the test of time. Aleksandr Pushkin was the first who, in a life tragically cut short, wrote literature that transcended its time and place. His oeuvre included both prose and poetry, but he produced no other novels besides the breathtaking *Evgenii (Eugene) Onegin*, a work in verse.

For it was especially in prose that Russian literature acquired worldwide fame in the nineteenth century. Apart from the craft Russian writers displayed in their works, they all shared a talent for depicting their times in a gripping, evocative manner. Their work is therefore all the more interesting to those interested in the Russian Empire's past. Thus in Onegin (the eponymous hero of Pushkin's novel) we meet a protagonist who epitomizes the indolence and boredom of the Russian nobleman of this "Golden Age of the Aristocracy." Onegin can idle his time away as he does not have a true occupation, living off the proceeds of the serfs on his estates.

The Russian effort to bridle the Caucasus forms the background of some other great works, such as Pushkin's story *Prisoner of the Caucasus*, Mikhail Lermontov's (1814–1841) novel *A Hero of Our Time*, and Lev Tolstoi's (1828–1910) novel *Hadji*

Figure 3.9.   The elderly Lev Tolstoi in his office of his Iasnaia Poliana estate, early twentieth century (Library of Congress)

Murat (based on a historical figure who was one of Shamil's allies). Here one meets the counterparts to the English works about British colonialism of writers such as Rudyard Kipling (1865–1936), E. M. Forster (1879–1970), or Joseph Conrad (1857–1924; himself a native of Russian-held Ukraine of Polish extraction). Conrad's oeuvre excepted, the Russian works outshine their British counterparts.

Mikhail Lermontov produced the first brilliant Russian prose novel (perhaps more a novella) with his *Hero of Our Time*. Lermontov, like Pushkin, died in a duel. Most accessible for today's reader is perhaps Nikolai Gogol's (1809–1852) work, of which the 1836 play *The Inspector-General* (*Revizor*) and the subsequent novel *Dead Souls* are the most renowned. Gogol was a full-fledged satirist, even if he appears toward the end of his life to have regretted his lampooning of Nicholas's Russia. Whereas Pushkin's work was personally vetted by Tsar Nicholas, Gogol's work caused the most controversy. Gogol mercilessly derided the sloth, incompetence, and corruption of the tsarist bureaucracy as well as the petty attitude of the provincial nobility (and their inhumane attitude toward their serfs), two groups that propped up the autocracy. Although the Ukrainian nationalist movement later sometimes claimed Gogol as one of their own,[11] his political convictions most closely resemble those of the contemporary Russian Slavophiles, in spite of his Ukrainian birthplace.

In their subtle questioning or deriding of their society, these early specimens of the golden age of Russian literature were possibly far more corrosive to the traditional order than any intentionally subversive nonfictional writing by people such as Herzen or Bakunin. These writers of fiction were not closely associated with the intelligentsia, which was per definition opposed to the tsar. This lack of evident political engagement may have given their works greater exposure than if they had been associated with the opposition to the autocrat. Pushkin, Lermontov, and Gogol found a reading public that had mushroomed thanks to the spread of education in Russia, even if by 1842 a mere one hundred thousand children attended public secondary-education institutes in the empire. If enrollment in military and girls' schools as well as private schools and church schools is counted as well, this number may have been twice as large, but this was out of a total of almost sixty million people. Illiteracy and half literacy remained extremely high, measured not only by today's standards, but even when compared to other European countries around 1850. Perhaps only one in forty adult Russians (as well as Ukrainians and Belarusyns) had received sufficient education to read Pushkin's work. In addition, literacy rates were far lower outside of European Russia, where, of course, few of those non-Russians who could read with ease knew the Russian language well enough to enjoy its literature.

But the works of Pushkin, Lermontov, or Gogol did not go out of fashion, and when literacy rapidly increased in the course of the subsequent decades, their audience continued to grow as well. In the Soviet Union, most people read works by these three writers, and their books continue to belong to the canon of Russian literature.

NOTES

1. Since Peter's reign, these families carried German-sounding noble titles rather than traditional Russian ones.

2. It is worth pondering that Catherine's accession to the throne coincided with the publication of Jean-Jacques Rousseau's *Social Contract*.

3. Even today, some Russian historians suggest that Aleksandr feigned his death in Taganrog in 1825, instead absconding to Siberia to take up the life of a humble carpenter (under the alias of Fyodor Kuzmich), and thus retreating into a life of a true Christian hermit and repenting for his sins (especially his complicity in his father's murder). The story has never been disproven, and it has remained mysterious that his successors made pilgrimages to Kuzmich's hut near Tomsk. Kuzmich died in 1864.

4. The aunt of Austria's emperor Franz II had been the beheaded French queen Marie Antoinette (1755–1793).

5. The tsar reminded one of the astonishingly popular literary character Werther, protagonist of a 1774 novel written by the German Johann Wolfgang Goethe (1749–1832).

6. The most important of these few battles occurred in August at Smolensk, which the Russians quickly abandoned after the first French attacks.

7. A minor French force did march toward Riga.

8. Both Pushkin and Goncharov wrote masterpieces in which an indolent aristocratic loafer was the protagonist.

9. And, of course, the Ottoman and Chinese Empires, too, collapsed around the same time as Romanov Russia, unable to transform themselves in timely fashion. This appears to indicate that reform was overdue in all of these empires.

10. The Russians tried to convert animists such as Mordvinians, Komi, or Mari peoples in the middle Volga region.

11. This was reinforced by Gogol's novel *Taras Bulba*, about a heroic Ukrainian Cossack fighting the Poles.

FURTHER READING

Translated Primary Sources

Davydov, Denis. *In the Service of the Tsar against Napoleon: The Memoirs of Denis Davidov, 1806–1814.* Translated and edited by Gregory Troubetzkoy. London: Greenhill Books, 1999.

Gogol, Nikolai. *Dead Souls: A Poem.* Translated by Robert A. Maguire. New York: Penguin, 2004.

———. *The Diary of a Madman, The Government Inspector and Selected Stories.* Translated by Ronald Wilks. New York: Penguin, 2006.

———. *Taras Bulba.* Translated by Peter Constantine. New York: Random House, 2003.

Herzen, Aleksandr. *My Past and Thoughts: The Memoirs of Alexander Herzen.* Translated by Constance Garnett. Berkeley: University of California Press, 1982.

Karamzin, Nikolai. *Karamzin's Memoir on Ancient and Modern Russia: A Translation and Analysis.* Edited by Richard Pipes. Ann Arbor: University of Michigan Press, 2005.

Lermontov, Mikhail. *A Hero of Our Time.* Translated by Paul Foote. New York: Penguin, 2001.

Nikitenko, Aleksandr. *Up from Serfdom: My Childhood and Youth in Russia, 1804–1824.* Translated by Helen Saltz Jacobson. New Haven, CT: Yale University Press, 2002.

Purlevskii, Savva Dmitrievich. *A Life under Russian Serfdom: Memoirs of Savva Dmitrievich Purlevskii, 1800–1868.* Translated and edited by Boris B. Gorshkov. Budapest: Central European University Press, 2005.

Pushkin, Aleksandr Sergeevich. *Eugene Onegin.* Translated by Stanley Mitchell. New York: Penguin, 2008.

Tolstoy, Leo. *Hadji Murad.* Translated by Richard Pevear and Larissa Volokhonsky. New York: Vintage, 2012.

Scholarly Literature

Berlin, Isaiah. *Russian Thinkers.* New York: Penguin, 2008.

Binyon, T. J. *Pushkin: A Biography.* New York: Vintage, 2004.

Bockstoce, John R. *Furs and Frontiers in the Far North: The Contest among Native and Foreign Nations for the Bering Strait Fur Trade.* New Haven, CT: Yale University Press, 2010.

Breyfogle, Nicholas B. *Heretics and Colonizers: Forging Russia's Empire in the South Caucasus.* Ithaca, NY: Cornell University Press, 2011.

Crews, Robert D. *For Prophet and Tsar: Islam and Empire in Russia and Central Asia.* Cambridge, MA: Harvard University Press, 2009.

Dennison, Tracy. *The Institutional Framework of Russian Serfdom.* Cambridge: Cambridge University Press, 2011.

Duffy, Christopher. *Eagles over the Alps: Suvorov in Italy and Switzerland, 1799.* Chicago: Emperor's Press, 1998.

Golden, Peter B. *Central Asia in World History.* New York: Oxford University Press, 2011.

Hoch, Steven. *Serfdom and Social Control in Russia: Petrovskoe, A Village in Tambov.* Chicago: University of Chicago Press, 1986.

Jersild, Austin. *Orientalism and Empire: North Caucasian Peoples and the Georgian Frontier, 1845–1917.* Montreal-Kingston: McGill-Queen's University Press, 2003.

Leatherbarrow, William, and Derek Offord, eds. *A History of Russian Thought.* Cambridge: Cambridge University Press, 2013.

Lieven, Dominic. *Russia against Napoleon: The True Story of the Campaigns of War and Peace.* London: Penguin, 2011.

Longworth, Philip. *The Art of Victory: The Life and Achievements of Generalissimo Suvorov, 1729–1800.* London: Constable, 1965.

Martin, Alexander M. *Romantics, Reformers, Reactionaries: Russian Conservative Thought and Politics in the Reign of Alexander I.* DeKalb: Northern Illinois University Press, 1997.

McGrew, R. E. *Paul I of Russia, 1754–1801.* New York: Oxford University Press, 1992.

Nabokov, Vladimir. *Lectures on Russian Literature.* Boston: Mariner, 2002.

Parkinson, Roger. *The Fox of the North: The Life of Kutuzov, General of War and Peace.* Philadelphia: David McKay, 1976.

Raeff, Marc. *Michael Speransky, Statesman of Imperial Russia, 1772–1839.* London: Hyperion, 1981.

Randolph, John. *The House in the Garden: The Bakunin Family and the Romance of Russian Idealism.* Ithaca, NY: Cornell University Press, 2007.

Riasanovsky, N. V. *Nicholas I and Official Nationality in Russia.* Berkeley: University of California Press, 1969.

Stites, Richard. *Serfdom, Society and the Arts in Imperial Russia.* New Haven, CT: Yale University Press, 2008.

Troubetzkoy, Alexis. *Imperial Legend: The Disappearance of Czar Alexander I.* New York: Arcade, 2002.

Vinkovetsky, Ilya. *Russian America: An Overseas Colony of a Continental Empire, 1804–1867.* New York: Oxford University Press, 2011.

Worobec, Christine. *Possessed: Women, Witches and Demons in Imperial Russia.* DeKalb: Northern Illinois University Press, 2003.

FILMS

The Star of Fascinating Happiness. DVD [Russian]. Directed by Vladimir Motyl. Moscow: Krupnyi Plan, 1975.

War and Peace. DVD. Directed by Sergei Bondarchuk. West Long Branch, NJ: Kultur, 2002.

4

Domestic Convulsions, 1855–1905

The comprehensive defeat in the Crimean War triggered significant reforms, the most important of which was the abolition of serfdom in 1861. The reforms, however, failed to have a truly political dimension; Aleksandr II and his successors stopped short of ending the one-man ruling system. Only the 1905 revolution forced Nicholas II's hand in this regard. Considering the historical experience of other industrializing countries, it cannot be doubted that Russia's industrialization would always have been a difficult transition period. But the half-baked nature of Aleksandr II's reform program and the obstinate refusal of his son and grandson to take any steps toward limiting the power of the monarch made the shocks that accompanied modernization everywhere reach an intensity in Russia that caused the collapse of autocratic tsardom.

THE WATERSHED

Neither the intelligentsia's deliberations nor Nicholas's commissions brought Russian serfdom to an end. The catalyst was a disastrous war, the Crimean War (1853–1856), in the midst of which the tsar died. The gravest danger for any one-person ruling system is a war gone badly, because most of the justification for absolute rule rests on the successful defense (or even expansion) of one's realm against foreign aggressors. If autocrats fail to acquit themselves well of this task, their governments are subject to criticism that may escalate into attempts to overthrow them. In modern times, this is all the more so the case, especially if the ruler can boast of few other accomplishments in furthering the "common good."

Domestically, Nicholas had changed little for the better during his thirty years on the throne. Care for the well-being of all subjects had never been an item on the tsars' agenda, nor had it been much of an issue for contemporary European counterparts of Aleksei, Peter the Great, or even Catherine the Great. But the French Declaration of the Rights of Man and Citizen of 1789 and the decapitation under the guillotine of King Louis XVI in 1793 heralded the arrival of a new perception about the role of the government among the Europeans. The conviction spread quickly that governments should be held accountable by their constituents. The British system, in which the king's government was controlled by parliament, was no longer an outlier after 1789. In addition, some sort of personal freedom became the norm for almost all Europeans as a consequence of the French Revolution. Even if the 1848 revolutions failed everywhere in their goal of implementing a parliamentary democracy, at least almost all adult men across Europe were legally free, while many enjoyed the right to vote for a legislature in their country.

But this was not so in Russia. The duty of the empire's inhabitants was to serve the state and the monarch, as Peter the Great's Table of Ranks, which survived until 1917, had underlined when it was introduced in 1722. This meant primarily working for the Russian military behemoth, whether as producers of food and other products to keep the army fed, clothed, and armed, or as soldiers, officers, or bureaucrats. The servants of the Orthodox Church (and the other religions in the empire) were to enforce obedience, by promising a better life after death to the meek and poor mass of the population, who performed the backbreaking work to keep the military machine running. Even merchants were valued primarily to the extent that they aided the state and the autocrat in waging war. Only the noble "estate" (*soslovie*) enjoyed any meaningful rights in exchange for discharging their duty.[1]

The tsars and tsaritsas had always been preoccupied with the defense of their realm. Most of the Russian government's expenditure had been on military matters, ever since Moscow wrested its independence from the Tatars around 1500. Before Catherine II's reign, it was not seen as a task of the government to improve its subjects' standard of living or to provide them with an education. Catherine the Great was the first monarch who accepted a role for the state in furthering the public good, but she had accomplished little in this respect. Apart from Aleksandr I's early years as tsar, her son and grandsons were far too absorbed by military matters to attempt to better in any sustained fashion the welfare of their subjects. For someone like Nicholas I, who saw everything through a sort of military prism, the public good was not a key concern for a Russian autocrat. But even he had intimations that serfdom's end was nearing.

That the system no longer worked, though, became evident only in the course of the Crimean War, during which the Russian military proved incapable of handling a foreign invasion. This was quite the contrast to the brilliant victory against Napoleon forty years earlier. Before 1853, the Russian army enjoyed the reputation of being the best of Europe. By 1856, those who had feared the "Russian bear" could defy it with impunity.

Comprehensive reform was urgently needed. The main obstacle to it, Nicholas I, died in 1855. Aleksandr II, albeit by temperament not fond of drastic change, saw no other way for Russia to prosper once again than by abolishing serfdom. He encouraged the emergence of a society in which the old elite was increasingly joined by newcomers, ruled by a government that at least at local levels behaved less arbitrarily than previously. He hesitated too long about surrendering some of his absolute power over his subjects, however, perhaps because he came to fear the social forces that his earlier reforms unleashed. At the moment that he seemed to have finally accepted that his autocracy should end, he was assassinated. This murder had a lasting and tragic impact on the subsequent course of Russian history. Aleksandr II's rule was probably the last best chance for Russia to embark on a relatively peaceful road toward modern society. The pig-headed stubbornness of his son and grandson in preserving the autocracy proved fatal, not just for the Romanovs, but also for the inhabitants of the Russian Empire, whose descendants are still recovering from that shortsightedness today.

THE CRIMEAN WAR

The casus belli for the Crimean War was the tsar's title of official protector of Christians and sacred Christian places in the biblical Holy Land, ruled by the Ottoman sultan. Russia had acquired this guardianship under the terms of the Treaty of Kuchuk Kainarji in 1774. But the Emperor Napoleon III (r. 1848–1870) attempted to have the sultan recognize France instead as the preeminent Christian champion in Palestine. Napoleon III tried to appease the more zealous Catholic faction in France, which considered it intolerable that Catholics had to defer to the Orthodox Christians in Jerusalem. Sultan Abdulmeçid I (1823–1861) moved back and forth between both countries but in the end decided that, because Russia infringed too much on Ottoman sovereignty, the time had come to end the tsar's (and the Orthodox) preeminent role. The Turkish sultan skillfully enticed the British and French to render him military support.

Subsequent Russian threats against the Ottoman Empire fell well within the usual pattern of Russians bullying the Turks, as had been most recently seen in the Russian support for the Greeks during the 1820s and 1830s. Then, the British and French had sided with the Russians against the Turks; in addition, none of the five Great Powers of Europe had ever seriously objected to Russia's periodic harassment of the Ottoman Empire, which had begun in earnest after 1750. But different from Abdulmeçid I, Nicholas failed to understand that a new international constellation had emerged by 1853. The French were willing to use force against the Russians in support of their claims as Christian champions in the Ottoman Empire. The Russian attempt at intimidation of the sultan caused the French (and, in their wake, the opportunistic British and Sardinians) to throw their weight behind the Turks.

While catering to the Catholics in his country was one motive for Napoleon III to challenge the tsar, the French emperor's desire to restore the grandeur of the Bonapartes added to his belligerence. Napoleon III was eager to prove his military mettle and honor the glory with which his name was identified. The British, meanwhile, were motivated by more sober calculations. They surmised that, whereas the Ottoman Empire (which by then acquired the nickname of being the "Sick Man of Europe") was not going to survive for much longer, for the time being they preferred the weak Turks over a strong Russia in the eastern Mediterranean. In addition, they worried about Russian expansion in Asia. For the British cabinet under Lord Aberdeen (1784–1860), the French-Russian quarrel seemed an excellent opportunity to cut the tsar down to size. Sardinia-Piedmont's prime minister Count Camillo Cavour (1810–1861) saw a chance to further his ambitious goals; supporting the already pro-Italian Napoleon III in the war on Russia would yield him the promise of French support for his project of Italian unification. He was indeed to receive French aid when he orchestrated Italy's unification around the house of Savoy, his monarch's dynasty, at the end of the 1850s.

In addition, whereas Austria remained neutral, its government made it evident to the Russians that it would not tolerate Russian annexation of the so-called Danubian principalities (today's Romania but without Transylvania). Russian expansion in this direction threatened Austria's plans to replace Ottoman Turkey as the dominant power in southeastern Europe. Austria's hostility took Nicholas aback, as he had recently been instrumental in helping the Habsburg Dynasty survive on the Austrian and Hungarian thrones. The Russian army had suppressed the 1848–1849 Hungarian Rebellion on behalf of the Habsburgs.

It was the Turks who attacked the Russians in late 1853. During the first months of the conflict, the Ottoman military was forced to retreat in Romania, and the sultan lost most of his Black Sea navy. Their hand thus forced, France and Britain came to the aid of the embattled Turks in March 1854. The French and British entry into the war was rather eager, as is underlined by the arrival in the course of 1853 of a combined British and French fleet at Istanbul, before the Turkish declaration of war. In the summer of 1854, this Western European navy landed an expeditionary force on the Crimean peninsula. The Russian defenders held out for a year at the Crimean naval port of Sevastopol, but by early 1855 the entire Crimea was in allied hands. Although on the other fronts the Russians held their own against the Turks, they hastened to conclude a peace treaty once the French and British began to threaten the mainland of Russian Ukraine.

The 1856 Treaty of Paris was a bitter pill to swallow for the Russians. The French were recognized as the protectors of Christians in the Holy Land, while the previous Russian influence over formerly Turkish Romania ended (with Romania gaining its independence in 1859). Russia lost territory (to the Turks) for the first time since Peter the Great's defeat at the Battle of Pruth in 1711. The country was banned from maintaining warships in the Black Sea (a stipulation slightly amended to Russian advantage in 1871). Meanwhile, Nicholas I had died in the midst of the siege of Sevastopol, a year before the peace was signed.

The Crimean War was in several ways a turning point in modern history. It was the first major war of which photographs survive, while it saw both sides making drastic improvements in terms of the treatment of battle wounded at the front and in the rear. Florence Nightingale's (1820–1910) name became legendary in this respect, while on the Russian side the medical doctor N. I. Pirogov (1810–1881) made a key breakthrough in using ether as an anesthetic in the field surgery he organized during the war. Alfred Tennyson's 1854 "Charge of the Light Brigade" became one of the most famous nineteenth-century poems. On the Russian side, Count Lev Tolstoi served as an officer on the Crimea; he went on to use his wartime experience in describing another military conflict (that of 1812) in one of the greatest novels ever written, *War and Peace* (1869).

In terms of military history, the war stands out as the first successful landing of a large expeditionary force in the modern age. The importance of military technology became apparent, as the victory of the allies over Russia was at least in part due to the use of superior weaponry. The Crimean War was also a key moment in the evolution of Austro-Russian relations. Russia and Austria had been allies for generations; suddenly, they found themselves on opposite sides. Whereas before the Habsburg and Romanov emperors had always been able to settle any serious disagreement amicably, the two empires now became increasingly embroiled in a conflict over the division of the spoils of the teetering Ottoman Empire in southeastern Europe. This dispute proved impossible to settle to mutual satisfaction. In the 1870s, 1900s, and early 1910s, war between the two powers was barely avoided; in 1914, war finally broke out.

Finally, the Crimean War had epochal consequences in Russia itself. It made Aleksandr II decide that his empire could survive only if serfdom disappeared. In the Russian analysis of the poor military performance during the war, the issue of the army's morale was seen as crucial. It was extremely difficult to keep motivated an army composed predominantly of serf soldiers, who served for twenty-five years (and were recruited on the basis of a quota system among serf households). In addition, it was evident that Russia had fallen woefully behind the other powers in technological terms. Although in the early 1850s the first railroad line from St. Petersburg to Moscow had been completed, industrialization had not yet taken off in Russia, and the troops had reached the front exceedingly slowly during the war, contributing to the defeat.

THE ABOLITION OF SERFDOM

Without the peasants enjoying the right to move, it would be difficult to find a large enough urban labor force if the Russian Empire were to embark on industrialization. It was not as if all enserfed peasants literally stayed in their villages, but permission to leave was usually granted only on a temporary basis by landowners, in exchange for monetary compensation by the itinerant serf. Collective responsibility for taxes and work for the landlord made village communities often resistant to the departure of their neighbors for employment elsewhere, too.

Factories and mines needed a permanent labor force, however, and a cheap one besides. If business owners could choose from only a small labor pool as existed in Russia before 1861, workhands would be insufficient and wages necessarily high. Meanwhile, even before serfdom's abolition, it was becoming apparent that parts of the Russian countryside were overpopulated. These surplus workers needed to be released from the restrictions of bondage. Thus, not merely concerns about poor morale in the army informed the decision to end serfdom.

Aleksandr II jump-started the work toward an emancipation settlement that had been languishing in his father's commissions. The key problem was how to ensure that the landowners were not deprived of most of their land as well as its cultivators in one fell swoop. It was concomitantly inconceivable to give the peasants their freedom without land, as this would likely trigger a rural uprising. The solution found was to allow the landowners to keep some of their land, with the rest given to the emancipated peasants. The peasants would have to reimburse their former masters for this land. As few peasants had any money readily available, a government bank would immediately compensate the landlords for the land they lost. The former serfs would then pay back their debt to this bank in installments.

On paper, the terms of the 1861 Emancipation Act seemed sound, but in practice few peasants proved capable of paying off their debt in the decades following serfdom's abolition. Because the redemption payments (as well as taxes owed to the government) were to be the collective responsibility of the village community, it remained difficult for peasants to leave for the city. Villagers feared losing their neighbors' share in remitting the compensation dues and taxes to the government.

Meanwhile, the government did little to encourage agricultural innovation by way of education (or through other means). The peasantry rarely learned about methods to increase yields by way of such things as crop rotation (with fodder crops alternating with grains) or fertilizing the soil. Crop yields remained low when the overwhelming majority of the peasantry was almost wholly illiterate. After general conscription was introduced in 1874, 75 percent of army recruits could neither read nor write. This percentage only slowly declined toward 1900.

The traditional manner of redistributing land, according to household need, also hampered agricultural efficiency. In much of European Russia, it was customary for village meetings (sel'skie skhody) to redistribute land according to the changes in family size every seven to ten years.[2] This saw all members of the village commune (mir or obshchina) temporarily enjoying access to the best land (or suffering through the use of poor land). But it meant that no family had the usufruct of a parcel of land forever. Since households cultivated their lots for only a limited amount of years, they lacked incentive to try to improve the soil. It is no surprise, then, that Russian agriculture failed to obtain significantly higher crop yields or a greater production of milk or meat during the second half of the nineteenth century.

Although agricultural productivity remained stagnant and many villages barely met redemption or taxation payments, a steep population growth occurred after

1850. Rural family size reached an all-time high during the last decades of Romanov rule. This was caused by rapidly improving health care (especially the spread of inoculation of children) and somewhat better nutrition (the consumption of potatoes increased rapidly in the course of the nineteenth century, adding greatly needed variety to a primarily grain-based diet). But the countryside could feed only a limited amount of mouths: yields remained far too low to nourish the rural population and remit redemption dues and taxes to the government. Rural overpopulation became a major problem in many parts of European Russia, where the population grew by 60 percent between the Emancipation Act and the 1897 census. When poor weather caused a series of misharvests in many regions, a devastating famine ensued in 1891 and 1892, killing millions. The government ultimately ended the debt problem in the wake of the 1905 revolution by abolishing the compensation payments. This reform was followed by other measures that promised to relieve some of the population pressure on the land.

Meanwhile, the Russian nobility did not thrive as landowners, despite receiving the reimbursements for the land they lost in the 1861 settlement. Few noble landowners had ever taken the trouble to investigate how to prosper as farmers. Their estates were usually run by bailiffs, while the owners preferred residing in the city for most of the year. Many nobles quickly spent the money they received in 1861 on things other than the improvement of their manors, and many sank further into a debt caused by a profligate lifestyle mandated by noble peer pressure. Foreclosures and bankruptcies became rampant. Thus, there was not much sign of the development of the type of farms that began to become typical in North America toward 1900, with ever-growing production levels generated by ever fewer workhands.

Subject to such financial difficulties, the nobility became increasingly dependent on state employment in the government or military in order to survive financially. Rather than accepting the landholding aristocracy's inevitable decline in their modernizing country, Aleksandr II's successors continued to rely on nobles as the mainstay of their government. The last two tsars seemed blind to the fact that, after 1861 (despite all the shortcomings of the Emancipation Act), their country's economy was rapidly changing from being predominantly agriculturally oriented to a mixed form in which the industrial and service sectors were increasingly important. They failed to realize that the estate society of the aristocracy's heyday was disappearing. Nicholas II was to pay a high price for this error.

Of course, the developments sketched above do not do justice to the enormous diversity among the rural dwellers of the late Russian Empire. In regions with better soil (such as the Black Earth zone that consisted of European Russia south of Moscow and northern Ukraine), peasants received smaller allotments in the Emancipation settlement than in the area around Moscow and to the north of the old capital. North of the Black Earth region, climate and soil made crop cultivation more arduous, negating the benefit of the reception of more land in 1861. Because of better soil and climate in the Black Earth area, peasants might have done better there than in the north after 1861. Such prosperity, however, was frequently short lived when, in the second half of the nineteenth century, more children than ever before survived the first few years of their lives.

The less friendly environment of northern regions further strengthened the trend among the local peasantry there to find employment as (often itinerant) artisans (*kustary*), seasonal workers (on larger estates, in the lumber industry, etc.), or as factory workers and miners. This income aided village household incomes, while many peasants returned home from employment elsewhere for the busiest period (especially harvesting) of the agricultural season. Some of the peasants, especially when faced with few prospects in their ancestral villages, settled permanently in the cities, becoming part of the industrial working class.

At the time of their serfdom's abolition (in 1863 in their case), peasants working the estates of the imperial family were given less onerous payment terms for the land they received. State peasants, who worked land usually located in more remote areas belonging to the state, had on the whole been treated better by the authorities than private serfs prior to 1861; by the decree of 1866 that formally released them, they were given somewhat better conditions in terms of land allotments and compensation fees. After another Polish revolt had been suppressed in Russian Poland, Polish peasants received a settlement in 1864 by which they did not have to pay any redemption payments. In the Baltic region, peasants had already been emancipated in the 1810s, albeit without land. According to an 1864 emancipation act in Georgia, local landowners received a far greater proportion of land than in Russia. Serfdom did not exist otherwise in the Transcaucasus region and was uncommon in Siberia and northern Kazakhstan (as far as it was under Russian rule in 1861).

In addition, whereas periodic repartition of village land within the *mir* was common in much of European Russia, in Ukraine and elsewhere this was much less the case. This and the more forgiving climate south of Moscow to some degree explain how, despite the difficulties encountered by most agriculturalists in the empire after 1861, there were some bright spots, and Ukrainian yields especially became quite bountiful. Thus "Little Russia," as the tsarist government preferred calling Ukraine, became by 1900 "Europe's granary," shipping much grain westward from Odessa and other ports.

OTHER REFORMS: THE COURTS AND LOCAL GOVERNMENT

Once the peasants received their freedom, several other reforms became imperative. As the aristocracy now no longer substituted for the government at local levels, the state had to step in to compensate for its retreat. In 1864, a system of courts was introduced in which independent judges, sometimes with the help of juries, were to dispense justice fairly, without regard for class (or, to be precise, one of the "estates" to which each Russian formally continued to belong). While the courts' independence was curtailed by the state of emergency that was introduced in the 1870s, the new courts constituted a dramatic improvement for many people, as henceforth, in theory, even the poorest person might turn to them to try to right a wrong. Accused people were entitled to legal support in court, another novelty.

Nonetheless, for the peasantry (the overwhelming majority of the population), litigation of most civil and criminal cases was usually pursued in district (*volost'*) courts, which had jurisdiction over several villages, rather than the new government courts. The district court officials were chosen from among the heads of households in the villages that made up the *volost'*, as were the local administrators of the districts. The latter were obliged to execute any decrees from the tsarist authorities without fail.

In the same year 1864, Aleksandr introduced bodies of local government in the various rural counties of which each Russian province consisted. In these *zemstva* (sing. *zemstvo*), representatives of all classes met to deal with issues ranging from health care (building and overseeing clinics and hospitals, hiring doctors and nurses, and providing inoculation) to education (building a network of schools, hiring teachers, and so on) and infrastructure (construction of roads and bridges, etc.). Local taxes were collected to pay the expenses toward these purposes. It is no coincidence that after 1864, literacy rates rose (although this was in part because the army began to educate its recruits). Elementary schools were founded in greater number and were better supervised thanks to the *zemstva*. *Zemstva* doctors (including the literary genius Anton Chekhov [1860–1904]) and other medical professionals oversaw the drastic improvement of the health of the rural population (even if this was to some degree due to better nutrition thanks to the cultivation of new crops such as potatoes). The rural population boom between 1850 and 1900 was to a significant extent due the beneficial activity of the *zemstva*, which genuinely concerned itself with people's well-being.

In 1870, a similar degree of self-government was given to the Russian towns. City councils (dumas) oversaw the construction of sewers, the opening of clinics and hospitals as well as schools, the paving of roads, the installation of street lighting, and so on. But following the time-honored practice of calibrating policies according to local conditions, the 1864 and 1870 reforms were not introduced everywhere in the empire. The predominantly non-Russian population of the empire's western borderlands (from Estonia to Polish Mazovia) was not allowed to elect *zemstva*, for example.

The great differentiation within Aleksandr II's Great Reforms reflects how much tsarist rule remained grounded in the idea of a composite empire (as argued by Matthew Romaniello for an earlier age), in which each distinct territory was governed in a specific manner. Before Aleksandr III's Russification policies of the 1880s, the government followed no coherent policy to impose a uniform political system across the empire, from Warsaw to Vladivostok. This respect for local custom and specific privileges was wise in a country that remained utterly vast in spatial terms and harbored more than 140 different ethnolinguistic groups. The tsar ruled nomads, hunters and gatherers, and sedentary crop cultivators as well as university professors, grand dukes, artisans, priests, monks, factory workers, miners, carters, and barge haulers. And to further complicate matters, Catholics, Lutherans, Orthodox, Shi'a and Sunni Muslims, Buddhists, and those adhering to shamanistic religions were all found among the tsar's subjects. Throughout most of Romanov rule, the government had shown a prudent sensitivity to the customs of each of the larger communities of which the population of the Russian Empire was composed. This time-honored tradition, however, was abandoned after 1881, when Aleksandr III tried to forge a more uniform national identity. Such shared national characteristics were considered an essential component of the modern state.

Some other reforms deserve mention because they indicate the drastic change that hallmarked Aleksandr II's early years. Preventive censorship was abolished, leading to a publishing boom. The universities were released from the utterly debilitating over-sight the government under Nicholas I exerted over their activities and were given significant autonomy in 1863. Meanwhile, a far greater number of secondary schools was introduced, and children of all social groups were encouraged to attend them.

THE CULMINATION OF THE REFORMS: THE ARMY

Aleksandr II's key assistants in implementing the reforms were the two brothers Miliutin. Nikolai (1818–1872), employed at the ministry of the interior, had been the tsar's key aide in implementing both the abolition of serfdom and the *zemstva*. The crucial reform of the armed forces, however, was overseen by his brother Dmi-trii (1816–1912), who was minister of war for twenty years (1861–1881). Since the reforms were triggered by the debacle of the Crimean War, the capstone reform was bound to be that of the military.

This was an age in which the European powers (Britain excepted) introduced general conscription for young males, creating enormous armies in reserve consisting of those who had gone through basic military training. In 1874, a decree made all male Russians, if in good health, liable to military service. The term of initial service was made dependent on the education levels of the draftee. Illiterate recruits were to serve six years, after which they stayed for nine years in the reserves. The army was meanwhile obligated to teach illiterate recruits reading and writing. Those young men who could boast of completed primary education (a four-year curriculum) were obliged to render four years of initial military service, while those with completed secondary education served two years, and university graduates a mere six months.

The age of mass conscript armies thereby arrived in Russia, eighty years after its first appearance in revolutionary France. The military became a modern mass in-stitution, the first of its kind in Russia. It strengthened the inculcation of a generic "Russian imperial" (*rossiiskii*) identity through the education of its recruits.[3] The army's role in strengthening a sense of "national" identity was mitigated by the fact that only Europeans were conscripted. The male population of Central Asia was ex-empted from military service until 1916, while ethnic units from the Caucasus or the

Cossacks served as soldiers under different terms (usually in separate units organized in a traditional fashion). The organization of such ethnic units was usually rooted in historical treaties that had been signed between ethnocultural groups and the tsar, when the former had recognized Russian sovereignty. This was another sign of the survival of the composite empire. From a strictly military viewpoint, the strong coherence of Cossack or Caucasian units in battle proved the soundness of this policy. But because of it, the empire's armed forces did not become a truly centripetal, or nationalist, force, encouraging non-Russian soldiers to adopt a Russian identity.

Regardless, Dmitrii Miliutin's reforms went some way toward making military service a burden shared by all, rather than an army organized around the nobility and assisted by men who had been unlucky enough to be selected for a twenty-five-year army stint. Before 1874, selection for military service had meant an almost certain death, as most succumbed to battle wounds or disease long before completing this lengthy term. The days when Russian villages organized funeral processions for the departing recruits were now gone forever.

THE POLISH QUESTION REVISITED

Aleksandr II inherited another complicated matter that was never resolved by his father: the fate of the Poles. Poland's autonomy had been heavily curtailed after the 1830–1831 rebellion, but in theory the country continued to enjoy the status of a distinct territory, with a measure of self-determination (as did several other parts of the empire, of course). Aleksandr eased the anti-Catholic policy followed by his father and allowed the opening of Polish postsecondary educational facilities. Despite the new tsar's display of goodwill, the cause of Polish independence continued to have the ardent support of a great number of Polish nobles, especially the university students and army officers among them. Similar to its Russian counterpart, the Polish intelligentsia was broadening its ranks and now began to include commoners. Most were fervent nationalists. Despite this growth of Polish nationalism, a significant part of the nobility remained in favor of collaborating with Russia.

Toward 1860, Tsar Aleksandr II asked Aleksander Wielopolski (1803–1877), his main advisor for Polish matters, to suggest measures to restore some of the Polish rights abrogated by his father in response to the risings of 1830–1831. But the tsar stopped far short of considering any steps toward full Polish self-determination. Aleksandr decided nonetheless to introduce a program (drafted by Wielopolski) that gave Poland greater autonomy. The tsar's brother Konstantin Nikolaevich (1827–1892), who had a liberal reputation, was dispatched in the capacity of viceroy to Warsaw in early 1862 to oversee the implementation of this plan. But a Polish nationalist tried to assassinate the viceroy within days after his arrival. Wielopolski, now the main advisor of Konstantin, decided to bridle the rebellious Poles by conscripting them to lengthy terms in the Russian army. Demonstrations broke out in Warsaw; they were suppressed at the cost of several dozen deaths.

This blew the lid off. Young men went into hiding to avoid the draft. Everywhere revolutionary committees were struck. On 22 January 1863, Poland was in full rebellion. It was the first broad-based nationalist uprising the tsars had ever faced (this Polish uprising had significantly more support from nonnoble groups, especially when compared to the previous rebellion of 1830–1831). It heralded the arrival of nationalism as one of the greatest challenges to face both the last tsars and the Communist bosses who succeeded them. Whereas the tsars managed to subdue domestic nationalism only to fall victim to insurmountable problems raised by nationalist movements abroad, nationalism at home was to doom Communist rule.

The 1863–1864 Polish revolt, however, even though supported by a broad layer of Polish society, failed to win much of the still enserfed Polish peasantry for its cause. The Polish leaders were wary of promising emancipation terms to the peasants that were unduly favorable, because key support for the movement came from aristocratic landholders. And the nationalists overreached in trying to entice historic Lithuania to join their rebellion, in an awkward genuflection to the joint past of the Polish-Lithuanian Commonwealth. The Russian government considered historic Lithuania a full part of the empire, not a territory with a separate status such as Poland. The few pro-Polish Lithuanian groups that did answer the Polish call to arms were ruthlessly suppressed.

In Poland itself the rebels once again stood no chance against the Russian armies, but Aleksandr II did not deal with the nationalists in an excessively harsh fashion. In something of a cunning move, the tsar emancipated the Polish serfs at fairly generous terms. This was aimed to harm the nobles, the mainstay of the nationalist movement. But in the following decades, thanks to the excellent network of schools set up by Polish nationalists, and thanks to the close alliance of the movement with the pro-Polish Catholic Church, the liberated Polish peasants chose to support the Polish rather than the Russian side that had treated them so benevolently in 1864.

COUNTERREFORM?

Aleksandr II was not a radical enthroned such as Peter the Great. Attempts to divide Aleksandr's rule chronologically into a good part (1856–1866) and a bad part (1866–1881), as is sometimes done for Aleksandr I (1801–1812 and 1812–1825), seem attractive but are ultimately too simplistic. As was the case with his uncle, Aleksandr II often alternated between more progressive and more conservative policies. Most of the tsar's actions responded to the political situation he faced, rather than being the fruits of a preconceived strategy. The exception to this was his bold proclamation of the Emancipation Act of 1861 (although it, too, was in a sense a response to the disaster of the Crimean War). Aleksandr II often appears to have embodied the ideal type of the Bismarckian "realpolitiker," the politician as a pragmatist, adhering to the principle that politics is the art of the possible. Even when contemporary revolutionary fanatics accused the tsar of following a program that amounted to the darkest reaction, Aleksandr II was actually attempting to inch forward, very slowly remaking his country into a modern state. Unfortunately for him and for Russia, however, he was not given sufficient time to bring this process to a successful conclusion.

Aleksandr II's measured response toward rebellious Poland shows some of his balanced approach, even if the suppression of the Lithuanian allies of the Poles may have been disproportionately harsh. He needed to respond firmly when in 1866 he was faced with the next crisis, triggered by the student Dmitrii Karakozov's (1840–1866) effort to murder him. Karakozov's attempt made evident that the opposition to the tsar was no longer confined to discussion circles. Some revolutionaries had concluded that the time for drastic actions had arrived. In response to Karakozov's action, the tsar appointed a notorious conservative, Dmitrii Tolstoi (1823–1889), as education minister. Universities were once again placed under strict government surveillance. But whereas Tolstoi placed strong emphasis on a curriculum that seemed out of touch with modernity (the study of Latin and Greek was prioritized at secondary schools), during his tenure as minister (1866–1880) the number of boys and girls attending such institutions quickly grew. Under Tolstoi, women gained access to special postsecondary schools that were affiliated with the universities of Moscow, Odessa, Kyiv, and Kazan.

Meanwhile, *zemstva* invested heavily in health care and primary education, even after Aleksandr II had allegedly turned into a reactionary. By the 1870s, the focus of the Russian local and central government undoubtedly had shifted. No longer was the state apparatus almost solely an instrument enabling the tsar to wage war. The government was now expected to improve popular well-being as well. This was quite the shift even from the recent past of Nicholas I's days. It shows how Aleksandr II was, far more than his father and uncle, or his son and grandson, attuned to his times.

The one piece missing in Russia's evolution from a premodern or early modern autocracy propped up by serf labor to a modern government of a society of free laborers was any institution by which the central government could be held accountable for its actions. The bell seemed to toll for the autocracy itself, for, by 1880, no other major European power (or the new budding power in North America) was ruled by an absolute monarch. Everywhere, the executive was held in check by some sort of a representative body elected by a part of the citizenry.[4] Even Russia's former conservative allies, the new German Empire (succeeding Prussia and founded by the Prussian prime minister Bismarck in 1871) and Austria-Hungary had parliaments. The byword for backwardness in Europe, the Ottoman Empire, had begun to experiment with constitutional rule (even if such experiments were brought to a halt by Sultan Abdülhamid II [r. 1876–1909]). Surely Russia was not to be considered more backward than its long-standing Turkish foe. It is moot in how far precisely Aleksandr II and his advisors were haunted by the growing sense of Western superiority over Eastern "others," but as is obvious from their justification of their colonization of Central Asia, the Russian tsar and his ministers did not want to be considered another "Oriental despotism," on par with the (Turkish) Sick Man of Europe or imploding Qing China.

Given this international context, Aleksandr's interest in a plan that would begin to curtail his omnipotence does not surprise (even if historians have pointed out that the proposals read by the tsar in his final days still fell far short of an actual constitution). In the midst of a crisis caused by revolutionaries who had embarked on a fanatic offensive to assassinate the tsar, Aleksandr had his main advisor Mikhail Loris-Melikov (1825–1888) developed a road map toward some sort of power-sharing agreement between him and his subjects. In the end, the terrorists won: in March 1881, before Aleksandr could take the first steps toward a constitutional monarchy, he was murdered. The killing of the tsar by the revolutionaries of the People's Will was a key moment in the chain of events that led to the catastrophic human tragedy that was to envelop the Russian Empire in the course of the subsequent century.

REVOLUTIONARIES

For the most radical members of the first generation of the intelligentsia, such as Aleksandr Herzen or Mikhail Bakunin, the pen was still mightier than the sword. After persecution by the tsarist authorities in Nicholas I's reign, both went abroad, never to come back to Russia. In his influential magazine *The Bell* (*Kolokol'*), Herzen preached a sort of peaceful transition to a new, socialist Russia. Bakunin, meanwhile, began to embrace the idea of a sort of cathartic violence through which humanity needed to move to reach the ideal of a world without government. Neither was a Marxist. Marxism began to spread in Russia only in the late 1870s, after Marx's *Capital* was (legally!) diffused among students and *intelligenty*.[5]

Herzen's socialism, while influenced by Western socialist thinkers, was a Russian ideology tainted by Slavophilism. He believed that Russia could become a society of equals because of the innate socialist character of the village commune, the *mir*. Although in the periodic repartition of land, for example, a sort of social justice could be recognized, this was based on myth rather than reality. In most villages, the shots were called by the (male) heads of the most prosperous households, who lorded it over their neighbors and behaved like patriarchs within their own families. Any true altruism was as hard to find in the village as it was in the rest of society.

Nonetheless, Herzen's convictions about a future socialist Russia composed of equal village communes remained influential. The Populists (Narodniki) of the 1870s "Going to the People" (*khozhdenie v narod*) movement believed in the socialist nature of the Russian peasant, as did, a generation later, the Socialist Revolutionary Party (founded in the early 1900s). Lenin (Vladimir Ul'ianov, 1870–1924), too, flirted with the idea of primordial peasant socialism in justifying his strategy to found a socialist country based on an alliance of hammer and sickle, of workers and peasants, who would find each other in their socialist mind-set. And at least in part,

Stalin (Iosif Dzugashvili, 1878–1953) may have genuinely believed that the innate socialist essence of the middle and poor peasants would make them understand the wisdom of his "dekulakization" (persecution of alleged rich peasants who exploited the labor of their neighbors) and embrace the collective farms he imposed on the Soviet countryside in 1929 and 1930.

The idea of a peaceful transition to a socialist Russia as entertained by Herzen lost its appeal fairly quickly. Urged on by inflammatory treatises as written by publicists such as Nikolai Chernyshevsky (1828–1889; his *What Is to Be Done?* became an inspiration to Lenin), Nikolai Dobroliubov (1836–1861), and Dmitrii Pisarev (1840–1868), the young men and women who formed the opposition of the 1860s and 1870s were impatient for a drastic change in their country's system of rule. Karakozov's failed attempt in 1866 was only the first of several. Illegal revolutionary groupings were organized across the country (although most of the fervor was limited to the towns and cities of the European parts and the Caucasus). In 1873 and 1874, hundreds of young zealots eager to preach the socialist gospel to the peasants traveled the countryside as part of the "Going to the People" movement. The peasants proved unreceptive to its message. Arrests followed, and this ended the Populist movement's first incarnation.

Some of those who had "gone to the people" then decided that more radical steps were necessary. They split off from the main organization (called Land and Freedom or Zeml'ia i Vol'ia) to form a terrorist group (the People's Will, or Narodnaia vol'ia) that aimed at, and succeeded in, assassinating the tsar.

Others, led by G. V. Plekhanov (1856–1918), fell under the spell of Karl Marx. They abandoned the idea of a specifically Russian path to socialism. The Russian Marxists suggested that Russia's socialist future would be brought about by its budding industrial working class, once its numbers had made it the dominant force in Russian society. But this would happen only in alliance with the proletarians of other (more advanced) industrialized countries, first and foremost those of Central and Western Europe. Plekhanov, together with two associates, Pavel Akselrod (1850–1928) and Vera Zasulich (1849–1919), voluntarily decided to go into exile to lead Russia's fledgling Marxist movement from abroad.

Zasulich had acquired almost legendary status in the revolutionary movement after her failed attempt in 1878 to kill the police chief of St. Petersburg, F. F. Trepov (1809–1889), for which deed she had been acquitted in a jury trial. Zasulich was not the only woman who came to the fore in the Russian revolutionary movement around 1880. Whereas women were clearly the "second sex" in nineteenth-century Russia, they began to find their own voice, first and foremost in the revolutionary movement. Vera Figner's (1852–1942) *Memoirs of a Revolutionist* is testimony to this process. In it, she presents one of the most evocative depictions of the revolutionary movement of the 1870s and 1880s.

Various theories about this public emergence of women have been proffered, none of them wholly convincing. Apart from the inspiration of the burgeoning women's movement in contemporary Europe, the example of the eighteenth-century empresses may have been a factor. As we saw earlier, in Slavic tradition the role of a sort of earth mother (and of mother earth) was pronounced, too. This Russian worship of a mother of creation, which resembles classical Greece's Gaia veneration, was never entirely erased by Christianity. In Russian Orthodoxy, the worship of the Mother of God (the Bogoroditsa) was intense, with Mary adopting some of the traits of the pagan earth mother.

It is certainly remarkable that so-called strong women came to the fore in many of the novels of the day. At the same time, however, women's lives remained harsh. In most villages, Russian men seem to have routinely beaten their wives, a practice that was rarely frowned on by their neighbors. In the primitive material circumstances of prerevolutionary Russia, many women died from complications while giving birth (or soon after).

Next to Zasulich and Figner, Sofia Perovskaia (1853–1881), daughter of a tsarist general, became famous as a revolutionary woman. She was one of the People's Will's key organizers of the tsar's assassination in March 1881. Perovskaia was among the five executed for this act of terrorism. She had worked closely together with Figner, who barely managed to avoid execution after her own arrest in 1883.

Figure 4.1.   Aleksandr II's assassins, Zheliabov and Perovskaia, sketched on the eve of their execution, 1881

CULTURAL BRILLIANCE

Despite the attempts by Nicholas I to prevent this from happening, a civil society had emerged in Russia during the first half of the nineteenth century. Intellectuals associated with each other in discussion circles and published in journals alongside like-minded souls (or those who disagreed with them), while scholarly and scientific groups met on their own initiative rather than that of the state. The government tried to monitor virtually every group activity of its subjects, through the Third Department and the Okhrana, which succeeded it in 1880. But this was no longer a society that had to be prompted to find its voice, as had been the case during Catherine the Great's reign. Despite the efforts of Dmitrii Tolstoi and others, the quickly increasing number of young people who received an education undoubtedly informed the spread of a critical mind-set in Russia after 1855.

Society's voice found its most eloquent expression in Russian literature (in other languages that could be found within the empire, writers were prolific, too, but their works do not enjoy similarly lasting, worldwide acclaim). Its golden age reached a climax during Aleksandr II's rule. Some of the radical political mind-set of the 1860s and 1870s has probably been most evocatively depicted in novels such as Ivan Turgenev's *Fathers and Sons* (1862) or Fyodor Dostoyevsky's *Demons* (1872). This was also the era of Lev Tolstoi's masterpieces *Anna Karenina* (1873–1877) and *War and Peace* (1869). In *Oblomov* (1859), Ivan Goncharov (1812–1891), oddly enough a government censor, depicted the twilight of the serf-owning nobility and its descent into lethargy. Poetry found some brilliant practitioners as well, such as Afanasii Fet (1820–1892) and Fyodor Tiutchev (1803–1873). Certainly, Pyotr Chaadaev's dismissal of Russia's failure to contribute anything substantially worthwhile for the benefit of humanity had been comprehensively countered by this literary brilliance.

In other areas of art, such as music and painting, a period of creative flourishing equally unfolded after 1850. In Glinka's wake, composers brilliantly succeeded in weaving Russian themes into classical music. Most famous became Pyotr I. Tchaikovsky (1840–1893), thanks to his music for the ballets *Swan Lake* (1877) and *The Nutcracker* (1892) and the opera *Evgenii Onegin* (1879), based on Pushkin's novel in verse. Tchaikovsky befriended a group of composers collectively known as "The Mighty Five" (a rather loose translation of "Moguchaia Kuchka," as they are called in Russian). They included Modest Mussorgsky (1839–1881), Aleksandr Borodin (1833–1887), and Nikolai Rimsky-Korsakov (1844–1908). Mussorgsky's opera *Boris Godunov* (1874, based on a Pushkin piece as well) remains a favorite the world over. His 1874 composition *Pictures at an Exhibition* aligned with other new trends in European art, such as French impressionism.

In painting, in which previously Karl Briullov (1792–1855) had been acclaimed for his work in the Romantic style, the "Peredvizhniki" ("Wanderers") emerged; they depicted scenes from the Russian past and present in a naturalist style. Il'ia Repin (1844–1930) became the most famous Wanderer, for works such as *Volga Barge*

Haulers (1872–1873) and *Procession in Kursk Province* (1881–1883). Vasilii Surikov's (1848–1916) historically inspired works have also remained popular. The Wanderers still practiced a realist style (and thus met approval in Stalin's Soviet Union), which was eventually challenged in the symbolist work of Mikhail Vrubel (1856–1910), who married Orthodox imagery with a more experimental style. Vrubel's art both recalls impressionism and seems to herald surrealism.

Russian genius was expressed not merely in arts and literature but in scientific research, too. The first great Russian scientist was the mathematician Nikolai Lobachevskii (1792–1856), who challenged several of the Euclidean axioms. In his wake, Dmitrii Mendeleev (1834–1907) became a giant in chemistry, responsible for developing the periodic table of elements. Another pioneer was Konstantin Tsiolkovskii (1857–1935), who designed rockets for space travel.

Nineteenth-century Russian historiography suffered from some of the same shortcomings as other European and North American history writing, with an unduly heavy emphasis on military and diplomatic history, and a particular preference to trace the development of the state in history (which was seen as a positive development, following Hegel's guidance). Neither women nor non-Russians received much attention, for example, and the incorporation of non-Russian areas by the Russian state was uncritically portrayed as beneficial to such regions. But work by some of the greatest historians of the age has to some degree stood the test of time. Even if it is in some ways a comment on the one-sided character and paucity of Soviet historiography, it is telling that in recent years the history of Russia by Sergei Solov'ev (1820–1879) has been translated in full into English for the first time. No one has rendered such a detailed picture of the Russian past since Solov'ev. Similarly, some of the insights of his pupil Vasilii Kliuchevskii (1841–1911) are still discussed by historians today, both inside Russia and elsewhere. Among the non-Russians, modern historiography developed as well and was to supply arguments for national self-determination, in response to those applauding the seemingly irresistible rise in history of the Russian state. Best known, perhaps, were the Ukrainians Mykola Kostomarov (1817–1885, who wrote most of his work in Russian) and Mykhailo Hrushevskyi (1866–1934), who was to become the head of the briefly existing Ukrainian state in 1917 and 1918.

FATAL CONTRADICTIONS; INDUSTRIALIZATION AND URBANIZATION

The Russian Empire embarked on full-scale industrialization at the time of Aleksandr II's murder. His death at exactly that moment was most unfortunate because the rapid changes that overcame the empire's economy and society needed to be guided by a responsive government. Aleksandr III's method of rule, instead, was inflexible and unresponsive. He resembled a despot of the premodern age, preferring things to remain as they were (or, indeed, had been). He was thoroughly out of touch with the modern society that was taking shape in Russia. And when Aleksandr

III suddenly died in 1894, his son and heir Nicholas was far from ready to take the throne. Nicholas had believed that his father had a good couple of decades ahead of him. Lacking imagination and boldness and without sufficient preparation for the task awaiting him, he decided to continue in his father's footsteps. Nicholas II was rudely woken up from his nostalgic reverie in 1905, when he was suddenly confronted by his entire country in rebellion. After it had been overcome, he never quite grasped its significance.

The first signs of industrialization in Russia appeared even under Nicholas I, when a railroad line was completed from St. Petersburg to Moscow in 1851. Its more than four hundred miles represented by far the longest double-track railway in the world. It was a prestigious accomplishment, but it was at the same time a mere drop in a bucket. Russia was vast, and railroad construction never fully acquired the momentum that would have provided the country with a sufficiently dense network (even if by 1876 track had grown more than tenfold). Apart from freight or passenger transport, this was required for fast troop movement, as was made once again evident in 1914 (it had already been apparent during the Crimean War). In the first days of the First World War, Germany moved its soldiers around fast enough to head off Russian offensives along the front line. More than sixty years after the first substantial rail line was completed, the development of Russia's railways was nowhere close to that of its German foe.

Besides railroad construction, early Russian industrialization occurred primarily in textile manufacturing. Even in the final years of serfdom, textile mills sprang up that were not unlike those of contemporary Manchester or Glasgow in Britain. They were founded in and around Moscow, St. Petersburg, and Ivanovo-Voznesensk in central Russia, as well as in Russian Poland. The workforce consisted of (former) peasants who already before the introduction of a mechanized production process had been earning supplementary income spinning and weaving at home, paying so-called quitrent to their lords. Outside of Poland, the textile workers hailed predominantly from the non–Black Earth zone, where people at best eked out a meager living in agriculture because of the poor soil and inclement weather. For decades, factory workers maintained fairly close ties to their ancestral villages, sometimes leaving their jobs at the looms to help out at home with farmwork in the summer.

Meanwhile, the abolition of serfdom and the steep decline in demand for Russian iron because of competition from technologically advanced mines in industrialized countries led to a decline in the production of the Ural metallurgical enterprises. Once they were liberated, the previously enserfed miners preferred to seek their luck in other pursuits, further encumbering the winning of ore. Altogether, industry under Aleksandr II grew very slowly. The number of factory workers and miners perhaps increased by 30 percent between 1860 and 1880, and barely surpassed one million workers by the latter year. In the 1870s, nevertheless, some groundwork was laid for the boom that was to follow, such as the completion of the railway link between the iron-ore and coal-mining districts in southern Ukraine, and the early exploitation of oil fields around Baku in Azerbaijan.

Figure 4.2.   Bashkir railroad switchman in the Urals, ca. 1910 (Prokudin-Gorskii Collection, Library of Congress)

But the real takeoff period for Russian industrialization was the 1880s and 1890s. It was funded by private initiative (including that of some foreigners), foreign loans, and comparatively high taxation, especially of those who could least afford it, the peasantry, and in part levied on consumer staples such as vodka. The government protected fledgling industries from foreign competition by way of high tariffs on imports while it provided required infrastructure and actively jump-started various enterprises, for example in mining. The ministers of finance of the era (among whom Sergei Vitte [1849–1915] deserves pride of place) who guided this economic policy thus tried to copy the successful German road to industrialization of the middle of the nineteenth century.

Railway building accelerated (albeit far from quickly enough). Its showpiece was the Transsiberian Railroad, which began to be built under Vitte's supervision in the 1890s. Railways linked key ports such as Odessa, Riga, and Novorossiisk with their hinterland, and budding industrial areas with each other. Coal and iron production boomed in the 1890s in the Donets Basin (Donbas), and oil production near Baku almost tripled during the same decade. Major cities in these booming regions, such as Baku or Ekaterinoslav (Dnipropetrovsk), saw their populations double in ten years. Still, much of the empire was hardly touched by the changes, for industry tended to be heavily concentrated in a few areas. By 1900, almost three times as many people worked as artisans (making products on a small scale without mechanized tools) than as industrial workers: eight to nine million were craftsmen and craftswomen, when approximately three million found employment in factories and mines.

Most of the new factories established in the final decades of the nineteenth century were large, employing thousands of workers. Their wages were low (partially because workers performed predominantly unskilled work), and labor conditions were harsh. The fluctuation of the labor force was high: many workers departed for their ancestral villages if their help was needed for farmwork back home. From fairly early on, the government countered the worst exploitation of workers by legislation. Legislation milestones included the outlawing of child labor in 1882 (for children younger than twelve); the limitation of the workday to a maximum of eleven and a half hours per day in 1897; and the 1903 decree that obliged employers to compensate those injured at work in their enterprises. Whereas government inspectors at first were often ignored or bribed, their honesty and the means to enforce factory legislation markedly improved during the 1890s.

Trade unions, though, were prohibited, and strikes forbidden, too. Work in factories and mines was dangerous for their labor force's health in the long and short term. Accidents were common, with hundreds of workers dying across Russia every year in industrial and railroad accidents. Housing was dreadful, with workers sleeping on bunks in barracks, which often lacked running water and sewers. Illness was common, even if epidemic diseases became rare after the spread of inoculation programs in the 1880s and 1890s. Alcoholism was rampant, as was violence in factory districts. Bereft of the support from their families or from fellow villagers (and often from any priest or other religious servant), workers sought solace in the promises and community offered by various socialist agitators and sometimes in informal mutual-aid organizations of workers who hailed from the same region.

Like anywhere else, modern mass society in Russia was not merely composed of the industrial proletariat and its employers, together with government officials overseeing the factories and facilitating their operation. Urbanization also involved a growth in the number of those engaged in the service sector, from artisans, shopkeepers, clerks, janitors, and teachers to transport workers. The 1897 census counted almost two million people as belonging to the nobility, most of whom lived at least part of the year in the empire's towns and cities as well. Three hundred and fifty thousand people were enumerated as clerics (many of whom lived in the countryside, but a significant number lived in the towns). Businessmen, lawyers, secondary-school teachers, professors, doctors, and so on, formed a predominantly urban upper middle class of slightly more than six hundred thousand people. With just as many rurally based as living in towns, artisans amounted to some 8 million people, while 2.6 million were enumerated as factory workers. Altogether, the empire's urban

Figure 4.3. Il'ia Repin's *Volga Barge Haulers*, 1872–1873

population amounted in 1897 to almost seventeen million people (the remaining 108 million were counted as rural dwellers). Such numbers remain tentative: millions were hard to categorize, as they lived for part of the year in their ancestral village and part in an urban community. In the census, 93.5 million peasants (including people who fished or hunted as a living) were counted, and almost 3 million people were identified as Cossacks.

Russia was thus a country in the throes of industrialization by 1900, but it was not an industrialized country. For example, in the United Kingdom, half the population lived in an urban environment by the middle of the nineteenth century, indicating that it had become an industrialized country with people finding employment primarily in the cities. In Nicholas II's empire, less than 10 percent did so in 1900. The early phase of industrialization is a most unsettling stage of development for any country, and this was certainly the case for Russia around 1900. The changes that this process wrought in the mushrooming cities were accompanied by a dire situation in much of the countryside, which was plagued by overpopulation and underproduction.

LAND HUNGER

Although the Russian peasantry cultivated half the available arable land by 1880 in European Russia, yields remained anemic. We saw earlier how rarely knowledge was diffused about more efficient methods of farming, and few advanced tools were in use. While the government was heavily involved in nurturing the empire's fledgling industry, it stood aside when it came to improving agriculture. Peasants bore much of the brunt of financing industry, through direct and indirect taxes, and compensation payments (which were sluiced into things such as infrastructure projects). Even if interested in sophisticated equipment, most peasants could not afford to purchase any advanced tools because high import duties were slapped on foreign imports and little farming machinery was made in Russia. Crop yields thus often did not surpass those common in Britain in the seventeenth century. In 1900, yields in Britain were four times as high as in Russia.

Because so much land was unsuited for agriculture as well, Russia faced rural overpopulation by 1900. This was the case even though the strong reliance on manual labor meant that farms needed far more workhands than in Western Europe or North America. The worst overpopulation was encountered in the region best suited for agriculture, that is, the Black Earth region, especially in the Ukrainian provinces of Chernigov (Chernihiv), Poltava, and Kharkov (Kharkiv) and the Russian provinces of Kursk, Oryol, and Tambov. Peasants tried to rent additional land from private landowners (apart from nobles, more and more middle-class town dwellers acquired land toward 1900), but this was expensive and few peasants had ready cash, given the meager surplus they marketed. In 1883, a special Peasant Land Bank began to operate, furnishing peasants with loans allowing them to buy more land, but it was difficult to qualify for these loans. In addition, many peasants were loath to take on further burdens in addition to the redemption fees and taxes they owed the government. Lacking sufficient land, families increasingly saw members leave the village to find part-time or full-time work in nonagricultural occupations. These people sought their luck as itinerant or sedentary artisans, as seasonal workers on the farms of richer neighbors or on noble and nonnoble estates, or as workers in the factories in the towns.

Gradually, too, some peasants moved from densely populated regions to areas where there was still sufficient land for farming, as was the case in western Ukraine, the Kuban, and Stavropol regions north of the Caucasus, or in western Siberia and northern Kazakhstan. Migration to Siberia and Kazakhstan stepped up with the expansion of the Transsiberian Railroad. The settlement of Slavic peasants there, however, came at the expense of the grasslands of the local nomadic population and led to sporadic clashes as well as smoldering resentment between settlers and nomads.

For years the government pondered the introduction of a policy that would end the periodic redistribution of land in the villages. Full perpetual ownership of a clearly demarcated piece of land might help peasants acquire a greater interest in improving their land, but nothing was undertaken in this regard until 1905.[6] Similarly, nothing substantial was undertaken to alleviate the burden of the compensation payments for the land received by the former serfs at the time of their emancipation. As with much else, of course, there were bright spots in agriculture, through which the Russian Empire was able to export agricultural products. The government's share of the proceeds from these transactions was sunk into the industrialization program.

MARXISM AND PEASANT SOCIALISM

By definition, an autocracy cannot tolerate political opposition. The autocrat is infallible, all seeing, and all knowing. Aleksandr III unhesitatingly subscribed to this theory. In his eyes, his father's murder confirmed that Russia needed to be ruled by a firm hand. The tsar ordered his security police to round up all Populists. Some were jailed and banished to Siberia; some went abroad. But the example of the People's Will nevertheless inspired others to continue to commit acts of terror. Among them was the biology student Aleksandr Ul'ianov (1866–1887), who hailed from the Volga town of Simbirsk. He unsuccessfully tried to assassinate the tsar in the spring of 1887. Ul'ianov was arrested and hanged. He had a younger brother, Vladimir (better known as Lenin), who at the time was preparing to study law at university. Vladimir became as fanatically opposed to the tsar as Aleksandr had been but decided that his older brother's methods to end the tsar's rule had been wrongheaded. Perhaps he had a point: after first acquiring power in Russia, Lenin had the last tsar killed in 1918.

The difference between the brothers Ul'ianov reflected the transformation taking place within the Russian revolutionary movement in the latter decades of the nineteenth century. The Populists remained faithful to the idea that Russia's peasantry consisted of budding socialists. It would be sufficient for revolutionaries merely to nudge them to see tsardom replaced by a decentralized state of equal peasant communes. This view was most eloquently expressed in the work of N. K. Mikhailovskii (1842–1904). But the wave of repression unleashed by Aleksandr III in response to the assassination of Aleksandr II was a setback for the revolutionary movement, as the tsarist authorities' arrest wave almost wholly eradicated the opposition. It made Populists such as Mikhailovskii reject the terrorism advocated by the People's Will as counterproductive. After 1900, however, when the Populists founded the political party of the Socialist Revolutionaries (SR), terrorism made a comeback as a revolutionary tactic. The impatient young leadership of the SR party considered it once again a valuable weapon in the fight for the overthrow of tsarism. The number of attempts on the lives of government dignitaries rapidly increased. In a few cases, perhaps, the terrorists may have actually triggered the desired effect; for example, the murder of the interior minister V. K. Pleve (1846–1904) ushered in a less repressive atmosphere in the country.

The infatuation with terrorism is of course not uniquely Russian. In the Russian case, it was unusually strongly developed, going back to Mikhail Bakunin's anarchism. Bakunin suggested that a society of equals would be brought about in one fell swoop, through a sort of purifying conflagration. It was not quite clear what this revolutionary catharsis would consist of, but Bakunin and his allies thought that it would entail some sort of violent orgy in which the oppressed settled scores with their oppressors. The murder of the symbol of inequality, the tsar, might bring about this transformative moment. Anarchists in other countries murdered dignitaries,[7] but nowhere did such assassinations have the desired effect. Quite the opposite, in fact, was usually the case, as it was in Russia. Apart from Aleksandr II's murder in 1881, the terrorist murder of prime minister Pyotr Stolypin (1862–1911) stands out as a supremely tragic moment in Russian history. Stolypin's death quashed perhaps the last chance for Russia to modernize in a relatively peaceful and gradual manner.

Few Populists, Socialist Revolutionaries, or anarchists believed in the possibility of a nonviolent transformation toward a society of greater justice. The world needed to be cleansed from the exploiters, who were not expected to surrender voluntarily. And terrorist violence, precisely because it led to harsher government repression, would awaken the toiling masses to their true friends and enemies, increasing their desire for an overthrow of the government and an end to the rule of the privileged classes. Finally, it should be noted that not all agreed that equality and justice would come about only through violence. The other great leader of Russian anarchism, Prince Pyotr Kropotkin (1842–1921), was a strong opponent of violent methods. His ideas seemed akin to the quirky Christian socialism championed by the writer Lev Tolstoi.

Certainly, the Marxists who organized themselves abroad under the lead of Plekhanov, Akselrod, and Zasulich rejected terrorism. They, too, believed that a better world could come about only through a violent overthrow of the bourgeoisie (or middle class composed of factory owners and their ilk) but argued that this revolution should begin only when society's support for socialism had become overwhelming. Then the proletarians (the industrial working class) would sweep away the bourgeoisie, ending its control over the economy (and therefore the government, in the Marxist view). But such a revolution could occur only if Russia was sufficiently industrialized and had such a proletariat, that is, if it could boast of an industrial working class that outnumbered all other social groups (including the allegedly backward peasantry). In addition, socialist agitators needed time to convince this proletariat that its true interest lay in the creation of a society of equals, who shared the fruits of their labor in an equitable manner. Since Russia was far from industrialized even in the 1880s, Plekhanov and company thus believed that patience was needed. Capitalism was in its infancy in the tsar's realm. Looking at the example of Britain or Germany, the Russian Marxist pioneers concluded that a level of modernization of the economy that would bring Russia to the brink of a socialist revolution might take half a century.

Although Marxist socialism was an attractive political philosophy, since it promised the arrival of a sort of paradise on earth and built its predictions on a supposedly scientific study of long-term historical trends (thus it was called "historical materialism" by Marx himself), some of its premises were murky. Marx suggested that the revolution would begin in the most advanced industrialized countries, after which the lesser-developed countries would follow suit. It would therefore be an international, global revolution. But it remained vague how many countries needed to be sufficiently industrialized and how such a level of industrialization could be measured. In addition, Marx had suggested that in mature capitalist societies capital would be increasingly concentrated in fewer and fewer hands. These capitalists would exploit their workers to the hilt. The vast majority of the population would sink into poverty and join the proletarians, who would realize that they had "nothing to loose but their chains." Vastly outnumbering the capitalists and their cronies in the government, the proletariat would start the inevitably triumphant socialist revolution.

But a countervailing trend could be discerned in the developed industrial countries in the late nineteenth century. Through trade union activism (as in Great Britain), the advocacy of strengthening socialist movements (in Germany or France), or positive government measures (as in the German Empire), the labor conditions and standard of living of the Central and Western European proletariat markedly improved. Pensions were introduced, as were accident and health insurance, while wages were rising and slums torn down and replaced by better housing. Education levels improved. And this occurred at a time when the world economy was mired in a long-term slump (1873–1896). Marxists such as Lenin and Trotsky later argued that these improvements in the mature capitalist societies were in effect meaningless. They argued that the workers remained powerless, bereft of any control over their labor. Only when workers owned their own factories would they be truly empowered and could the vagaries of the free market and capitalist competition be overcome. Purist Marxists such as Lenin argued that capitalist businessmen, and their allies who ran the government, attempted to distract the proletarians from pursuing their true interest by making a few cosmetic concessions. Only socialism would bring true relief from capitalist oppression.

A new generation of Marxists appeared in 1890s Russia that witnessed firsthand the industrialization boom and the dreadful labor conditions and living circumstances of the workers who were employed by the factories. This second generation (not unlike those who led the SR after 1900) was much less patient than Plekhanov and company. Since workers were not allowed to form trade unions that could defend their interests and bargain for better wages and labor conditions, exploitation was indeed frequently extreme, despite the government's efforts to overcome the worst excesses. Owners often hired and fired at will, as the labor pool seemed inexhaustible. The workers lacked almost any means of defense against such practices, although strikes broke out with regularity. In these dire circumstances, socialist agitators seemed to offer solace and even ultimate salvation.

Driven by the impatience of youth, the young Lenin, together with such allies as Yuli Martov (1873–1923), worked hard at whipping up the revolutionary inclinations of St. Petersburg's proletariat. Lenin's activities quickly drew the attention of the tsarist authorities, who sent him for several years of exile to Siberia during the late 1890s. Deciding that the danger of renewed arrest would be too great if he stayed in Russia and that his writings could influence the Russian working class more profoundly if he lived abroad, Lenin joined the Plekhanov group in Switzerland upon his release in 1900. Meanwhile, the tsarist government was fighting a many-headed Hydra in its attempts to suppress socialist agitation. For every one socialist rounded up, another two cropped up.

LIBERALISM AND CONSERVATISM

Because of the ultimate outcome, a socialist (or communist, as the Bolsheviks preferred to call their state) Soviet Union, historians used to neglect the considerable support in late Imperial Russia for political movements that took their cue from Western-style democracies. Both democratic liberalism and conservatism might have worked in Russia in the long term, if the country had been given sufficient time to adjust to the promising changes brought about from 1905 onward. Instead, however, the First World War terminated the brief Russian experience with constitutional government.

Nonetheless, before August 1914 it had become obvious that the tsarist regime, although no longer ruling unchecked, was even reluctant to work with the conservatives. The tsar and his advisors preferred to seek advice from extremist politicians and political movements, believing that they represented the "healthy viewpoint of the common folk" (as the Nazis called it a generation later[8]). It was undoubtedly true that still after 1905 many peasants had little political awareness and that their lodestars were the little lord (the tsar, or "Tsar-Batiushka") on earth and the great lord in heaven. But the tsar mistook the political demagoguery of the leaders of the Union of the Russian People (also known as the Black Hundreds) as the voice of the people. Nicholas was even loath to condemn the flaring up of pogroms of Jewish communities in the Pale of Settlement (which became a recurring phenomenon from 1881 onward), as they, too, were seen as expressing authentic popular sentiments. No one was prosecuted for forging the notorious *Protocols of the Elders of Zion* (a document about an alleged Jewish world conspiracy that was to be used by Hitler), and no one was convicted for conjuring up the ritual murder that placed Mendel Beilis (1874–1934) on trial in Kyiv, both signs of an utterly vile anti-Semitism. Compared to the perverse ravings of the Black Hundreds' ringleaders, Grigorii Rasputin's (1869–1916) advice to the imperial couple was far less baneful, but contrary to Aleksandra's and Nicholas's beliefs, the Siberian monk's views hardly reflected those of the majority of the tsar's subjects.

In seeking advice, Aleksandr III and Nicholas II could have turned to people of liberal or mainstream conservative convictions, if they had cared to find them. Once in a while, a more enlightened figure was appointed to a ministry, such as Vitte or Stolypin. Even though these men were utterly loyal servants, the monarchs never listened very well to them. And these ministers lacked any sort of backing by a broad-based political movement within Russian society. Instead, the key advisor of the last two tsars before 1905 was an archreactionary who rejected the modern world wholesale. Konstantin Pobedonostsev (1827–1907) was the former tutor of Aleksandr III and subsequent lay chief (Oberprokuror) of the Russian Orthodox Church. Pobedonostsev wanted Russia to revert to a state in which religion combined with autocracy existed in a felicitous harmony and to a country in which all accepted their station in life without complaint, selflessly serving their sovereign and awaiting their rewards in the hereafter. Such ideas were pleasing to Aleksandr and Nicholas, but they were wholly out of touch with reality.

The problem for those who could have formed his tsarist majesty's "loyal opposition" was that political opposition was outlawed. Thus, mild critics might be treated like rabid revolutionary firebrands. Liberal critics sometimes found an outlet in journals and magazines, but even then they had to avoid bringing down the censor's wrath on themselves and their publications. Eventually, Pyotr Struve (1870–1944) organized the Soiuz Osvobozhdenie (Union of Liberation) abroad; members of the liberal party that in 1904 emerged from the Union of Liberation were known as Constitutional Democrats, or for short, K-D or Kadets. One of the key leaders of the Kadets was the historian Pavel Miliukov (1859–1943). The liberal leaders, unfortunately, were so traumatized by more than twenty years of tsarist persecution that they missed the chance to lead Russia to a better future when it was offered to them. When they and their sympathizers received more than half of the seats in elections for the new Duma (parliament) in 1906, they did not trust the tsar's offering of an olive branch and instead boycotted the proceedings.

Their competitors, the Octobrist Party, were willing to work with the tsar, but they were backed by a rather smaller part of the electorate.[9] When they received a greater share of the vote after the franchise was restricted for the elections of the Third Duma in 1907, the Octobrists (led by Aleksandr Guchkov, 1862–1936) were not invited to join the government. Instead, they became a very critical, albeit loyal, opposition.

One can easily imagine a government made up of elected liberal or conservative leaders ruling Russia in the name of a constitutional monarch, a more conciliatory or enlightened character than Aleksandr III or Nicholas II. After all, governments of such persuasions alternated in the United Kingdom and other countries around 1900. But Russia's misfortune was to be ruled by men who somehow had convinced themselves that they possessed a sort of superhuman charisma and wisdom, thanks to their divine appointment. God's will obliged them to rule as autocrats in the image of the Byzantine emperors. In the half millennium that had passed since the fall of Constantinople, however, the world had evolved beyond such concepts of sacred kingship.

NON-RUSSIAN NATIONALISM

According to the 1897 census, out of a total of 125 million inhabitants of the tsar's empire, approximately 84 million people spoke an Eastern Slavonic language (the breakdown was made according to mother tongue), of whom 55.7 million were Russians, 22.4 Ukrainians, and 5.9 million Belarusyn. Numerically, the third-largest group was the almost 8 million Polish speakers. Five million Yiddish-speaking Jews lived in the empire. The 1.8 million German speakers outnumbered Latvians (1.4 million), as well as the Georgians, Lithuanians, Moldavians, or Estonians, each of which nation numbered slightly more than a million people. Almost 14 million Turkic-Tatar speakers (4 million Kazakhs and 3.7 million Tatars among them) were enumerated. The exact breakdown of this group (who spoke related, albeit different, languages) remains vague, since census takers often failed to grasp the distinction between Kyrgyz and Kazakh, or Uzbek and Tajik. It is more than likely than many Central Asian Muslims avoided the census takers (and some numbers were forged), as was the case for the Caucasian mountain dwellers (a million were counted) and Azeris (of whom 380,000 were counted). There were identified several million others whose mother tongue was a language spoken by fewer than one hundred thousand people. Ninety three and a half million people lived in European Russia (excluding the Caucasus), with slightly over thirty million in Asiatic Russia. Seventy percent were Orthodox believers, 11 percent Muslim, 9 percent Catholic, and 4 percent Jewish, with many belonging to smaller religious groups.

The 1897 census was the first and last comprehensive counting in the history of Imperial Russia that detailed the linguistic and cultural allegiances of the tsar's subjects as well as their places of residence. Its staging reflected how, toward the end of the nineteenth century, matters such as religious affiliation or mother tongue had suddenly acquired importance for the Russian Empire's authorities. During Nicholas I's rule, when the official ideology was one of "nationality," "autocracy," and "Orthodoxy," the tsar's subjects' common bond was primarily their loyalty to the monarch, whose empire they had joined, forcibly or voluntarily, across the centuries. "Nationality" did not mean much beyond a certain recognition that the monarch and the state (and the administration's language) were Russian. "Orthodoxy" was not meant to be exclusive, and the tsar's flock harbored millions of Muslims, Lutherans, animists, and Catholics.

Before 1880, only perhaps the Poles living in historical Poland had adopted modern mass nationalism. Especially by way of Polish-language schools and to some extent through the Polish-Catholic clergy, a belief about their nation's unique shared cultural and historical identity had spread among all social strata in Poland. This sort of conviction usually implies a sense of superiority. As a result, Poles proved highly resistant to any government efforts to have them adopt a Russian identity (so-called Russification) after 1881. But this policy did not meet with much success among other non-Russians either.

With Russification, the archconservative Aleksandr III offered one truly novel major policy to his peoples. The tsar tried to Russify the non-Russians by abolishing many of the special rights and privileges various ethnocultural groups had historically enjoyed in Russia's composite empire. Clearly, in some places that were less diverse, nationalism could be a unifying force strengthening allegiance to the state. Such was the case in Imperial Germany, where it was manipulated by Chancellor Otto von Bismarck (1815–1898).

In post-1870 Germany, Bismarck galvanized German nationalism in several ways, most notoriously by scapegoating certain allegedly disloyal groups, such as the Catholics and socialists. During his campaigns against these "un-German" elements, the German chancellor invited those who did not belong to the Catholic Church or the socialist movement to join his attacks on the "enemy within." After Catholics (in 1878) and socialists (in 1890) had been pardoned for their alleged flirtation with disloyalty, they made sure that they behaved like good Germans, chastised by Bismarck's offensive. The genius of his strategy became apparent in July 1914, when almost all Germans supported their government's decision to go to war.

More subtly, Bismarck compelled all German citizens to receive a primary education that followed curriculum taught in High German (Hochdeutsch). Subjects such as geography and history were taught in a manner that depicted the creation of a united Germany with its 1871 borders as the goal of history. Military conscription, too, increased German citizens' inclination to obey their authorities loyally. What perhaps was least obvious at the time was that Bismarck's social insurance program and the general economic boom of his country made many Germans feel that they had a vested interested in the country that had so drastically improved the material condition of their lives.

In their Russifying policies, Aleksandr III and his advisors appear to have taken their cue from Bismarck (who once had been Prussian ambassador to St. Petersburg). But it should have given them pause that Bismarck was least successful in "Germanizing" the two largest non-German groups residing in Imperial Germany, the Poles and Alsatians. Neither group was numerically very large, however, and the failure to turn these people into loyal Germans did not seem to matter much in the German Empire. In contrast, as the census numbers show, the tsar ruled a country in which less than half of the population spoke Russian as its mother tongue. After all, although the tsarist government denied that they spoke a distinct language, the more than one-fifth who spoke Ukrainian or Belarusyn should not be counted as Russian. In addition, a fair number of Ukrainians belonged to the Uniate Church, a sect that since 1596 recognized the Catholic pope as their spiritual leader (even if it continued to observe Orthodox rituals), and thus did not share a common religion with the Russians either. Already among the Eastern Slavs, therefore, any Russification proved to be problematic. And then there was the one-third of the population that was neither Orthodox nor Eastern Slav.

In addition, Aleksandr III's government lacked the means to Russify the non-Russians. The Russian Empire was still far from implementing an all-encompassing system of primary education. Although a Russifier, Aleksandr III did not want to oblige all pupils in the non-Russian regions of his empire to learn their lessons in Russian, fearing that this would provoke an anti-Russian reaction, but this watered down Russification even further. Most non-Slavs were exempt from the basic training and garrisoning that came with the Slavs' military conscription after 1874. Furthermore, late Imperial Russia's standard of living was far lower than that in contemporary Imperial Germany. With the exception of a few prosperous businessmen, very few of Aleksandr III's subjects enjoyed unprecedented economic prosperity.

The tsar's strategy to Russify his peoples, therefore, could hardly go beyond singling out saboteurs who were accused of doing harm to the cause of Russia for ethnic, religious, or political reasons. This was a weak echo of Bismarck's campaign against Germany's Catholics or socialists. Such scapegoating was an easy strategy. Catholics, Jews, socialists, and so on, were thus targeted in efforts to rally people behind the tsar. But this policy had its limitations: it was hard to convince any non–Eastern Slavic speaker or Orthodox believer that the government's fury might not soon fall on them as well.

Lacking positive incentives to encourage non-Russian to Russify, the government relied on coercion. It had been tried earlier in Poland, where it had been shipwrecked on the rather more subtle strategy by Polish nationalists to cultivate a Polish identity through concerted educational efforts. In the course of the nineteenth century, most Poles came to believe that they shared a glorious historical past and boasted of a language and civilization superior to that of Russia. In other regions, however, Russification also faltered, often having the opposite effect from that intended. In this way, the Finns, who had without protest joined the Russian Empire in 1809, were faced with the loss of their extensive autonomy.[10] Instead of meekly submitting to the tsar and Russifying, they formed an articulate and well-organized nationalist movement, which was sophisticated and popular enough to achieve Finnish independence in 1918. In other non-Russian regions, nationalist movements often linked with socialist movements in protest to Russification policies.

Rather than galvanizing a shared sense of Russian identity, then, Aleksandr III (and Nicholas II, who continued these policies until 1905) frequently accomplished quite the opposite. In response to the Russification campaign, in many regions a nationalist movement took shape, gaining enough strength to proclaim the independence of the majority ethnocultural group in 1917 and 1918, as happened in Poland, Lithuania, Estonia, Latvia, Finland, Ukraine, Georgia, Armenia, Azerbaijan, and all of Turkestan.

Only at the cost of a strenuous effort (and with much bloodshed) did the Soviet successors of the tsars manage to patch back together an empire in which most of those territories were reabsorbed. But the Soviet leaders realized that they needed to propitiate the newly awakened nationalist sentiments that had been provoked by the Russification policies of the tsars. Stalin returned after 1929 to the tsarist Russification policies with ever greater conviction, but the consequences of his offensive, too, were ultimately counterproductive. His brutal enforcement of pro-Russian policies corroded the promising potential of the "affirmative action" policies of the 1920s, as Terry Martin has convincingly argued. By 1991, few outside Russia mourned the collapse of the multiethnic Soviet Union.

NOTES

1. And the clerics of the Orthodox Church and other religious dignitaries enjoyed some sort of autonomy, but the state could easily strip them of their privileges.

2. This was probably a habit rooted in Peter the Great's taxation system.

3. In the Russian language, a distinction was (and sometimes still is) made between an "all-Russian" or "Russian imperial" identity (in Russian, *rossiiskii*) and a strictly ethnocultural and linguistically based Russian identity (in Russian, *russkii*).

4. No country yet had a full democracy, of course. France came closest, but all her women were excluded from the vote, as they were in the United States, where Jim Crow laws were spreading as well.

5. Marx's first part of *Capital* was published in the original German in 1867. The censors deemed the book too difficult for a Russian audience to be subversive.

6. In 1903, the commune's collective responsibility for taxes was abolished, and the next year peasants were no longer to be subjected to corporal punishment.

7. For example, anarchists murdered the French president Sadi Carnot (1837–1894) and the American president William McKinley (1843–1901).

8. In German, this viewpoint was called *Gesundenes Volksempfinden*.

9. The Octobrist Party was named after the tsar's 1905 October Manifesto, the realization of which it took as the party's platform.

10. The Finns' move to join the empire was one of the consequences of the Tilsit Treaty between Aleksandr I and Napoleon I.

FURTHER READING

Translated Primary Sources

Denikin, Anton I. *The Career of a Tsarist Officer, Memoirs, 1872–1916.* Translated and annotated by Margaret Patoski. Minneapolis: University of Minnesota Press, 1975.

Dostoyevsky, Fyodor. *Demons.* Translated by Robert A. Maguire. Edited by Ronald Meyer. London: Penguin, 2008.

Figner, Vera. *Memoirs of a Revolutionist.* DeKalb: Northern Illinois University Press, 1991.

Goncharov, Ivan. *Oblomov.* Translated by David Magarshack. New York: Penguin, 2005.

Gorky, Maxim. *Autobiography of Maxim Gorky.* Translated by Isidor Schneider. Amsterdam: Fredonia Books, 2001.

Kanatchikov, Semen I. *A Radical Worker in Tsarist Russia: The Autobiography of Semen Ivanovich Kanatchikov.* Translated and edited by Reginald E. Zelnik. Stanford, CA: Stanford University Press, 1986.

Semyonova Tian-Shanskaia, Olga. *Village Life in Late Tsarist Russia.* Translated and edited by David L. Ransel. Bloomington: Indiana University Press, 1993.

Turgenev, Ivan. *Fathers and Sons.* Translated by Rosemary Edmonds. New York: Penguin, 1982.

Scholarly Literature

Avrutin, Eugene M. *Jews and the Imperial State: Identification Politics in Tsarist Russia.* Ithaca, NY: Cornell University Press, 2010.

Brower, Daniel, and Edward Lazzarini, eds. *Russia's Orient: Imperial Borderlands and Peoples, 1700–1917.* Bloomington: Indiana University Press, 1997.

Confino, Michael. *Russia before the "Radiant Future": Essays in Modern History, Culture and Society.* New York: Berghahn, 2011.

Eklof, B., J. Bushnell, and L. Zakharova, eds. *Russia's Great Reforms, 1855–1881.* Bloomington: Indiana University Press, 1994.

Emmons, Terence, and Wayne Vucinich, eds. *The Zemstvo in Russia.* Cambridge: Cambridge University Press, 2011.

Engel, Barbara Alpern. *Breaking the Ties That Bound: The Politics of Marital Strife in Late Imperial Russia.* Ithaca, NY: Cornell University Press, 2011.

Engelstein, Laura. *Slavophile Empire: Imperial Russia's Illiberal Path.* Ithaca, NY: Cornell University Press, 2009.

Grant, Jonathan A. *Big Business in Russia: The Putilov Company in Late Imperial Russia, 1868–1917.* Pittsburgh: University of Pittsburgh Press, 1999.

Henze, Charlotte E. *Disease, Health Care and Government in Late Imperial Russia: Life and Death on the Volga, 1823–1914.* New York: Routledge, 2011.

Herlihy, Patricia. *The Alcoholic Empire: Vodka and Politics in Late Imperial Russia.* New York: Oxford University Press, 2002.

Khachaturian, Lisa. *Cultivating Nationhood in Imperial Russia: The Periodical Press and the Formation of a Modern Armenian Identity.* New Brunswick, NJ: Transaction, 2009.

Khalid, Adeeb. *The Politics of Muslim Cultural Reform: Jadidism in Central Asia.* Berkeley: University of California Press, 1999.

Klier, John. *Imperial Russia's Jewish Question, 1855–1881.* Cambridge: Cambridge University Press, 2005.

Lincoln, W. Bruce. *The Great Reforms: Autocracy, Bureaucracy and the Politics of Change in Imperial Russia.* DeKalb: Northern Illinois University Press, 1990.

———. *In the Vanguard of Reform: Russia's Enlightened Bureaucrats, 1825–1861.* DeKalb: Northern Illinois University Press, 1986.

Moss, Walter. *Russia in the Age of Alexander II, Tolstoy and Dostoyevsky.* New York: Anthem, 2002.

Nathans, Benjamin. *Beyond the Pale: The Jewish Encounter with Late Imperial Russia*. Berkeley: University of California Press, 2004.

Plokhy, Serhii. *The Cossack Myth: History and Nationhood in the Age of Empires*. Cambridge: Cambridge University Press, 2012.

———. *Unmaking Imperial Russia: Mykhailo Hrushevsky and the Writing of Ukrainian History*. Toronto: University of Toronto Press, 2005.

Pomper, Philip. *Peter Lavrov and the Russian Revolutionary Movement*. Chicago: University of Chicago Press, 1972.

Radzinsky, Edvard. *Alexander II: The Last Great Tsar*. New York: Free Press, 2006.

Raeff, Marc. *Russia Abroad: A Cultural History of the Russian Emigration*. New York: Oxford University Press, 1990.

Schrader, Abby M. *Languages of the Lash: Corporal Punishment and Identity in Imperial Russia*. DeKalb: Northern Illinois University Press, 2002.

Venturi, Franco. *Roots of Revolution: A History of the Populist and Socialist Movements in Nineteenth-Century Russia*. Chicago: University of Chicago Press, 1983.

Verhoeven, Claudia. *The Odd Man Karakozov: Imperial Russia, Modernity and the Birth of Terrorism*. Ithaca, NY: Cornell University Press, 2011.

Wcislo, Francis. *Tales of Imperial Russia: The Life and Times of Sergei Witte*. New York: Oxford University Press, 2011.

Worobec, Christine, et al., eds. *The Human Tradition in Imperial Russia*. Lanham, MD: Rowman & Littlefield, 2009.

Yekelchyk, Serhy. *Ukraine: Birth of a Modern Nation*. New York: Oxford University Press, 2007.

WEBSITE

Russia photographed by S. M. Prokudin-Gorskii around 1900: http://www.loc.gov/exhibits/empire

FILMS

The Brothers Karamazov. DVD. TV series. Directed by Yury Moroz. Russia: RBC Video, 2008.
Oblomov. DVD. Directed by Nikita Mikhalkov. New York: Kino Video, 2004.

5

Fatal Foreign Entanglements and a Failed Revolution, 1877–1914

Although Russia was seething around 1900 with industrialization, cultural modernization, the spread of socialist movements, and nationalism all engulfing the empire at the same time, the deathblow to Romanov rule was the war that broke out in 1914, which was in considerable measure due to the disastrous foreign policy pursued by Nicholas II. The revolution of 1905 stopped short of ending Romanov rule because on that occasion the tsar extricated his country from war with Japan in a timely fashion. The 1917 Revolution, however, ended tsardom because Nicholas doggedly wanted to fight the war to a "victorious conclusion." Although nationalism and socialism gave the last two tsars and their advisors fits, the undoing of the house of Romanov was its foreign policy. Because foreign affairs played such a decisive role in the fate of tsarist Russia, they are the primary focus of this chapter.

THE RUSSO-TURKISH WAR AND PAN-SLAVISM

Despite some setbacks, Russian diplomatic and military fortune from Aleksei's reign until Nicholas I's last years had been unusually good. From 1654 to 1856, the country grew massively in size, and few significant battles were lost. The worst defeats came in 1711 at the Battle of Pruth against the Turks and in 1805 and 1807 at, respectively, Austerlitz and Friedland against the French. But in both cases the setbacks were brief, and the Russians quickly recovered from them. From the loss in the Crimean War, however, Imperial Russia never quite recuperated. It is true that after 1856 the empire further expanded toward the Iranian and Afghan borders, but in Europe little was gained.

In 1877, Russia went to war with Ottoman Turkey. The ultimately comprehensive military victory (even if the Turkish defense proved stronger than anticipated) in this

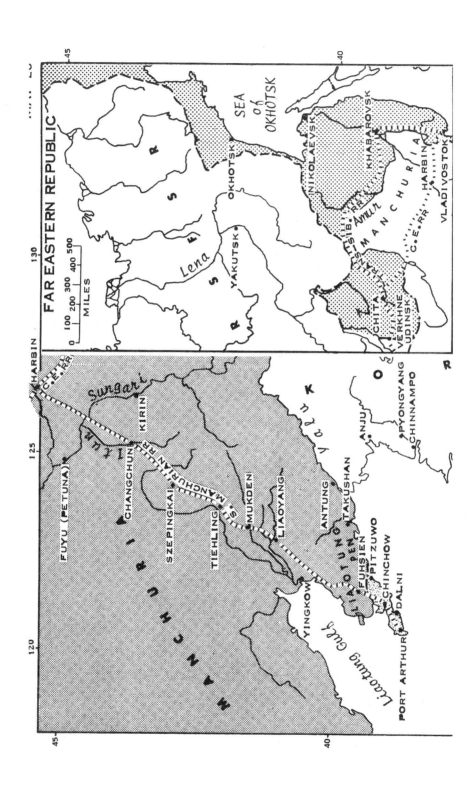

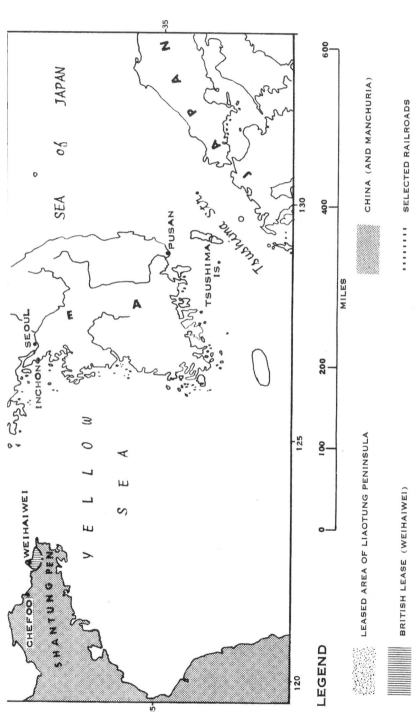

LEGEND

LEASED AREA OF LIAOTUNG PENINSULA

BRITISH LEASE (WEIHAIWEI)

CHINA (AND MANCHURIA)

SELECTED RAILROADS

Map 5.1. Russian Far East, 1898–1945 (From Allen F. Chew, *An Atlas of Russian History*, New Haven, CT: Yale University Press, 1967. Used by permission.)

conflict was reflected in the advantageous terms of the Treaty of San Stefano, concluded in early 1878. But the Russian gains were reduced to a much less favorable outcome by the Congress of Berlin later that year. At Berlin, the powers decided to delete from the map a large independent Bulgaria, created at San Stefano as a client state of Russia (within a few years, the Turks nonetheless gave a smaller Bulgaria its independence). Of even greater consequence was the Berlin Congress's handing over of the Turkish provinces of Bosnia and Herzegovina to Austrian-Habsburg administration. This was territory the small Orthodox and Slavic kingdom of Serbia (with whom the Russians had allied in the war) coveted, too. In Serbian eyes, Bosnia-Herzegovina's award to the Habsburgs was an unforgivable injustice, even if Serbia was officially recognized as an independent state by the Congress of Berlin. Some minor territorial gains along the Black Sea coast for Russia itself hardly compensated for the treatment the Berlin Congress meted out to its "little Slav brethren" on the Balkans. Russian Pan-Slavists in particular decried the concessions made at Berlin as an outrageous humiliation. But Aleksandr II and his foreign minister Aleksandr Gorchakov (who was the key Russian negotiator at Berlin in 1878) sensibly decided that this was the maximum their country could receive: the United Kingdom and Austria-Hungary seemed poised for war with Russia, if it was to insist on maintaining the terms of San Stefano.

After the loss in the Crimean War, then, the Russo-Turkish War was a case of a war won and a peace lost. For Russia, the settlement of the Congress of Berlin was, at the time and later, often seen as a further international humiliation on top of the Crimean War. After 1878, the Russians became impatient for an opportunity to recover some of their lost reputation as a military powerhouse. And Russian ire was ever more directed at Habsburg Austria. The Habsburgs had betrayed the Romanovs in the Crimean War and had been instrumental in forcing the Russians to accept the terms of the Treaty of Berlin. A series of further embarrassments worsened the Russian itch to settle the scores with the Austrians. Well aware of the impossibility of going to war on their own against any of the other Great Powers in Europe, the Russians concluded a firm military alliance with another power, France, which was joined by the United Kingdom in 1907. Once the Russian government was assured of allied backing, the tsar and his advisors felt sufficiently confident in the summer of 1914 to let the Sarajevo crisis escalate and embark on a fatal attempt to settle scores with the Habsburg Empire.

The thirst for revenge on the Austrians (and the desire for international rehabilitation) was intensified by Pan-Slavists. The aim of Pan-Slavism was to create a state in which all Slavic peoples would be united and, in its Russian iteration, specifically under Russian rule. Its key ideologue had been Nikolai Danilevskii (1822–1885), who in his *Russia and Europe* (1869), argued that the "Slav moment" in history was imminent. For Danilevskii, Slavs were the chosen people. Their Orthodox emperor would govern the rest of the world from his seat at Constantinople, after it was recaptured from the Turks. In some ways a nineteenth-century version of Catherine the Great's Greek Project, Pan-Slavism was infused by quasi-scientific biological and social Darwinist ideas. Although a pipe dream, this ideology suited the last tsars rather well in its fanning of the flames of Russian belligerence. Since the Pan-Slav program in many respects aligned with the

Russification policies of the last two tsars, Pan-Slav leaders were among the few "representatives of society" whom the tsars lent a willing ear (while some sympathetic to Pan-Slav ideas served in high positions within the tsar's government).

During the final decades of the nineteenth century, European nationalism everywhere took on an extremist guise, categorizing peoples as those born to rule and those born to be led, whether in Europe or in the overseas European empires. Using spurious scientific findings to justify the concept of a hierarchy of human races, racism and nationalism merged. Pan-Slavism was a Russian iteration of the various theories that propagated that some peoples were culturally and even biologically further advanced than others. It provided an important impetus for those (among whom tsars themselves might be counted) who wanted Russia to seek revenge for the humiliations it had suffered since 1853. Pan-Slavism was racist, claiming a sort of biological as well as cultural Slavic superiority over Germanic-speaking and Romance-speaking peoples. Pan-Slavists considered non-Christians even more inferior to Slavs than Germans, British, French, or Italians.

RUSSIA AS AN IMPERIALIST POWER IN EAST ASIA

While some of Aleksandr II's generals laid claim to Central Asia in the wake of the Crimean War, other officers led campaigns that underlined Russia's role as an East Asian power. In 1689, the early Qing (Chinese rulers from 1642 to 1911) and Romanov dynasties had concluded the Treaty of Nerchinsk. It regulated the borders, trade, and communication between the two empires, and its stipulations were more or less followed for the next one and a half centuries. Before 1800, the Russians were not strong enough to encroach any further on Chinese power in the Far East. Along the Pacific coast, they were forced to limit their presence to areas that were located too far north to be of any other use than as collection points for fur. The local population, as well as some Russian trappers, hunted the pelts.

But in the First Opium War (1839–1842), the British taught Qing China a bitter lesson. While the Qing had to open their huge market to British trade (especially in opium), the other Great Powers understood that they could force their way into China. In 1854, Britain and the United States concluded treaties with Japan, opening it up for Western goods as well. And in 1855, Russia signed an agreement with Japan that split the Kurile archipelago into two, with the northernmost islands going to Russia; the large island of Sakhalin was placed under a sort of joint rule. Russian merchants were now allowed to trade with Japan.

During an 1858 pause in the Second Opium War (which pitted both Britain and France against China from 1856 to 1860), Russia joined the Western powers at the negotiation table with the Chinese; underscoring Russian demands were troops under the command of Nikolai Muravyov (1809–1881), who threatened military action against China. A treaty between Russia and China was concluded, yielding Russia substantial territory along the Amur River near the Pacific coast. As with Sakhalin and the Japanese, however, the status of some territory remained in limbo.

The Russians then proceeded to build their first substantial Pacific port, which was given the presumptuous name of Vladivostok ("Lord of the East"). However, it was not wholly ice free throughout the year. Therefore, Russia continued to pursue a navigable harbor in the region farther south.

By 1875 a compromise was struck; it saw Russia gain all of Sakhalin and Japan all of the Kuriles (Japan's current claims to the Kuriles, which Stalin confiscated in 1945, go back to this treaty). But whereas most of the borders between Russian and Japanese East Asia were now clearly defined, the countries remained at odds over Korea and China. In the second half of the nineteenth century, the Qing government grew too weak to support its traditional claims on Korea, which had historically been a Chinese protectorate ruled by a native dynasty. Both the Russians and the Japanese desired to take over Korea from the Chinese. At first Japan weaned Korea from China by signing a diplomatic treaty with its royal government, implying that Korea was an independent kingdom rather than a Chinese satellite state. But many Koreans disagreed with their country departing the Chinese orbit and entering that of Japan. Korean protests were expressed in violent clashes, and attacks on Japanese diplomats erupted in the early 1880s. The Chinese army restored order, thus underlining continued Chinese suzerainty over Korea. Tension between pro-Chinese and pro-Japanese Korean factions nevertheless continued. The Chinese government could not prevent Korea from opening its borders to the Western powers as well as Russia (in 1884), a move that seemed to underline Korea's drifting away from China.

During the 1890s, using a variety of pretexts, various European powers (in addition to Japan) began to help themselves to territory in China itself. In 1891, a decree of Aleksandr III announced the plan to build a railroad across Siberia, underlining the Russian desire to become far more of a player in the Far Eastern theater. How far south the Russian ambitions extended in the region was not even clear to the tsar or his ministers themselves, but the Transsiberian Railroad would undeniably facilitate Russia's ability to meddle in East Asian affairs. Apart from expressing Russia's East Asian ambitions, the railroad's construction was triggered by economic motives. It had by then become clear that Siberia's soil contained almost inexhaustible raw materials that could feed the factories of the tsar's industrializing empire.

In 1894, renewed tension in Korea escalated into a Chinese-Japanese war. The Chinese were no match for the modern Japanese army, and by 1895 Korea (as well as part of Chinese Manchuria) was occupied by Japanese troops. Russia stood by on this occasion. But in 1898, in concert with France and Germany, Russia forced the Japanese to cede Chinese Manchurian territory to Russia. The Chinese government (still formally ruling Manchuria) was subsequently pressured to lease the Liaodong Peninsula and its ice-free port of Port Arthur (Lushun) to Russia. In the view of the Russian government, all of Manchuria now fell within the Russian "sphere of influence." But Russia's stubborn refusal to relinquish its desire for a slice of Korea prevented the Japanese from recognizing Russian authority in Manchuria. Russia began to lay tracks for a branch of the Transsiberian Railroad across the province. Meanwhile, Russia continued to intervene in Korea, adding to the Japanese irritation with St. Petersburg. Clearly, the Russians were contemptuous of both Koreans and

Chinese. Although many Russian diplomats treated the Japanese as equals, Russian racism, too, increasingly influenced the Russian attitude toward Japan.

Meanwhile, Britain, which continued to be Russia's antagonist across Asia, became sufficiently worried by the Russian moves. By 1902, the United Kingdom signed a pact with Japan. When the Russians did not withdraw in a timely fashion their military from Manchurian territory (where they had dispatched troops during the 1900 Chinese Boxer Revolt), Japan decided to go to war. Tacitly supported by the British, the Japanese decided that the moment had arrived to check the Russian appetite for expansion. Thus the Japanese navy attacked Port Arthur in February 1904.

THE RUSSO-JAPANESE WAR

From a military point of view, the war with Japan was a disaster for Russia. Although the initial damage wrought by the Japanese stealth attack on the Russian fleet at Port Arthur was not especially great, foolhardy decisions ensured further severe Russian losses at sea in the subsequent months. In April and May 1904, neither Russian land forces nor Russian warships could prevent Japanese troops from crossing into Manchuria on land and across the sea from Korean positions. Port Arthur was encircled on its land side by June. In August and September 1904, the Russians were beaten back in their attempts to break the siege of Port Arthur. Finally, in the first days of January 1905, Port Arthur surrendered to the Japanese. Russia's last serious offensive on land occurred in the Battle of Mukden in February and March of 1905. This battle involved six hundred thousand men in total, setting the record as the largest land battle in recorded history. It ended with a Russian retreat. A few months later, the Russian Baltic fleet (which had to sail around southern Africa, as the British refused to let it use the Suez Canal) reached the war zone, completing an eight-month journey. But before reaching its destination of Vladivostok, the Russian squadron was destroyed in the Battle of the Tsushima Straits (May 1905).

Militarily, Russia had comprehensively lost the war. After the disaster at the Tsushima Straits, the tsar needed a quick peace, as at home a revolution had broken out, threatening the survival of his regime. Despite their victories, the Japanese were close to exhaustion themselves, for their government teetered on the verge of bankruptcy because of the war's cost to them. With the aid of President Theodore Roosevelt,[1] the two countries swiftly concluded a peace at Portsmouth, New Hampshire, on 6 August 1905. Sergei Vitte led the Russian delegation in New England. Aware of the Japanese conundrum, Vitte managed to limit the damage. The Liaodong Peninsula and the Southern Manchurian Railway were lost to Japan, which Russia now also recognized as Korea's overlord. South Sakhalin went to the Japanese as well. But it could have been far worse had it not been for Vitte's negotiating skills.

It is clear that the budding anticolonial movements in Asia and Africa gained some confidence from the Japanese defeat of Russia. The Japanese triumph was generally read as a victory of an Asian country over a European empire, rather than one of an Asian power over a Eurasian (or only partially European) empire. But

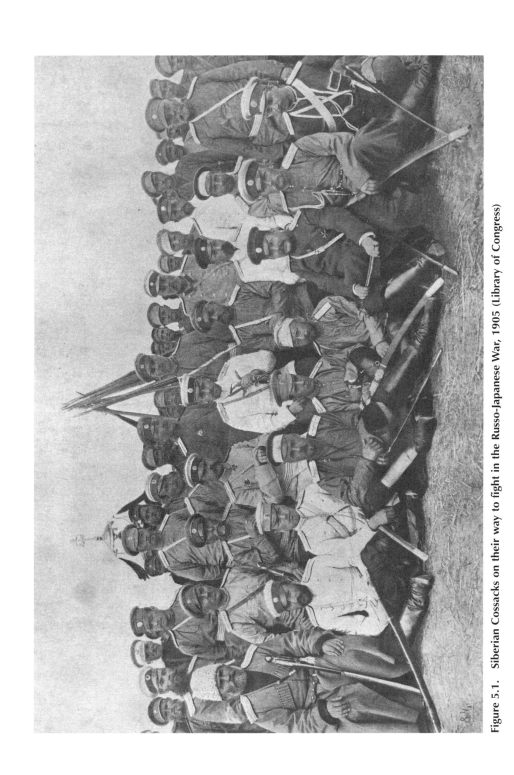

Figure 5.1. Siberian Cossacks on their way to fight in the Russo-Japanese War, 1905 (Library of Congress)

still some decades passed before European powers were confronted with broad-based uprisings against their rule in their overseas colonies. Japan, meanwhile, had now entered the path that was to lead to its ruin in 1945. Military historians have pointed at the parallel between the surprise attack on Port Arthur and that on Pearl Harbor. Whereas the first announced the arrival of Japan as a Great Power, the second ushered in its fall as an empire.

For the Russian government and military, the defeat in the war was obviously traumatic. A military overhaul was undertaken, and it was not quite finished in 1914. It is odd that in August 1914 St. Petersburg felt sufficiently confident to wage a war against the world's supposedly best military, that of Germany, having been taken to task not long before by a military of such an "inferior nation" as Japan. The Russian armed forces redeemed themselves in the First World War, in fact, although this was masked by the implosion of the 1917 Revolution and subsequent German rout.

The Soviet leadership (which had also been confronted with a Japanese intervention in the Civil War) did not repeat the mistake of underestimating Japan. In 1938 and 1939, Stalin made sure that probing Japanese moves testing Soviet military strength were comprehensively rebuffed. Japan was sufficiently rebuked and declined to join the Nazi-led assault on the Soviet Union on 22 June 1941. Stalin, furthermore, showed great diplomatic skill (not always his strong suit) in capitalizing on the opportunity offered by the Japanese collapse in 1945. The Red Army occupied Manchuria, North Korea, Sakhalin, and the Kuriles in a matter of weeks. North Korea was given its independence (as a Soviet satellite), and Manchuria given back to China, but the Soviet Union kept Sakhalin and the Kuriles. Japanese resentment about this continues to cloud Russo-Japanese relations today.

POLITICAL OPPOSITION

The outbreak of a countrywide rebellion against the autocracy in 1905 appears unsurprising in light of another war gone awry. Different from the relatively tranquil 1850s (through which Aleksandr II was spared a revolution), 1900s Russia was a country already in turmoil because of the modernization it had embraced in the previous twenty years. The dramatic changes in the country's economy and society caused great insecurity, not only among the uprooted peasants who had flocked to the cities to find work in the factories, but also within a regime that looked to the past rather than to the present (let alone the future) in making its decisions.

One could restate the American historian Leopold Haimson's argument that the 1917 Revolution was inevitable irrespective of the First World War by suggesting that a revolution like the one in 1905 would have broken out even if Russia had not gone to war in 1904. Of course, both arguments belong to that attractive albeit pointless exercise beloved by popular historians and their readers: counterfactual history. In the case of the 1905 conflagration, it can be said that there are some strong parallels with the period following the Crimean War, when the tsar decided to change his country from above rather than wait for the moment when his sub-

Figure 5.2.   Prison in Siberian Irkutsk in 1885 (Library of Congress)

jects would change it from below. But Nicholas II was not as sober an observer of the circumstances as his grandfather had been. Rather than taking the initiative, he awaited events in 1905; as a result, he only barely survived on the throne. During the next crisis in 1916–1917, he was to show that he had learned nothing from his lack of decisiveness in 1905. This cost him his head.

Before 1905, unrest had plagued Nicholas II's Russia as much as his father's. Aleksandr III's regime faced a severe crisis in 1891–1892, when a famine broke out. It showed that Russian agriculture remained unduly vulnerable to the vagaries of climate, while the country's infrastructure appeared inadequate to supply timely relief. The government failed to offer much aid to the sufferers, even if it could now at last ship some emergency food supplies across the railways. Perhaps five hundred thousand people died of hunger and diseases associated with the famine. The government's failure in coping with the crisis caused a renewed upsurge in oppositional activity, negating Aleksandr's painstaking campaign of the previous decade to weed out most revolutionaries. Nicholas II, therefore, succeeded his father at a time when strikes were on the rise, students were restless, revolutionaries became bolder, nationalist movements were growing, and unrest in the villages was increasing.

Channeling the oppositional voices, Russian exiles organized political parties with an underground network within the empire from the late nineteenth century onward. In 1902, various factions of Populists founded the Socialist Revolutionary Party (SR). The SR remained faithful to the Populist ideal of a decentralized Russia made up of primarily peasant communes, although it now acknowledged the emergence of the industrial working class by calling for workers' control over their factories. The SR had

Figure 5.3.   Convicts in Siberia, late nineteenth century (Library of Congress)

a terrorist section (the "Combat Organization") that killed a great number of tsarist officials, even if it was run for years by a tsarist double agent, Yevno Azef (1869–1918).

The Marxists formed the Russian Social Democratic Labor Party (RSDLP or SD) in 1898. As Marxists, of course, the SD championed the cause of the urban working class. Since the party's founders were (with one exception) immediately arrested upon the conclusion of its first congress in Minsk, the Social Democrats staged a second congress in Western Europe in 1903. This gathering first met in Belgian Brussels before moving on to London, after the Belgian authorities asked the Russian socialists to leave.

At their second party congress, the Social Democrats immediately split into two main factions: Bolsheviks and Mensheviks. The Bolsheviks, led by Lenin, believed in an elite party made up of professional revolutionaries. This so-called vanguard would lead the naive proletariat to the revolution. The revolutionaries themselves were to obey loyally the party's highest leadership, its Central Committee. In contrast, the Mensheviks had in mind a mass membership party, which would routinely hold the leadership accountable. They were much more willing to champion the prole-tariat's short-term wishes and desires, such as higher wages, better labor conditions, accident-and-illness insurance, or pensions. As with the SR, almost all SD leaders were middle-class intellectuals who claimed to speak in the name of the oppressed masses. They tacitly agreed with Lenin that it was best if actual toilers let others speak for them, as the Russian proletariat and peasantry lacked political sophistication.

A third political party deserves mention because of its influence on the events of 1904–1905 and beyond: the liberals, or Kadets. They stood for a constitutional monarchy on the British model, with an elected government chosen by a broad franchise. They supported the capitalist development of Russia but tended to advocate social legislation to protect workers and others against ruthless exploitation. The Kadets also advocated self-determination for the largest of the empire's non-Russian peoples.

Some of the other political movements that cropped up were the nationalist parties (strongest of which was the Polish) and the Muslim-Tatar parties, as well as the parties of the extreme right. On the left, various smaller groups besides SR and SD can be identified, including a non-Marxist Labor Party, to which the future premier Aleksandr Kerensky (1881–1970) belonged, and the uncompromising anarchists. It should be noted here that, until 1917, sections that disagreed with their leadership's policies often peeled off from their various parties, proceeding to establish themselves as independent parties. The Russian political landscape, underground before 1905, and mostly legal thereafter, rapidly acquired a bewildering complexity.

Before 1905, trade unions were prohibited, but in order to preempt the emergence of an illegal trade union movement, tsarist officials began to experiment with organizing government-controlled quasi unions in the early 1900s. Combining a defense of workers' rights with loyalty to the autocracy, their founders (foremost among them was Sergei Zubatov [1864–1917], an Okhrana official) believed that these organizations would deprive workers of their militancy by wresting various concessions from their employers. Higher wages, sick leave, shorter workdays, and pensions would keep the working class away from the radical solutions advocated by the socialist activists.

The idea was not altogether outlandish: in 1902, the Bolshevik leader Lenin warned in his foundational pamphlet *What Is to Be Done?* that factory workers give in to a "trade-union consciousness," if left to their own devices. The proletariat, Lenin argued, was inclined to acquiesce in its fate, once it accepted concessions regarding wages or labor conditions made by employers. Workers then lost sight of their real interest, which was ousting their bosses and taking control of their factories and society at large. Socialist agitators were to explain to the workers that such short-term gains changed nothing fundamentally in the long term. Raises and benefits would be taken away whenever owners deemed this necessary for their bottom line (and workers, obviously, were always in danger of being fired if they did not "have control over the means of production," i.e., owned their own workplace). This is why Lenin emphasized the need for professional revolutionaries to be the mainstay of the Social Democratic Party (and why he polemicized so heavily against the Mensheviks).

Meanwhile, Zubatov's scheme was not well liked even within the tsarist government (as some felt that it forced owners to make far too many concessions to their workers). In early 1905, the experiment with government-controlled trade unions ended abruptly in the bloody snow in front of St. Petersburg's Winter Palace. Ironically, it was copied by the Bolsheviks after they gained power.

THE 1905 REVOLUTION

Even by traditional Russian standards, the legitimacy of Nicholas II's rule was jeopardized by the defeat at the hands of the Japanese. Presumably all seeing and all knowing, the tsar's regime failed in its key task of defending the realm (even if Port Arthur had been a rather recent Russian acquisition). The situation appears akin to Nicholas I's autocracy losing its infallible aura because of Russia's defeat in the Crimean War.

The first trigger for the revolution was the bad news from the Far East. In the summer of 1904, SR terrorists assassinated one of the tsar's key aides, the interior minister V. K. Pleve (1846–1904), who had stood for a policy of no compromise with the growing opposition. Faced with an increasingly restless public, the tsar inched toward granting concessions. With Nicholas's blessing, Pleve's successor Pyotr Sviatopolk-Mirskii (1857–1914) began to consider the inclusion of some elected members to the tsar's main advisory body, the State Council, which would be given more power over government policy. But the burgeoning opposition dismissed Sviatopolk-Mirskii's proposals as too modest, when the government's credibility sank further with news of each defeat in the East. In the fall of 1904, the liberals, in tandem with the *zemstva*, began to organize banquets across the empire that demanded substantial change. Initially, they backed Sviatopolk-Mirskii when the minister began to develop bolder plans for reform.

Then Bloody Sunday led to a radical turn. In the wake of a citywide strike in St. Petersburg, a demonstration was organized in January 1905 in the capital. The marchers voiced very mild demands regarding better working conditions and profusely professed loyalty to the dynasty (although a few demonstrators carried banners that called for general elections and an end to the war with Japan). The protest was inspired by one of the government's trade union organizers, the priest Georgii Gapon (1870–1906). The protesters marched toward the Winter Palace, in the hope of delivering a petition to the tsar. The monarch, however, was absent. Misinterpreting the crowd's mood as hostile, the governor of St. Petersburg ordered his troops to disperse the demonstration by using live ammunition. Dozens, possibly hundreds, of demonstrators were killed. Across the country, many held the tsar responsible for this excessive use of force against a peaceful demonstration. Strikes broke out from Riga to Vladivostok, expressing solidarity with the St. Petersburgers killed on Bloody Sunday.

Sviatopolk-Mirskii, responsible for public order as minister of the interior, was blamed for Bloody Sunday and resigned. He was succeeded by Aleksandr Bulygin (1851–1919). Tension further intensified when SR terrorists murdered the governor-general of Moscow, Sergei Aleksandrovich Romanov (1857–1905), the tsar's uncle, in February 1905. Two weeks later, Nicholas II ordered Bulygin to draft a series of significant political reforms. Bulygin set to work but was still held to a very limited agenda. The tsar was now prepared to allow an elective assembly and to introduce the principles of freedom of speech and religious tolerance. Peasants' compensation payments were to be reduced. But the assembly was to have only consultative powers. In other words, the tsar could ignore its advice whenever he pleased. When these proposals were published in August 1905, the unrest across the country escalated.

Strikes and peasant uprisings were rampant across Russia after Bloody Sunday. The crew of one of the Black Sea fleet's battleships, the *Potemkin*, famously mutinied in June 1905. The *zemstva* became ever more vociferous in demanding change. Students had gone on strike in January 1905 and were still on strike in August. The Bulygin Constitution was soon followed by the news that peace with the Japanese had been concluded, but that, too, failed to calm the situation. The *zemstva* rejected the Bulygin concessions in September, and in October a railway strike was developing into a general strike. The end of the Romanov dynasty seemed near. Sergei Vitte, who as head of the Russian delegation at Portsmouth had acquired renewed clout and had just returned home in the early fall of 1905, implored the tsar to grant a constitution as soon as possible.

Rejecting the possibility of establishing a military dictatorship (in Vitte's view the only other option the tsar had), Nicholas II issued a manifesto on 17 October 1905 that pledged far-reaching changes that would end the autocracy. The October Manifesto was, however, not a constitution but only the promise of it. Adding to the earlier concessions of the freedom of speech and religion were the assurance of equality before the law and an end to the prosecution without trial of those accused of political crimes. But the signal promise in the manifesto was for a parliament (Duma), elected by a broad franchise. The Duma was to vet every bill proposed by the government and oversee the executive's operation. Nonetheless, it was the tsar who was to appoint this government.

The tsar's concessions satisfied neither most of the liberals nor any of the socialists. But liberals and socialists fell out with each other, and the opposition to the tsar fatally weakened because of squabbles between various political parties. The socialists allied with councils of workers' deputies (called *sovety*, or soviets) that began to emerge across the country. These councils were chosen from among industrial workers and functioned as a sort of local workers' government or legislature. The most important soviet was that of St. Petersburg. Its leadership, the executive committee, consisted of representatives from the capital's major factories and (now officially allowed) trade unions as well as the socialist political parties. Meanwhile, peasants, too, organized in unions. Local peasant unions united into a countrywide organization that was heavily influenced by the SR (whereas the urban soviets were more strongly influenced by the Marxist SD). The liberals, meanwhile, had no truck with the soviets, which they saw as a dangerously radical form of direct democracy in which the untempered and impulsive desires of the rabble found expression.

The October Manifesto's promises peeled off the conservatives in the *zemstva* movement and elsewhere among the public. In the days following the manifesto, on the right side of the political spectrum the Octobrists parted way with the liberals. They were now willing to give the tsar the benefit of the doubt and await the implementation of the concessions made in the October Manifesto. Stauncher supporters of the tsar came to the fore after 17 October as well. Extremist right-wing movements had formed earlier in the year but had kept a low profile before the October Manifesto was issued, as the political pendulum was clearly swinging in the direction of the left. But upon the manifesto's release several parties rose to prominence and postured as die-hard defenders of the tsar.

Especially notorious became the ultra-right-wing Union of the Russian People, led by Aleksandr Dubrovin (1855–1921) and Vladimir Purishkevich (1870–1920). It was soon better known as the Black Hundreds, after the moniker given to its violent activists. The Black Hundreds were resolute supporters of the autocracy. They were strongly anti-Semitic, Great Russian nationalists, who rejected any autonomy for non-Russian regions. They organized a series of pogroms in the fall of 1905 and spring of 1906. This violence not only intimidated the Jews in the Pale of Settlement but also distracted the attention of many people everywhere from developments in St. Petersburg. Nicholas, meanwhile, believed he heard the voice of the people in the vicious roar of the Black Hundreds, and their activities helped the tsar regain his confidence after October.

Whereas the Union of the Russian People was an extreme Russian nationalist party, in 1905 several nationalist parties of non-Russian groups were set up as well. The Polish National Democratic Party led by Roman Dmowski (1864–1939) was the most powerful one. It advocated a Poland united with Russia only through the person of the tsar, as head of the Polish state. Nationalist parties also arose in Ukraine, Belarus, and Moldavia (then called Bessarabia, a largely Romanian-speaking territory along the Black Sea coast in the country's southwest), but different from Dmowski's National Democrats, they obtained limited support, primarily from intellectuals (including students).

A Muslim League was organized as well, led by Tatars residing in European Russia. Its program (loosely based on the Muslim renewal movement called Jadidism, which sought to marry Islam with modernization) was directed mainly toward cultural change, such as the introduction of Muslim schools and the spread of literacy. Ideas about autonomy of Muslim areas were not yet diffused to any significant extent, but some Muslim leaders began to ponder so-called Pan-Turanianism. This called for a unification of all Muslim Turkic-speaking peoples into a reinvigorated Muslim empire. It would replace the decrepit Ottoman Empire and the khanates and emirates of Central Asia that had submitted to the tsar after 1850.

THE END OF THE REVOLUTION

The split among the revolutionaries, the October Manifesto's promise, and Nicholas's renewed sense of self-confidence led to a waning of the revolutionary mood. By the end of 1905, the tsarist authorities began to arrest radicals, including the executive committee of the St. Petersburg soviet,[2] without encountering much resistance. In Moscow a similar operation was undertaken, but there it provoked an uprising that saw tsarist forces kill hundreds of soviet supporters. It became evident that the tsar could call on sufficient numbers of loyal troops (who had now returned to Europe from the East Asian front) to restore order.

The tsar's circle (especially Vitte, who for several months was prime minister) understood that, once the Duma convened, one of the key clashes between parliament and government would be over the budget. The tsarist ministers proceeded to do their best to limit the Duma's clout in this regard. Electoral rules for the Duma were announced in February 1906. The bicameral parliament was to be elected in a complicated manner that still gave the nobility and those with property much greater weight in the voting process. In March, when the elections for the First Duma were staged, budgetary rules were announced that removed any Duma control over the greatest share of the budget, which was the money allotted to the armed forces. In April, just before the Duma met for the first time, "Fundamental Laws" were proclaimed, purporting to be the "constitution" as promised in the October Manifesto.

The Fundamental Laws conceded much less than had been hoped for by those who had given Nicholas the benefit of the doubt in October 1905. Only the tsar could amend the constitution itself. Ministers were appointed and dismissed by the tsar, without any input from the Duma. The Duma could merely indicate its displeasure with a minister's performance. The Duma, then, remained a consultative body, with few legislative powers and very little right of oversight.

Despite its limitations, though, the establishment of the Duma was a major step forward in Russian political history. Elsewhere in Europe, the role of legislatures had only gradually been broadened after 1850. In Germany or Austria-Hungary in 1905, the government likewise could avoid being held accountable by elected representative bodies. Even in the 1900s, in most European countries the franchise remained restricted to men, with greater weight given to those with property. If developments in Europe were at all a reliable gauge, it was reasonable to expect that the Duma's power was to grow after its establishment in 1906.

In the spring of 1906, Vitte managed to borrow an enormous sum of money from France. This allowed the government to ignore the Duma even more, because the government did not need to go to the Duma to have its budget ratified. Immediately before the Duma convened in April 1906, Vitte, who was loathed by the reactionary members of the government and by the tsar himself, resigned from the government. While a placeholder by the name of Ivan Goremykin (1839–1917) became prime minister, the leading light of the new government was the minister of the interior, Pyotr Stolypin (1862–1911).

STOLYPIN AND THE TSAR

Although Aleksandr II's murder may have thwarted the best opportunity to reform Russia in a gradual and peaceful manner, not all was lost yet for the Romanovs in 1906. But the survival chances of Nicholas II on the Russian throne took a decidedly bad turn with another assassination, that of Pyotr Stolypin in 1911, exactly thirty years after the murder of the tsar's grandfather.

In the Soviet-invented tradition that demonized late tsarism as pure evil, Stolypin was singled out as one of its great villains. He gave his name to no few than two hated symbols of tsarist repression, that of the hangman's noose (the "Stolypin necktie") and the railroad boxcars transporting prisoners ("Stolypin wagons"). The suppression of revolutionary mood in 1906 and 1907 was indeed accompanied by the hanging of several hundred ringleaders under martial law. Although even regular courts might have sentenced some of the condemned for their crimes to death, this undeniably was a heavy hand. Thousands of others were sentenced to jail or Siberian exile, the first convicts in Russian history to be transported by train in great numbers. Of

Figure 5.4.   Pyotr Stolypin, ca. 1905

course, latter-day admirers of Stolypin compared these numbers to those who fell victim to the Soviet, and especially Stalin's, regime, which make the tsarist prime minister seem like a veritable humanitarian.[3]

After Stolypin replaced Goremykin (mere months after the latter's appointment), he maneuvered the ship of state with great skill. Stolypin imposed his own agenda, often facing down the opposition of both the tsar and the Duma (as well as "public opinion," now fully given a voice in the press). He had no patience for socialist radicals, who tried to assassinate him by blowing up his house (and killed twenty-seven people in the process). But he also defied the "real voice of the Russian people," in other words, that of the Black Hundreds, despite the tsar's fondness for their crackpot ideas. And although overseeing the disbanding of the first two Dumas, he did attempt to establish some sort of regular process by which the Duma was given a part in overseeing government policy. Most important was his effort at resolving the problems plaguing the Russian peasantry.

Stolypin was promoted to prime minister when the revolutionary wave still had force. In the first elections ever held in Imperial Russia in March 1906, a restricted franchise returned a parliament in which more than half of the seats were held by leftist parties, largest among which were the Kadets. If they allied with a group of moderate socialists, the liberals held the majority of seats in the First Duma, which gathered in St. Petersburg in April. Given this strength, the Kadet leaders (among whom Pavel Miliukov was recognized as chief) demanded that the Fundamental Laws be revised. They called for a government responsible to the Duma, reflecting the views of a majority of Duma representatives. But the tsar and Stolypin refused this demand, dissolving the Duma in July. Many of the liberal parliamentarians protested this dissolution by calling on the population to refuse to pay taxes or avoid the draft. Such defiance of the law was as illegal a move as Stolypin's dissolution of the parliament. The perennial theme of disregarding the law in Russian history resurfaces here. Both sides undermined the principles of a *Rechtsstaat* (a state built on the rule of law).

New elections were staged in early 1907. The SD, which had largely boycotted the first elections, now participated, as did a number of SR candidates (although the party as such still refused to take part). Socialist gains caused the Kadets to lose their majority. But altogether, left-wing parties still occupied some 60 percent of the seats in the Second Duma. And the "nationalist" parties (Polish National Democrats, Ukrainian nationalists, and Muslim-Tatars) agreed with most of the left's agenda. The Second Duma thus proved as uncollaborative as the first. Stolypin used the pretext of an SD conspiracy against the tsar's life to dissolve the Second Duma in June 1907.[4]

Stolypin then further restricted the electorate: in the next election, the upper 1 percent of the population chose approximately two-thirds of the parliamentary representatives. The vote for the Third Duma was more pleasing to Stolypin. Octobrists and groups to their right were in the majority. This meant parliamentary representatives who would behave, at a minimum, as a loyal opposition to the government.

This Duma, indeed, served the length of its five-year term. Although the Duma was dominated by Russia's high and mighty, public discussion of politics continued in print. And even if the Duma was composed mainly of representatives of a narrow elite who were in theory loyal to the tsar, it often proved difficult to handle for the government. The parliament frequently used its right to call the tsar's ministers to account, even if it had no power to dismiss them.

Stolypin accepted the end of autocracy, but his tsar did not. Nicholas II was not fond of Stolypin, partially because the prime minister was willing to work with the Duma, partially because Stolypin rejected the extreme right wing's bizarre ideas, and partially because the tsar thought that Stolypin was trying to outshine him. Nicholas II tried to avoid contact with the Duma politicians as much as possible. The tsar preferred to rule by decree. A loophole had been left in the Fundamental Laws that allowed the tsar to issue laws when the Duma was not in session. This strategy undermined the trust between government and parliament, preparing the ground for the Duma's ultimate rebellion in 1917.

For advice, the tsar sought out some of the most reactionary characters. Increasingly, he followed his wife Aleksandra (1872–1918) in trusting the charismatic Siberian monk Grigorii Rasputin. Rasputin came to the couple's attention in 1905, when he proved able to stop the bleedings that could be lethal to the heir to the throne, the hemophiliac tsarevich Aleksei (1904–1918). In Rasputin, Aleksandra and Nicholas thought they had met the Russian people personified. The eccentric monk's advice began to be sought in political matters. Although Rasputin's influence should not be exaggerated, his presence at the court and political influence was symptomatic of the sort of unsound advice the tsar was inclined to seek.

PEASANTS INTO FARMERS

While Stolypin made significant progress in implementing an educational system in which all children would enjoy at least some years of primary schooling, his most imaginative policy was in the field of agriculture. Compensation dues were finally abolished in November 1905. At the end of 1906, Stolypin introduced a law that aimed at ending the communal tenure of land, with its periodic repartitions. Peasants could apply to own outright the soil they tilled. Stolypin expected that full ownership would give them far more incentive to improve their plots. The law was popular, but its complications slowed the process of individuals' acquisition of consolidated parcels of land in private ownership. Still, by 1915 in European Russia (in which Belarus and Ukraine were then included), more than 20 percent of peasants had abandoned communal farming and established themselves as private farmers. These were promising signs for the government, but the trend toward private ownership was interrupted by the war that had broken out in the previous year.

Stolypin, too, improved the credit system for the peasants, so that money was made available for those keen on innovation of their farming operation. Furthermore, he began to offer attractive support programs for those who were willing to migrate from the densely populated rural areas to arable land in Siberia and Kazakhstan. Migration in that direction acquired significant momentum, easing the pressure on the land in the Black Earth zone.

While his policies were far more ingenuous than those of previous tsarist ministers, who had banked on industrialization at the expense of the peasants, Stolypin's motivation for his pro-peasant strategy was political, rather than rooted in any great love of the Russian *muzhik*. Taking a cue from postrevolutionary France, he believed that the restless French peasantry, a driving force behind the unrest in France from 1789 to 1795, had become a solidly conservative segment of society, once the revolution gave the peasants title to the land they cultivated. In nineteenth-century elections, time and again, the French farmers voted for maintaining the status quo by electing the most conservative politicians to parliament. Stolypin announced that he was banking on the strong, on those who would be able to make a success out of their agricultural enterprise and would then want to keep the fruits of their labor. The revolutionary sting would be taken out of the countryside once it was populated by small property owners. As in France, they would be loyal backers of the Russian government that had made their success possible.

Stolypin's reforms stood every chance of succeeding, were it not for the outbreak of war in 1914. It is counterfactual history to speculate on what would have happened if his policies had continued in peacetime, but their apparent success before August 1914 leads one to suspect that, even at that very late moment in the history of Romanov Russia, it was not too late to stave off revolution. Stolypin himself, meanwhile, did not live to see the outbreak of war. In September 1911 he was assassinated in Kyiv by a confused SR terrorist, Dmitrii Bogrov (1887–1911), who was also in the service of the Okhrana. Although Bogrov appears to have operated on his own, many continue to speculate to this day that his act was orchestrated by the secret police. The Okhrana was not fond of the straitlaced prime minister, who objected to some of the secret police's more eccentric deeds (such as inciting pogroms). It is at least odd that Bogrov shot Stolypin rather than the tsar, who had been present as well in the Kyiv Opera House on the night of the prime minister's murder.

INDUSTRIALIZATION AND ECONOMIC GROWTH: STRIKES

The global economy underwent a veritable boom during the last two decades before the First World War. Russia very much partook in this growth. Its economic expansion was further encouraged when the peasantry was freed from the previous restriction on its mobility. After 1905, the mass of the population was no longer held back by the burdens of compensation payments or collective responsibility for taxes. Across the country, purchasing power increased and a significant rise in consumption occurred in the last years before the First World War. But even if wages were sometimes rising and new legislation further improved working conditions in industry, the industrial sector of the economy remained the most volatile. In 1912, an upsurge of strikes followed a massacre of strikers who were employed in the gold mines along the Siberian Lena River. This strike wave continued all the way until July 1914.

In part, workers protested the continued restrictions on their freedom to organize themselves. Whereas trade unions had become legal in 1905, the government prohibited unions or strikes that followed a "political" agenda. Unions were to restrict themselves to bargaining for economic improvements in the workplace. Furthermore (as in parts of the United States in those days), the police often colluded with owners in breaking up strikes, locking out workers, and so on.

The economic boom was accompanied by various developments that are encountered in periods of rapid economic growth in most places. The cities could not readily absorb the arrival of numerous workers, whose housing was extremely poor. Workers, with or without their families, shared one-room apartments, while others bunked in barracks. Without proper sewage, water supply, or electricity,[5] this was no improvement over the village hut. In these slum-like conditions, people lived in a highly agitated state of mind. This frenzy was not mitigated by ministrations from priests or cautionary words from neighbors or family members, as had been the case in the villages in times of crisis. Inebriation, illness, violence, and even rape were common. The factory workforce in the textile centers (around Moscow, in Poland, and in Ivanovo-Voznesensk) was often predominantly female, and women workers' fate was usually worse than that of men, although both sexes fell victim to industrial accidents at an alarming frequency.

This restless and even chaotic atmosphere became muted in the first years of the world war, but violence and anger continued to simmer underneath the calm surface of the home front, and the radical mind-set resurfaced emphatically in 1917. Outside of working-class neighborhoods, Russia was a sort of work in progress on the eve of the First World War, too. With the limitations on the Duma's role; the unequal representation of the various social strata in the local *zemstva* (which had still not been introduced everywhere in the empire); the restrictions on personal freedom; and the lack of accountability of government officials at all levels, extensive change was still necessary if Russia was to become a truly constitutional monarchy, with a government representing all of the empire's inhabitants. Frustration among the intelligentsia remained high. The liberals, who in the 1912 elections were returned to the Fourth Duma in a somewhat higher number, clamored for a government that "enjoyed the country's confidence," and even the Octobrist leader Aleksandr Guchkov (1862–1936) expressed similar ideas.

Apart from widespread anger at the tsar's obstinacy in St. Petersburg or Moscow, the authorities did not gain popular support by some of their actions at the local level. In this sense, the trial against the Kyivan Jew Mendel Beilis (1874–1934) in 1913 was symptomatic. Whereas the prosecution of a Jew for ritual murder gained the approval of the rabid right extremists, the majority of the educated public was appalled by the obscurantist accusations against Beilis, which reeked of the superstitious Middle Ages. The government's prestige suffered further through such incidents. Although the outbreak of war led to almost all social groups in European Russia and Siberia rallying behind the cause of tsar and country, support began to waver when the government (and its military) proved incapable of winning the war.[6] After more than two years of unprecedented bloodshed, the belief in the government's incompetence and arbitrariness was rekindled and the call for a government "enjoying the public confidence" resurfaced and was louder than ever before.

THE BOSNIAN CRISIS OF 1908 AND THE BALKAN WARS; THE ALLIANCE SYSTEM

Russia's road to the First World War was a lengthy and twisted one. Russia's belligerence (or, to be more precise, that of the tsar's government, some of its military commanders, and a minority of its articulate citizenry, i.e., the extreme right and Pan-Slavists) in 1914 was rooted in an intense desire to restore the country's damaged reputation as a Great Power. Although the majority of the empire's inhabitants never strongly cared about this issue, those who had been indifferent to it came to believe that it was their patriotic duty to answer the call to arms issued in the name of the tsar and the motherland in the summer of 1914.

The longest festering wound informing the government's behavior in the crisis of the summer of 1914 was the humiliation of the Crimean War. In that conflict, Russia's reliable ally Austria had unexpectedly turned against Russia. The Habsburg emperor (Franz Josef I, r. 1848–1916) and his advisors had become worried about Russia's designs regarding the southeastern European possessions of Turkey, commonly known as the Balkans. No attempt to reconcile the two sides succeeded thereafter, although during his tenure from 1871 to 1890, the German chancellor Otto von Bismarck exerted himself toward this goal. But even Bismarck favored the Austrians over the Russians. With Bismarck's connivance, at the 1878 Congress of Berlin the dual monarchy of Austria-Hungary gained more than Russia, again without spilling any blood.[7] This had been a hard pill to swallow for, in defense of the Balkan Christians, the tsar's army had fought the Turkish army for almost a year.

In the second half of the nineteenth century, the Habsburgs, more than the Romanovs, were increasingly confronted by nationalist movements that made their empire ever harder to rule. Hungarian discontent had been appeased by the creation in 1867 of the dual monarchy of Austria-Hungary. By way of the 1867 Compromise (*Ausgleich*), Hungarians had become equal partners of the German speakers in Emperor Franz Josef's realm. But Franz Josef and his ministers proved incapable of placating many of the southern Slavs—Croatians, Serbs, and (Muslim) Bosnians—who lived inside their borders. Most Croatians lived within the Hungarian half of the empire, as did a good number of Serbians. In the middle of the nineteenth century, meanwhile, the Serbians established a monarchy of their own outside Austro-Hungarian borders, which was recognized as independent by the powers at Berlin in 1878. Unfortunately, the Treaty of Berlin also awarded Bosnia and Herzegovina to

Austria-Hungary, which led to a sharp increase in the number of Croats and Serbs inside the Habsburg Empire. The Bosnian Serbs in particular cast a longing eye across the border, preferring to join a state in which Serbs ruled themselves.

Since the Croatians were subjected to attempts to "magyarize" them, that is, make them Hungarian, a policy bearing resemblance to "Russification," they were tempted to join the Serbs in a common cause. Serbs were religiously Eastern Orthodox, and Croatians Catholic, but the two groups shared a common language, which the Serbians wrote in the Cyrillic script (similar to Russian script) and the Croatians in Latin script. Joining the Serbian monarchy seemed to promise more equitable treatment to the Croatians (although many, probably rightfully given subsequent developments, were skeptical about this). For the Habsburgs, any satisfactory solution to the south Slav problem was difficult to conceive, but the best option seemed to incorporate all southern Slavs (with the possible exception of the Bulgarians, because of their remote geographical location) into their empire and to give them a measure of autonomy. To allow the creation of a greater Serbia that united all Serbs as well as many Croats and Bosnian Muslims would merely replace the old Turkish foe with one that was likely more formidable than the tottering Ottoman Empire.

After 1856, the Austrian(-Hungarian) government detected a growing Russian involvement in fanning the flames of south Slav nationalism. Russian diplomats, as well as the Pan-Slavists who influenced them, did not provide much reassurance to the Habsburgs in this regard. Russia championed the cause of their little Slav brethren on the Balkans (especially the Orthodox ones), playing on the contempt for the "barbaric" Muslim Turks in Western public opinion. But Russian support for the southern Slavs was inconsistent. Ham-fisted behavior cost them much Bulgarian sympathy even before 1885, in which year, during another crisis that engulfed the Turkish Empire, the kingdom (or tsardom) of Bulgaria received what amounted to full independence.

After "losing Bulgaria," Russia proceeded to do its utmost to cultivate its friendship with Serbia. Different from Austria, the Russian claim on the Balkans was not based wholly on strategic considerations. There was the centuries-old Orthodox bond between the Russians, Greeks, Serbians, Montenegrans, and Bulgarians. All had been struggling to overcome the rule of Islamic potentates, and all shared a memory of a lost Eastern Orthodox Empire. The Russians had cast covetous eyes on Tsargrad, Constantinople, since Peter the Great's days.

The Habsburg aims toward the Balkans were much more pragmatic: to ensure peace within their borders and replace an allegedly uncivilized government with one that was to bring enlightenment and economic development to the region. But the Austro-Hungarians did face the dilemma of where to draw the borders of their expanded empire. Besides the uncertainty of whether to annex independent Serbia, the cultural or ethnic identities of territories such as Montenegro, Albania, or Macedonia were moot. To complicate matters further, there was Orthodox Romania, which might claim part of Habsburg Transylvania. In Transylvania, a plurality of the population consisted of Romanian-speaking Orthodox believers. Should Romania then be incorporated into the Habsburg Empire as well?

Russian designs were likewise muddled. Catherine II had conceived of her re-stored Greek Empire as an independent country. Pan-Slavists, however, advocated the annexation by Russia of Romania (as an Orthodox country with a language heavily influenced by a Slavic vocabulary), Bulgaria, Serbia, and so on, further adding to the plethora of peoples populating the tsar's empire. A large independent Orthodox empire rivaling Russia was not something the Pan-Slavists desired.

Meanwhile, both military strategy and economic reasons made the Russian government and army command desire control over the straits that linked the Black Sea to the Mediterranean Sea (and separated Europe from Asia) at Istanbul. In 1856, Russia had been prohibited from keeping a war fleet in the Black Sea, a ban soon (in 1871) rescinded, but Russian access to the Mediterranean remained restricted. The Russian navy could easily be holed up in the Black Sea, for, according to the 1878 Treaty of Berlin, if war broke out involving any of Europe's Great Powers, the Turks were supposed to close the straits to all belligerents. Russia's diplomats continued to seek freer access for their navy into the Mediterranean Sea.

Mutual distrust between Vienna and St. Petersburg always prevented a durable solution from being negotiated. But there were moments when most problems between the two countries seemed close to being resolved (as when Franz Josef visited St. Petersburg in 1897). Especially after 1900, however, attitudes hardened.

The Russian government had for the longest while been distrustful of France, the country that had invaded it in 1812, defeated it in 1856, and had become a republic in 1870. But both France and Russia were hostile to Britain by the early 1890s (because of clashes over Africa and Asia respectively), while Russia's antagonism to Austria-Hungary was matched by the French thirst for revenge on Germany for the loss of the eastern provinces of Alsace and Lorraine in 1871. Meanwhile, Germany and the dual monarchy had become close allies after the creation of the German Empire in 1871. Thus, France and Russia concluded that the enemy of their enemy should be their friend. The vast gulf that separated an autocracy from a parliamentary republic based on the principles of liberty, equality, and brotherhood was conveniently ignored. France, too, helped matters along by financing Russia's industrialization with generous loans from 1888 onward. Many small investors bought Russian government bonds that were floated on the French financial markets.

In 1891, Aleksandr III listened to a rendition of the "La Marseillaise," the national hymn that was a symbol of the French Revolution, on a French warship visiting the Russian naval harbor of Kronstadt. At that time, the first agreement between France and Russia about mutual defensive aid was concluded. The terms of military collaboration in case either country was attacked by Germany and its allies (Austria and, at the time, Italy) were ever more precisely determined in the following few years. By 1894, the agreement had become a full-fledged military alliance.

Meanwhile, Germany's attitude toward Russia was ambiguous and inconsistent. Emperor Wilhelm II (r. 1888–1918) and Nicholas were cousins, and their empires had few territorial or other disputes. They agreed on the delineation of their mutual border and in keeping their Polish minorities subjugated. They respected each other's sphere of influence elsewhere in the world. The Russians did not object to the German economic penetration of the Ottoman Empire, of which the construction of a railroad from Berlin to Baghdad became the most celebrated example. In exchange, the Germans promised to leave northern Iran to Russia. They supported each other in China.

In the midst of the 1905 revolution, Nicholas seemed close to reversing his alliances and joining Germany in a pact against France. But the tsar decided against this, in part because his country was deeply indebted to France (and Wilhelm, too, was dissuaded from a German-Russian pact by his strongly opposed government). French money kept the Russian government afloat throughout the revolutionary crisis at home in 1905.

Soon after the revolutionary mood in Russia calmed down, the tsarist government began to make overtures toward Britain, aiming to resolve the various disputes regarding Asia. In 1907, a treaty was concluded that split Iran evenly into two zones, with the north primarily given over to Russian influence and the south designated as a zone for primarily British economic penetration. The Russians allowed the British to deal with Afghanistan and Tibet in a manner that they saw fit. With British encouragement, Russia and Japan improved their relationship in the Far East by ironing out some problems that had not been resolved by the Treaty of Portsmouth of 1905. The two countries firmed up the division between a Japanese sphere of influence in Korea and southern Manchuria and a Russian one in northern Manchuria and (Outer) Mongolia. Mongolia declared its independence from China in 1912 (capitalizing on the opportunity provided by the fall of China's Qing dynasty the previous year) and became a Russian protectorate, which it was to remain until 1991. At the same time, Britain oversaw the separation of Tibet from China.

Meanwhile, in 1908, the Russian conflict with Austria-Hungary over the Balkans took on a renewed acuity. The catalyst was a rebellion against the sultan in Istanbul by the Young Turks, military officers who had been converted to modern-style nationalism. They planned to reinvigorate the Ottoman Empire through economic modernization and rallying its population behind Turkish nationalism. It appeared that part of their program was to reincorporate the provinces of Bosnia and Herzegovina, still formally under Turkish rule, even if they had been administered by Austria-Hungary since 1878. Citing the alleged breakdown of public order that attended the Young Turkish coup, however, Austria-Hungary quickly annexed the two southern Slav provinces instead. This met with strong protest from the kingdom of Serbia and among those Bosnians and Herzegovinians who identified with the Serbian cause. The Serbs believed that Russia supported them.

In fact, the Russians abided by an agreement between the Habsburg and Romanov empires that was more than a quarter century old. It had the Russians accede to the Austro-Hungarian annexation of Bosnia-Herzegovina in exchange for Austrian support to force the Turks to allow the Russian navy to enter the Mediterranean from the Black Sea (even when Russia was at war with the other Great Powers). But when the Austro-Hungarian government announced the annexation of the two provinces, the Russian foreign minister Aleksandr Izvolskii

(1856–1919) encountered strong British opposition to any resolution of the straits issue to Russian advantage. While Bosnia-Herzegovina became Austrian in 1908, neither Russia nor Serbia received any compensation.

Diplomatic maneuvering led to the subsequent creation of an anti-Turkish alliance of Balkan states. This alliance declared war on the Ottomans in the fall of 1912. The aim was to conquer the last pieces of territory in Europe still in Turkish hands. While Russia backed the Serbs, Greeks, and Bulgarians in their effort, Austria made it clear that it would not allow Serbia to establish a bridgehead on the Adriatic Sea, preferring to keep Serbia landlocked. The Turks quickly surrendered in this Balkan War, but soon quarrels between the victors broke out over the division of the spoils. Austrians and Russians meddled in this conflict as well and threatened each other with war.

A compromise was stuck regarding the Adriatic coastline by creating an independent state of Albania in the spring of 1913. An Albanian port connected by rail to Serbia gave the kingdom access to the sea. In the early summer of 1913, war broke out anew, mainly about the division of Macedonia, between Bulgaria, Serbia, and Greece. This time Romania, desirous of some territory on its southern border that was part of Bulgaria, sided with Serbia and Greece, and Turkey saw its chance to recover some of the land lost the previous year on the embattled (and ultimately defeated) Bulgarians.

On the eve of the 1913 Balkan War, the Bulgarian government, which had enjoyed some Russian support until that time, had managed to antagonize the Russians. Russia thus stood aside, and at the conclusion of the war, it was evident that Russia's most consistent ally in the region remained Serbia. In the course of 1913, Russian relations with Bulgaria's foe Romania also improved. Romania was, as we saw previously, eager to defend the interests of the Romanian speakers in Hungarian Transylvania, and thus hostile to the Habsburgs.

Meanwhile, Russia became suspicious of the German designs in Ottoman Turkey, where German military advisors were becoming prominent alongside German civilians modernizing the empire's infrastructure. Toward 1914, not all politicians in St. Petersburg, however, supported the alliance with France and Britain, despite the humiliations to which the Russians had been exposed at the hands of the Austrians (often with forceful German backing). Some on the political right advocated the revival of the post-Napoleonic pact of the conservative powers of Eastern Europe and abandoning the far too liberal British and French. As the former interior minister Pyotr Durnovo (1845–1915) pointed out in early 1914, no real conflict existed between Russia and Germany.

But when faced with the crisis caused by the assassination in Bosnian Sarajevo in late June 1914 of Franz Ferdinand, the Habsburg heir to the throne, the alliance system worked better than some had anticipated. What started out as a Serbian-Austrian conflict quickly escalated into a war that pitted Germany and Austro-Hungary against Russia, France, and Britain, with each side being joined by numerous other countries in the course of the war.

WOMEN

As elsewhere in Europe, the "women's question" was raised in late Imperial Russia. As elsewhere, too, women were disenfranchised, although before 1905 they were of course in this regard no different from men in the tsar's empire. In some respects, Russia's women may have been marginally better off than their counterparts in other European countries or North America around 1900. Educational institutions for women had existed since the reign of Catherine the Great. While women did not gain access to university education until the 1870s, in 1881 already two thousand women studied at universities. This was a number that compared well to the rest of Europe. But in 1897, the literacy rate among Russian women was three times lower than among Russian men, and six times lower among Ukrainian women when compared to Ukrainian men.

Legally women were not considered the equal of men. The degree to which the law treated women as inferior to men depended on the social stratum to which they belonged, as well as their marital status. Widows in villages sometimes wielded remarkable power as de facto heads of households, as did female landowners. But female professionals remained rare before 1900 in Russia, most of them being schoolteachers. The first female member of the Academy of Sciences was Lina Shtern (1878–1968), but this genius of medical research received her education in Switzerland, and her election to the academy occurred only in 1939.

Certainly, apart from class and gender, women's lives were calibrated by their ethnicity and religion. Especially in Central Asia, hardly any women escaped the restrictions placed on their public role, while, as a rule, the opportunities for women to carve out a more independent existence were greater in European Russia. Nonetheless, along the Volga, among such non-Russian groups as the Chuvash or Mordvinians, women were universally illiterate in 1897 (although a mere 10 percent of their men could read and write). Meanwhile, literacy rates among (Muslim) Tatar women in the Volga area were actually higher than among their Russian counterparts.

Of course, whether living in steppe nomad communities or Ukrainian or Russian farming villages, or employed in factories or as shopkeepers, most women worked. In some branches of industry, such as in the textile mills, women sometimes made up the majority of the workforce. With the accelerated urbanization that accompanied the postemancipation era, and especially once industrialization took off, came a growth of prostitution, which was legal. It is with great empathy portrayed in novels such as Dostoyevsky's *Crime and Punishment*. Even though writers such as Dostoyevsky admired "strong women," it is evident that many women were brutally treated, with beatings and rape being a rather common occurrence in the burgeoning cities.

In the countryside, women's fate was unenviable, for physical abuse was common; few frowned on men beating their womenfolk. And everywhere Russian health care lagged compared to that of Western countries. Therefore, infant mortality was high, as was the death of women in childbirth or as a result of complications afterward.

Frequently, this was the result of a lack of understanding about the key importance of hygiene (and the inability to maintain any decent hygienic standards).

Notwithstanding the presence of several women among the leadership of the Russian political parties in the 1900s, women remained deprived of political rights, with one important exception. In 1905–1906, the autonomous rights of the Grand Duchy of Finland were restored for a while (only to be abolished again later), and Finnish women received not only the right to vote but also the right to be elected, one of the first places in the world where this was the case.

Despite this not particularly bright picture of women's lives in late Imperial Russia, women did begin to find a voice. Female authors and artists began to emerge, such as the poets Zinaida Gippius (1869–1945) and Anna Akhmatova (1889–1966), the painter Liubov Popova (1889–1924), the pianist Anna Yesipova (1851–1914), and the ballet dancers Matilda Kshesinskaia (1872–1971) and Anna Pavlova (1881–1931).

RELIGION

The 1897 census enumerated eighty-seven million Eastern Orthodox believers. Some two million people belonged to one of the many sects that had sprung from the Old Belief, although it is likely that a number of Old Believers, suspicious of authorities who had persecuted them across the centuries, may have called themselves Orthodox in fear of repercussions (while others may have evaded the census takers).

Almost forty million non-Orthodox inhabitants resided in Russia in 1897. Eleven and a half million people were Roman Catholics, and 3.5 million were Lutherans. Other Protestant sects were small, having fewer than one hundred thousand adherents. More than five million people professed the Judaic faith, and fourteen million were Muslims. Half a million were (Lama) Buddhists, and some three hundred thousand belonged to "other non-Christian" religions. The Ukrainian Catholics (or Uniates) were not separately distinguished in the census: some of them seem to have been counted as Orthodox (they had been subjected to a long-term campaign by the Russian Orthodox Church to leave the Catholic Church), although others were counted as Catholics.

The census takers apparently did not find atheists among the almost 126 million subjects of the tsar. This omission was of course not reflective of reality. Certainly since the rise of the intelligentsia, atheism had spread and was especially strong among left-wing revolutionaries toward 1900. But it remained primarily a worldview popular among intellectuals, and their proportion of the general population was relatively low. It is interesting that even Lenin seems to have married before an Orthodox priest, perhaps partially because his marriage could otherwise not be registered in the late 1890s, when civil unions did not legally exist.

Historians today are interested in questions of identity and have pondered what was more important to the tsar's subjects in identifying themselves, nationality or religion. Projecting back from later evidence and through comparison with other countries, it seems that around 1900 most of the empire's inhabitants first saw themselves as members of their religious community. In Russian-speaking Orthodox villages, the standard answer before 1917 (or even 1929[8]) to the question to which larger community one belonged seems to have been "*Ia pravoslavnyi/pravoslavnaia*" ("I am Orthodox"), not "*Ia russkii/russkaia*" ("I am a Russian"). Apart from Poland and Finland, one surmises that elsewhere in the empire the mass of the population similarly identified with religion rather than nation. This, too, shows the short-sighted side of the last tsars' Russification policies in non-Russian areas. Mass nationalism had still not arrived in a country in which "mass media" had yet to arrive, and in which the means of communications and transport remained far less advanced than in contemporary Europe or North America. Even more important in preventing nationalism's spread were the low levels of literacy. Thus, the population's "cosmology" was determined by long-standing tradition, passed on through the generations, and the religious concepts taught by priests, rabbis, shamans, or mullahs.

This lack of nationalism has at times been linked to the ultimately faltering performance by the Russian army during the First World War. One reason Russian morale flagged, according to this hypothesis, was the insufficient nationalist enthusiasm among the troops, which was far lower than among, particularly, the highly motivated German soldiers who faced them. But why did Russian morale begin to weaken only after more than two years of warfare, as recent studies have found? And since Russian nationalism clearly had not made much headway, why did the Russians (including the Ukrainians, etc.) answer the call to arms in 1914 without much demurring?

There was indeed very little protest against the mass mobilization of the summer of 1914. Enthusiasm to go to war at the time was as great (or as decent) as it was elsewhere in Europe. In the first place, support for the dynasty may have been stronger than has been suggested ever since 1917. This challenges the Soviet-infused conventional wisdom that the tsar had lost his subjects' trust through Bloody Sunday (and that in 1914 most soldiers only very reluctantly went to war). Additionally, given the evidence regarding the manner in which people identified, support for the Orthodox cause against heretics may have played more of a role than previously thought. Perhaps, then, a sort of premodern nationalism that combined a defense of the Orthodox patrimony, Holy Russia, and the semidivine monarch held most Russian troops under its spell until the home front (more than the actual front) became fed up with the war.[9]

Meanwhile, the importance of nationalism in motivating soldiers to go to war in the massive conscript armies of modern times may have been exaggerated. Military historians have found that localized loyalties played an important role in morale in both world wars: soldiers tended to be markedly more tenacious if they fought shoulder to shoulder with their fellow villagers or high school classmates than if they ended up in units in which troops did not know each other before being deployed. Such loyalties might trump loyalty to the abstract concept of the nation. Because of the Russian soldiers' low level of schooling and lack of exposure otherwise to nationalist propaganda before 1914, the soldiers' almost unwavering cohesion before 1917 might be explained by such solidarity and other hitherto underestimated factors.

Historians need to investigate further the reasons behind the continued Orthodox allegiance of the absolute majority of the Russian or Ukrainian population. The church had been bereft of a patriarch since 1700, and the tsarist authorities used the church as if it was a branch of government. Priests read government decrees from the pulpit and were even asked by the government to inform on their flock's political mood. The church was supportive of the society of inequality that was tsarist Russia, preaching acceptance of the status quo (it was no coincidence that one of its last secular chiefs was Konstantin Pobedonostsev). Priests and monks were often corrupt or imbibed heavily (Rasputin was by no means an exception), hardly setting an example of a true Christian life in their communities. Saintly figures as can be found in Dostoyevsky's great novels (Father Zosima, Alyosha Karamazov) were rare in late Imperial Russia.

At the same time, religious belief remained strong among the non-Orthodox, often in the teeth of discrimination and harassment by the authorities, which especially befell the Jews and the Catholics. Apart from this intimidation strategy, the Russian government offered little incentive to wean people away from the religion of their ancestors. In sum, the 1897 census numbers, showing a country in which every inhabitant was religious, were inflated, but there is no denying that religious belief remained quite important in the lives of almost all of the tsar's subjects. As elsewhere, such beliefs began to wane only before the combined onslaught of education and industrialization, accompanied by the idea that people are called on to make a better world for themselves and others in this life, rather than meekly await improvements in the afterlife.

BALLETS RUSSES, SILVER AGE: DECADENCE, THE EMPIRE'S LAST HURRAH, OR CASSANDRA

Perhaps great social turmoil is conducive to great art. In the waning days of the Russian Empire, this was certainly the case. The period was given the modest epithet of the "silver age" in Russian literature, giving pride of place to Pushkin's era, but in truth Russian creativity in all the arts was never as flourishing as it was around 1900. Some of the great composers of the previous age were still at work, but it was also the age of Igor Stravinsky (1882–1971), composer of the ballet scores *Petrushka*, the *Rites of Spring* and *The Firebird*, staged by Sergei Diaghilev's (1872–1929) *Ballets Russes*. Diaghilev's troupe showcased dancers such as Vachlav Nijinskii (Nizhinskii; 1890–1950) and Anna Pavlova. Diaghilev's work was seen as the epitome of the avant-garde, as were the paintings and designs by Russian visual artists such as Vasilii Kandinsky (1866–1944), Marc Chagall (1887–1985), Kazimir Malevich (1879–1935), and Liubov Popova. Russian poetry was at its height, as can be seen

Figure 5.5. Jewish schoolboys in Samarkand, ca. 1910 (Library of Congress)

from the works by futurists Velimir Khlebnikov (1885–1922) and Vladimir Maia-kovskii (1893–1930), and the symbolists Aleksandr Blok (1880–1921) and Zinaida Gippius, or the more classical lyrical poetry by Sergei Esenin (1895–1925), Anna Akhmatova, Marina Tsvetaeva (1892–1941), and Osip Mandelshtam (1891–1938). In prose, Ivan Bunin (1870–1953; the first Russian winner of the Nobel Prize for Literature, in 1933), Fyodor Sologub (1863–1927), and Andrei Bely (1880–1934) stood out. In literary criticism, Boris Eikhenbaum (1886–1959) and Roman Jakob-son (1896–1982) developed the study of semiotics. Around 1900, Russian science could boast of the physiologist-psychologist Ivan Pavlov (1849–1936), among many others who continued to be active, such as Tsiolkovskii.

It is of note that a great number of the scientists, scholars, and artists, even if criti-cal of the political and social environment in which they worked, turned away from monistic political theories that promised to bring revolutionary salvation for the op-pressed masses. The most famous critique of the intelligentsia as the beacon leading Russia to a radiant future came from a group of former left-wing theorists (including Pyotr Struve) in an essay collection called *Milestones* (*Vekhi*), which was published in 1909. They argued that Russia could only improve through a moral regeneration of the individual and harshly criticized the idea that the implementation in practice of some sort of enlightened political philosophy would bring salvation. They seemed to imply that matters might even turn out worse if such an effort were undertaken. Their words proved prophetic. Indeed, in Russian art and literature some sense of impending doom and premonition can be discerned, although here the benefit of hindsight undoubtedly influences us, who know about what unfolded in the Russian Empire from the summer of 1914 onward.

NOTES

1. Roosevelt went on to win the Nobel Peace Prize for his efforts.

2. One of the committee's chairs was the young Marxist Lev Bronshtein, better known as Trotsky (1879–1940).

3. Among these admirers of Stolypin was the writer Aleksandr Solzhenitsyn, the Russian Nobel Prize winner.

4. Such a conspiracy was an unlikely scenario, as the Marxists rejected terrorism as a tactic.

5. Grids for electricity began to be installed around this time in middle-class neighborhoods.

6. Central Asia remained almost oblivious to the war until conscription was introduced there in 1916.

7. The Habsburg Empire had split into two equally sized parts in 1867.

8. A census was staged in the Soviet Union in 1926.

9. This premodern nationalism was not unlike Nicholas I's and Uvarov's ideology propa-gated in the first half of the nineteenth century.

FURTHER READING

Translated Primary Sources

Berdyaev, Nicholas. *The Origin of Russian Communism*. Translated by R. M. French. Ann Arbor: University of Michigan Press, 1960.

———. *The Russian Idea*. Westport, CT: Praeger, 1979.

Miliukov, Pavel. *Political Memoirs, 1905–1917*. Translated by Carl Goldberg. Edited by Arthur P. Mendel. Ann Arbor: University of Michigan Press, 1967.

Shulgin, V. V. *Days of the Russian Revolution: Memoirs from the Right, 1905–1917*. Translated and edited by Bruce F. Adams. Gulf Breeze, FL: Academic International Press, 1990.

Scholarly Literature

Ascher, Abraham. *P. A. Stolypin: The Search for Stability in Late Imperial Russia*. Stanford, CA: Stanford University Press, 2002.

———. *The Revolution of 1905*. 2 vols. Stanford, CA: Stanford University Press, 1994.

Bernstein, Laurie. *Sonia's Daughters: Prostitutes and Their Regulation in Imperial Russia*. Berkeley: University of California Press, 1995.

Brower, Daniel R. *Turkestan and the Fate of the Russian Empire*. New York: Routledge, 2003.

Crews, Robert D. *For Prophet and Tsar: Islam in Russia and Central Asia*. Cambridge, MA: Harvard University Press, 2010.

Ely, Christopher. *This Meager Nature: Landscape and National Identity in Imperial Russia*. DeKalb: Northern Illinois University Press, 2009.

Engelstein, Laura. *The Keys to Happiness: Sex and the Search for Happiness in Fin-de-Siècle Russia*. Ithaca, NY: Cornell University Press, 1994.

Frank, Allen J. *Muslim Religious Institutions in Imperial Russia*. Leiden, Netherlands: Brill, 2001.

Fuhrmann, Joseph T. *Rasputin: The Untold Story*. Boston: Wiley, 2012.

Geraci, Robert. *Window on the East: National and Imperial Identities in Late Imperial Russia*. Ithaca, NY: Cornell University Press, 2009.

Gerasimov, Ilya. *Modernism and Public Reform in Late Imperial Russia: Rural Professionals and Self-Organization, 1905–1930*. Houndsmills, UK: Palgrave Macmillan, 2009.

Gleason, W. E. "Alexander Guchkov and the End of the Russian Empire." *Transactions of the American Philosophical Society*, New Series, 73, no. 3 (1983): 1–90.

Haimson, Leopold H. "The Problem of Social Stability in Urban Russia, 1905–1917." Part 1, *Slavic Review* 4 (1964): 619–42; part 2, *Slavic Review* 1 (1965): 1–22.

Heywood, Anthony, and Jonathan Smele, eds. *The Russian Revolution of 1905: Centenary Perspectives*. New York: Routledge, 2012.

Hiro, Dilip. *Inside Central Asia: A Political and Cultural History of Uzbekistan, Turkmenistan, Kazakhstan, Kyrgyzstan, Turkey and Iran*. New York: Overlook, 2011.

Jukes, Geoffrey. *The Russo-Japanese War, 1904–1905*. Oxford, UK: Osprey, 2002.

Khalid, Adeeb. *The Politics of Muslim Cultural Reform: Jadidism in Central Asia*. Berkeley: University of California Press, 1999.

Morrissey, Susan. *Suicide and the Body Politic in Imperial Russia*. Cambridge: Cambridge University Press, 2012.

Paine, S. C. M. *Imperial Rivals: China, Russia and Their Disputed Frontier, 1858–1924*. Armonk, NY: M. E. Sharpe, 1996.

Perrie, Maureen. *The Agrarian Policy of the Russian Socialist-Revolutionary Party: From Its Origins through the Revolution of 1905–1907*. Cambridge: Cambridge University Press, 2009.

Pleshakov, Constantine. *The Tsar's Last Armada: The Epic Voyage to the Battle of Tsushima*. New York: Basic Books, 2003.

Rogger, Hans. *Russia in the Age of Modernisation and Revolution, 1881–1917*. New York: Longman, 1989.

Sahadeo, Jeff. *Russian Colonial Society in Tashkent, 1865–1923*. Bloomington: Indiana University Press, 2010.

Scheijen, Sjeng. *Diaghilev: A Life*. New York: Oxford University Press, 2012.

Schimmelpenninck van der Oye, David, and Bruce Menning, eds. *Reforming the Tsar's Army: Military Innovation in Imperial Russia from Peter the Great to the Revolution*. Cambridge: Cambridge University Press, 2004.

Siegel, Jennifer. *Endgame: Britain, Russia and the Final Struggle for Central Asia*. London: I. B. Tauris, 2002.

Steinberg, Mark D. *Proletarian Imagination: Self, Modernity and the Sacred in Russia, 1910–1925*. Ithaca, NY: Cornell University Press, 2002.

Steinberg, Mark D., and Heather Coleman, eds. *Sacred Stories: Religion and Spirituality in Modern Russia*. Bloomington: Indiana University Press, 2007.

Stites, Richard. *The Women's Liberation Movement in Russia: Feminism, Nihilism and Bolshevism, 1860–1930*. Princeton, NJ: Princeton University Press, 1978.

Tolz, Vera. *Russia's Own Orient: The Politics of Identity and Oriental Studies in the Late Imperial and Early Soviet Periods*. New York: Oxford University Press, 2011.

Uyama, Tomohiko, ed. *Asiatic Russia: Imperial Power in Regional and International Contexts*. New York: Routledge, 2012.

Weeks, Theodore R. *Nation and State in Late Imperial Russia*. DeKalb: Northern Illinois University Press, 2008.

Wolff, David, Bruce Menning, et al., eds. *The Russo-Japanese War in Global Perspective*. Leiden, Netherlands: Brill, 2007.

FILMS

Battleship Potemkin. DVD. Directed by Sergei Eisenstein. Berlin: Kino International, 2007.

Dersu Uzala. DVD. Directed by Akira Kurosawa. New York: Kino Video, 2003.

Prisoner of the Mountains. DVD. Directed by Sergei Bodrov. Beverly Hills, CA: MGM, 2003.

6

Forging Soviet Civilization, 1914–1924

The utter disregard for human life that was a key feature of the ruling style of the Bolshevik leaders was to a significant degree an echo of the massacre of millions of soldiers on the orders of their political leaders and military commanders in the First World War. It is therefore not amiss to start this chapter about the beginnings of the Soviet Union with a discussion of Russia in the "Great War," even when its primary focus is on the manner in which the Bolsheviks took power and established a political dictatorship that would lead Russia and the world to the radiant future of communism. Early on, however, the survival of the dictatorship at any price replaced the Marxist goal of the creation of a society of equals whose human rights and freedoms were meticulously protected.

THE FIRST WORLD WAR

On the eve of the Sarajevo assassination in June 1914, a number of Russian politicians (including the former ministers Vitte and Durnovo) warned the government against Russia's entry into any major European war. The fiasco of the Russo-Japanese War indicated that the Russian military performance in such a conflagration might be anything but impressive. By 1914, there was little reason to believe that Russia's armed forces would fight substantially better against the armies of Germany and Austria-Hungary, which would probably be supported by those of the Ottoman Empire and one or more Balkan states. But pride and honor trumped common sense in St. Petersburg in 1914. In the expectation of Russian support, in July Serbia defied Austria-Hungary's government ultimatum that Serbia surrender its sovereignty to allow Habsburg officials to hunt down on Serbian soil the conspirators who had organized Archduke Franz

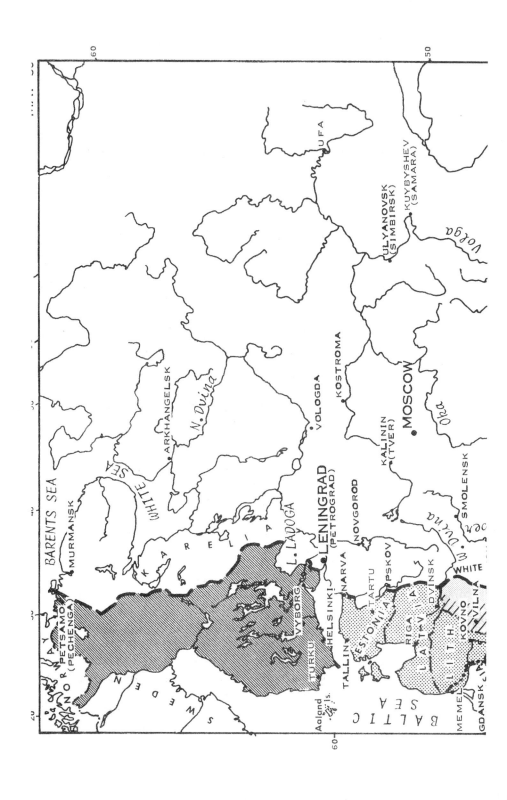

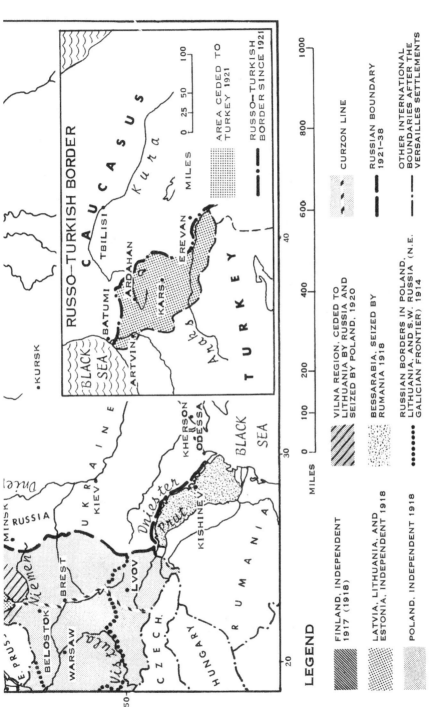

Map 6.1. European Russia, 1918–1938 (From Allen F. Chew, *An Atlas of Russian History*, New Haven, CT: Yale University Press, 1967. Used by permission.)

Figure 6.1.   Minsk in 1912 (Library of Congress)

Ferdinand's assassination. The tsar and his advisors, backed by most of Russian public opinion, ordered first a partial and then a full mobilization.[1]

Having been recently forced to back down to Austria-Hungary in the Bosnian Crisis (1908) and the Balkan Wars (1912–1913), the Russian government refused to accept another humiliation at the hands of the Austrians. The Serbian "little Slavic brethren" needed to be rescued, even if this would come at the price of a war with Austria and the German Empire, the staunch Habsburg ally. The tsar rejected German demands to rescind the mobilization order. War with the Central Powers thus became inevitable.

During the next three years, the Russian armed forces often fought as well as their foes. Indeed, they won major battles both against the Ottoman Turks and the Austrians. Crucial errors were made by Russian commanders in a number of other battles (most famously at the Masurian Lakes in August–September 1914), however, and luck was not on the Russian side in the fighting. When in the spring of 1915 the Russians were forced into a sustained retreat along the entire front, the tsar, convinced that his presence at general headquarters would turn the tide, decided to take personal control at the front. Nicholas thus decamped to Mogilev (Mohiliau). The enemy advance did indeed grind to a halt at the very moment the tsar appeared at the command post, but this had little to do with the monarch's physical proximity to the fighting.

Figure 6.2. Russian POWs during the First World War (Library of Congress)

Nicholas's departure meant that the government in Petrograd fell into the hands of querulous and incompetent ministers.[2] They primarily sought to curry favor with Tsaritsa Alexandra and Grigorii Rasputin. In military terms, the Brusilov Offensive, which was waged from June to August 1916 on the southwestern front, may have been the last best chance for the tsarist regime. However, the Austrians and Germans ultimately managed to stop the Russian advance.

After more than two years of warfare that had cost Russia millions of casualties and prisoners of war, the voices of opposition in the Duma were raised again. Prior to the second half of 1916, the Duma membership had observed a patriotic loyalty; criticism of the tsar's government was muted. In the fall of 1916, however, the Kadet leader Pavel Miliukov delivered a speech in the Duma in which he asked whether the government's failure to achieve any meaningful victory in the war was due to the ministers' incompetence or their treasonous activity. He demanded the appointment of a government that would be responsible to the Duma (as he had in 1906, after the Kadet triumph in the first Duma elections). Desperate monarchists decided soon thereafter that the quagmire was all the fault of Rasputin. But the murder of the monk in December 1916 came too late (and he did not enjoy as much influence as was suspected).

In February 1917, people took to the streets in the capital to protest bread shortages. Street fighting and plundering ensued, and the Petrograd garrison as well as Cossack detachments refused orders to suppress the unrest. On 1 March, the general staff and monarchist politicians prevailed on the tsar in Mogilev to abdicate in favor of his brother. But Grand Duke Mikhail refused the throne. The Romanov dynasty had come to an end.

PROVISIONAL GOVERNMENT AND SOVIETS

The government that replaced the tsar claimed its authority from being selected by and among the leadership of the moderate Duma factions (Kadets and Octobrists). Thus Kadet leader Miliukov became minister of foreign affairs of this Provisional Government (whose prime minister was a moderate public figure, Prince G. E. L'vov [1861–1925]). It remained moot, however, whether the Provisional Government really enjoyed a mandate from the Russian citizenry. The Duma had been elected by a very small franchise in 1912. At the time of the organization of the Provisional Government, a rival emerged for political power, when the Petrograd soviet of workers', soldiers', and sailors' deputies was resurrected. The soviet claimed greater legitimacy than the Provisional Government, for it was elected by all working in industry or serving in the armed forces. The Petrograd soviet initially merely represented the industrial proletariat and armed forces of the capital, but it acquired ever greater prestige. Within weeks it was recognized as the country's leading soviet among the hundreds of its counterparts that sprang up in the rest of Russia.

Figure 6.3.   The beginnings of the Provisional Government in 1917 (Library of Congress)

After a rapid turnover during the very first days of its existence, the Petrograd soviet's elected leadership consisted of leaders of the entire spectrum of left-wing political parties. It included, in the beginning, the moderate Laborites (Trudoviki). They were a sort of "SR light," which rejected the terrorism of the Socialist Revolutionary Party. Their main leader was Aleksandr Kerensky (1881–1970). Then there were the SR themselves, led by Viktor Chernov (1873–1952), and the Mensheviks, whose leaders were such men as the Georgians Nikolai Chkheidze (1864–1926) and Irakli Tsereteli (1882–1959), as well as Lenin's old comrade, Yuli Martov. Finally, the Bolsheviks in the capital were in the first days led by an actual factory worker, Aleksandr Shliapnikov (1885–1937), but he was soon replaced by the more senior Viacheslav Molotov (1890–1986), Yakov Sverdlov (1885–1919), and Iosif Stalin, once they had reached Petrograd from their former places of exile in Siberia. In April, Lenin arrived at the Finland railway station in the capital; he took firm control over the faction that he had founded in 1903.

Immediately after its formation on 1 March, the Petrograd soviet issued decrees that expanded the democratic program that the Provisional Government promised to implement, while the soviet actually issued legislation that bypassed the Provisional Government as well. The Provisional Government itself, meanwhile, promised more than it delivered in the eyes of many of the impatient revolutionary-minded population; thus, free elections by universal suffrage were announced, but only after the war "had been brought to its victorious conclusion."

In early March 1917, the Petrograd soviet issued a decree that was understood as allowing troops to refuse orders of their commanding officers. This was to lead to the collapse of military discipline in subsequent months and sabotaged any chance of a Russian victory over the Central Powers. The political mood among the masses of the Russian Empire, whether in uniform, in the factories, or in the villages, quickly radicalized during the months following the tsar's abdication. Most of the ministers of the Provisional Government's various iterations failed to understand this impatient mind-set. The first Provisional Government was forced to stand down when in May it was made public that it pursued the same war aims as its predecessor. These goals included the Russian annexation of Constantinople and the straits linking the Black Sea with the Mediterranean Sea.

The second Provisional Government added several socialists to the one left-wing representative, Kerensky, who had been a government minister since March. These socialist ministers represented the strongest parties, that is, the SR and Mensheviks, in the Petrograd soviet and the all-Russian congress of soviets, which met in June. The Bolsheviks stayed out, unwilling to collaborate with the "bourgeoisie" in the Provisional Government and calling for an all-socialist government chosen by the soviets. Kerensky, who had become minister of defense, decided in June to prove Russia's continued significance as a valuable ally to the French, British, and Americans. He ordered an offensive on the southwestern front (where Austro-Hungarian units, considered to be weaker, outnumbered German troops). This offensive, once it met with determined resistance, collapsed after a few days. Subsequently, Russian troops did not just fall back to their former positions but decided to desert altogether and return to their ancestral villages. There, peasants were busy confiscating land from noble, monastic, and middle-class proprietors and distributing it among their households. As Lenin declared, the soldiers "voted with their feet" for a Russian departure from the war.

THE BOLSHEVIKS

The call for peace became much louder in the summer months of 1917, while the growing contingent of socialist ministers in the Provisional Government failed to initiate any peace talks. More and more Bolshevik representatives were being elected to the soviets, indicating increasing frustration with the government's lack of steps toward ending the war. The Bolsheviks called for an immediate peace and demanded that all political power should be transferred to the soviets. Already in July, they may have toyed with the idea of taking power but decided that the moment was yet too early. After riotous demonstrations in the early days of the month, Bolshevik leaders were accused of treason, and whereas Lenin went into hiding in Finland, several of his comrades were arrested.[3] But they enjoyed considerable freedom in their confinement to communicate with the outside world and were subject to a very humane prison regime.

In August 1917, an odd attempt to restore discipline and order in Petrograd with the aid of a section of the army (commanded by General Lavr Kornilov and with the possible connivance of Kerensky) failed. When news spread of Kornilov's progress toward the capital, most Bolsheviks were released from jail. A renewed effort was made to restore the left's unity of prerevolutionary days, this time to face the threat of a right-wing or military coup. But Kornilov's forces never even reached Petrograd, abandoning the campaign without a fight. On Lenin's instigation, the Bolshevik Party's leadership decided to capitalize on the opportunity that had arisen in the evident absence of any significant political or military support for the Provisional Government. The Bolsheviks began to prepare for an insurrection.[4] In September, Bolsheviks acquired a majority in the soviets of both Petrograd and Moscow. The onetime chairman of the St. Petersburg soviet, Lev Trotsky, who had joined the Bolsheviks only in the summer, was elected chairman of the Petrograd soviet. He used its Military-Revolutionary Council, formed to protect the revolution against the Kornilov coup, in planning a takeover.

After weeks of incessant cajoling by Lenin (who traveled incognito to Petrograd, fearing that the arrest warrant for him remained in force), the Bolshevik Central Committee (the party's leading body) agreed to move during the night of 25–26 October. Strategic points in the city (railway stations, telegraph and telephone exchanges, the post offices, and army barracks) were occupied by so-called Red Guards (worker volunteers) and soldiers or sailors; the Provisional Government's ministers were arrested (with Kerensky making a narrow escape). The coup succeeded virtually without any bloodshed.

The Bolshevik putsch had been planned to coincide with the opening of the second all-Russian congress of soviets. A triumphant Lenin mounted its stage in the early hours of 26 October 1917. He announced that from then on all power in the former tsarist empire was in the hands of the soviets. In protest to the overthrow of the Provisional Government (in which several of their leaders had been ministers), a majority of Menshevik and SR delegates left the congress. The rump that stayed behind ratified the coup that had ostensibly been executed on the orders of the Petrograd soviet's Military-Revolutionary Council. In reality, the Bolshevik Central Committee had been its organizer. It established a communist tradition: behind a facade of legitimacy and a genuflection to democratic process, the Communist (Bolshevik) Party ruled in dictatorial fashion.

GOING BOLDLY WHERE NO ONE WENT BEFORE

Undeniable historical continuity exists between the tsarist regime and the new Bolshevik regime that established its rule in the Russian Empire from early November 1917 (New Style[5]) onward. One pertains to the utter disregard for human life. The massive slaughter of the First World War in Europe, in which millions of men died, led to a political mind-set in which a person's life could easily be sacrificed for an allegedly greater good. The Russian revolutionary leaders proved to be as merciless in this regard as the tsarist politicians and generals had been from August 1914 onward. Suddenly, the killing of human beings in unprecedented numbers was accepted as a normal part of modern warfare and even of peacetime politics.

Of course, the Russian iteration of this sort of brutality was but one of many. A series of twentieth-century governments showed utter disregard for human life, going to the length of even massacring their own subjects in peacetime, as was to occur not just in the Soviet Union but also in China and Rwanda. Historians now link the First World War's battles of the Masurian Lakes or Somme with the Armenian genocide (1915), Stalin's massacres, the Holocaust, China's Great Leap Forward and Cultural Revolution, the killing fields of Cambodia (1975–1977), and the extermination of the Tutsis in Rwanda (1994) in a chain of ghastly mass crimes against humanity. In their utter disregard for human life, Lenin and Stalin seem to have adhered to what Stalin allegedly argued, that "one death is a tragedy, but a million deaths is a mere statistic." He was, alas, not the only one capable of such cynicism in this, the bloodiest century of human history.

Despite the Communist leadership's attempt to disown the entire tsarist involvement in the war, it adopted, in another instance of historical continuity, its predecessor's wartime mass mobilization and conscription of young men. The bulk of the Red Army in the Civil War that broke out in 1918 was created by a massive call-up of young men, while the economy of Bolshevik Russia was placed on a wartime footing. After some tentative probing, Lenin's successors (among whom Stalin stood out as the unrivaled leader) mobilized all their subjects once again in 1929 for an unprecedented effort to forge a new civilization. This enlistment of all people in the grandiose effort to realize the Soviet project lasted from the first two Five Year Plans (1929–1937) through the Second World War and the postwar reconstruction all the way until Stalin's death in 1953. Mass-mobilization campaigns disappeared only after Stalin's death. The last wave constituted the Virgin Lands project of the middle of the 1950s.

Nevertheless, the 1917 Revolution was at the same time a watershed, a radical departure from the historical past, and not just for Russian history. The scale of the Communist dictatorship's efforts to build a new society of equals and its intense desire to remake humanity into a different species made the Union of Socialist Soviet Republics (the official name of the country from 1922 onward, abbreviated as USSR) into something radically different from tsarist Russia. Soviet society (and a world that was destined to be communist as well) was to be modern and urban. In this (as in much else) they followed the ideas of Karl Marx and his close collaborator Friedrich Engels (1820–1895), who had forecasted that distinctions between city and countryside would disappear in the perfectly harmonious global society of the future. This communist world would be populated by fully conscious and enlightened people, living a life in a society of plenty, in effect a modern utopia.[6]

Some contours of this "radiant future" had taken shape by 1960, when more than half of the Soviet population lived in cities rather than villages; for any country, this may count as a milestone on the road to modernity (it had been reached first in industrializing Britain around 1850). Urbanization continued apace for the subsequent half century in the Soviet Union and the post-Soviet successor states. Today, the countryside of the former USSR is indeed littered with abandoned villages. But it was rather the individual desire for a better life with modern amenities that eventually sustained the migration from the countryside to the cities, after the enforced mobilization waves began to wane. Enthusiasm for the cause (some of which was present in the Five Year Plans and quite pronounced in defending the country during the Second World War) eroded after 1953, when individualism and acquisitiveness of the modern kind became the prime movers for Soviet citizens as much as their counterparts in the capitalist world. Most shockingly, however, in their attempts to build a perfect modern society of happy equals, Marx's faithful Soviet disciples eliminated, executed outright, exiled to remote and inhospitable regions, or confined to labor camps millions who were thought to stand in the way of its construction.

Scholars are fascinated by the problem of historical continuity. Thus, apart from the debate about the link between tsarist and Soviet Russia, another long-term and unresolved historiographical debate (actually originating with Soviet critics such as Stalin's rival Trotsky) has been waged about Stalin being Lenin's "true heir," especially in executing his Great Turn from 1929 onward.[7] In order to make up our mind about this question, we should first investigate what Lenin did (try to) accomplish in the few years that he stood at the helm of his Soviet Russia. It should meanwhile be remembered, too, that the idealistic Lenin of November 1917 was a rather different character from the sober Lenin of 1921–1922. By the end of his active political life, his revolutionary optimism had been chastened by the trials and tribulations of the Civil War (1918–1921), the war with Poland (1920–1921), and a massive famine (1921–1922). Even at the time of his death in January 1924, a rebellion against Russian rule that originated in 1916 was still smoldering in Central Asia. It was a last reminder of the utter chaos and lawlessness into which the Russian Empire sank in 1917–1918, from which it resurfaced only by 1922.

HOW TO BUILD A COMMUNIST SOCIETY

Whereas Vladimir Lenin displayed a brilliant political instinct in taking power in November 1917, neither he nor his Bolshevik comrades had a blueprint for the construction of a socialist or communist, classless society. They had no models after which they could fashion their realm and, of course, no experience in governing a country of some 140 million people. Stumbling along the imagined road to communism, their rhetoric sometimes betrays a rather desperate quest to find historical analogies to guide them. They thus frequently referred to the dictatorship of Robespierre's Committee of Public Safety (1793–1794) or the Paris Commune (1870–1871) in France. Neither had been attempts, however, at establishing a communist proletarian dictatorship based on Marxist theory. In addition, whereas 1870s France resembled the tsarist empire in 1917 in terms of its level of industrialization, France was demographically and geographically a far smaller and less diverse country. It showed great historical naivety to think that truly useful lessons could be drawn from the French example.

At first, the Bolsheviks seemed in fact wholly unconcerned with steering the country into any clear direction, instead encouraging (and surrendering to) the utter dissolution of the tsarist state and economy. In this, they were led by their reading of Marx's historical determinism. Marx had predicted that the socialist revolution would unfold (as anything of true historical importance did) through the workings of impersonal forces, over which individuals had no control. Trotsky, the first People's Commissar (PC) of Foreign Affairs and subsequent architect of the Red Army's victory in the Civil War, had worked this out somewhat more concretely. Before the 1917 Revolution, Trotsky suggested that, once the capitalist chain was broken at its weakest link (as it was in Russia in October 1917), the rest of the fully or half-industrialized world would follow suit and be engulfed by a socialist revolution similar to Russia's. Therefore, all the Bolsheviks had to do after coming to power was to await events elsewhere.

Lenin himself had outlined in his *State and Revolution* (written mainly while he was in hiding in 1917) how, after a brief transitional period of a proletarian dictatorship, the state would "wither away." At that point, the enlightened masses would voluntarily live by the principles of "each working according to her abilities" and "each receiving according to his needs." In this classless society, the conscious proletarian would work as a streetcar driver or haul garbage on some days, while on others she would write poetry or study, when others took their turn performing menial labor. Children would be raised by the community, primarily in day-care centers and schools, and nutritious meals would be shared with other people in large communal halls.

Soon after the Bolshevik takeover, certain signs seemed to herald a global communist juggernaut: In 1918, mutinies spread in the German army, and councils of soldiers' and sailors' deputies were set up in several German cities. In 1919, Communists ruled the German state of Bavaria for a short while. In Hungary, a Communist republic was proclaimed not long after the November 1918 armistice. And whereas this latter truce led indeed to the guns being silenced on the Western front, in Eastern Europe a variety of smaller territorial conflicts erupted into local wars, fertile grounds for revolutionary developments. Western colonialism, too, was coming under attack. In China and India, revolutionary stirrings against Western tutelage occurred, while the Vietnamese politician Ho Chi Minh (1890–1969) attempted to plead for the independence of his country during the peace negotiations held in Paris in 1919.

Lenin and Trotsky soon gave up on the idea of a spontaneous transition to communism in Russia and took the reins firmly into their hands in the first months of 1918. But they did not discard their expectation of an imminent global wave of revolutions ushering in a communist world. With the example of the French revolutionary armies in mind, Soviet leaders began to believe that their Red Army might help to impose communism on other countries. In the summer of 1920, the Red Army advanced to the gates of Warsaw, the capital of newly independent Poland, after a foolish attempt by the Polish government to lay claim to most of Ukraine during the chaos of the Russian Civil War. Again, hope grew in the new capital of Bolshevik Russia, Moscow, that the revolution would sweep away all capitalist opposition in all of Europe, now with the aid of the triumphant Red Army marching westward. But the Poles stopped the Red Army's advance in August and September of 1920.

This setback confirmed to the ever more realistic Lenin that it was rather naive to expect a performance from his ragtag military that resembled the astonishing success of the French revolutionary soldiers in Europe during the 1790s. By 1921, the failure of revolutions elsewhere and the utter exhaustion of their country convinced Lenin and his comrades that it was best to await another wave of revolutionary stirring abroad. Building up their strength at home would allow them to come to the aid of future foreign revolutions with as much force as possible.

DESTROYING AN EMPIRE

Lenin and his comrades in the Bolshevik Party's Central Committee believed that they needed only to stay at the helm of their new empire until the global communist revolution engulfed the world. This explains why they promised everything to almost everyone after they took over in November 1917. First, land was "given" to the peasants of Russian Europe and Russian Asia. In truth, it became public property to be used by those who cultivated it, but few in the villages noticed at the time how this differed from full ownership. Second, peace was promised to the soldiers. True to their word in this respect, Trotsky was immediately dispatched to Brest-Litovsk to begin armistice negotiations with the Central Powers. Third, the Bolsheviks promised bread to all, for shortages of this staple food appeared to have triggered the March revolution. This was a promise much harder to keep given the breakdown of the empire's distribution system in the second half of 1917. Furthermore, in honor of their Marxist-proletarian essence, workers' control over factories was introduced. This proved to be unpractical and, in fact, detrimental to workers. Finally, the various non-Russian ethnic groups were promised "self-determination." These groups were called "nations" in the initial proclamation of the new Bolshevik government in November 1917, even if most of the members of these ethnocultural groups had yet to develop a sense of national identity. The Bolshevik leaders had hardly reflected on the practical consequences of granting some two hundred ethnic groups such self-determination. Their proclamation of independence for all non-Russians was at the time to provoke a response especially among the inhabitants of the European colonies and inspire them to rise up and overthrow their Western rulers.

These measures were faithful to Marxist ideals with their breathtakingly optimistic view of human, and especially working-class, nature, but they completely ignored the less-than-exemplary nature of human beings as recorded in history; as the German philosopher Immanuel Kant (1724–1804) had once written, "Out of the crooked wood of humanity no straight timber can be made." Despite arguing earlier (beginning with his *What Is to Be Done?* of 1903) that a "proletarian vanguard" (meaning his party) needed to lead the blue-collar workers to the light they would not be able to see on their own, Lenin and his circle preserved a strong belief in the innate transformative character and wisdom of factory workers. As long as they were given strategic posts in the economy, society, and the government, the rest of the population would follow their lead and recognize how the "radiant future" of communism was awaiting them. According to the Bolsheviks, open-minded proletarians, who had lost nothing but their chains in 1917, would be able to build this ideal society from scratch. Such had been the predictions of the prophet Marx.

In practice, Lenin was soon forced to conclude that his prerevolutionary doubts regarding the exceptional nature of the factory workers had not been groundless. For the radical policies announced in 1917, which aimed to discard the entire past of the tsarist regime, led to chaos and lawlessness. The necessary cohort of class-conscious and emancipated proletarians unerringly leading Russia to the promised land failed to materialize. Even in running their factories, workers turned out to be flawed human beings: once they had been given control over management, they often worked as little as possible, while giving themselves exorbitant pay raises. They also pilfered away the equipment, fuel, raw materials, and manufactured output. And they could not stop the gradual collapse of much of the communication-and-transport system, which deprived factories of supplies and the ability to distribute their goods.

But there were also too few proletarians to lead the former tsarist empire to a life of equality and justice for all. Only a few regions of tsarist Russia had industrialized, some of which were lost in the war (such as Poland). Factory work or mining was the occupation of a considerable amount of people in these pockets of industrial development,[8] but most of the empire's population was rurally based and engaged in agriculture. Many non-Slavic population groups had remained wholly untouched by the modernization that had spread in the empire for a mere few decades.

It all forced Lenin, Trotsky, Stalin, and the other leaders to make a choice: repeat the heroic example of the Paris Commune and refuse to compromise any ideals and be inevitably vanquished by foreign and domestic foes, or hold on to power by compromising many of the ideals held dearly by them throughout their entire adult lives. Lenin and Trotsky believed that Marx had discovered the laws of historical development. It seemed a shame to give up power to those who did not know those laws. That would allow, too, the reestablishment of a regime that was exploitative of the masses. In March 1918, after another heated debate in the party's Central Committee, the decision was therefore made to buy time by signing the Peace of Brest-Litovsk with the Central Powers. The Bolsheviks decided to regroup in the much-reduced territory that the Germans, Austrians, and Turks left them under the terms of this agreement. While awaiting the revolution elsewhere, Communist Russia was to try to survive, surrounded by hostile capitalist states. But until a series of strokes in 1922–1923 put him out of commission, Lenin seems to have believed that the wait would be short.

Although peace was concluded at Brest-Litovsk, chaos reigned in the former tsarist empire in the spring and summer of 1918. The economy slowly ground to a halt, and the shortages of foodstuffs in the cities that had plagued the country during the war further intensified: most peasants turned away from the market and limited themselves to cultivating only as much as was necessary to feed their own households. The Bolshevik Central Committee saw capitalist conspiracies behind the faltering industrial production and decided to nationalize every larger business in the course of 1918. But public ownership did not jump-start the economy, for the Bolsheviks could not find the managerial talent to keep the factories running after the owners had been ousted. Workers' management proved an inadequate substitute. The growing unrest across the country wreaked havoc with transport routes and communication lines. This further diminished supplies reaching their destinations and products reaching their markets. Productivity collapsed.

EMPIRE AND COMINTERN

By the summer of 1918, Ukraine was under German occupation; it was to be torn apart by its own civil war and by foreign invaders long after the November 1918 armistice made the Central Powers lay down their arms. Other parts of Imperial Russia besides Ukraine broke away. National governments in the Transcaucasus region declared independence. First they continued to fight the Ottoman Turks and then defied the Soviets for several years. Poland and Finland gained a more durable independence, initially under the terms of the Brest-Litovsk Treaty and subsequently when they were recognized by the Allies and Soviet Russia (and Poland was to rule a good part of formerly tsarist Ukraine and Belarus until 1939). Latvia, Lithuania, and Estonia seceded from the empire at the same time. After the German surrender in November 1918, German free corps and tsarist officers helped to maintain the independence of these Baltic states.

After the rebellion of the Fergana Valley in 1916 had received a tremendous boost from the events of 1917, it was for several years wholly unclear who ruled across large stretches of Central Asia. The Bolsheviks were in charge of the Ural region and Siberia for about half a year after their coup, but by the end of the summer of 1918 most of those areas broke away from Communist rule. A variety of rebels, collectively known as the Whites, replaced the Communists. The Whites ran the gamut from left-wing Socialist Revolutionaries to sadistic sympathizers with the Black Hundreds. As a result, from August 1918 to the summer of 1919, Communist-controlled Russia was about the size of pre-Petrine Muscovy. Nevertheless, after the Red Army beat back a final offensive by the White armies to capture Moscow in the fall of 1919, the Bolshevik troops managed to secure most of the territory that had been ruled by the tsars in Asia, the Caucasus, and Ukraine before 1914.

In most non-Russian territories that Soviet Russia annexed, the pattern of the Communist takeover was similar. A coup was staged by the local Communist Party (often led by Russian speakers) in the capital of the region, which set up a military-revolutionary council. The new government would ask Soviet Russia for aid, which was furnished by way of the Red Army's entry into the region. After this, the Communist leaders in Moscow welcomed the newly "liberated people" into their state. Belarus and Ukraine were the first to be "sovietized" in this manner at the end of 1918. Nevertheless, in Ukraine civil war (which eventually became entangled with a Polish invasion) continued to rage for almost two years after the first attempt to establish Bolshevik power. From early 1920, the mountainous regions of the Caucasus, such as Chechnya, Azerbaijan, Armenia, and Georgia, were annexed following the same recipe, and in 1922 Central Asia was also thus "sovietized."

Usually, sustained resistance to the reimposition of Russian rule was slight: the great majority of the population from Ukraine to Kyrgyzstan had not developed any meaningful sense of national identity. Illiteracy levels remained extremely high, and mass nationalism was therefore at best in its infancy. Nationalism was not even fully articulated among the small group of intellectuals who tried to articulate it and spread its message. Suppression of nationalist governments was thus relatively easy. This was all the more so because the champions of national independence lacked any military muscle. Most officers from the former tsarist army who staffed the White armies championed a "Russia One and Undivided." They had no tolerance for movements trying to establish independence from the Russian Empire.

During the Civil War, efforts were made to expand westward to recover some of the territory lost at Brest-Litovsk; for example, in 1918 a brief civil war ended with the defeat of the Communists in newly independent Finland.[9] Likewise, the Soviet Communists contemplated expansion into Turkey (which seemed on the verge of disappearing from the map around 1920), Iran, and Afghanistan. In September 1920, a "Congress of the Peoples of the East" met in Soviet Azerbaijan's capital Baku, which declared a "Holy War against British Imperialism." But the efforts to export Communism across Asia were abandoned once it appeared that nowhere on the continent (except in Outer Mongolia) did there emerge a Communist movement that was sufficiently viable to establish a Communist republic propped up by Soviet military, financial, and political aid.

Instead, Soviet aid was transferred to generic anti-Western resistance groups such as that organized by Mustafa Kemal (Atatürk; 1881–1938) in Turkey. The only successful foray was into (Outer) Mongolia, where the first Soviet satellite state arose in 1921 in the chaos that ensued following the collapse of Imperial China in 1911 and the Russian Empire in 1917. Its first leader was Suhe Bator (1893–1923), who was succeeded upon his death in 1923 by Khorloogiin Choibalsan (1895–1952). Both had spent their formative years in Imperial Russia. By early 1921, then, internationally recognized borders had been determined for the Soviet republic in Europe. By 1924, most of the rebellious Fergana Valley had been brought back under Bolshevik military control, and the Soviet Union obtained clearly defined international borders in Asia as well.

In the midst of the Civil War in March 1919, the Bolsheviks founded an international organization of Communist Parties, the Third or Communist International (Comintern). It was modeled after the international organization of socialist parties known as the Second International but rejected its policies as too conciliatory toward capitalism. The Second International had deemphasized Marx's premise that the proletariat could gain power only through revolutionary violence. It believed that socialists could gain power through parliamentary means and democratic elections. The Comintern seemed no more than a marginal organization of revolutionary fanatics at the time of its founding. At its second meeting in July 1920, however, it had become a rather more dynamic organization. By then a much more stable Russian-Soviet government backed it. At the second Comintern congress, strict regulations (the "Twenty-One Conditions") were laid down for Marxist parties who wanted to join. These rules subordinated foreign Communist Parties to Moscow's firm hand.

Whatever semblance of independence thereafter remained to foreign Communist Parties was gradually pared down during the 1920s through the exclusion of all those who were critical of the policies of the Communist leaders in Moscow. By 1929 the Comintern did Stalin's bidding as much as the Soviet Communist Party itself. Gradually Stalin was to prefer to work directly with the leaders of foreign Communist Parties without the Comintern operating as an intermediary. The organization was eviscerated in purges of alleged opponents during the 1930s, and in 1943 Stalin had no qualms about dissolving it altogether, as a conciliatory gesture toward his Western allies in the Second World War.

CHEKA AND GULAG: THE BEGINNINGS

Even before the hostilities had begun in earnest in the Civil War, the Bolshevik regime had increasingly turned to violent enforcement of its authority. This use of force fell primarily to the "Extraordinary Commission for Combating Counterrevolution, Speculation, and Sabotage," known by its Russian abbreviation as Cheka. It was founded on 7 December 1917, when it replaced the early enforcers of Communist rule, which had been irregular paramilitary forces such as the Red Guards. While the Red Guards had been made up of workers, soldiers, and sailors who volunteered, the Cheka was instead a professional political police. From the beginning, it took hostages from allegedly class-hostile people, such as tsarist officers, members of the aristocracy, middle-class intellectuals or businessmen, and leaders of other political parties. Those apprehended were often guarded in jails in appalling conditions, although outside of the jails poverty and destitution, malnourishment, and famine were just as much the norm between late 1917 and the summer of 1922. From the outset, the Cheka engaged in executing hostages, too, even if the scale of these operations became massive only when the so-called Red Terror was introduced. The Bolsheviks unleashed this merciless offensive against internal enemies in response to attempts on the lives of Bolshevik leaders, including one on Lenin in August 1918.

As Aleksandr Solzhenitsyn (1918–2008) points out in his *Gulag Archipelago*, almost from the beginning, too, concentration camps were organized for the confinement of those opposing the Bolsheviks. One of the most notorious early camps

Figure 6.4.   The first chief of the Cheka, Feliks Dzerzhinskii, ca. 1920 (Slavic and Baltic Division, New York Public Library, Astor, Lenox, and Tilden Foundations)

was the former monastery complex on the Solovetskii Islands in the White Sea. Conditions there during the 1920s proved nonetheless rather benign in comparison with the brutality of the massive camp complex that arose across the Soviet Union from 1929 onward.

Not just the Cheka terrorized Communist opponents in the Civil War: Bolshevik army commissars ordered Red soldiers to deal mercilessly with opponents. At one point, Stalin, the highest-ranking Bolshevik in 1919 on the southern front, had several dozen captives drowned in the hold of a boat that was sunk in the Volga. And on another occasion, to set an example that would inspire fear in the Communists' enemies, Lenin ordered the shooting of "rich peasants and other counterrevolutionaries" by the hundred. Any admiration for the (often praised) military commander Mikhail Tukhachevskii (1893–1937) should be tempered by the knowledge that he ordered his troops to bomb peasant rebels with mustard-gas grenades in 1921. In the Civil War, however, equally brutal repressions were committed by the Whites. Thus, historians have sometimes excused the Red Terror as a response to extremely trying circumstances. Participants in such civil conflicts tend to fight without much regard for human life.

But some of the brutality seems utterly excessive and gratuitous. For example, Lenin and Trotsky were at a minimum aware of the order to execute the former tsar and his family in the cellar of the house in Ekaterinburg in which they were held in July 1918. A convincing case may be argued that Nicholas and perhaps his meddling wife deserved the death penalty. The argument is rather more difficult to uphold that their children deserved death by firing squad because they might fall into the hands of the Whites and thus become a rallying point around which the Bolshevik opposition could unify. It suggests excessive Bolshevik bloodlust.

The order to liquidate the tsarist family was probably signed by the then official head of state in Soviet Russia, Yakov Sverdlov. Sverdlov was instrumental in organizing the Soviet state after the first months of chaos. He stood at the apex of the network of soviets that formally governed Russia. He died of Spanish influenza in

Figure 6.5.   Aleksei Nikolaevich and Tat'iana Nikolaevna interned after the tsar's abdication, ca. 1917 (Library of Congress)

Figure 6.6.   Yakov Sverdlov in 1919

1919, when he was succeeded by Mikhail Kalinin (1875–1946). Kalinin, a much more peripheral figure than Sverdlov, remained Soviet "president" until his death.

A SHAM DEMOCRACY

The outbreak of civil war in 1918 put paid to experiments toward the immediate realization of a stateless society. War led instead to a hypertrophied bureaucracy that was geared to wage war. Throughout the existence of the Soviet Union, this administration consisted of two parts. A formal government, organized on paper in a genuinely democratic way, existed along a centralized and autocratic Communist Party organization. The party made all the decisions in reality. They were then rubber-stamped by the various (elected) soviets that made up the official government.

In November 1917, Socialist Revolutionaries and Mensheviks left the second All-Union congress of soviets in protest to the Bolshevik coup that had abolished the Provisional Government. The soviet congress, now a rump parliament, officially confirmed Lenin's Council of People's Commissars (Sovnarkom) as the new government. The Sovnarkom included, in fact, even non-Bolsheviks: intermittently, left-wing Socialist Revolutionaries participated in it until July 1918. And the Sovnarkom remained officially the executive branch of the government, formally held accountable by the official legislature, the All-Union congress of soviets. The central executive committee of soviets (from 1936 called the Supreme Soviet), which the congress elected, represented the congress between full sessions. This parliament was quickly turned into a rubber-stamp body, as were the soviets at lower levels.

The Communist Party was pulling the strings and vetted every member of every soviet at every level; indeed, the vast majority of soviet delegates, with the exception of certain rural regions, were trustworthy members of the All-Union Communist Party (which adopted this name in the spring of 1918). The chairman of the central executive committee of soviets (first Sverdlov and then Kalinin) was a merely symbolic head of state. Power was concentrated in the hands of the leader of the party, at first Lenin (who had no official party post except his memberships of its Central Committee and, after its foundation in April 1919, of its Political Bureau, or Politburo) and then, after an uncertain interregnum, by the first or general secretary of the party: Stalin, Nikita Khrushchev (1893–1971), Leonid Brezhnev (1907–1982), Yuri Andropov (1914–1984), Konstantin Chernenko (1911–1985), and Mikhail Gorbachev (b. 1931), respectively.

Since Lenin's establishment of a Bolshevik faction in 1903, the party had been highly centralized and hierarchically organized. Before the 1917 coup, Lenin's authority was hardly challenged, or, if it was, his opponents usually left the Bolshevik faction. But Lenin led the party through the Central Committee (rather than imposing his will on it in dictatorial fashion) and did not always immediately get his wishes granted. This was evident in the lead-up to the October 1917 coup, when Grigorii Zinov'ev (1883–1936) and Lev Kamenev (1883–1936) publicly denounced the Bolshevik plans to take power. Once again, the Central Committee proved divided in March 1918 when it voted on the peace treaty with the Central Powers. And Lenin continued to have to persuade or cajole his fellow leaders on a variety of issues during the Civil War.

Because the Central Committee was faced with a prohibitive workload, the leaders created an official Secretariat to deal with the Central Committee's paperwork, as well as political and organizational bureaus (Politburo and Orgburo) after a party congress in 1919. The division of tasks between the Orgburo and Secretariat was not always clearly defined, but ultimately almost all paperwork that was sent to the Central Committee was handled in the Secretariat's departments. The Secretariat also dealt with personnel matters, propaganda, and with executing, and checking on, decrees emanating from the Politburo. The Politburo meanwhile became the ultimate political authority in Soviet Russia after 1919 (it remained so until 1989). The men (only once did a woman briefly serve on it) who served on it—initially a handful and never more than a dozen—became almost all powerful in the Soviet Union (and, after 1945, in the Soviet Bloc).

In an age that predated the modern use of computers, the tentacles of the Politburo did not reach everywhere across a country that covered one-sixth of the earth's landmass and had never many fewer than two hundred million inhabitants. Nevertheless, the Politburo decided on a remarkable number of issues affecting the USSR. To give a fairly typical idea of its workload and widespread responsibilities, in less than three weeks in the spring of 1937, the Politburo rendered well-nigh two hundred decisions. These involved issues such as the completion of the Volga–Moskva canal (built by political prisoners); the development of the Far Eastern Construction Project in eastern

Siberia (Dalstroi, an industrial-and-mining complex using camp labor); the extension of a research visit by a Soviet engineer to the United States; and the bust that was to be placed on the grave of the agronomist I. V. Michurin (1875–1935).

By the 1930s, many of the Politburo's decisions were in fact no longer handled in official meetings but in written fashion. Usually, decisions were formally rendered after Stalin together with his four or five closest friends had predecided them in his office, Kremlin apartment, or increasingly, at his nearby country house (dacha). Only after Stalin's death was a rule instituted that the Politburo was to meet in the Kremlin every Thursday.

The rulers of the Soviet Union, therefore, can more often than not be identified as the members of the Politburo. Among them, however, some individuals stood out as more powerful than others. For long periods, one person lorded it over all the others, as did Lenin from 1919 to 1922, Stalin from 1929 to 1953, Khrushchev from 1957 to 1964, and Brezhnev from about 1970 to 1982. No one, however, enjoyed anything close to the unbridled power of Stalin in his heyday. He repeatedly had fellow Politburo members (or their wives!) arrested and executed in the 1930s and 1940s, without anyone raising objections. This was a feat only once achieved otherwise, when Lavrentii Beria (1899–1953) was arrested in 1953.

VICTORY IN WAR, RETREAT IN PEACE

The outcome of the Civil War was uncertain until deep into the fall of 1919. Prior to that, various offensives by the White armies nearly vanquished the Communist regime. The Reds barely held on to their control over Central European Russia. Thanks to a great extent to the organizational genius and brutal methods of the People's Commissar of War, Lev Trotsky (who had moved there from foreign affairs in the spring of 1918), the Red Army ultimately emerged victorious. Trotsky masterfully used the railroads to shift troops at the crucial moment, while former tsarist officers commanded his army in a reasonably competent fashion. These officers were accompanied by Communist watchdogs (called "political commissars") and were threatened by reprisals against their family members, whom Trotsky ordered to be held hostage.

In addition, the Reds had something tangible to offer to the inhabitants of the territories they ruled or conquered. It may be doubted that many quite believed or understood Communist promises of equality, freedom, or workers' rule. The Reds did, however, concretely offer land to the peasantry (although not quite in full ownership, but few bothered to explain or understand the difference), who still formed the great majority of the population of the former tsarist empire. The White generals did not match that offer, merely suggesting that they stood for a "Russia One and Undivided." Their slogan seemed to suggest a return to pre-1917 large landownership. The Whites rejected as well any calls for greater local autonomy for non-Russians, to which the Bolsheviks at least paid lip service.

Figure 6.7. Trotsky, Lenin, and Kamenev, ca. 1920 (Slavic and Baltic Division, New York Public Library, Astor, Lenox, and Tilden Foundations)

By the late fall of 1919, the Whites were on the retreat almost everywhere, but the war was prolonged because of the conflict with Poland that raged from April to October 1920. This allowed the Whites to regroup for one final stand. It ended on the Crimea in November 1920, when thousands of Whites escaped overseas to Istanbul in Turkey.

When the fighting was finally over, the former tsarist empire was on its knees. A famine in 1920–1921 (accompanied by epidemics) that followed in the wake of the Civil War may have cost ten million people their lives. It added to the millions of deaths from the First World War, Civil War, and the concomitant Spanish influenza epidemic of 1918–1919. Realizing that in the midst of such human suffering, devastation, and scarcity no socialist society of plenty could be erected, Lenin and his closest comrades postponed some of their goals until a more propitious moment arose. For the time being, they were content with creating a federalized state that had a mixed or quasi-capitalist economy. Nonetheless, politics were to be the exclusive preserve of the Communist Party. Its Tenth Congress in March 1921 decided on Lenin's urging to introduce the New Economic Policy (NEP), which allowed peasants to sell their products for market prices, and small businesses (shops, restaurants, etc.) to reopen. But this retreat from socialism was always meant to be temporary. Whereas it was already obvious that no other parties (left wing or not) would be tolerated, the Tenth Congress even prohibited the formation of dissenting factions *within* the party. Policy suggestions, criticism, grievances, and so on had to be directly submitted to the Politburo via the Secretariat. Any organization of oppositional groups by people at lower levels in the party would be considered sedition and might lead to suspension of party membership or even exclusion from its ranks.

THE SOVIET FEDERATION

Meanwhile, as we already saw, the non-Russian areas that had proved determined enough to resist a return of Russian rule had been grudgingly allowed their independence (Poland, Finland, and the Baltic countries). But several others were brought back to the fold, as happened with Ukraine, the Caucasus, and Central Asia. Nevertheless, in honor of the promise of national self-determination made in November 1917, the territory of the new state was organized to accommodate the expression of national identity among the non-Russian ethnic groups. This underscored that Soviet Russia resembled neither the tsarist "prisonhouse of nations" nor the Western imperialist powers' colonial empires. Granting non-Russian "nations" some of the trimmings of independence, the Soviet Union could posture as a postcolonial power.

In the view of Marxists such as Lenin and Trotsky, nationalism was a transient phenomenon in history. Nationalism emerged during the historical phase of capitalism in which a national bourgeoisie (middle class) controlled the means of production in the economy and was hegemonic in other areas of life (politics and culture). It would disappear once the internationalist proletariat overthrew their capitalist exploiters. Nevertheless, every society needed to pass through this bourgeois stage. Even during the next, socialist, phase, the Communists recognized that some of the "remnants of the past" would linger in people's view of the world, such as religious or nationalist sentiment. But neither was going to survive against the all-powerful truth of internationalist and atheist communism.

Among the senior Communist leaders, one specialist had in November 1917 been designated as People's Commissar to oversee the country's interethnic relations. This man seemed well equipped to deal with the delicate matter of the relationship between the "nationalities." In 1913, he had been the author of one of the few papers that outlined the Bolshevik position on the relationship between Marxism and nationalism in the Russian imperial context. He was a Georgian native by the name of Iosif Vissarionovich Dzugashvili and had spent years in the Bolshevik underground and in tsarist jails. He was better known as Stalin, his revolutionary alias. Apart from his treatise *Marxism and the National Question*, Stalin seemed eminently suited to deal with the hoary issue of nationalism because he had spent his formative years as a revolutionary traveling around the multicultural mosaic that was the Caucasus region. He was familiar with the delicate and combustible coexistence of languages and cultures in this mountain range. It, perhaps, could be seen as a microcosm of multinational character of the Soviet Union in its entirety.

During the first years of Bolshevik rule, Stalin did not have much time to focus on the question of the Communist state's territorial organization. He was involved in a myriad of other tasks, as political commissar on the various fronts in the Civil War (including the war with Poland and the reconquest of the Caucasus) and as party official (he sat on the Politburo from its inception in 1919). But by 1921 the People's Commissar of Nationalities could dedicate far more time to the development of a federal organization for the new Soviet state. In developing an organizational structure for this state, Stalin and the other Bolsheviks were guided by the principle that no nation was to be privileged over the others. All Communist leaders, however, agreed that, no matter how much the formal government was going to be decentralized, the Central Committee and Politburo of the all-Soviet Communist Party were to decide any matter of importance for the constituent republics that were to make up the Soviet federal state.

Despite this consensus, toward the end of Lenin's life in 1922, a quarrel erupted between Stalin and Lenin on the issue of the precise definition of the relationship between the federal and republican governments within the Soviet Union. Lenin was far more worried than Stalin about preserving the appearance of a state of which the units had *voluntarily* united in a federation. And Lenin, in this as in other matters on the eve of his death, was suddenly plagued by worries that his proletarian dictatorship was developing into a dictatorship of a few men in Moscow. These half dozen men laid down the law for hundreds of millions of subjects without being accountable to anyone. This was not what Marx, or Lenin himself for that matter, had had in mind.

To their closest comrades, Lenin's carping about Stalin's overemphasis on centralization in his plans for the federal Soviet state appeared somewhat overanxious hairsplitting. To appease the now deathly ill Lenin, some of Stalin's proposals for a more centralized state were amended to allow a greater measure of local decision-making power, but the difference was more a question of degree than of substance. Education, health care, and culture would be primarily the affair of local government, but the organization of the economy and economic planning, defense, foreign policy, and so on remained the domain of the Sovnarkom. And this body was of course guided by the directions emanating from the Central Committee and Politburo of the Communist Party.

But even in matters of education, health care, or culture, the hypercentralized Communist Party—rather than the official government of the various Soviet republics or autonomous regions—had the last word. Encouragement of national self-expression by the Bolsheviks was thus selective and restrained and, in practice, privileged Russian culture and the Russian language, the language of communication within the Communist Party. But Bolshevik support for a sort of "affirmative action" program in non-Russian territories did nonetheless have some significant long-term consequences. In Ukraine, Belarus, and elsewhere, the introduction of education in the local language and the permission to allow cultural production in the local tongue (from the staging of theater plays to the printing of texts) nurtured a much more defined national identity. Here can be found the roots of the nationalism that has sustained the independent states that succeeded the USSR in 1991.

Certain tragic developments of the (subsequent) Soviet period, however, also galvanized rudimentary nationalist sentiments among the non-Russians, such as the Holomodor (the Ukrainian famine of 1932–1933), or the deportation of Chechens, Ingushetians, and others to Siberia and Kazakhstan at the end of the Second World War. Undeniably crucial, too, was the role played by an exiled diaspora, made up of a first wave of emigrants fleeing the revolution and Civil War and a second wave that escaped during the chaos of the Second World War. These émigrés kept the nationalist flame alive for many of the subject peoples. It was, however, especially Communist cultural and repressive policy that galvanized rudimentary sentiments into a growing sense of nationhood among the non-Russians.

In December 1922, the first congress of the soviets of the Union of Socialist Soviet Republics gathered in Moscow. It ratified the establishment of the USSR, a country with almost 140 million inhabitants.[10] At first it consisted of four republics (Russia, Ukraine, Belarus, and Transcaucasia), a number that was to grow to fifteen after the Second World War. Within these republics, smaller autonomous units were created in areas in which an ethnic group other than the "titular nation" of the republic was in the majority. Slightly more than half of the USSR population considered themselves Russian, with 20 percent Ukrainian; 42 million people belonged to the well-nigh two hundred other nationalities that were identified. The largest ethnic groups among the latter were the 4 million Belarusyn, 3.5 million Uzbeks, 2.5 million Tatars, 2.4 million Jews, and 1.5 million Armenians, Georgians, and Azeris each.

In January 1924 (coinciding with Lenin's death), the USSR adopted a constitution that declared in its preamble how "the States of the world have divided into two camps. . . . Capitalism and . . . Socialism." It also maintained that in the USSR reigned "mutual confidence and peace, national freedom and equality, . . . and the brotherly collaboration of peoples." Equality, fraternity, and liberty, the keywords of the Declaration of the Rights of Man and Citizen of the French revolutionaries in 1789, were thus presented as the fundamental principles guiding the Soviet Union. In reality, however, the Politburo hardly practiced what it preached. Despite its antagonistic view of a world divided between capitalists and socialists, the Soviet Union was recognized by the United Kingdom, China, France, and Italy in 1924 (Germany and Turkey had done so even earlier).

SOVIET WOMEN

Already in the first provisional constitution of Soviet Russia of 1918, women were proclaimed legally equal to men. This principle was upheld in subsequent USSR constitutions (1924, 1936, and 1977). Women therefore enjoyed in theory equal rights and opportunity. In practice, however, in the course of the history of the Soviet

Union, only a few token women reached the highest echelons of the Communist Party, the Soviet government, academe, the economy, or the fields of art and literature. A glass ceiling existed. In professions in which women formed a majority, such as in teaching or among general practitioners of medicine, pay was often remarkably low (factory workers earned considerably more than those professionals). Women, too, were expected to perform heavy physical labor on the farms and in the factories. They were spared military conscription and were usually allowed to retire somewhat earlier (unless they were collective farmers, as we will see). In addition to their full-time employment, women were expected to do most of the child rearing (sometimes taking care of their grandchildren) and the household tasks. Some scholars, therefore, speak of women carrying a triple burden in the USSR.

One unsettling element of Soviet women's life was the manner of birth control practiced throughout most of the Soviet era. Although condoms were not unknown, very few were available in the Soviet Union, as were contraceptive diaphragms and the like (they belonged to the sort of consumer goods given low priority by economic planners). The birthrate in the initial years of Soviet power was still quite high, especially because the Soviet Union was a predominantly rural country. But with urbanization, the birthrate dropped drastically because housing was cramped, and most parents could barely raise two children in the communal apartments (let alone factory barracks) that were their homes. This led to abortion becoming the common method for practicing birth control. Adult women in the Soviet Union thus underwent numerous abortions, often in extremely poorly equipped and staffed hospitals.

In one sense, perhaps, being a woman in the Soviet Union had an advantage: as women seldom occupied positions of leadership in politics, the economy, or society, and served in the armed forces only by exception (even if many women served in the Soviet army in the Second World War), women escaped most of the waves of persecution of alleged political opponents unleashed under Stalin. In the labor camps of the Gulag in the 1930s and 1940s, perhaps only 5 percent of inmates were female, while a similar, comparatively small, proportion of women were executed.

As a final point regarding the status of women in the Soviet Union, it may be telling that the Soviet authorities outlawed male homosexuality in the middle of the 1930s but refrained from doing so in the case of lesbianism. Female homosexuality was apparently not seen as something that might hinder the emergence of the new Soviet woman. This appears reflective of the subordinate role women played in Soviet society. Gay men were far more dangerous, as their presence threatened the exemplary heterosexual masculinity of the Stakhanov worker and Red Army soldier alike.

NOTES

1. The tsar's military advisors soon prevailed on him in suggesting that a partial mobilization (for which no clear plan existed) would lead to chaos.

2. Petrograd had been rebaptized with the more Russian-sounding name in 1914.

3. Communists preferred to address each other with the word "comrade" (*tovarishch*), which sounded more egalitarian than "Mr." or "Mrs." (and was gender neutral).

4. When indicating the Bolshevik or Communist Party from here onward, I will use the uppercase; so, "Communists" with a capital denotes members of the Communist Party rather than adherents in general to the idea of communism.

5. In February 1918, the Soviet government introduced the Gregorian Calendar (New Style) in the Russian Socialist Federated Soviet Republic (RSFSR), replacing the Julian Calendar (Old Style), which had been thirteen days behind the Gregorian Calendar used in the Western world.

6. Despite Karl Marx's contempt for "utopian socialists," he did believe that the endpoint of history would be a sort of paradise on earth. The "utopian socialists" just did not understand how this would come about, in his view.

7. We will return to this in the next chapter.

8. These areas were Petrograd, Moscow and some of the cities that surrounded it, eastern Ukraine, part of the Urals, and some part of western Siberia.

9. Many of the border changes made in the Brest-Litovsk Treaty were adopted by the Allied victors during the Paris peace negotiations in 1919.

10. The United States had a population of approximately 115 million at the time.

FURTHER READING

Translated Primary Sources

Babel, Isaac. *Red Cavalry and Other Stories*. Edited by Efraim Sicher. Translated by David McDuff. New York: Penguin, 2006.

Got'e, Iu. V. *Time of Troubles: The Diary of Iurii Vladimirovich Got'e; Moscow, July 8, 1917 to July 23, 1922*. Translated and edited by Terence Emmons. Princeton, NJ: Princeton University Press, 1988.

Pasternak, Boris. *Doctor Zhivago*. Translated by Richard Pevear and Larissa Volokhonsky. New York: Vintage, 2011.

Steinberg, Mark D., and Vladimir M. Khrustalev. *The Fall of the Romanovs: Political Dreams and Personal Struggles in a Time of Revolution*. Russian documents translated by Elizabeth Tucker. New Haven, CT: Yale University Press, 1997.

Sukhanov, N. N. *The Russian Revolution, 1917: Eyewitness Account*. Edited, abridged, and translated by Joel Carmichael. 2 vols. New York: Harper, 1962.

Trotsky, L. *History of the Russian Revolution*. Translated by Max Eastman. New York: Pathfinder, 1980.

Zamyatin, Yevgeny. *We*. Translated by Mirra Ginsburg. New York: Harper, 2001.

Scholarly Literature

Abraham, Richard. *Alexander Kerensky: The First Love of the Revolution*. New York: Columbia University Press, 1990.

Barnes, Steven A. *Death and Redemption: The Gulag and the Shaping of Soviet Society*. Princeton, NJ: Princeton University Press, 2011.

Dowling, Timothy. *The Brusilov Offensive*. Bloomington: Indiana University Press, 2006.

Edgar, Adrienne. *Tribal Nation: The Making of Soviet Turkmenistan*. Princeton, NJ: Princeton University Press, 2006.

Figes, Orlando. *A People's Tragedy: The Russian Revolution, 1891–1924*. New York: Penguin, 1998.

Getzler, Israel. *Martov: A Political Biography of a Russian Social-Democrat*. Cambridge: Cambridge University Press, 2003.

Healey, Dan. *Homosexual Desire in Revolutionary Russia: The Regulation of Sexual and Gender Dissent*. Chicago: University of Chicago Press, 2001.

Hirsch, Francine. *Empire of Nations: Ethnographic Knowledge and the Making of the Soviet Union*. Ithaca, NY: Cornell University Press, 2005.

Holquist, Peter. *Making War, Forging Revolution: Russia's Continuum of Crisis, 1914–1921*. Cambridge, MA: Harvard University Press, 2002.

Hosking, Geoffrey. *Rulers and Victims: The Russians in the Soviet Union*. Cambridge, MA: Harvard University Press, 2009.

Kenez, Peter. *The Birth of the Propaganda State: Soviet Methods of Mass Mobilization, 1917–1929*. Cambridge: Cambridge University Press, 1985.

Lieven, D. C. B. *Russia and the Origins of the First World War*. Houndsmills, UK: Palgrave Macmillan, 1983.

Lincoln, W. Bruce. *Red Victory: A History of the Russian Civil War, 1918–1921*. New York: Da Capo, 1999.

Lohr, Eric. *Nationalizing the Russian Empire: The Campaign against Enemy Aliens during World War One*. Cambridge, MA: Harvard University Press, 2003.

Martin, Terry. *An Affirmative Action Empire: Nations and Nationalism in the Soviet Union, 1923–1939*. Ithaca, NY: Cornell University Press, 2001.

Mawdsley, Evan. *The Russian Civil War*. New York: Pegasus, 2009.

Menning, Bruce. *Bayonets before Bullets: The Russian Imperial Army, 1861–1914*. Bloomington: Indiana University Press, 2000.

Pereira, Norman. *White Siberia: The Politics of Civil War*. Montreal-Kingston: McGill Queen's University Press, 1996.

Pipes, Richard. *The Russian Revolution*. New York: Vintage, 1991.

———. *Russia under the Bolshevik Regime*. New York: Vintage, 1995.

Rabinowitch, Alexander. *The Bolsheviks Come to Power: The Revolution of 1917 in Petrograd*. Chicago: Haymarket Books, 2009.

———. *The Bolsheviks in Power: The First Year of Bolshevik Rule in Petrograd*. Bloomington: Indiana University Press, 2007.

Radkey, Oliver. *Russia Goes to the Polls: The Election to the All-Russian Constituent Assembly, 1917*. Ithaca, NY: Cornell University Press, 1990.

Reed, John. *Ten Days That Shook the World*. New York: Penguin, 2007.

Robinson, Paul. *The White Russian Army in Exile, 1920–1941*. New York: Oxford University Press, 2002.

Sanborn, Joshua. *Drafting the Russian Nation: Military Conscription, Total War, and Mass Politics*. DeKalb: Northern Illinois University Press, 2011.

Service, Robert. *Lenin: A Biography*. Cambridge, MA: Harvard University Press, 2000.

Smith, Douglas. *Former People: The Final Days of the Russian Aristocracy*. New York: Farrar, Straus and Giroux, 2012.

Smith, Scott B. *Captives of the Revolution: The Socialist-Revolutionaries and the Bolshevik Revolution*. Pittsburgh: University of Pittsburgh Press, 2011.

Solzhenitsyn, Aleksandr. *August 1914*. New York: Farrar, Straus and Giroux, 2000.

———. *November 1916*. New York: Farrar, Straus and Giroux, 2000.

Stites, Richard. *Revolutionary Dreams: Utopian Vision and Experimental Life in the Russian Revolution*. New York: Oxford University Press, 1991.

Stockdale, Melissa K. *Paul Miliukov and the Quest for a Liberal Russia*. Ithaca, NY: Cornell University Press, 1996.

Volkogonov, Dmitri. *Lenin: A New Biography*. New York: Free Press, 1994.

White, Elizabeth. *The Socialist Alternative to Bolshevik Russia: The Socialist-Revolutionary Party, 1921–1939*. New York: Routledge, 2010.

Wildman, Alan. *The End of the Russian Imperial Army*. 2 vols. Princeton, NJ: Princeton University Press, 1979, 1987.

Wood, Elizabeth. *The Baba and the Comrade: Gender and Politics in Revolutionary Russia*. Bloomington: Indiana University Press, 2000.

WEBSITE

Seventeen Moments in Soviet History (much more than that!): http://www.soviethistory.org/

FILMS

Agony: The Life and Death of Rasputin. DVD. Directed by Elem Klimov. New York: Kino, 2005.

Mother. DVD. Directed by Gleb Panfilov. Netherlands: Homescreen, 2009.

October. DVD. Directed by Sergei Eisenstein. Chatsworth, CA: Image Entertainment, 1998.

Strike. DVD. Directed by Sergei Eisenstein. Berlin: Kino International, 2011.

Tsar to Lenin. DVD documentary. Directed by Herman Axelbank. Oak Park, MI: Mehring Books, 2012.

7

The Inevitable Triumph
of Stalinism? 1924–1941

Even before Lenin's death in 1924, when he lay ailing in his dacha (from late 1922 onward), a struggle developed between his lieutenants about his succession. By the late 1920s, it was evident that Stalin had outfoxed his rivals. Once he was the uncontested boss, Stalin unleashed a political program that had as its goal the establishment of a socialist society in the Soviet Union. As a consequence, the Soviet Union was much more of an industrialized country toward 1940, but this was virtually the only achievement of Stalin's "Great Turn." This success came at an appalling price, causing extreme hardship in the countryside and in the towns. Millions died during the 1930s. Whereas the Soviet Union's ultimate victory over the Nazis in the Second World War may be attributed to the industrial plant built up during the first Five Year Plans, the Soviet military performance was crippled by Stalin's purges and misreading of Hitler's intentions, almost leading to a Soviet defeat. Much of the backbreaking work performed by Soviet citizens to transform their country into an industrialized society was thus wasted. It is a virtual certainty that any of Stalin's rivals of the 1920s would have done better if they had succeeded Lenin. But it is moot how much more humane they would have been, since all had adopted a ruthless style of rule during the revolution and civil war.

LENIN AND STALIN

Lenin's imprint on the twentieth century was deep, but his time at the helm of the Soviet Union was short. His health had already begun to deteriorate in late 1921. This was partially the result of the strain of the previous five years of intense activity, but his father, too, had died in his early fifties, exhibiting the same symptoms to which his son was to succumb. In May 1922, Lenin suffered the first of a series of strokes. By October he had recovered, but in December of that year he suffered another brain hemorrhage that partially paralyzed him. After this, he no longer took any active part in the government. He lay ill in his Kremlin apartment for several months until a new stroke in March 1923 robbed him of his speech altogether. He was then transferred to his country estate near Moscow, where he died in January 1924.

Even if he did not rise from his sickbed after the second stroke, Lenin did compose, with the help of a few secretaries and his wife Nadezhda Krupskaia (1869–1939), a series of papers that conveyed his final thoughts about several developments in his country that had begun to worry him in the course of 1922. He also reflected on the qualities of the leading personalities with whom he had worked in the Communist Party and Sovnarkom in recent years. Because of Lenin's illness and death, Lenin's notes were only conveyed to the Thirteenth Party Congress of May 1924.[1] Long after, around the time of the collapse of the Soviet Union, it became evident that Lenin had asked Lev Trotsky to succeed him as Soviet leader. Trotsky himself, however, rejected the offer, since he believed that the Soviet population would not accept a Jew as its leader. He implied that the Slavic population in particular had been conditioned by a long history of anti-Semitism. But Trotsky does not seem to have suggested an alternative successor to Lenin.

Lenin dictated in the fall of 1922 a few observations about the six men whom he thought would play leading roles in the Soviet leadership after his death. People's Commissar of War Trotsky, obviously, was among them. Lenin thought the Soviet "Organizer of Victory" brilliant but deemed him to be unduly fond of coercive methods.[2] In addition, Lenin implied that as a late arrival to the party, Trotsky was too much of a free spirit, insufficiently trained in seeing the world in Bolshevik terms and reluctant to submit to Bolshevik discipline when he disagreed with the majority.[3] Politburo members Grigorii Zinov'ev, the Leningrad party chief and Comintern head, and Lev Kamenev, Lenin's deputy as Sovnarkom chairman and Moscow party boss, were accused of lacking stamina and determination, as they had shown in October–November 1917, when they had publicly protested the plans for a Bolshevik coup. By this, Lenin meant that this duo harbored certain moral scruples and showed possible signs of cowardice, qualities that would hinder a Communist leader in exerting power. The young (alternate) Politburo member Nikolai Bukharin (1888–1838) was a charming fellow, Lenin admitted, but he went on to argue that Bukharin's reputation as a leading Marxist theorist was undeserved because he did not really understand Marxist dialectics. Central Committee member Yuri Piatakov (1890–1937) was another young prodigy whom Lenin deemed talented enough to be considered as a potential Soviet leader; he, too, was not quite the ideal Bolshevik boss, since he lost himself too much in paperwork and lost track of the big picture.[4]

Finally, then, Lenin recognized in this "Testament" Stalin as the most outstanding leader next to Trotsky. Lenin praised the talent Stalin exhibited as a chief but suggested that he occupied too many posts in the party and government. Most problematic was his new role as general secretary of the party, which he had become at the Eleventh Party Congress in 1922. This position, Lenin implied, might offer too much opportunity for manipulation and intrigue. And Lenin was also concerned about Stalin and Trotsky's strong mutual dislike, since they were the senior chiefs in his absence.[5] Lenin seemed to conclude, nevertheless, that, for the moment, the ship of state could be steered by this sextet despite their disagreements and former quarrels.

Ten days later, however, Lenin wrote a postscript that was to become famous because of its prophetic quality (even if it was suppressed in the Soviet Union after Stalin's autocracy was firmly established):

> Stalin is too rude and this defect, although quite tolerable in our midst and in dealings among us Communists, becomes intolerable in a Secretary-General. That is why I suggest the comrades think about a way of removing Stalin from this post and appointing another man in his stead, who . . . differs from Comrade Stalin in . . . being more tolerant, more loyal, more polite, and more considerate to the comrades, less capricious, etc. This circumstance may appear to be a negligible detail. But I think that as precaution against a split, and considering what I wrote previously about the relationship between Stalin and Trotsky, it is not a detail, or it is a detail which can assume decisive importance.

Apparently, Lenin's change of heart (or his sudden alarm) about Stalin had been brought about by a falling-out between Stalin and Lenin's wife Nadezhda Krupskaia. In 1922, the Politburo had appointed Stalin as the sick Lenin's guardian. The Politburo had ordered that the excitable Lenin should not be disturbed by affairs of state to avoid having his condition deteriorate. When Stalin found out in December that Lenin was still being informed about politics, he proceeded to blame Lenin's wife over the phone for this trespass and used some choice words in rebuking her. Lenin, son of a nineteenth-century landowning aristocrat, adhered to an honor-and-behavioral code perhaps poorly suited to the crude twentieth century. In contrast, Stalin, son of a cobbler, proved to have a coarseness offensive to aristocratic sensibilities but necessary to survive and thrive in that cruel age. Lenin was aghast with Stalin's rudeness and suddenly recognized in Stalin fatal character flaws. But he became utterly powerless when, not long after dictating his "Testament," he suffered another stroke.

Even before Lenin died, Stalin had become the most important leader of the Communist Party, to a significant degree because as general secretary he could manipulate the appointment system (called *nomenklatura* in Russian) used by the party through the Central Committee's Secretariat. Candidates for the several thousand senior positions in the country's party and state apparatus were vetted by department heads in the Secretariat and the secretaries who oversaw them, among whom the general secretary was the final arbiter. Unassuming and hardworking, Stalin proved an outstanding patron of a variety of clients who were dependent on him for their political careers by his skillful use of this system. Stalin selected and cultivated the party's elite so ably that by 1929 he became the unchallenged leader of the Soviet Union.

His rivals, who were wont to believe that they were locked in an ideological struggle with Stalin for Lenin's succession, wrote essays and books and gave speeches in
which they decried Stalin's political ideas. The general secretary's manipulation of the
nomenklatura system, however, was far more than any political argument responsible
for his emergence as a one-man ruler. Despite Lenin's warnings in his "Testament,"
none of the other ranking leaders seems to have understood after 1922 that the post
of general secretary of the party was the key to power.

If ideas had truly mattered, the party faithful might have asked why Stalin first had
condemned Trotsky (in 1923–1924) and Zinov'ev and Kamenev (in 1924–1925) for
their "leftist" ideas, only to adopt several of those very ideas in advocating rapid industrialization and collectivization of agriculture in 1928–1929. And few questioned
why he condemned in 1928–1929 his former ally Bukharin for his "rightist devia-
tion" of defending the New Economic Policy (NEP). After all, Stalin had wholeheartedly sponsored the NEP before 1928 against Trotsky, Zinov'ev, and Kamenev.

Rather than attacking Stalin for such inconsistencies, the delegates at party congresses of the 1920s and the members of the Central Committee at their meetings
successively attacked Trotsky (as well as Piatakov), Zinov'ev and Kamenev, and
Bukharin and his allies, Sovnarkom chairman Aleksei Rykov (1881–1938) and
trade union boss Mikhail Tomskii (1880–1936). Stalin's deft use of the *nomenklatura* system is evident. Local party organizations delegated their leaders to party
congresses, but Stalin and his assistants in the Secretariat had vetted these local
chiefs before appointing them to lead these party branches. Few questioned the
bosses that Moscow had dispatched to lead them, partially because such criticism
might be considered the factionalism prohibited by the Tenth Party Congress of
1921. At the congresses of the 1920s, these delegates elected a Central Committee of like-minded people who equally benefited from their support for Stalin and
basked in his benevolence.

Stalin's most loyal and influential cronies of the 1920s still boasted of having been
personally acquainted with Lenin, but those who joined his inner circle after 1930
were upstarts who had played no significant role in the revolution or Civil War.
Conveniently, the second group had not witnessed Stalin's quarrels with Lenin and
thus did not suspect their "Boss" (as he became known) of ever being anything less
than Lenin's best pupil. Most important among the first group were the Central
Committee secretaries Viacheslav Molotov and Lazar Kaganovich (1893–1991); the
Transcaucasian chief and All-Union economic boss Grigorii (Sergo) Ordzhonikidze
(1886–1937); the Leningrad party boss Sergei Kirov (1886–1934); and the People's
Commissar of Defense Kliment Voroshilov (1881–1969). Among the second group
were the security police chief and Central Committee secretary Nikolai Yezhov
(1895–1940); his successor Lavrentii Beria (1899–1953; chief of the Transcaucasian
region in the first half of the 1930s); the Central Committee secretary and Leningrad boss Andrei Zhdanov (1896–1948); the Ukrainian and subsequently Moscow
party chief Nikita Khrushchev (1894–1971); and the Central Committee secretary
Georgii Malenkov (1900–1988).

THE 1920s INTERMEZZO AND THE GREAT TURN

While the supreme leaders of the Soviet Union were wrangling about Lenin's mantle, the country enjoyed several years of comparative tranquility. This allowed the population to recover from the devastation of war, revolution, and civil war. After the worst effects of the famine were overcome in the course of 1922, agriculture recovered fairly swiftly. Industrial production lagged behind, but it, too, began to reach pre-1914 levels by the late 1920s. Foreign countries began to accept the existence of a "Red Russia," and no genuine threat of war loomed. But it was difficult to find foreign credit. In 1918, Lenin and his comrades had renounced the foreign debt contracted by the tsarist government and had defaulted on any payment of foreign- or domestic-owned bonds after nationalizing the banks. So few investors trusted the Soviet government with their money, except such daredevil entrepreneurs as the American businessman Armand Hammer (1898–1990). Without foreign credit, it was difficult to pay for modern machinery that could be used in Soviet factories and mines. Some relief was found in selling off the tsarist gold reserves on the international market, or parts of the art collections and jewelry owned by the former aristocracy or house of Romanov, but such sources were not inexhaustible.

In the second half of the 1920s, the Soviet leaders decided to lower the prices they paid to the peasants on agricultural products, especially grain. This lowered the cost of living for blue-collar workers and thus increased real wages without pay raises. It further permitted the regime to sell grain on the international market with a greater profit margin and thus generate revenue to pay for the importation of foreign-made technology. This was not unlike the tsarist finance ministers' policies of the 1890s. But the peasants responded in 1927 and 1928 by hoarding their grain, awaiting higher prices. The Soviet authorities in their turn fell back on forced grain requisitioning. As in the Civil War, armed detachments of Red Army soldiers, party and government workers, and secret-police officials visited the villages, where they forced peasants to give up their grain. This policy, however, had not worked in the longer term in the Civil War, for peasants eventually shut down production altogether or turned to armed resistance.

Therefore, in the course of 1928, and with ever greater conviction in 1929, Stalin and his followers decided that the time had come for a radical policy switch. First a Five-Year Plan of economic development was drafted by the State Planning Bureau (Gosplan). In 1929, the plan was retroactively announced to have started on 1 September 1928. Its production targets and construction plans were continuously increased in the course of 1929, until they aimed at economic growth levels that were unprecedented in human history. Indeed, when in late 1932 the plan was declared to have been fulfilled in four years (and a few months), in reality almost none of the goals had been met.

Twice during the unfolding of the plan, Stalin went on record to explain the epochal importance of the plan to the Soviet citizens and the world. In December 1929, he noted in the national newspaper *Pravda* how the Soviet Union had embarked on "the Great Turn of socialist construction." He further explained to a meeting of Soviet engineers in February 1931 that the Soviet Union was "fifty or a hundred years behind the advanced countries. We must overcome this backwardness in ten years. Either we do it, or they will crush us."

The theory indeed had an elementary logic to it. Here was the only Communist country in the world, surrounded by capitalist foes who could not but wish for its destruction. How could capitalists tolerate the existence of a country that was run by the people they exploited elsewhere across the globe? The Soviet Union could survive only by developing rapidly into a country that had reached the same degree of industrialization as the leading capitalist states. Only then could it afford an army that could defend its border (or aid Communists who tried to take power elsewhere). And only by industrializing quickly could the Soviet Union point the way to the radiant future of a communist horn of plenty.

There was a great deal of enthusiasm in 1929 for the project, and many people proved willing to work tirelessly and for virtually no reward to lay the basis for the promised society of plenty. Urban young men and women in the boomtowns and cities identified with the proletarian cause, and many rural youth flocked from the countryside to the cities to build socialism. Fortified by their idealism, they selflessly toiled, surviving on badly prepared food in large canteens and meager supplies to which ration cards entitled them, sleeping on bunk beds in poorly heated army-style barracks, and working endless shifts constructing new plants, at textile looms, digging ore in mines, and so on. But the population of the Soviet Union did not quite become a harmonious commune of worker bees willing to sacrifice their health and well-being for the good of the cause indefinitely.

BOLSHEVIK FARMING

Far from everyone was convinced that such a paradise on earth was in the offing, given sufficient effort and planning. In the first place, a generational gap made many urban citizens in their thirties and older far less keen on the Great Turn than the young. The lives of those who vividly remembered the catastrophe that began in 1914 and ended in 1922 had been hard enough. In their experience, radical change had not always been for the better. But far greater than the doubts about the transformation in the cities was the general reluctance in the Soviet countryside about the transformation of agricultural production. And whereas party activists managed sometimes in Russian-speaking rural communities to drum up a degree of enthusiasm for the cause of collectivization, in non-Russian areas party activists were hard to find in the countryside before 1930.

This rural skepsis was of great significance, for the great majority of the Soviet population (around 120 million people out of 155 million) lived in villages. In some parts of the Russian countryside, people seem to have been at least willing to entertain the concept of collective farms because individual farms had traditionally

Figure 7.1. A newly finished collective-farm hut, 1930s (Library of Congress)

hardly yielded a profit there. As we saw, in order to make ends meet in north and central Russia, many peasants departed the villages to work as itinerant artisans or, in the winter, as seasonal workers in towns where such work was in demand. In addition, in most parts of the Soviet Union some farming jobs had been undertaken collectively from time immemorial; in theory, villagers were therefore not averse to working as a team. For example, climatic circumstances made harvest time exceedingly brief in central and northern Russia, where rye, potatoes, and flax were grown. The whole village together hauled in everyone's crops in a matter of days. Combining one's efforts in these regions was further sensible because their soil was poor, too. Few efforts to improve soil quality had been made in the tsarist era or 1920s because peasants could not afford such improvements on their own, or did not know about them. Even animal manure was in short supply, as most peasants had at best one dairy cow. Because of its high cost, peasants by themselves could not easily purchase mechanized agricultural equipment, and in central and northern Russia as much as elsewhere, horses provided the main draft power for plowing or transport.

But in other parts of the country, agricultural production might yield more than just a basic livelihood to a family, sometimes because of better soil and climatic conditions, and sometimes because production had specialized in the exclusive cultivation of one crop, in dairy cattle, or in meat production. By the eve of the First World War, tsarist Russia had become a substantial exporter of grain. This surplus originated mainly in the Black Earth zone in the borderlands of Russia and Ukraine south of Moscow. While some of these regions were lost to Poland in the Russian-Polish peace treaty of Riga in 1921, Ukrainian farms in particular remained capable of growing a considerable surplus. But the Ukrainians were far less in the habit of working their lands collectively than those tilling poorer soils.

Collective or communal farms were not entirely new to the Soviet Union in 1928 or 1929. Various socialist thinkers had vaguely written about them. Most of the experimental collectives founded before 1929 had failed, however. Any profound understanding of farming was uncommon among Bolsheviks, or, for that matter, other Marxists, who believed that the solution to the world's problems was to be found in the cities. Indeed, at one point during the preparation for the grandiose changes in the countryside, a leading party boss, Andrei Andreev (1895–1971), who had been assigned a key agricultural portfolio, admitted in a Central Committee meeting that he knew little about farming. His comrade Ordzhonikidze put Andreev at ease by assuring him that none of the other leaders knew much about farming.

Agricultural cooperatives had existed in prerevolutionary Russia and existed during the 1920s. Often, peasants had teamed up to sell their products. This was more efficient than selling them individually. They also joined up to purchase expensive equipment that was to be shared by several households. The Communists interpreted such collaboration as promising signs of the alignment of Marxist theory with economic practice; such cooperation suggested to them that the way of the future was the replacement by individual farmsteads with collective ones.

The collective farm envisioned by the Communists was a type of farm that was a supposedly more comprehensive version of an agricultural cooperative. The combined effort of the peasants on the collective farm (kolkhoz) would lead to a more efficient production and a greater surplus, which state-procurement agencies would collect and ship to the towns. Some of this anticipated surplus would then be sold on the international market. Its proceeds would be used to buy sophisticated foreign technology for Soviet industry.

In addition, the Soviet leaders applied a sort of Marxist class analysis to the countryside. Exactly why Stalin and his ilk believed this to be so crucial is not clear. The Boss himself had inspected the halting grain deliveries in Siberia in early 1928 and may have locked on to complaints about more affluent villagers employing their neighbors as hired hands. He may have concluded that these "capitalists" were in the process of marginalizing the poorer peasants.

In 1928–1929, the party identified these rich peasants as kulaks, a term that had stood for greedy and exploitative farmers before 1917. These prerevolutionary kulaks had the reputation of squeezing out their fellow peasants by any means available, including strong-arm tactics and violence. Perhaps that was why they had acquired the moniker, which literally meant "fist." But such early capitalist farmers had been expropriated and chased from the villages in 1917–1918. The so-called kulak of the 1920s was usually barely better off than his neighbors. He might have been lucky in having several able-bodied sons, whereas his neighbor had no children and had to provide for his enfeebled parents. With the help of such a comparative abundance of labor, the rich peasants were able to market more crops and cattle products than their neighbors. Sometimes, the 1920s Soviet "kulak" owned two horses rather than the usual single nag owned by most peasants. Some peasants had little or no land and could not survive other than by hiring themselves out to richer peasants. Rather than capitalist exploitation, such labor relations amounted to symbiotic mutual support between the slightly richer and the slightly poorer.

COLLECTIVIZATION AND DEKULAKIZATION

The gap between rich and poor was thus much greater in the party's imagination than in the daily experience of the Soviet peasantry. Barely perceptible, the differentiation between rich and poor in the villages was nevertheless the basis for the Marxist class analysis applied by the Communists. Stalin and his followers argued that kulaks were capitalists, who exploited a rural proletariat of poor peasants and landless laborers. Between these two groups existed a fairly large group of middle peasants who could just make ends meet on their own because they wielded enough (albeit not abundant) land, equipment, and animals. This middling group was allegedly in danger of becoming proletarianized, since it would not be able to survive against kulak competition, according to Communist logic. The undeniable truth of the party's Marxist analysis would help the middle peasants recognize that their interests lay with the poor peasants and that collectivization was to their benefit.

The Communists began in the course of 1929 to encourage a solution to the supposed class conflict in the villages between kulak capitalists and poor and middling peasants: the "liquidation of the kulaks as a class" accompanied the organization of the collective farms. Party and soviet activists, Red Army detachments, and state security officers "helped" or "encouraged" villagers to force kulak households to give up all their property. The collective farms became the new owners of houses, barns, horses, plows, and so on. Kulak families were exiled to remote areas, sometimes in their own province, but more often far away. So-called special settlements were designated by the Soviet regime in 1929 and 1930, to which during the First Five Year Plan perhaps five million people who had been driven from their ancestral homes were exiled. The victims were transported in railroad boxcars and dropped in the most inhospitable areas of northern Russia or Siberia in the middle of winter. Mortality rates were staggering. The Communist authorities used a quota system (imposed from above) to ensure that sufficient kulaks were apprehended and banished. About 5 percent of villagers were thus dispatched. If kulak numbers fell short, people could be arrested as "kulak helpers" to make up the quota. Priests were usually singled out as such.

"Dekulakization" provided collective farms with the buildings, equipment, animals, and land of their unfortunate exiled neighbors. But such proceeds were meager and far from a sufficient basis for the creation of a modern collective farm. The sudden decision to complete the collectivization of all peasant households as soon as possible in the fall and early winter of 1929–1930 complicated matters further. Most peasants slaughtered their horses (and sometimes oxen) during these months, for many were unwilling to surrender their animals to the "socialization" process. Others appear to have believed that the state would provide them with the necessary draft animals and machinery for their farm's socialized sector before spring sowing. By March, draft power on the farms had dropped drastically: only in the 1950s would Soviet farms once again have as many horses as in 1928. And very few harvest combines or tractors appeared at first in the villages.

Rather than taking any personal blame for the chaos, in a *Pravda* editorial of March 1930 Stalin personally criticized overzealous activists for being "Dizzy with Success" in collectivizing the peasants. He suggested that these zealots had violated the "voluntary principle" that was supposed to be the premise of joining the kolkhoz. At first, many peasants left the collective farms after Stalin's criticism, but most soon concluded that they had no alternative but to return. Survival on an individually run farmstead, bereft of draft power and faced with far higher taxation in kind than the kolkhoz, was made virtually impossible. By 1932 the vast majority of Soviet peasants farmed on the kolkhoz.

Meanwhile, few knew how to organize an efficient collective farm. Peasants had not been schooled in drawing up plowing, sowing, and harvesting plans, in soil amelioration, or in ways to improve yields from dairy or meat cattle. Some relief was intended to be offered by regional machine-tractor stations (MTS). These stations housed mechanized equipment (tractors, harvest combines, etc.) and their operators, and rented out their equipment and technological expertise to the kolkhoz (against payment in kind or money). But besides its woefully insufficient stock of tools, machinery was produced in factories according to uniform standards that hardly took into account local circumstances. Machines easily broke down, and usually MTS mechanics hardly knew how to repair or adjust the equipment.

Socialized cattle herds were often neglected at the expense of the one private dairy cow that most households were allowed to keep by law. Collective farmers (kolkhozniks) often gave it no more than a token effort when working in the socialized sector of crop cultivation or animal husbandry. Peasants preferred spending time on the small private plots on which they could grow crops (private cultivation of grain was usually prohibited) for their own consumption. Sometimes the yields of these plots were good enough to sell some surplus crops or milk in nearby town markets.[6]

Kolkhozniks were supposed to work a set amount of hours in the socialized sector of the farms. A record of these hours was kept by their foremen or forewomen[7] (called brigadiers) and the collective farm director and bookkeeper. At the end of the fiscal year (usually in the early months of the calendar year), the farmers received remuneration for the total amount of "workdays" they had earned in the socialist sector of their farm. This wage was partially paid out in kind, from the farm's production, and partially in money, from the miserly payments made by state procurement agencies for delivered products (and after the kolkhoz had remitted a variety of dues, such as to the MTS for their services). If planned production targets were not met (and grain deliveries to the agencies thus fell short), no money was paid by those agencies. Even in good times under Stalin, collective farmers made less than two hundred rubles per year, which amounted to a quarter of the monetary income of a textile worker in the city. The private plot and private cow came to the kolkhozniks' rescue, but even they proved sometimes insufficient (and many peasant households had no private cow before the early 1950s). Deprivation and malnourishment were the lot of many.

FAMINE

This pattern showed of course great regional variation, for the climate, soil, and the agricultural traditions across the former tsarist empire remained vastly different. Traditionally the population of what is Kazakhstan today had survived primarily by way of transhumance, that is, they lived as nomads, moving their cattle between summer and winter grazing grounds. Such a way of life did not suit the modern mind-set of the Soviet regime. It preferred to have its subjects reside in the same place, so it could count and control them. The Kazakhs were thus forced to give up their itinerant cattle driving. They slaughtered some of their herds around 1930, while many of the other animals starved, after exhausting the local grazing lands to which their herders were now consigned. Knowing little to nothing about crop cultivation, for which their arid steppe lands were rather poor to begin with, the Kazakhs had no substitute for cattle farming. By 1933, probably one-quarter of the Kazakh population (one million people) had died as a result.

In 1932–1933, another famine raged in Ukraine and southern Russia. Crop yields fell to exceedingly low levels because of a misharvest in 1932. This did not stop the Soviet authorities to demand crop deliveries that were not much lower than in previous years. To collect as much grain as possible, the goverment introduced draconian laws in August 1932 against the "theft of socialist property." They introduced mandatory sentencing to ten years in labor camp of people who gleaned grain left behind on the fields after harvest. In December 1932, internal passports were introduced; these were issued only to inhabitants of the Soviet Union who were not engaged in agricultural work. Kolkhoz members could thereafter leave their villages only after receiving from the local authorities special permits to depart. They remained without passports until 1977. A second serfdom had descended on the Soviet countryside.

When planning targets were not met in the fall of 1932, grain-requisition units once more appeared in the villages. They sometimes stripped peasant households of the last foodstuffs they had, accusing the peasants of hoarding and sabotage. Perhaps four million people died, most of them in Ukraine. Stalin did not order ruthless treatment of the Ukrainians primarily because he suspected them of harboring anti-Russian sentiments. After all, similar treatment was meted out to Russian peasants living immediately to the north of the Caucasus. But the cruel action against the Ukrainian peasants was at least partially inspired by a desire to browbeat the Ukrainians about their alleged anti-Soviet (anti-Russian) sentiments and stubborn independent spirit.

At one of their meetings in Moscow during the Second World War, Stalin apparently astonished British prime minister Winston Churchill (1874–1965) in stating that the early days of the German attack on the USSR were not the worst crisis of his political career: the days of collectivization had been far worse, for then ten million people had died. Stalin did not exaggerate this number. Meanwhile, no serious threat to overthrow him between 1928 and 1934 seems to have materialized.

It is moot whether Stalin and his cronies actually believed that they were creating a socialist kind of agriculture with their crude and callous methods. Cynics might say that the hidden agenda behind collectivization and dekulakization was instead different: the Bolsheviks had followed Marx in mainly showing contempt for the peasants (Marx had in 1848 written of the "idiocy of rural life"). They believed in the superiority of a modern urban culture and set about in 1929 to modernize their country at breakneck speed at virtually any cost in human terms. They needed cheap food for the burgeoning urban working class and goods that could be exported to buy scarce technology abroad. Stalin was apparently fond of the Russian saying "When wood is chopped, chips fly," a version of "You cannot make an omelet without breaking eggs." Even more than in Lenin's case, for Stalin the socialist end justified any means. That socialist modernity was to be accomplished over the dead bodies of some bumpkins should be of no great concern in Stalin's view, which took into account the greater scheme of human progress.

INDUSTRIALIZATION

One can make a compelling case that the Soviet Union could have industrialized as well as, or even better than it did, without the astonishing sacrifice made by the peasantry. During the Five Year Plans (even if the targets set for the first plan were not met, as even official Soviet numbers showed), quantity often came before quality in measuring results in industry. As a result, "Stalinist" industrialization was extremely wasteful.[8] Far too many projects were begun at the same time, spreading investments and resources thin. Engineering expertise was in short supply as well. In many of the regions designated as prime centers of industrialization, factory buildings had been erected by 1933. The production of industrially manufactured goods had often barely begun, however, because crucial components of machinery were missing. Such was the case with the Molotov automobile works in the city of Nizhnii Novgorod. There the first cars (which were based on blueprints provided by Ford Motor Company) rolled out of the factory gates more than three years after the first spade went into the ground. A better husbanding of available means might have allowed for a much less tyrannical treatment of the peasants who furnished the food and funds for this crazed industrialization drive.

But the process set in motion in 1929 irreversibly set the Soviet Union on the path to a modern, primarily urban society. During the First Five Year Plan, the working class probably doubled in number, even if the urban proletariat still represented only about a third of the total Soviet workforce by 1932. And the demand for labor was high, as many enterprises were built from the ground up, often largely by hand. Therefore, unemployment, which reached disastrous proportions in the West as a result of the Great Depression at this time, did not exist in the Soviet Union. Naturally, the Soviet leadership trumpeted this allegedly great accomplishment to audiences at home and abroad.

As we saw above, living conditions in the rapidly expanding towns were dire, but it appeared as if in certain parts of urban life a glimpse of the future society of plenty could be had. Public transport and health care were free, even if the quality of both left much to be desired. Factories and mines established day cares for (tellingly) female workers, even if many preferred to leave the care of their offspring to a grandmother. Education was free until the seventh grade, and for talented pupils, scholarships paid for further schooling. Indeed, in 1929 compulsory education for a minimum of four years became mandatory for all children, while in the cities virtually all children attended school for at least seven years. Workers' clubs organized amateur theater performances and film showings, and in most cities urban workers had a choice of drama theaters and concert halls at nominal prices. Libraries mushroomed. Books, newspapers, and magazines were available at very low costs, and sometimes for free, as were newspapers exhibited on the walls of factories.

CULTURE AND RELIGION

Historians, foremost among whom has been Sheila Fitzpatrick, have therefore argued that the Soviet population, at least in the cities, was in the throes of a cultural revolution in the years of the Great Turn (1929–1933 or even 1929–1939). A Soviet version of modern man was forged in this radical upheaval. Whereas the Soviet regime made a variety of cultural amenities available to their subjects, it also actively suppressed cultural manifestations with which it disagreed. Books, theater plays, films, and so on were censored. Eventually, most art was judged according to a rigidly defined aesthetic called socialist realism. In fiction, in a usually linear narrative, protagonists made their appearance as positive and optimistic builders of socialism. These model socialists defied and defeated the leftover specimens of depraved capitalism (and their foreign puppet masters).

Equally important was a full-fledged assault on organized religion, especially on Eastern Slav Orthodoxy and other forms of Christianity. Religion was for the Communists "the opium of the people," as Marx had called it. It diverted people from understanding their true interest, which was building a good life for everyone in the here and now. Lenin had already begun the attack on the Orthodox Church. At first, the Bolsheviks strictly separated church and state. Then they deprived the Orthodox Church and other religions of all their privileges in 1918 and eventually confiscated the wealth of many religious institutions. In the famine of 1921–1922, silver and gold ornaments, precious icons, and so on were sold abroad in exchange for food.

Priests and other religious officials who protested against this "socialist expropriation" were either summarily executed or dispatched to the first labor camps.

In 1929, the antireligious offensive resumed with new force. In most villages, churches were closed (and often converted into storage barns or the administrative and cultural centers of the kolkhoz) and priests arrested as "kulak helpers." Most monasteries and convents were closed as well, and their occupants were likewise dispatched to camps. Atheism (often entailing the diffusion of scientific ideas about nature and evolution) was heavily propagated by organizations such as the Society for Militant Atheists. By the late 1930s, only four Orthodox bishops remained at liberty.

This recurring antireligious offensive did not remain without effect: by the 1960s few denizens of the European part of the USSR considered themselves Christians, although it is hard to gauge how many preferred to profess atheism publicly while secretly worshipping as Christians. Western visitors to the Soviet Union in those days usually encountered empty churches, in which only a few elderly women seemed to pray. But churchgoing continued to be actively discouraged in the 1960s and 1970s as well, and throughout Soviet history one's career was jeopardized if one was identified as a religious believer.

What applies to Orthodoxy applies even more strongly to Judaism, Catholicism, or Lutheranism. In the case of Judaism, it should be remembered that the majority of Soviet Jews resided before the Second World War in territories that fell under Nazi occupation after 22 June 1941. Virtually only those Jewish men who served in the Red Army and evaded German capture survived the Holocaust. Synagogues were not rebuilt after the Soviet army drove out the occupiers from areas previously inhabited by Jews. In those territories that escaped Nazi occupation, only a handful of Jewish temples remained open after the Second World War. In contrast, after the war the Soviet Union harbored a fair amount of Catholics and Lutherans who resided in its newly acquired western regions (western Ukraine and the Baltic republics). Religious persecution along the lines of the oppression of the Orthodox Church became common there, even if believers held on to their faith with somewhat greater tenacity than in Russia or Ukraine.

Soviet authorities were more circumspect with Islam, or perhaps somewhat less strenuous in their efforts to destroy this religion. This was more out of necessity than out of choice. Communism never quite gained the same sort of intensively fanatical support in predominantly Muslim regions that it acquired among residents of culturally "European" or Christian regions. Mosques were closed at times as often as churches, but it was evident that many Muslims managed to remain loyal to their faith. They adhered in private to certain crucial rituals behind a loyal and even atheist exterior. Stalin had been familiar with Islam since his childhood and had witnessed its powerful hold in the Caucasus, a fact that perhaps explains a certain roundabout way in his efforts toward its eradication. At the same time, the predominantly Islamic areas of the Soviet Union were usually far more rural than non-Islamic territories, and in the countryside of European Russia, too, Christianity proved more resilient than in the cities. But if need be, Stalin could be just as brutal with Muslims as with

Christians. He thus deported all Tatars living on the Crimea (more than 350,000 people) when he decided that they had been collaborating with the Nazis during the war. Several Caucasian Muslim nations, such as the Chechens and Ingush, shared the fate of the Crimean Tatars. But since Stalin also had all Buddhist Kalmyks or Orthodox Crimean Greeks and Bulgarians deported as Nazi collaborators, the marker that doomed these "punished peoples" was ethnicity rather than religion. All these groups ended up in inhospitable regions in Central Asia, where many succumbed.

The cultural revolution thus included enforced atheism. It does seem clear that many Soviet citizens embraced a scientific and nonreligious worldview, once they became acquainted with its outlines, without much coercion. The spread of a secular mind-set among the USSR's population reflects a more commonly observed trend in modern industrial countries, as in most of Europe or Canada. In this sense, the United States is more of an outlier, for it has until recently avoided this sharp increase in irreligiosity. Meanwhile, one wonders how many Soviets agreed with those who argued that God could not exist, because no god could be so cruel as to allow the boundless human suffering twentieth-century Soviet Russia experienced.

THE GULAG ARCHIPELAGO

After 1929, a burgeoning network of concentration camps appeared across the Soviet Union. The Great Turn made the number of camps balloon, as millions rather than thousands were sentenced to camp for a variety of "anti-Soviet" or "counterrevolutionary" crimes. Few were released as innocent, and courts began to process cases of political or other crime in the manner of Soviet factory workers handling goods on conveyor belts fulfilling or overfulfilling the plan. A great variety of courts, meanwhile, sentenced people. Some fell under the auspices of the State Procuracy. Military courts dealt with cases that involved state treason, a loosely defined rubric applied to many of those prosecuted. Others were processed by special tribunals of the State Political Administration (Russian abbreviation: GPU), the secret or political police, which from 1934 was known as the People's Commissariat of Internal Affairs (NKVD). It was then rechristened the Ministry of Internal Affairs (MVD) in 1946. Finally in 1953, it became the Committee for State Security (KGB); despite its notoriety in the West, the KGB was by far the most benevolent incarnation of the Soviet security police.

The NKVD arrested people and confined them in jails to await trial. Prisons became ever more crowded during the 1930s. To speed up the processing of cases by the courts, and to justify their feverish activity uncovering treasonous conspiracies (for which they almost always lacked convincing material evidence), NKVD agents usually tried to force the accused to sign a written confession. In almost all such statements, the accused admitted to a host of crimes against the Soviet state and implicated a great number of others. The latter could then be arrested in their turn.

Such confessions, however, were seldom signed voluntarily. The NKVD became extremely adept at wearing down those awaiting trial and coercing them to admit

Figure 7.2. Book cover celebrating building the White Sea Canal, in fact built by prisoners, 1930s (Slavic and Baltic Division, New York Public Library, Astor, Lenox, and Tilden Foundations)

to things of which they were innocent. Harmless conversations were turned into evidence of plotting terrorism and the overthrow of the regime. But apart from sophistry, torture of the accused was the norm. Sleep deprivation was a mild example of the methods the security police applied. Interrogations were conducted during the night, and inmates were not allowed to lie down in the daytime. Reprisals against family members were threatened. Many of the accused were mercilessly beaten. Sharing cells with people maimed by NKVD officers convinced many to avoid being tortured by placing their signature at the end of a statement in which they confessed to a welter of fictive crimes. Armed with such confessions, the NKVD had little problem in having the courts dispatch the accused to a lengthy term in labor camps.

The labor camps also fell under the authority of the NKVD. They were organized in its Main Administration of camps, abbreviated in Russian as Gulag. Concentration camp inmates built houses and factories in cities, dug canals, laid down railroad track, cut trees, and mined ore. They were fed meals that left them severely malnourished. They worked in freezing temperatures, lacking adequate warm clothing and footwear. Convicts slept in barracks that were insufficiently heated. Camps were guarded by NKVD troops, but the camp administrations left much of the pecking order to the convicts themselves. Among them, the so-called social deviants (ordinary criminals) ruled through violence and intimidation. Criminal gangs lorded it over the "political" convicts, forcing the latter to give up their warm clothing and boots, and to perform most of the hard physical labor. The camps thus became death traps, and the mortality reached enormous proportions during the 1930s and 1940s. Because trustworthy statistics do not exist, we can only guess at the number of people who died in the camps between 1928 and 1953–1954. The camp population rose from tens of thousands in early 1929 to more than two million before, and three million after, the Second World War, and perhaps twenty million people spent some time in a camp between 1929 and 1953. That amounts to one in eight or one in nine Soviet inhabitants; how many of them died is unclear. Of course, many others lived in special settlement regions, as did many of the kulaks arrested around 1930 and the "punished peoples" deported at the end of the Second World War.

Chilling accounts about the Gulag camps have been produced by Soviet writers, such as the former camp inmate Aleksandr Solzhenitsyn. He suggested that if one looks at a representation on a map of the USSR of the thousands of labor camps, it resembles an island archipelago. Thus he named his magnum opus *The Gulag Archipelago* (published in the West in the 1970s, after Solzhenitsyn's deportation from the Soviet Union, and in Russia and the former Soviet states in 1988–1989). Besides Solzhenitsyn's work, equally terrifying accounts have been written by Aleksandr Gorbatov (1892–1973), Varlam Shalamov (1907–1982), Evgeniia Ginzburg (1896–1980), Lev Kopelev (1912–1997), and others. And Anna Akhmatova's "Requiem" may be the emblematic poem representing the anguish of those left in uncertainty about the fate of their loved ones after their arrest. Similarly harrowing are the memoirs of Nadezhda Mandelshtam (1899–1980) about her life with her husband Osip, who died on his way to the Kolyma camps in 1938.

THE GREAT TERROR

Solzhenitsyn has argued that no one single period in Stalin's lifetime stands out as a period of exceptionally harsh repressive policies. He identified various waves of increased mass arrests, either across the country, as in 1932–1933 and 1937–1938, or in certain regions, as in western Ukraine and western Belarus (then newly annexed to the USSR) in 1939–1941, and in the Baltic republics in 1940–1941 (incorporated into the USSR in 1940). But Solzhenitsyn argued that arrests of those opposed to the Soviet regime were always a normal part of Soviet life between 1917 and 1956. For Solzhenitsyn, arbitrary arrest predated and postdated Stalin. The Russian writer thereby took exception to a historical narrative imposed by the Soviet leaders after Stalin's death. It suggested that all was going well in the Soviet Union until Stalin began to order the arrest, sentencing, and execution of former Communist Party members in 1936.

Stalin's successor Khrushchev presented this reading of Stalin's failings during his "Secret Speech" at the Twentieth Party Congress in February 1956.[9] Khrushchev argued that the policies of collectivization and industrialization had been correct and set the USSR on the road to communism. If he had criticized Stalin for the human suffering and economic fiasco that those policies entailed, he would have pulled the rug out from under his own feet and from that of his comrades in the post-Stalin leadership. Thus, Khrushchev's criticism was highly selective. As Western observers pointed out in 1956 after the Secret Speech was leaked, Khrushchev did not even admit to the farcical nature of the show trials held in Moscow in 1936, 1937, and 1938, and the innocence of the accused who were convicted and sentenced by them. In these trials, some of Lenin's closest comrades, such as Zinov'ev, Kamenev, and Piatakov, confessed of having plotted against the Soviet Union under the command of the exiled Trotsky. In 1956, those accused were not reinstated, at least in part because they had questioned the necessity of the Great Turn in 1929.

Solzhenitsyn's argument about the constant nature of arrests of alleged (and sometimes real) opponents of the Soviet Union is largely correct. Records made available to historians in the 1990s and 2000s tell of staggering numbers of people being persecuted by the GPU or NKVD in the 1930s and 1940s. They also attest to Lenin's bloodlust. But Lenin's ruthlessness (as evident especially in the Civil War but also in episodes after that conflict had ended) pales against Stalin's. Even if in 1922 Lenin ordered a trial staged against some of the leaders of the Socialist Revolutionaries (SR), who were accused and convicted of imaginary plots against the government, the SR leaders were still allowed to deny the charges and received mild sentences. In Stalin's trials, the accused (who had been tortured and blackmailed) admitted to heinous crimes and received the "highest measure," execution by firing squad.

While the Moscow Trials of 1936, 1937, and 1938 were almost verbatim reported in *Pravda*, waves of mass arrests of staggering proportions were unleashed, intended to catch any potential or real, current or former, foe of the regime. There were thus mass arrests of Poles, Germans, Koreans, Finns, Latvians, and Estonians who lived in exile, or had merely found employment, in the Soviet Union. The rationale behind these campaigns seems to have been that they might form a "fifth column" if the USSR went to war with their countries of origin (doubly ironic in the Korean case, as their country was occupied by Japan). There were mass "operations" conducted by the NKVD against "former kulaks," former tsarist officials decried as "Whites," economic "saboteurs" and "wreckers," and former political opponents such as surviving ex-Mensheviks and SRs. Those identified as supporters of former opponents of Stalin—the "Trotskyites," "Zinov'evites," "right deviationists," or as state prosecutor Andrei Vyshinskii (1883–1954) said at one show trial, "left-right-wing freaks"—were rounded up as well. Arrest in 1937–1938 virtually always meant conviction, even if the only pieces of evidence entering the record of most cases were the confessions by the accused. It is certain that in 1937 and 1938 minimally 692,000 Soviet residents were executed, and more than 1.7 million people arrested. Those who avoided execution ended up in camps. The numbers were likely higher, for some cases did not even enter the records (for example, if the accused died under torture). The scale of this butchery was a world record in absolute numbers; no rulers had ever killed so many people in any country during peacetime. Soon, however, others were to rival and surpass Stalin as the bloodiest mass murderer ever known.

The Gulag camp inmates became so numerous that the NKVD was a substantial contributor to the economic production of the USSR. At the same time, the massive campaigns of arresting, processing, and guarding hundreds of thousands absorbed a lot of labor. Tens of thousands of NKVD operatives and guards were deployed to handle arrests as well as those in prison, on transport, or at the camps. And a considerable number of NKVD agents were busy shooting people (the average number of executions in the USSR during the height of the purge neared 1,500 per day!). This was a rather costly use of valuable manpower and added nothing to the country's economic productivity.[10] The yield from slave labor is low, according to most economists (including Marx). It certainly was in the Soviet labor camps, because most work was done manually, without machinery. People suffered from exposure to the brutal climate and received extremely low food rations. In addition, the arrests of 1937–1938 disproportionally affected the better educated, such as engineers, and other highly skilled employees and workers. This brain drain, too, began to undermine the economy.

In November 1938, Stalin (as general secretary of the party) and Molotov (as Sovnarkom chairman) announced to party organizations and NKVD agents that the "mass operations" had ended. In a telegram to the highest local leaders throughout the country, they stated that the goal of the purges had been accomplished and added that evidence had emerged that arrests had become indiscriminate and excessive. In other words, Stalin pretended that, as during the early stages of collectivization, enthusiasm had once more gotten the better of officials involved in the campaigns. A scapegoat was found in NKVD People's Commissar Nikolai Yezhov, who was arrested in early 1939, after many of his subordinates had already been apprehended. Others committed suicide before they could be captured. Yezhov's successor, Beria, restored the more routine manner of police operations in the Soviet Union that had prevailed before 1937.

The so-called Great Terror, as the British historian Robert Conquest dubbed the massacre in the 1960s, thus came to a close in late 1938. Solzhenitsyn was correct, however, in suggesting that mass operations did not cease; they just became more selective, singling out various groups rather than singling out the entire country. Meanwhile, almost all of those accused of conspiring against Soviet power did in fact no such thing as it was by the middle of the 1930s wholly impossible to engage in plotting in this police state. As an act of protest by a desperate individual, the murder of Sergei Kirov in Leningrad in 1934 was the last of a kind. The great majority of those apprehended therefore never saw their arrest coming: most were taken by surprise when they heard the usually nocturnal knock on the door.

The Great Terror appears to have targeted primarily urban residents.[11] The countryside had already been "purged" between 1929 and 1933. In the close quarters of the cities, any plotting was difficult. Everywhere informers lurked, egged on by their handlers in the NKVD who tried to meet the arrest quotas that had been imposed on them (indeed, ultimately by Stalin himself, as archival documents show). Although the evidence about police informers is somewhat sketchy, it is likely that from the middle of the 1930s onward, at least one in ten adults, forcibly or voluntarily, regularly delivered reports about "sedition" to the NKVD. Most of this amounted to passing on incautious remarks, malicious gossip, and even made-up stories. Failing to notice any dissent could lead to the arrest of the informer on suspicion of harboring an anti-Soviet attitude. Few, meanwhile, were unaware of the presence of these stool pigeons.

Historians continue to debate how much those who stayed outside of the claws of the NKVD believed in the guilt of their friends, neighbors, and coworkers, or of those about whose arrest they read in *Pravda*. No uniform answer can be given to this question, it appears. Factories and institutions organized mass meetings of workers and employees, during which party activists tried to whip up a frenzy among their audience.[12] Sometimes, indeed, participants in such meetings demanded in a sort of trance the heads of the exiled Trotsky and his fellow conspirators who had admitted to heinous crimes at the Moscow Trials.

Soviet citizens did not have any other means to help them assess the veracity of the news about the show trials than what was fed to them by the Soviet media. Nowhere were reports published about the scale of the arrests in 1937 and 1938. Undoubtedly, people witnessed or heard about the arrests of colleagues, acquaintances, friends, and relatives, but many were apprehended during the night, darkness hiding the massive scale of events. Even to close family members, the NKVD divulged little to nothing about the reasons someone had been hauled off to jail. Many seem to have thought that those arrested probably had been guilty of some sort of trespass, while relatives usually believed in the innocence of their spouse, children, sibling, or parent who had been apprehended. They earnestly awaited their release, usually to no avail.

What was behind the "purge" of Soviet society and the Communist Party during the Great Terror? As with many things about the Great Terror, we do not have a fully convincing answer to that question. Yet it seems that Molotov may have been frank when, long after his ouster in 1957 from the leadership, he declared that the arrests and executions of 1937–1938 had a preventative purpose. In the middle of the 1930s, Stalin, together with people such as Molotov, Kaganovich, Voroshilov, and Zhdanov, believed that the Soviet Union housed countless people who hated the regime. These foes were primarily those who had lost out in the grandiose transformation of the country since its foundation in 1917. They ranged from monarchists to kulaks to Trotskyites. If the Soviet Union were confronted by a major crisis such as a foreign invasion, these people might betray it, as they were bound to feel little loyalty to a country that had ruined them. In league with the foreign enemy, they would work toward the collapse of the country from the inside. According to Molotov, it was better to rid the Soviet Union of these people before war broke out.

And by late 1936, war seemed in the offing because of the saber rattling by the Nazis and the outbreak of a civil war in Spain. Stalin had read the relevant parts of Hitler's *Mein Kampf*. He anticipated that Hitler, sooner than later, would attempt to destroy the "Jewish-Bolshevik" state the book had denounced, where "Jewish vermin" lorded it over Slavic and other "subhumans." Hitler further announced in *Mein Kampf* that he would enslave the Soviet citizenry and work most of Eastern Europe's population to death. The vacuum thus created was then to be filled by the German "master race."

Ultimately, Stalin was to make a crucial error regarding Hitler, but this was not because he ever discounted the German threat. The mistakes Stalin made in 1941 show instead how on more than one occasion flights of fancy replaced a sober assessment of the reality of the situation. In the spring of 1941, Stalin convinced himself that Hitler would not attack the Soviet Union but would wait at least another year. This was what Stalin wanted to happen, for his country would be ready for war only by 1942. Once the last days of spring arrived in 1941, he seemed to be proven right; by the third week of June, it surely was too late in the year for an invasion, given the merciless Russian climate and difficult terrain. Although Stalin did not believe that Hitler would scrupulously honor the Ten-Year Non-Aggression Pact concluded in August 1939, he deluded himself in wishing for a later German attack. As a result, his country was ruefully unprepared for war to break out on 22 June 1941.

Apart from ignoring the extensive intelligence that came to his desk about an impending German invasion in 1941, Stalin also undermined his country's readiness for war in another crucial respect. As part of the Great Terror, he ordered widespread arrests within the senior brass of the Red Army. Military officers who had earned their stripes in the Civil War and who had often attended German military exercises that were (in defiance of the terms of the Versailles Treaty) conducted on Soviet soil before 1933 were killed in great number. By the end of the army purges, Stalin had killed not only one of the earliest and best military theorists on tank warfare, Mikhail Tukhachevskii, but also Vasilii Bliukher (1889–1938), who had defeated the Japanese armies invading the Soviet Union at Lake Khasan in 1938, and Iakov Smushkevich (1902–1941), an air force commander who had organized the Spanish Republic's air force in the civil war in 1937 and 1938. Grigorii Shtern

(1900–1941), a general who had organized the Spanish Republican defense and beat back another Japanese invasion in 1939 at Khalkin Gol, was murdered in a later purge. And these were only the most senior brilliant commanders Stalin had killed. He was left in 1941 with an army commanded by officers loyal to him but bereft of the talent of such military experts.

A POTEMKIN COUNTRY

While standards of living were abysmally low during the second half of the 1930s and millions languished in labor camps or jails, the Soviet leadership announced that it was making great strides on the road to a free society of equals. Full employment prevailed; health care and education were free and available to all. A facade was upheld that tried to advertise the Soviet Union as the most democratic country in the world.

Measures were taken to make the Soviet Union into an exemplary democracy and thus increase the population's sense of belonging. Perhaps some Soviet citizens looked no further than the Potemkin village that was the new (Stalin) Constitution promulgated in 1936, but this set of basic All-Union laws seems to have been introduced primarily for foreign consumption. The Stalin Constitution granted the right to vote to all adults, irrespective of gender. It did away with the greater weight that had been given to working-class votes and the exclusion of certain "former people" (tsarist officials, priests, etc.) from the right to vote. The membership Union parliament, the Supreme Soviet, was from 1936 directly chosen by the Soviet population. Elections took place every four years for its Soviet of the Unions (a sort of lower house or chamber of deputies) and its Soviet of Nationalities (a sort of upper house or Senate). These All-Union soviets rarely met and were usually represented by a much smaller body, the Presidium of the Supreme Soviet, of whom the chair was the official Soviet head of state (until 1946, Mikhail Kalinin, and from 1946 to 1953, Nikolai Shvernik [1888–1970]). The Supreme Soviet formerly appointed the Sovnarkom, legislated, and officially held the government accountable for its policies. There were also soviets of the republics and of rural districts and cities, which were also elected every four years.

But this highly democratic structure was a sham in practice. The Communist Party handpicked all candidates for the soviets at all levels. In every election, only one candidate (representing a "bloc of party and nonparty communists") stood for office per electoral district. And whereas "former people" received the right to vote under the new constitution, few of them remained at liberty or were even alive after the Great Terror. The Stalin Constitution explicitly recognized the Communist Party as the leading force in society. The party, it stated, was made up of the most advanced representatives of the working class, collective farmers, and "toiling intelligentsia." The party, meanwhile, met less and less often in All-Union gatherings. In the 1930s, only three party congresses were staged, and the number of Central Committee plenary meetings fell drastically. Even the Politburo decided most matters by correspondence or telephone calls rather than in formal meetings. In effect, four or five men who gathered in Stalin's proximity (in his Kremlin office, on his Moscow estates, or at his holiday resort in the Caucasus) decided most of the important matters, on the basis of materials submitted to them by the departments of the Central Committee Secretariat.

The Stalin Constitution claimed that all different ethnic groups in the USSR were great friends of each other. The example set by the Russians led them in gentle fashion to a radiant future. It was argued that the Russians were destined to be such a beacon because they were slightly farther ahead on the road to universal enlightenment than the other Soviet peoples. It is not quite certain why Stalin began to soft-pedal the previous strictly observed equality of all Soviet nations in official rhetoric. Apart from his growing worry about Stalin's acquisition of too much power, Lenin had been worried at the end of his life about Stalin's "Great Russian chauvinism," as well as that of other non-Russian Soviet leaders. In a sharp observation, Lenin argued that those who adopted the Russian language and culture such as Stalin were in the habit of becoming more Russian than the Russians themselves. They identified too strenuously with Russia to prove that they belonged.

This ultra-Russian quality of Stalin (whose spoken Russian meanwhile betrayed a clear Georgian accent) began to leave a more marked imprint on Soviet cultural policy in the 1930s. At the same time, the language of communication within the All-Union Russian Communist Party was Russian, and in most republics Russian was the second language. Russian was the lingua franca through which an Azeri could communicate with a Kazakh or Ukrainian. It was, in other words, practical to have Soviet citizens learn Russian. In the 1930s, education, literature, and theater in the national languages lost terrain to the propagation of accomplishments of the Russian nation and culture in the present and past. No longer were Russians portrayed as imperialist oppressors of the non-Russians, or tsarist Russia as a prisonhouse of nations. Thus, many of the tsars were rehabilitated in the Soviet version of Imperial Russia's past. The expansion of the Russian Empire was interpreted as a positive step that allowed non-Russians to ascend to a higher stage of civilization. Artists from Pushkin to Tchaikovsky became All-Union cultural icons rather than specific Russian ones. Since most Soviet inhabitants learned Russian, Russian literature was far more frequently read by non-Russians than non-Russian literature was read by Russians (and translations into Russian were not as numerous as the other way around). Soviet culture blended therefore with Russian culture in many respects.

WAS STALINISM REALLY NECESSARY?

Academic historians do not usually believe that history is predestined, for such a view amounts to believing in a sort of predetermined unfolding of a divine plan. Perhaps this allows us to ponder some counterfactual history. This is useful, because voices (including Stalin's own in the official party history issued in 1938[13]) argue that the Great Turn and the accompanying massacre were inevitable. They draw comparisons with the industrialization of Western countries, which also involved prohibitive human cost in the form of slums, abysmal wages, child labor, disease, early deaths, and so on. Many have pointed out that by the middle of the 1950s, the Soviet Union definitively overcame periodic famine and achieved universal literacy as a result of the profound transformation of the previous thirty years. Everyone had some sort of housing in the Soviet Union and had access to some basic health care that was free. There was virtually no unemployment. The Soviet record outshines that of countries such as Brazil, India, Pakistan, or Mexico, according to this analysis.

And, in addition, the Soviet Union had been responsible for the ultimate defeat of the formidable Nazi war machine. In sum, for many politicians in the past and even for a few historians today, the Soviet Union did offer a model of development that offered a viable alternative road to modernization different from Western-style capitalist industrialization. The Soviet model certainly attracted many political leaders in the Third World of developing countries during the 1960s and 1970s, who often adopted economic policies that took their cue from the Soviet Five Year Plans (as in India, for example). Some went further and created a one-party state, where political freedom took a backseat to economic priorities (in Ghana or Syria, for example). Others went even further than that and adopted the Soviet model wholesale, including the killing of numerous opponents (North Korea, Ethiopia, Cuba, and Cambodia). While government economic planning is not without its use, the necessity of a country's modernization can never justify such "killing fields": from 1917 to 1953, as we saw before, countless millions of inhabitants of the Soviet Union lost their lives to domestic conflict or regime policy.[14] The Soviet model of development was a fiasco, and it certainly has been an unmitigated disaster wherever else it was copied. The famines of Communist Ethiopia, North Korea, China, or Cambodia align with those of Soviet Ukraine and Kazakhstan.

And although the Nazis and their allies should be primarily blamed for the indiscriminate slaughter on the "Eastern Front" between 1941 and 1945, Stalin could hardly have done worse on the eve of the Nazi invasion in terms of preparing his country's defense. A greater degree of readiness would likely have saved millions of lives, as would have judicious retreats of the Soviet military before the advancing Germans in 1941. An acknowledgment that millions of Soviet troops had been captured, so that they could be considered POWs and treated under the protection of the International Red Cross, would have additionally saved countless lives. Thus, apart from the deaths from the Civil War, the 1921–1922 famine, the 1929–1930 dekulakization, the 1932–1933 famine, the 1937–1938 Great Purge, and various subsequent waves of killing, millions of war deaths can be blamed on Stalin's failings. Such a massacre would not likely have taken place if Lenin had accepted the results of the elections for the Constituent Assembly in November 1917, which gave a majority to the Socialist Revolutionaries, and had resigned with his government. Instead, Red sailors sent the deputies home.

The question lingers: what would have happened if Stalin had died in 1925 or 1926, like Trotsky's successor as People's Commissar of War, Mikhail Frunze (1885–1925), or the founder of the Cheka, Feliks Dzerzhinskii (1877–1926)? Would Zinov'ev and Kamenev, or Trotsky, or Bukharin have unleashed a modernization program that involved so much suffering and violence? It seems highly plausible that the first three and even Bukharin would have engaged in a renewed offensive in the countryside to increase grain deliveries and "socialize" farming in one form or other; they harbored such plans in the 1920s, and it is difficult to see how they could have otherwise found the resources to fund any stepped-up industrialization.

But would they have decided to exterminate the kulaks or to leave the starving Ukrainians, Russians, and Kazakhs to their fate in 1932–1933? Perhaps because of the contents of the massive amounts of writing Trotsky produced after he was exiled in 1929, one likes to believe that he had maintained some semblance of a moral being, and to answer in the negative. Certainly, unleashing the Great Terror seems something that only Stalin could have concocted among the Soviet chiefs of the 1920s who fought for Lenin's mantle. One can be more firmly convinced than in the case of collectivization that Trotsky or Bukharin would not have acted as rashly and cruelly as Stalin did. Trotsky and the others, finally, might also have been more vigilant in tracking, and realistic in interpreting, Hitler's moves.

A perhaps more intriguing question occupies historians as well: what if the revolution of 1917 had never happened? For that to have transpired, the tsarist empire should probably not have entered the First World War. The Russian filmmaker Stanislav Govorukhin (b. 1936) and, again, Solzhenitsyn have argued that in that event Russia might have been able to modernize in another, less radical way, avoiding all the bloodshed of the Stalinist path to modernization. They appear to have had a point.

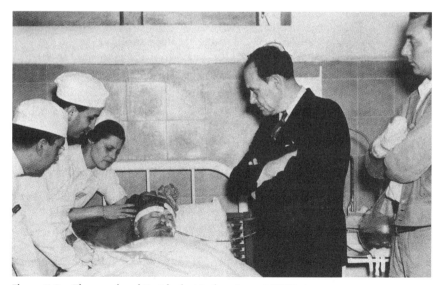

Figure 7.3. The murdered Trotsky in Mexico, August 1940

NOTES

1. In Soviet parlance, the party congresses were referred to in capital letters as, allegedly, their convocation often marked important milestones on the road to communism; this habit has been adopted here.

2. This was the name of honor given to Lazare Carnot (1753–1823), who organized the French revolutionary armies into a force that defeated the best-drilled armies of Europe in the 1790s.

3. Perhaps this explains why Trotsky felt obliged to declare during the 1920s that he lived by the maxim "my party, right or wrong," which seemed somewhat unnatural to say for such an arrogant type.

4. Piatakov's name as one of the future leaders was surprising, since he did not occupy any senior leadership post at the time.

5. Their enmity originated in the Civil War and the Soviet-Polish War, when Stalin had repeatedly disobeyed orders by commander in chief Trotsky.

6. These markets were permitted because they offered foodstuffs otherwise unavailable, as the state distribution system failed to supply most cities adequately with a diverse assortment of goods.

7. After the Second World War especially, many kolkhozes were almost entirely dependent on women's labor. But whereas many women became brigadiers, few were appointed to direct the farms.

8. "Stalinist" was a laudatory term that came into Soviet use in the early 1930s.

9. To Stalin's crimes Khrushchev added his strategic blundering during the lead-up to the German invasion of the USSR in 1941 and some of his postwar "purging" of close comrades in whom Stalin suddenly lost faith. See also the next chapter.

10. A few women worked for the NKVD, but they formed a very small percentage.

11. The exception is some of the persecution campaigns of certain nationalities, such as the Koreans.

12. This induced frenzy inspired George Orwell for certain episodes in *1984*.

13. This was the *History of the All-Union Communist Party (Bolsheviks): Short Course*, published in installments in *Pravda* in 1938 and in book form in multiple editions and languages from 1939 onward. Stalin was its main editor, even if he preferred to have the work appear as collectively written by a "commission of the Central Committee," whose composition was not further identified.

14. The term "killing fields" derives from the locations where the remains of victims of the ultra-Communist Khmer Rouge were found after the fall of that particularly odious Cambodian regime.

FURTHER READING

Translated Primary Sources

Bulgakov, Mikhail. *The Master and Margarita*. Translated by Diana Burgin and Katherine Tiernan O'Connor. New York: Vintage, 1996.

Dimitrov, Georgi. *The Diary of Georgi Dimitrov*. Translated by Jane T. Hedges, Timothy D. Sergay, and Irina Faion. Edited by Ivo Banac. New Haven, CT: Yale University Press, 2003.

Getty, J. Arch, and Oleg V. Naumov. *The Road to Terror: Stalin and the Self-Destruction of the Bolsheviks, 1932–1939*. Translated by Benjamin Sher. 2nd ed. New Haven, CT: Yale University Press, 2010.

Ginzburg, Evgeniia. *Journey into the Whirlwind*. Translated by Paul Stevenson and Max Hayward. New York: Harcourt, 1967.

History of the All-Union Communist Party (Bolsheviks): Short Course. London: Greenwood Press, 1976.

Khlevniuk, Oleg. *The History of the Gulag: From Collectivization to the Great Terror*. Translated by Vadim A. Staklo. New Haven, CT: Yale University Press, 2004.

Mandelshtam, Nadezhda. *Hope against Hope: A Memoir*. Translated by Max Hayward. New York: Atheneum, 1970.

Shalamov, Varlam. *Kolyma Tales*. Translated by John Glad. New York: Penguin, 1995.

Solzhenitsyn, Aleksandr I. *The Gulag Archipelago, 1918–1956*. Translated by Thomas P. Whitney. 3 vols. New York: Harper & Row, 1974, 1978.

Stalin, Joseph. *The Stalin-Kaganovich Correspondence, 1931–36*. Translated by Steven Shabad. Edited by R. W. Davies et al. New Haven, CT: Yale University Press, 2003.

———. *Stalin's Letters to Molotov, 1925–1936*. Translated by Catherine A. Fitzpatrick. Edited by Lars T. Lih, Oleg V. Naumov, and Oleg V. Khlevniuk. New Haven, CT: Yale University Press, 1995.

Trotsky, Leon. *My Life: An Attempt at an Autobiography*. Translation of Moia Zhizn'. New York: Pathfinder, 1970.

Scholarly Literature

Alexopoulos, Golfo. *Stalin's Outcasts: Aliens, Citizens and the Soviet State, 1926–1936*. Ithaca, NY: Cornell University Press, 2003.

Chatterjee, Choi. *Celebrating Women: Gender Festival Culture and Bolshevik Ideology, 1910–1939*. Pittsburgh: University of Pittsburgh Press, 2002.

Conquest, Robert. *The Harvest of Sorrow: Soviet Collectivization and the Terror-Famine*. New York: Oxford University Press, 1987.

Davies, R. W., and Stephen G. Wheatcroft. *The Years of Hunger: Soviet Agriculture, 1931–1933*. Houndsmills, UK: Palgrave Macmillan, 2004.

Fitzpatrick, Sheila. *The Cultural Front: Power and Culture in Revolutionary Russia*. Ithaca, NY: Cornell University Press, 1992.

———. *Stalin's Peasants: Resistance and Survival in the Russian Village after Collectivization*. New York: Oxford University Press, 1996.

Halfin, Igal. *From Darkness to Light: Class, Consciousness and Salvation in Revolutionary Russia*. Pittsburgh: University of Pittsburgh Press, 2002.

Hellbeck, Jochen. *Revolution on My Mind: Writing a Diary under Stalin*. Cambridge, MA: Harvard University Press, 2009.

Hoffmann, David. *Peasant Metropolis: Social Identities in Moscow, 1929–1941*. Ithaca, NY: Cornell University Press, 2000.

Keller, Shoshana. *To Moscow, Not Mecca: The Soviet Campaign against Islam in Central Asia, 1917–1941*. New York: Praeger, 2001.

Khlevniuk, Oleg. *Master of the House: Stalin and His Inner Circle*. New Haven, CT: Yale University Press, 2008.

Kotkin, Stephen. *Magnetic Mountain: Stalinism as a Civilization.* Berkeley: University of California Press, 1997.

Kuromiya, Hiroaki. *Freedom and Terror in the Donbas: A Ukrainian-Russian Borderland, 1870s–1990s.* Cambridge: Cambridge University Press, 2003.

———. *Stalin: Profiles in Power.* New York: Longman, 2005.

Lewin, Moshe. *Lenin's Last Struggle.* Ann Arbor: University of Michigan Press, 2005.

Petrov, Nikita, and Marc Jansen, *Stalin's Loyal Executioner: People's Commissar Nikolai Ezhov, 1895–1940.* Stanford, CA: Hoover Institution Press, 2002.

Ree, Erik van. *The Political Thought of Joseph Stalin: A Study in Twentieth-Century Revolutionary Patriotism.* New York: Routledge, 2002.

Scott, John. *Behind the Urals: An American Worker in Russia's City of Steel.* Bloomington: Indiana University Press, 1989.

Service, Robert. *Stalin: A Biography.* Cambridge, MA: Belknap, 2005.

———. *Trotsky.* Cambridge, MA: Belknap, 2009.

Viola, Lynn. *The Unknown Gulag: The Lost World of Stalin's Special Settlements.* New York: Oxford University Press, 2009.

Voslensky, Michael. *Nomenklatura: Anatomy of the Soviet Ruling* Class. London: Bodley Head, 1984.

Weiner, Douglas R. *Models of Nature: Ecology, Conservation and Cultural Revolution in Russia.* Pittsburgh: University of Pittsburgh Press, 2000.

Werth, Nicolas. *Cannibal Island: Death in a Siberian Gulag.* Princeton, NJ: Princeton University Press, 2007.

WEBSITE

"Memorial," society to commemorate the victims of Soviet communism and defense of human rights and freedoms: http://www.memo.ru/ (in Russian)

FILMS

Bed and Sofa. DVD. Directed by Abram Room and Vsevolod Pudovkin. Chatsworth, CA: Image Entertainment, 2012.

Burnt by the Sun. DVD. Directed by Nikita Mikhalkov. Culver City, CA: Sony, 2003.

Ivan the Terrible, parts 1 and 2. Amazon Instant Video. Directed by Sergei Eisenstein. Venice, CA: Egami, 2012.

Man with a Movie Camera. DVD. Directed by Dziga Vertov. New York: Kino, 2010.

Quiet Flows the Don. DVD. Directed by Sergei Gerasimov. New York: Kino, 2007.

Rossiia, kotoruiu my poteriali [The Russia That We Lost]. Documentary (Russian only). Directed by Stanislav Govorukhin. Moscow: Mosfilm, 1992.

Vlast' Solovetskaia. VHS documentary. Directed by Marina Goldovskaia. Moscow: Sovexport-film, 1988.

8

The Great Patriotic War and the Cold War, 1941–1953

The Soviet Union may have lost twenty-seven million people during the Second World War. Most of them can be blamed on Adolf Hitler and his murderous hordes, who invaded the Soviet Union on 22 June 1941. Stalin's Red Army purges, his obstinate refusal to accept intelligence about an impending German invasion in the spring of 1941, and his foolish strategic decisions after war broke out caused the death rate to be much higher than necessary, however. Not without reason, some critics have argued that Stalin could have prevented this catastrophic tragedy. In the early 1930s, the Soviet leaders ordered the German Communist Party to reject any political alliance with the German Social Democrats; this move paved the way for Hitler's rise to power.

Despite Stalin's blundering, the war was nonetheless won by the Soviet armed forces, and by its end the Soviet Union and the United States seemed the only powerful states left standing in the world (when Great Britain, economically crippled, became embroiled in extricating itself from its vast colonial empire). Although Soviet leaders had always admired the U.S. economic might and technological ability, they saw the United States as the epitome of capitalism. Because of that perception, as well as the hostile view of Stalin's empire harbored by most American politicians, the wartime alliance was doomed once peace descended on Europe and Asia in 1945. Within a mere three years, the two wartime allies had become each other's inveterate foes in a Cold War, which threatened to become hot at any moment.

THE SECOND WORLD WAR

When war broke out in 1939 in Europe, Stalin believed he had outfoxed the capitalist leaderships of France, Britain, and Nazi Germany, setting them against each

other. According to his thinking, the war was the logical outcome of capitalist con-
tradictions. In his Marxist worldview, he made little distinction between the three
countries, since parliamentary democracy was just as much as fascism a bourgeois
sham. He hoped that the Western powers would exhaust themselves fighting each
other, while he kept his powder dry. In a sense, Stalin was right in believing that the
war would lay waste to the three Great Powers of Europe. The French and British
overseas empires proved unsustainable, after the moral abyss of Nazi-ruled Europe
had put paid to Western concepts of "civilized Europe" and the war effort had
emptied the imperial coffers. Thus, the Western Europeans were forced to grant
independence to their colonies decades before the Russians had to give up most of
theirs between 1988 and 1992. But despite the war's ultimate outcome of the fall of
France, Britain, and Germany as Great Powers, Stalin did come to rue the absurd
confidence he developed in his ability to manipulate the capitalist countries and to
predict Hitler's every move. Dismissing the threat of a German invasion in 1941
as nonsense, Stalin's lack of preparation for the Nazi invasion had devastating consequences for the Soviet population. Perhaps one-sixth of them died between June
1941 and September 1945.

THE MOLOTOV-RIBBENTROP PACT

Historians these days no longer adhere to the idea that the Second World War began
with the Nazi invasion of Poland on 1 September 1939. Instead, many argue that the
conflict began with the Japanese invasion of China in 1937. Certainly, in the Soviet
case that might be a good point to start, for the Red Army fought two major battles
with the Japanese at Khalkin Gol and Lake Khasan in 1938 and 1939, even if both
countries remained formally at peace. In some ways, too, the Spanish Civil War that
raged from 1936 to 1939 was a prologue for the carnage in Europe. The war in Spain
was in part a proxy war, in which one side (the democratic-republican) received military support from the USSR, while its opponent, the insurgent military-fascist coalition under General Francisco Franco, was (more substantially) aided by Fascist Italy
and Nazi Germany. Stalin's support for the Spanish Republic was never enthusiastic,
even after he had received the Spanish gold reserve for safekeeping. Already then he
was suspicious of the motives of France and the United Kingdom, whose governments found pathetic excuses not to support Spain's legitimately elected government
against Franco's hordes. Marxism-Leninism (or Stalinism) was of course an already
morbidly suspicious creed, as we saw, and its paranoia about capitalist collusion was
fed by inaction of the Western democracies in the Spanish Civil War.

Increasing Stalin's apprehension about their motives, at the Munich Conference in September 1938 the French and British prime ministers conceded parts
of independent Czechoslovakia to Hitler. The German dictator claimed that the
territory he demanded was populated primarily by German speakers, which was
true; the elevated region in which they resided, however, was the key strategic area

Figure 8.1. Molotov signs Nazi-Soviet Non-Aggression Pact, August 1939 (Picture Collection, New York Public Library, Astor, Lenox, and Tilden Foundations)

from which the Czechoslovak government planned to defend its country in case
of a foreign attack. With a stroke of the pen at Munich, this Czechoslovak defense
was erased. Neither Czechoslovak nor Soviet leaders had been invited to the Munich Conference. And its agreement negated the military alliance that the USSR
and France had concluded to defend Czechoslovakia in 1935. Stalin's trust in the
Western powers further diminished.

In 1939, relations between Nazi Germany and France and Britain rapidly deteriorated. In the spring, Hitler helped himself to the defenseless Czech plain and
made Slovakia into an independent satellite state; he made a sidestep by taking over
a coastal part of helpless Lithuania (the Klaipeda, or Memel, area). He also began
to utter threatening sounds toward Poland, demanding the territory that separated
eastern from western Prussia (the so-called Polish Corridor). The Polish government
was caught between a rock and a hard place: most of the members of its military dictatorship had personally fought the Soviets in 1919–1920 and saw no reason to trust
Stalin's good faith any more than Hitler's. The Soviets had claims on eastern Poland,
on the grounds that the majority of the population in this region was Belarusyn and
Ukrainian (which means that the residents spoke those languages as their mother
tongues) rather than Polish. In April, a desperate Poland gained the Western democracies' guarantee that, if it were attacked by Nazi Germany, they would declare war
on the Reich. Stalin now faced a complicated situation. It did seem, however, that
if he played his cards right, the Soviet Union could recover some of the substantial
territory lost in the chaos of the Russian Civil War.

By 1939, Stalin had abandoned any reliance on the Comintern as an instrument
of Soviet foreign policy. It had enjoyed no success in fostering Communist revolutions, and its existence riled most governments. More useful to him was the foreign
branch of the People's Commissariat of Internal Affairs (NKVD). It was rather skillful at gathering crucial intelligence, but its foreign-espionage branch had been gutted
in the Great Terror. In addition, some of its efforts abroad were frivolously wasteful,
such as the operations hunting down Soviet enemies like Trotsky and his family.
Trotsky was finally murdered in Mexico City in August 1940. But despite the purges
of NKVD ranks in the Great Terror and the distraction provided by the organization
of Trotsky's assassination, Soviet agents continued to gather accurate information
about Nazi plans. Crucially, however, Stalin was inclined to disbelieve unwelcome
information he received from Soviet agents, which was to have tragic consequences.

Downplaying the Comintern's existence also meant that Stalin began to rely
more and more on old-fashioned diplomacy. His ideas about the conduct of Soviet
foreign policy took on a rather traditional shape. Perhaps, since he was now in his
sixties and a child of the nineteenth century, he unwittingly reverted to the principles and goals of the tsarist diplomatic and imperialist game before 1914; perhaps
he was fully aware of using this blueprint. Regardless of his aims and motivations,
he did have to deflect any involvement of his country in a major war in 1939. First,
the USSR had undergone a decade of epochal change from which the dust had
not yet settled. Second, Stalin had himself undermined his country's defense by

liquidating the majority of the senior army officers during the Great Terror. Their successors were young and unproven, even if a few gained some experience fighting the Japanese in 1938 and 1939.

It is thus no great surprise that Stalin in the summer of 1939 rejected Western overtures to join their guarantee to Poland and instead struck a deal with Hitler. France and Britain had little to offer the Soviet dictator and, possibly, preferred to have the USSR fight their war against Hitler. After all, the Soviet Union bordered Poland and could therefore much more readily than the Western powers offer concrete military support to the Poles. In contrast to the Western powers' ostensibly self-serving attitude, the Führer was willing to make the far-reaching territorial concessions that Stalin sought, once Hitler realized that the Soviets were willing to deal. Although the territorial barter remained secret, in August 1939 the formal announcement of a Non-Aggression Pact astounded a world that believed Nazis and Communists were each other's archenemies.[1]

One puzzle remains in this otherwise logical lead-up (from the Soviet viewpoint) to the Molotov-Ribbentrop Pact (which was named after the foreign ministers of both countries). The dissolution of Poland to which Hitler and Stalin agreed created a very long common border between Nazi Germany and the Soviet Union that did not exist before. This allowed a Nazi invasion of the Soviet Union along a very lengthy front, as did indeed materialize in June 1941. Perhaps Stalin would have been better off after all in joining the tepid French and British instead in 1939. Having read *Mein Kampf*, Stalin knew of Hitler's desire to destroy the Soviet Union: why did Stalin in 1939 make it easier for the Germans to invade the Soviet Union by acquiring a lengthy border with the Reich that had not existed before?

BEFORE BARBAROSSA

The Molotov-Ribbentrop Pact allowed Hitler to move his forces into Poland on 1 September 1939 without any fear of having to face the Soviet army as well on the battlefield. On 17 September, Soviet troops advanced into eastern Poland without encountering resistance. Polish army units were interned. Soon Nazi and Soviet troops shook hands. The occupation was celebrated in the Soviet papers, in film, and on radio as the reunification of the Ukrainian and Belarusyn nations and a liberation of their workers and peasants from Polish aristocratic oppression. In this newly annexed territory, the NKVD immediately began to arrest those whose support for the Soviet cause might be dubious. By mid-October, once western Poland was under firm German control, Stalin began to contemplate the execution of further territorial moves that Hitler had allowed him under the terms of the Non-Aggression Pact.

Pressure was applied on Finland to surrender border territory near Leningrad. But the Finns refused to budge. In late November 1939, Soviet forces crossed into Finnish territory, allegedly provoked by Finns, in a cheap Soviet imitation of the Nazi excuse to invade Poland. Perhaps Stalin should have studied the rather messy advance of his own troops into Poland instead of copying Nazi stunts, since his army proved unprepared for the stubborn Finnish resistance and the merciless climate in which it had to operate. Finland, with a population that amounted to 1.5 percent of the Soviet population, checked the Soviet military progress until February 1940. Red Army losses were so great that Stalin called off pursuing the Finns after a breakthrough of Finnish defensive lines was finally accomplished. Stalin had to settle for a minor territorial gain at Finnish expense in the peace treaty that ended this Winter War in March 1940.

For reasons that have never been quite explained, somewhere in the weeks following the peace with Finland in March 1940, Stalin ordered Lavrentii Beria to have all Polish officers executed who after the Soviet occupation of eastern Poland had been interned. Some fifteen thousand were shot at Katyn, Starobel'sk, and Mednoe in April 1940. Most of these officers were reservists who had occupied positions of middle-level leadership in Polish society (lawyers, doctors, teachers, and so on) and might become leaders of a Polish nationalist resistance against the Soviet occupiers.

There was, however, no chance in the spring of 1940 that anything of an anti-Soviet movement would emerge in the former eastern Poland. And besides, the officers were in Soviet confinement. Did Stalin already then believe that Poland would eventually fall within the Soviet orbit and want to preempt any opposition arising against a Communist regime in Poland? The mass murder can then be seen as another preventative measure: Stalin had now gotten used to the habit of killing anyone who might at some point in the future oppose him.

From early April to mid-June 1940, meanwhile, Hitler's soldiers conquered with ease Denmark, Norway, the Low Countries, and most of France. Far from engaging in any exhaustive internecine capitalist conflict, the Germans effected their campaigns without encountering much resistance. Stalin took fright at the apparent ease with which Hitler had rolled westward and now decided to press his luck. He first forced the Baltic countries to surrender. Without a shot having been fired, the countries' new Soviet bosses saluted Red Army victory parades in the Baltic capitals in June 1940. Romania, a reluctant ally of Germany, was forced to give up most of Moldavia (Bessarabia) in August, while the Luftwaffe was pounding England in the Battle of Britain. The German air war against Britain was somewhat of a desultory affair, a fact that has caused some historians to argue that Hitler only tried to soften up the British. He had reserved a place in his new World Order for these Anglo-Saxons, whom he admired as rulers of a vast overseas empire. No such place was set aside for the Soviet Union in the long term.

In November 1940, Molotov visited Berlin to appease the growing German complaints about the somewhat overbearing Soviet behavior in East-Central Europe. The Germans refused any further concessions to the Soviets in Europe, suggesting flippantly that the USSR should move toward British India. Soon after this visit, Hitler gave the green light to develop a comprehensive plan for the invasion of the Soviet Union, which came to be known as Operation Barbarossa.

BARBAROSSA AND BEYOND

Military historians suggest that Hitler lost several crucial weeks in the spring of 1941. The German dictator had to postpone the invasion of the Soviet Union in order to subjugate Yugoslavia (which had left the Nazi camp) and Greece (where an Italian invasion had gone awry). Rather than in early May 1941, as was the original plan, the Nazis attacked on 22 June, the very same day on which in 1812 the emperor Napoleon had invaded tsarist Russia. Even with the aid of the mechanized equipment that the French emperor had lacked, the German advance was not to proceed fast enough over the course of the next months. The Germans failed to encircle and capture Moscow before first the muddy fall (*rasputitsa*) and then the bone-chilling winter descended on the Eastern European plains. But less cautious than Mikhail Kutuzov and Aleksandr I, Stalin traded blunders with Hitler in the immediate lead-up to the war and in the first year of its unfolding. The Soviet Union then went on to win the war because Stalin was eventually prepared to listen to the advice of his military brass, whereas the longer the war lasted, Hitler listened less and less to his generals.

One could argue, however, that the postponement of Operation Barbarossa until 22 June 1941 may have been to Hitler's advantage. There is evidence that Stalin did not discount the chances of a German invasion until the middle of spring in 1941. Once an invasion did not occur at the expected moment (mid-May at the latest), he seems to have become increasingly confident that nothing was to happen during that year. An invasion that began at the start of summer, he concluded, would not have sufficient time to penetrate deeply enough into Soviet territory. Stalin somehow expected the Germans to draw the same conclusion and postpone their invasion to 1942. Unfortunately, an impatient Hitler thought otherwise.

Stalin thus ordered in the spring of 1941 to continue to move the primary Soviet defensive line of fortifications westward, closer to the new border. It might have been better instead to shore up the previous line located along the pre-September 1939 border. In case of a German invasion, the former eastern Poland, Bessarabia, and the Baltic region could then first be ceded to the Nazis, who would have subsequently slammed into this defensive line, at a time when they had traversed considerable territory. But Stalin was clearly unconcerned: another sign of his careless attitude was the Soviet airplanes, waiting to be painted, sitting out on the airfields on 22 June. They were only in the process of being camouflaged. And on the day before the German-led forces crossed the Soviet border, he granted his ailing favorite Andrei Zhdanov, the party's propaganda chief and boss of the crucial strategic region of Leningrad, leave to recover at a spa in the Caucasus.

The Soviet surprise at the German attack of 22 June was almost total. At first, Stalin refused to believe the news that an invasion had begun, and for some hours commanders of border units lacked orders to fire back. Most Soviet airplanes were destroyed while parked outside on their airfields. Whole divisions and armies were encircled by German pincher movements when, in subsequent weeks, Stalin refused to accept that the Nazi forces advanced at lightning speed. By early September, the Germans (and Finns and Romanians, who had joined them) reached the outskirts of Kyiv and Leningrad. The commander of the central front, Dmitrii Pavlov (1897–1941), committed suicide in August, while some of his staff was arrested for criminal incompetence. Kyiv fell soon after the Germans reached it.

By the time of the conquest of the Ukrainian capital and the beginning of the German siege of Leningrad, Hitler had decided to execute his plans to exterminate Europe's Jews. Behind the advancing armies, special detachments of SS (Schütz-staffel, the paramilitary Nazi elite force), aided by local guides, formed so-called Ein-satzgruppen, which began to round up Jews and execute them to the last person. At Kyiv, all Jews who had failed to escape with the retreating Red Army were rounded up and machine-gunned at the edge of the ravine of Babi Yar. Thirty thousand bodies piled up there in a matter of days in September 1941. Eventually, at the Wannsee Conference of January 1942, the SS decided on a more clinical method to accomplish the so-called Final Solution of the Jewish Question in Europe. Gas chambers were constructed in extermination camps, which were equipped with ovens to dispatch the bodies of the victims. Oddly, the first victims on whom the gas chambers were tried out at Auschwitz-Birkenau (Oswieçim, near Krakow), the largest death camp, were several thousand Soviet prisoners of war (POWs).

Hitler could proceed so brutally against the Soviets because their government had not joined the International Red Cross. It had therefore forfeited any authority to monitor German compliance with the Geneva Conventions regarding the humane treatment of POWs. Indeed, Stalin considered the five or six million POWs who surrendered to the Nazi-led forces as cowardly traitors. He did not care about their fate and remained unmoved when he received word that his eldest son had been shot trying to escape from a German POW camp.

SOVIET RESOLVE

Despite the magnitude of the Soviet defeats, the Red Army somehow managed to wage a spirited fight (echoing its tsarist counterpart in the First World War). In the early days of the war, even Stalin himself despaired and retreated briefly to one of his dachas near Moscow. According to one of his cronies, when Stalin's comrades in arms came to visit him to persuade him to return to his desk in the Kremlin, the dictator was relieved to find out that they had not come to arrest him. His first radio speech after the war's outbreak (not delivered until 3 July 1941!) betrayed some of this temporary insecurity as he modestly addressed his listeners as his "brothers and sisters."

The Germans and Finns failed to capture Leningrad in early September, even when they encircled the city except for a corridor linking it to Lake Ladoga. They ended offensive operations at the second-largest Soviet city because they were convinced that the city's surrender would follow its isolation from the rest of Russia.

Bereft of food reserves because of German bombardments and poor preparation, Leningrad could for a long while be supplied only across the water of Lake Ladoga. Even that route became impassable for many weeks in the fall of 1941, before the ice on the lake had frozen solidly enough to send trucks across it. From early December 1941 onward, famine laid waste to the city, and during the next half year at least one million inhabitants died of hunger. Leningrad, however, did not surrender.

Apart from being checked at Leningrad, the Nazi forces also met determined Soviet resistance elsewhere. This resolve had not been anticipated by Hitler, who believed the Soviet Union to be a house of cards. Competent commanders began to replace the bumbling types who had often led the Soviet army in the first days of the war. While it took some time for the Soviet air force to recover from the devastation at the very outset of the war, in quantity and quality Soviet tanks and artillery proved a match for their German counterparts. Above all, the Soviet population proved capable of a superhuman effort in what now began to be called the Great Patriotic War. Apart from desperate fighting at the front, the Soviet industrial plant was with considerable success evacuated eastward to the Urals and Siberia and rebuilt there. Women "manned" the posts left open in the defense factories by those who departed for the front, and thousands of women saw active duty in the armed forces. In German-occupied territory, a growing partisan movement sabotaged German supply lines.

These efforts proved stubborn enough to slow down the German advance in the fall of 1941, even if on occasion some luck aided the Soviets as well. Then the autumn rains turned much of the terrain into deep mud, which further hindered German progress. By late November 1941, the temperature along the front fell to minus 40 degrees Fahrenheit. German equipment began to malfunction when exposed to such extreme cold, and German soldiers lacked proper winter dress. German planes flew over Moscow, and artillery exchanges could be heard in the center of the city, but the German forces never came closer than some twenty miles from the capital. Suddenly, in early December, they were faced with several fresh Soviet divisions, which Stalin had transferred by rail from the Far East.

This reinforcement had been made possible because of the Japanese refusal to come to the aid of their German allies. In April 1941, Japanese foreign minister Yosuke Matsuoka (1880–1946) had visited Moscow in an effort to normalize the relations between the two countries. The negotiations were concluded to the satisfaction of both sides, and Stalin was so delighted that he made the unusual move to say good-bye personally to Matsuoka at the railway station. In the course of the fall of 1941, it became clear that Japan was indeed not going to launch another attack on the USSR. Thus, even before Pearl Harbor, Stalin ordered some of his Siberian divisions to redeploy in Europe.

The Battle of Moscow raged until February 1942 and was the first real setback for the Germans in the Second World War. Soviet success was modest, but the Germans were pushed back several tens of miles along a fairly broad front. The year 1942 saw renewed German advances, predominantly along the southern front, with German troops reaching the mountains of the Caucasus. In August, German forces reached the city of Stalingrad on the Volga. Its fall might enable the Germans to execute a pincher movement that would meet behind Moscow. Stalingrad, however, was stubbornly defended by the Soviets. Gradually, Soviet units gained the upper hand in this battle, supported by an industrial juggernaut that turned out ever more tanks and airplanes, to which the Germans had no answer. The Soviets, too, were aided by the many convoys that reached Murmansk and Arkhangel'sk with supplies (especially of American-made half-tracks and trucks) under the terms of the Lend-Lease agreement (which was concluded with the United States even before Pearl Harbor). Stalin, who hosted British prime minister Winston Churchill for the first time in Moscow in 1942, was, however, displeased by the Anglo-American inability to open a second front in Western Europe. He had to wait until June 1944 before the Western Allies landed in Normandy and thus penetrated German-occupied Europe. True to form, Stalin suspected deliberate capitalist lingering.

THE VICTOR'S SPOILS; TEHERAN, YALTA, AND POTSDAM

In January 1943, it became apparent that Soviet forces had encircled the German Sixth Army at Stalingrad. Hitler had refused to allow its commander Friedrich von Paulus to retreat his forces in time. By early February, German and Romanian forces surrendered, and hundreds of thousands of soldiers became Soviet POWs. The Soviet armies now began to drive the Germans back to their homeland. During 1943, the Germans slowly retreated. The massive tank battle at Kursk in July was a signal Soviet victory. By January 1944, Soviet forces reestablished a corridor connecting the rest of the country by land with Leningrad. Ukraine was liberated by the early fall. Stalin ordered a pause to regroup before the final assault on the Reich. This halting of the advance coincided with an uprising by Polish nationalists in Warsaw. Soviet troops stood idly by. They saw through their binoculars how SS detachments reduced the Polish capital to ruins and exterminated the Polish resistance. This Soviet inaction has been interpreted as another sign of Stalin's strategy to sabotage the formation of a strong and independent, "bourgeois," government leading a resurrected postwar Poland. He preferred to deal with the government of Soviet straw men he had organized in the summer of 1944, the so-called Lublin Committee. These Polish "fellow travelers" did not raise awkward questions about the mass graves discovered at Katyn in 1943. There, on invitation of the Nazis, a neutral Red Cross investigative commission had used forensic evidence to determine that the bodies dressed in Polish uniforms were of people killed in 1940, long before Barbarossa unfolded.

Apart from trouble brewing in Poland, Stalin also faced opposition to the reimposition of Soviet power in the USSR. He interpreted information about the collaboration with the Nazi cause by certain members of ethnic groups as if their entire community had been pro-Nazi. Stalin therefore had already in 1943 ordered the deportation of ethnocultural groups thus identified. These deportations assumed massive forms: for example, a whole NKVD division (some sixty thousand troops) deported the several hundreds of thousands of Chechens from the Caucasus to special settlements in Central Asia. The Crimean Tatars were sent eastward in 1944. In western Ukraine and the Baltic states, meanwhile, guerrilla warfare against the Soviets persisted until 1948, three years after the Nazi collapse. The Soviets fought the Ukrainian and Baltic partisans with massive NKVD-led military operations. Many of the captured "bandits" were executed, but thousands were arrested and sent to labor camps. There they were to form an unruly lot, who on several occasions staged revolts in the Gulag.

Meanwhile, Stalin tried to maneuver on the diplomatic front to gain maximum geopolitical advantage out of a war that had been so extraordinarily costly to his subjects. After the preliminary talks with Churchill, the Big Three (including U.S. president Franklin Roosevelt) met at Teheran (Iran) in 1943 to discuss the pursuit of the war (including that against Japan) and the postwar settlement that was to follow the conclusion of hostilities. At Teheran and the later conferences at Yalta and Potsdam, Stalin's secret police seems to have rigged the premises of the Western Allies with ample listening devices. It is not clear if Churchill and Roosevelt realized this. But even if they did, it did not change the substance of their arguments very much. Anglo-Americans and Soviets treated each other with suspicion.

In the discussions between the Big Three, Stalin behaved as if he was negotiating at a stand on a Russian *bazar* (open-air market). He quasi-generously suggested that he was perfectly willing to join the proposed United Nations if he would receive territory in exchange and was allowed to expand the Soviet sphere of influence in Europe and Asia. In another cheap token of his supposed good faith, Stalin disbanded the Comintern in 1943. The organization had outlasted its utility a long time before. President Roosevelt was nonetheless impressed.

A side deal struck in 1944 between Stalin and Churchill in Moscow combined with the military situation on the ground to determine the postwar settlement in East-Central Europe. The British prime minister was willing to forego any say in the fate of Romania and Bulgaria, and to some extent of Hungary and Czechoslovakia, if the Soviets allowed the British to control Greece. The Baltic countries were not even mentioned by Churchill: it was a foregone conclusion that the USSR was allowed to reincorporate them. Poland, however, remained a delicate matter, for the British had gone to war in defense of its independence. Stalin continued for a while to communicate with the official Polish government-in-exile, which resided in London. He maintained the mien of an accommodating fellow until the end of the war in Europe. Probably because it had in effect little strategic significance, the Soviets treated defeated Finland mildly after it surrendered in the summer of 1944. In another gesture to the Western allies of Soviet goodwill, Finland was not strong-armed into becoming a Soviet satellite.

Stalin also had some vague designs on a variety of western Asian countries, but developments soon after the war appear to indicate that he considered them mere bargaining chips, like Finland. Thus, cautious Soviet moves to perpetuate a presence in Iran or take over part of Turkey were halted by about 1947. No attempt was made to increase Soviet influence in Afghanistan, although, after the British retreat from India and Pakistan in 1947, it began to slowly gravitate toward the Soviet orbit. In China, a sort of Soviet protectorate over Xinjiang province and Inner Mongolia was established in 1945, while the Red Army occupied Manchuria during a successful campaign against the Japanese in a mere few weeks in August 1945 (on the day the second atomic bomb fell on Nagasaki, the Soviets invaded Japanese-held Manchuria). The Soviets, too, were given the supervision over northern Korea after the Japanese withdrawal there.

It was the Soviet army rather than the Anglo-American military that occupied Berlin in early May 1945, to the dismay of Winston Churchill, a lifelong foe of Communism. At Potsdam in the summer, the Big Three decided that Germany and Austria were each to be divided into four occupation zones (as were their two capitals, Berlin and Vienna). Churchill insisted on giving France, led by General Charles de Gaulle (1890–1970), a place at the victors' table. France, too, together with China, became a permanent member of the UN Security Council, enjoying veto power. Stalin was not unduly disturbed by all of this: he appears to have thought that the occupation of Germany would not last very long and that the country was to become once more a great industrial power in the near future. At first, he did not plan for a divided country, as he hoped that the German Communists might come to power in a united Germany. And he had no particular faith in international organizations such as the UN, as he probably remembered the failure of the League of Nations, the Second Socialist International, or the Comintern. Thus, he too did not object when the UN was given its headquarters in the United States.[2]

In Potsdam in July 1945, Stalin was unpleasantly surprised by news of a successful test of the atomic bomb in the United States, especially when secretary of state James Byrnes began to use the American monopoly on the bomb as a means to gain advantage in the negotiations. Once the devastating consequences of the bomb's detonation became apparent at Hiroshima and Nagasaki in August, Stalin ordered his security chief Lavrentii Beria to oversee a Soviet atomic bomb project, using whichever means available to develop a nuclear weapon. Even if Beria used hundreds of thousands of people (many of whom were camp inmates) in this enterprise, he showed his administrative adroitness (and how much espionage, threats, force, and fear may accomplish). In August 1949, a Soviet bomb was successfully detonated, sending shivers throughout the Western world. In hindsight, then, the Potsdam Conference might be seen as the moment when the Cold War began, even if the causes of the Cold War can be traced all the way back to 1917. It is significant that the Big Three would never meet again after they had decamped from the Berlin suburb.

POSTWAR RECONSTRUCTION

At the 1945 Yalta and Potsdam conferences, it became abundantly clear that the Soviet wartime alliance with the British and Americans had been no more than temporarily expedient to both sides. Stalin ruled a country that had been bled white and needed as much support as he could get in rebuilding his country. But after the United States canceled Lend-Lease immediately upon the victory in Europe and the Soviet leadership was confronted with the existence of a deliverable atomic bomb, Stalin probably realized that no Western aid was further forthcoming.

The Soviet populace's effort during the postwar reconstruction period thus almost equaled the Soviet population's selfless heroism during the war itself or the First Five Year Plan. The Fourth Five Year Plan that was announced in early 1946 once again targeted the development of heavy industry (machinery, defense, mining, and, indeed, the construction of an atomic bomb) rather than the production of consumer goods or the increase of agricultural production through greater investment. A misharvest in 1946 led to another famine in Russia and Ukraine, which may have cost some two million people their lives in 1946 and 1947.

Some Soviet intellectuals hoped at the end of the war that a new era of greater freedom had dawned. During the war, certain writers who had been gagged before 1941 were once more allowed to publish because of more relaxed censorship rules. Churches had been allowed to open, and the Orthodox Church had even been permitted to elect a patriarch in 1943, the first since the death of Patriarch Tikhon (1865–1925). In the countryside, collective farms, faced with severe labor shortages because of wartime mobilization, had been given leeway to allow for a greater share of state deliveries to be produced by individual, rather than socialized or collective, effort.

But from the spring of 1946 onward, the liberties that had been allowed were quickly reduced. Private plots on collective farms were standardized and the kolkhoznik was once again forced to work primarily in the socialized sector on pain of being evicted from the farm as a shirker. After the early months of 1947, no further houses of worship were given the right to open their doors. And artists, musicians, writers, and scientists were berated for straying from the party's line in a series of campaigns that were often associated with Andrei Zhdanov, who spearheaded them publicly.

Zhdanov, too, called the Eastern European (as well as the French and Italian) Communist Parties to order in the context of a smaller version of the defunct Comintern, called the Cominform. And Zhdanov and Mikhail Suslov (1902–1982), who succeeded him as chief of the party's propaganda apparatus after Zhdanov's death in August 1948, created a comprehensive system of ideological schools in which party officials went to study the Holy Writ of Marx, Engels, Lenin, and Stalin. This indoctrination was all the more necessary because the party had seen a wholesale renewal of its membership during the war, when entry requirements had been relaxed and many front soldiers had joined, even those who were virtually clueless about Marx.

Of course, for people who defied the regime from a political point of view or as common criminals, the labor camp system continued to operate. In addition, POWs were put to work to help rebuild the country. Nothing like the Great Terror recurred, but regularly plots within the party or Communist Youth (Komsomol) organizations were detected, with its plotters condemned as enemies of the people

Figure 8.2. Celebrating forty years of Soviet power, 1947 (Slavic and Baltic Division, New York Public Library, Astor, Lenox, and Tilden Foundations)

or counterrevolutionaries. In the very leadership of the party after Zhdanov's death, most of those who had been associated with the deceased ideologue at some point in their career were arrested. Some two hundred people may have perished in this Leningrad Affair.

Despite all these efforts at rooting out political opposition, subversive acts continued and sometimes remained undetected. One of them was Boris Pasternak's (1890–1960) writing of *Doctor Zhivago*, a novel that expressed grave doubts about the blessings of the 1917 Bolshevik takeover and Civil War victory. Rather than submitting his novel to the editors of one of the state publishing houses, a sensibly cautious Pasternak placed his manuscript in a drawer, awaiting freer times.

FOREIGN AFFAIRS

Foreign Communists also proved to be less pliable than Stalin liked. In 1948, Stalin berated the Yugoslav Communist leader Josip Tito (1892–1980), who had engaged in unauthorized discussion with the Bulgarian party boss Georgi Dimitrov (1882–1949) about the formation of a federalized southern Slavic state. Stalin was not keen on this plan, as it might create in southeastern Europe a rather powerful Communist state (Albania was also to be added) that might challenge Moscow's dominance over the Communist world.

Rather than apologizing to Stalin (as Dimitrov did), Tito defied Stalin and demanded that the Soviets stay out of Yugoslav affairs. By the summer of 1948, the rift became public. Yugoslavia was the first country that defected from the fledgling Soviet Bloc. Despite threats, Stalin refrained from an invasion. The Yugoslav Communists had largely on their own strength defeated the Nazis and Italian Fascists (and their Yugoslav allies) during the Second World War. Any Soviet armed engagement in Yugoslavia might prove to be risky.

At about the same time as the Yugoslav defiance, the Soviet Union virtually ruptured relations with the West. In 1947, the wartime allies had still found enough common ground to sign peace treaties with Germany's former allies, Hungary, Romania, Finland, and Bulgaria. In the summer of that year, however, the Soviets marched out of negotiations in Paris about a vast economic stimulus package offered to Europe by the United States, known after one of its architects as the Marshall Plan.[3] Soviet negotiators, headed by Molotov, claimed that U.S. terms for eligibility for aid under the plan amounted to an infringement on sovereignty, for it would allow U.S. monitors, ostensibly assigned to check on the distribution of the funds, to spy on the Soviet Union and its allies.

In February 1948, the Czechoslovak Communist Party ousted all parties from the government in Prague that did not wholly agree with its program. After Poland, Hungary, Yugoslavia, Romania, Bulgaria, and Albania, as well as the somewhat special case of Eastern Germany, this made Czechoslovakia the final East-Central European country to become a "people's democracy." This was a euphemistic term for countries ruled by Soviet-style dictatorships. In the spring of that year, around the time when Yugoslavia broke off relations with the Cominform and Moscow, the Soviets decided to close all entryways that led through Soviet-occupied Eastern Germany to the Western-occupied sectors of Berlin. Stalin's motives behind this move are not fully clear. Indeed, the decision to "blockade" Berlin appears to have been made somewhat whimsically. Stalin seems to have hoped for the imminent restoration of a united Germany (and Berlin) that would eventually fall into Communist hands. But the Western Allies supplied the inhabitants of their sectors of Berlin with food and other basic necessities through an airlift. In the spring of 1949, Stalin allowed the railroad and highway that normally supplied West Berlin to reopen, just as rashly as he had decided to close them a year previously. In a further response to the Berlin Blockade, meanwhile, the British and Americans had sponsored the formation of the North Atlantic Treaty Organization (NATO), a military alliance in which all member countries were to defend any of their number if attacked by a third party.

Perhaps Stalin decided that he could afford to give way somewhat on the German issue because of his acquisition of the atomic bomb and the triumph of the Chinese Communists over their adversaries in a civil war in 1949. The Chinese Communist leader Mao Zedong (1893–1976) visited Stalin in late 1949. The Soviet boss made clear who was the leader of world Communism by having Mao cool his heels in Moscow for two weeks before receiving him. But he did return Xinjiang province as well as Inner Mongolia and Manchuria to the Chinese. Otherwise, he had little aid to offer, partially because the USSR still was a patient on the mend from its own war wounds, while it had strained itself to test its first nuclear device a few months earlier. But Stalin also recalled how his own country had pulled itself up by its bootstraps in the Great Turn around 1930. Surely China could accomplish the same feat, for there were no fortresses, as the saying went, that the Bolsheviks could not storm.[4]

Stalin's last significant foreign policy move concerned Korea, where the Cold War turned hot in the first of a series of proxy wars between Soviet and U.S. clients. Here the Soviets had sponsored the Communist dictatorship of Kim Il-Sung (1912–1994) in their zone of occupation (the north of the peninsula) after 1945. Kim was an ambitious man who managed to persuade both Stalin and Mao in early 1950 that he could easily conquer South Korea (which was ruled by a right-wing dictator). This seemed all the more feasible, when in January 1950 U.S. secretary of state Dean Acheson (1893–1971) implied in a public speech that South Korea was not considered a vital ally by the United States. Stalin gave Kim the green light to invade the south, but at the same time he told Kim that no open Soviet support would be rendered (Soviet pilots did fly North Korean planes). After a rapid initial advance, the North Koreans were surprised by a counteroffensive led by the U.S. military. It almost caused Kim to flee his country, but at the eleventh hour the Korean dictator was bailed out by Chinese "volunteers" dispatched on Mao's command. They pushed back the U.S.-led force to the thirty-eighth parallel, where the front stabilized until a shaky truce was concluded in 1953. Several million Koreans and foreign troops died in the fracas.

NOTES

1. The Soviet regime continued to deny the clause's existence until the very last months of the Soviet Union's existence. The clause divided up East-Central Europe.

2. The renaming in early 1946 of the Council of People's Commissars (Sovnarkom) into Council of Ministers (Sovmin), adopting the traditionally Western name of the government's executive branch, seems to have been another whimsical move on Stalin's part to propitiate the Western Allies.

3. General George C. Marshall (1880–1959) was U.S. secretary of state from 1947 to 1949.

4. And surely the East-Central European countries, which received precious little Soviet economic aid as well, could turn themselves around, too.

FURTHER READING

Translated Primary Sources

Bidlack, Richard, and Nikita Lomagin, eds. *The Leningrad Blockade, 1941–1944: A New Documentary History from the Soviet Archives.* Translations by Marian Schwartz. New Haven, CT: Yale University Press, 2012.

Chuikov, Vasily. *The End of the Third Reich.* Translated by Ruth Kisch. London: MacGibbon, 1967.

Grossman, Vasily. *Life and Fate.* Translated by Robert Chandler. New York: New York Review Books, 2006.

———. *A Writer at War: A Soviet Journalist with the Red Army, 1941–1945.* Edited and translated by Antony Beevor and Luba Vinogradova. New York: Vintage, 2007.

Kopelev, Lev. *To Be Preserved Forever.* Edited and translated by Anthony Austin. New York: Lippincott, 1977.

Meretskov, K. A. *Serving the People.* Translated by David Fidlon. Moscow: Progress, 1971.

Solzhenitsyn, Aleksandr I. *In the First Circle.* Translated by Harry T. Willetts. New York: Harper, 2009.

Scholarly Literature

Berkhoff, Karel. *The Harvest of Despair: Life and Death in Ukraine under Nazi Rule.* Cambridge, MA: Belknap, 2008.

Boterbloem, Kees. *Life and Death under Stalin: Kalinin Province, 1945–1953.* Montreal-Kingston: McGill Queen's University Press, 1999.

———. *The Life and Times of Andrei Zhdanov, 1896–1948.* Montreal-Kingston: McGill Queen's University Press, 1999.

Edele, Mark. *Soviet Veterans of World War Two: A Popular Movement in an Authoritarian Society, 1941–1991.* New York: Oxford University Press, 2009.

Erickson, John. *The Road to Berlin: Stalin's War with Germany.* Vol. 2. London: Cassell, 2004.

———. *The Road to Stalingrad: Stalin's War with Germany.* Vol. 1. New Haven, CT: Yale University Press, 1999.

Filtzer, Donald. *The Hazards of Urban Life in Late Stalinist Russia: Health, Hygiene and Living Standards, 1943–1953.* Cambridge: Cambridge University Press, 2010.

Glantz, David. *The Battle for Leningrad, 1941–1944.* Lawrence: University Press of Kansas, 2002.

———. *Colossus Reborn: The Red Army at War, 1941–1943.* Lawrence: University Press of Kansas, 2005.

———. *Stumbling Colossus: The Red Army on the Eve of World War.* Lawrence: University Press of Kansas, 2011.

Gorodetsky, Gabriel. *Grand Delusion: Stalin and the German Invasion of Russia.* New Haven, CT: Yale University Press, 2001.

Gross, Jan T. *Revolution from Abroad: The Soviet Conquest of Poland's Western Ukraine and Western Belorussia.* Princeton, NJ: Princeton University Press, 2002.

Holloway, David. *Stalin and the Bomb.* New Haven, CT: Yale University Press, 1994.

Khlevniuk, Oleg, and Yoram Gorlizki. *Cold Peace: Stalin and the Soviet Ruling Circle, 1945–1953.* New York: Oxford University Press, 2005.

Kirschenbaum, Lisa. *The Legacy of the Siege of Leningrad, 1941–1995: Myth, Memories and Monuments.* Cambridge: Cambridge University Press, 2006.

Kostyrchenko, Gennadi. *Out of the Red Shadows: Anti-Semitism in Stalin's Russia.* Amherst, NY: Prometheus, 1995.

Krementsov, Nikolai. *The Cure: A Story of Cancer and Politics from the Annals of the Cold War.* Chicago: University of Chicago Press, 2002.

———. *Stalinist Science.* Princeton, NJ: Princeton University Press, 1997.

Kuznetsov, Anatoli. *Babi Yar: A Document in the Form of a Novel.* New York: Farrar, Straus and Giroux, 1970.

Marshall, Alex. *The Caucasus under Soviet Rule.* New York: Routledge, 2010.

Merridale, Catherine. *Ivan's War: Life and Death in the Red Army, 1939–1945.* New York: Picador, 2007.

———. *Night of Stone: Death and Memory in Twentieth-Century Russia.* London: Granta, 1999.

Nekrich, Aleksandr. *The Punished Peoples: The Deportation and Fate of Soviet Minorities at the End of the Second World War.* New York: Norton, 1981.

Polonsky, Rachel. *Molotov's Magic Lantern: A Journey in Russian History.* New York: Faber and Faber, 2011.

Polyan, Pavel. *Against Their Will: The History and Geography of Forced Migrations in the USSR.* Budapest: Central European University Press, 2003.

Pons, Silvio. *Stalin and the Inevitable War, 1936–1941.* New York: Routledge, 2002.

Slepyan, Kenneth. *Stalin's Guerillas: Soviet Partisans in World War II.* Lawrence: University Press of Kansas, 2006.

Snyder, Timothy. *Bloodlands: Europe between Hitler and Stalin.* New York: Basic Books, 2012.

Solomon, Peter H. *Soviet Criminal Justice under Stalin.* Cambridge: Cambridge University Press, 1996.

Veidlinger, Jeffrey. *The Moscow State Yiddish Theater: Jewish Culture on the Soviet Stage.* Bloomington: Indiana University Press, 2006.

Watson, Derek. *Molotov: A Biography.* Houndsmills, UK: Palgrave Macmillan, 2005.

Weiner, Amir. *Making Sense of War: The Second World War and the Fate of the Bolshevik Revolution.* Princeton, NJ: Princeton University Press, 2002.

Werth, Alexander. *Russia at War, 1941–1945.* New York: Dutton, 1964.

Yekelchyk, Serhy. *Stalin's Empire of Memory: Russian-Ukrainian Relations in the Soviet Historical Imagination.* Toronto: University of Toronto Press, 2004.

Zubkova, Elena. *Russia after the War: Hopes, Illusions and Disappointments, 1945–1957.* Armonk, NY: M. E. Sharpe, 1998.

Zubok, Vladislav M. *A Failed Empire: The Soviet Union in the Cold War from Stalin to Gorbachev.* Chapel Hill: University of North Carolina Press, 2008.

Zubok, Vladislav M., and Constantine Pleshakov. *Inside the Kremlin's Cold War: From Stalin to Khrushchev.* Cambridge, MA: Harvard University Press, 1997.

FILMS

Ballad of a Soldier. DVD. Directed by Grigorii Chukhrai. New York: Criterion, 2002.

The Cranes Are Flying. DVD. Directed by Mikhail Kalatozov. New York: Criterion, 2002.

Katyn. DVD. Directed by Andrzej Wajda. New York: Koch Lorber, 2009.

9

Embattled Leader of the "Second World," 1953–1982

After Stalin's death, his successors continued to rule his far-flung empire for another three and a half decades, successfully conveying the image that the Soviet Union and the Eastern Bloc were a serious rival of the Western world led by the United States. But in reality the effort to catch up and overtake the Western capitalists became increasingly strained. The planned economy and tightly controlled society of the Soviet Union left too little room for the creativity and innovation needed to shepherd the country into the postindustrial world that began to take shape by the 1970s. The regime's planning straitjacket stalled the development of a consumer society, and its unduly centralized distribution system hindered the availability of goods for sale (and even of materials needed by Soviet industry to manufacture its products). And even in terms of industrial modernization the Soviet regime missed out: whereas it lavishly funded the use of computers in military endeavors (to which the Soviet space program belonged as well), the Soviet Union missed out on developing computers for personal use. By the 1980s, the Soviet leaders belatedly admitted that their country had dangerously fallen behind. Ultimately, the disappearance of the Soviet Union in its rigidly regulated Stalinist form seemed inevitable to Mikhail Gorbachev and his allies.

AT THE APEX

If Stalin had been able to trust anyone, he might have bequeathed his empire to his successors with some confidence. From the Boss's perspective in the early 1950s, Soviet Communism had made massive strides since he had replaced Lenin. When Stalin died in 1953, about one-third of the global population was ruled by Soviet-style Communist regimes. This "Second World" was quickly developing in

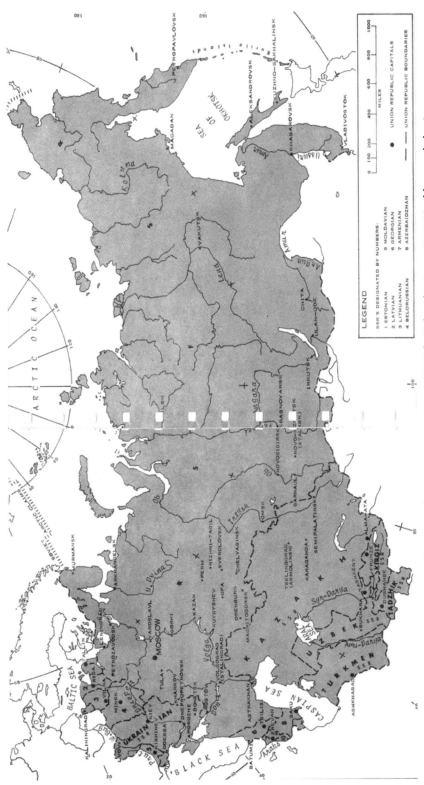

Map 9.1. USSR (From Allen F. Chew, *An Atlas of Russian History*, New Haven, CT: Yale University Press, 1967. Used by permission.)

Figure 9.1. First woman in space, Valentina Tereshkova, 1960s (RIA Novosti archive)

terms of its economic might. Soviet boasting that the country would catch up and overtake the United States seemed more than empty rhetoric after the launch of the satellite *Sputnik* in 1957.

By 1960, the Soviet Union was a country in which the majority of the population lived in an urban environment. Still, according to the 1959 census, well-nigh half of the Soviet population of slightly more than two hundred million people lived in villages in the countryside, a far higher proportion than in the contemporary Western world (in the United Kingdom, the urban population had surpassed the rural population around 1850, and in the United States around 1920). And this percentage was higher among the non-Slavs, who formed about one-fifth of the Soviet population at the time.[1] But a radiant future, as it was called, seemed to beckon to the true believers, and Stalin, despite his otherwise twisted mind, remained one of them.

Stalin, however, did not have faith in other human beings. Toward the end of his life, he greatly worried about his successors' capacity to rule his empire in an authoritative fashion. Indeed, he had surrounded himself with a rather mediocre set of yes-men because of his habit to eliminate talented figures in his surroundings, as he had recently done in the 1949–1950 Leningrad Affair. In a sense, Stalin's anxiety was appropriate, for it took his successors barely longer to dismantle his empire (1953–1991) than the amount of time it had taken to build it under his leadership (1922–1953). Still, upon Stalin's death in 1953, such a speedy unraveling seemed remote from the viewpoint of the Soviet leaders, their subjects, and foreign observers. True believers in the radiant future of communism were plentiful, not least at the very top: the dynamic Nikita Khrushchev, who emerged as Stalin's heir by 1956, attempted to rekindle the enthusiasm of the early days of revolution and Five Year Plans among Communist Party members and Soviet citizens. Khrushchev strenuously appealed to the newly emerging Third World of former colonies in Asia and Africa to follow the Soviet Union as the global leader of the formerly downtrodden and encouraged them to adopt the Soviet model of development. He even meddled in the "American backyard" of Middle and South America.

But the Soviet economy in most of its sectors proved to be incapable of moving beyond a certain level of technological sophistication. Defense was the exception (and the Soviet space program was a spin-off of this branch) but swallowed up greater and greater amounts of budgetary expenditure. After the global oil crisis of 1973 and the worldwide economic downturn that followed it, the Soviet standard of living stagnated as well. Across the Soviet Union and in the countries of East-Central Europe in the second half of the twentieth century, most people lived in crowded dwellings and survived on a minimally adequate household budget. Meanwhile, the Soviet penchant to achieve economic growth at any cost began to lead to extensive environmental damage. The Chernobyl disaster ultimately became the symbol of Soviet ecological neglect.

THE STRUGGLE FOR STALIN'S MANTLE

While Stalin did not leave a testament such as Lenin had in 1924, another succession struggle that resembled the first years after Lenin's demise developed upon his death in 1953. At first, the chief contenders publicly announced that they would lead collectively, implying that none of them was to be the first among equals. The Politburo was reduced from the inflated size Stalin had introduced in his dotage to the normal number of eight to ten full members.[2] All the survivors were long-term apprentices of Stalin, who had served the dictator in high posts since at least the 1930s. During that time, they had become patrons of a large network of clients: to outmaneuver their rivals, they now strategically joined their networks during crucial votes in the Central Committee. Thus, Georgii Malenkov's and Khrushchev's group teamed up in causing the dismissal of Lavrentii Beria.

Resuming full control over the secret police upon Stalin's death, Beria was feared by almost all his Politburo colleagues. They suspected that he kept compromising material about all of them, which he could use against them in the power struggle for Stalin's mantle. In the spring of 1953, as vice premier, Politburo member, and police chief, Beria initiated a series of policies that aimed to end some of the worst features of the Stalinist system, including an amnesty of well-nigh one million camp inmates. He further tried to counter the hypercentralized ruling system by advocating the replacement of Russians with representatives of the local population to lead the republican Communist Parties. Furthermore, Beria suggested to his colleagues that the East-Central European satellites should be given a greater measure of freedom from Moscow. But Beria failed to see how his liberalized version of Communist despotism lost him the support of virtually all his Politburo comrades.

Nikita Khrushchev, who had become the first secretary of the party following Stalin's death, led the operation that dethroned Beria. In tandem with military commanders, he conspired to have Beria arrested at a Politburo meeting. The hero of Stalingrad, Marshal Georgy Zhukov himself, did the honors. A Central Committee meeting ratified Beria's arrest in July 1953. Beria was now accused of having been a British spy and (with apparently solid evidence) of raping young women whom his bodyguards plucked from the streets of Moscow. After an investigation that lasted about half a year, he was convicted with several of his assistants in a secret trial. His crimes included espionage, counterrevolution, and being an "enemy of the people," standard Stalinist clichés. Stalin's ghost was to haunt the Soviet leadership and Soviet society until its very end and beyond.

Following Beria's fall, Prime Minister Malenkov seemed the leading light among the Soviet bosses, but this was more apparent than real. Khrushchev controlled the crucial party apparatus and manipulated the *nomenklatura* appointment system just as skillfully as had Stalin in the 1920s. Malenkov did not aid his own cause by making a couple of ill-advised public announcements. In August 1953, at a session of the Soviet parliament (the Supreme Soviet), the prime minister announced that the burden carried by the collective farmers would be considerably lightened. Prices paid by the state for kolkhoz deliveries would drastically increase, while debts incurred by the farms would be written off. In the eyes of his colleagues, the agricultural policy Malenkov advocated reversed too strongly the previous policy of prioritizing investment in heavy industry. It was "corrected" at a Central Committee meeting in September 1953, even if this gathering agreed to alleviate the burden placed on the kolkhozniks as well.

In March 1954, Malenkov made a second cardinal error in publicly declaring that a nuclear war between East and West could not be won. This last point flew in the face of Marxist beliefs, which held that the historical triumph of communism was inevitable. In January 1955, Malenkov was forced out as prime minister. His demotion went at least in part back to the distrust he had brought on himself by his previous friendship with Beria (and his implication in the latter's crimes as secret police chief). His alleged incompetent management as prime minister and his lust for power were, however, especially singled out. His so-called demagoguery about agricultural prices and the impossibility of nuclear war was cited as proof of the latter trait.

In retrospect, it appears that Beria and Malenkov shared an outlook that was too pragmatic for the Soviet Union's elite in the 1950s. Senior Communist Party leaders had participated in the Great Turn and had faithfully memorized the relevant passages from Stalin's *Short Course*. They saw the outside world as implacably hostile to their sacred cause. They believed that any compromise with the non-Communist world could only be temporary, in anticipation of the next Communist advance. This followed a tried-and-true recipe. Such tactical truces with capitalism had been agreed to at Brest-Litovsk in 1918, in signing the Molotov-Ribbentrop Pact in 1939, and in concluding the alliance with the Western Allies from 1941 to 1945. But actually retreating from territory that was firmly in Communist hands went too far. Therefore, Eastern Germany should remain Communist rather than unifying with Western Germany, unless a united Germany was a Communist-controlled country.

Nevertheless, Nikita Khrushchev, who remained a true believer in the Communist cause until his death in 1971, was willing to concede minor points to the American-led Western Bloc in the Cold War. He had personally participated in the slaughter at Stalingrad and had taken stock of the utterly devastated Ukraine as its party chief during the Second World War. If at all possible, Khrushchev preferred that his country stay out of any war, despite the saber-rattling in which he occasionally engaged. The new Soviet leaders persuaded North Korean leader Kim Il-Sung and his Chinese backers to agree to an armistice on the peninsula in 1953. Viacheslav Molotov, once again foreign minister, agreed in Geneva in 1955 to the withdrawal of Soviet forces from Austria. Relations with Josip Tito's Yugoslavia were normalized, although the Yugoslavs stayed outside of the Warsaw Pact, the military alliance of Eastern European Communist states created as an answer to NATO in 1955.

CHAMPION OF THE THIRD WORLD

Khrushchev and the new Soviet prime minister, Nikolai Bulganin (1895–1975), visited newly independent India, Afghanistan, and Burma in 1955. They portrayed their country as an anti-imperialist state that had successfully broken free from the Western economic stranglehold after the 1917 Revolution. The Soviet path of development, with its planned economy, was held up to the postcolonial states as the road to full freedom from ongoing Western economic dominance. The cost of Soviet industrialization in human terms was muffled. Twenty-five years after the Great Turn began, Khrushchev boasted of some significant tangible results, not in the least the victory in the Second World War. He omitted to mention that all of it cost several dozen millions their lives.

Khrushchev believed that his courtship of the "Third World" would prepare the ground for the next phase of Communist expansion, which was envisioned as the addition to the camp of most postcolonial states in Asia and Africa. He was not just deluding himself by wishful thinking. For example, the Communist Party of Indonesia numbered hundreds of thousands of members, North Vietnam had been Communist since 1945 (and had successfully forced the French from Indochina), and several states within India's federation were ruled by the Communist Party. In the Middle East, various nationalist Arabic movements adopted quasi-Communist policies, such as the Ba'ath Party in Syria and Iraq, or Gamal Abdel Nasser's (1918–1970) regime in Egypt. When other African countries received their independence, their political leaders, too, established one-party states that introduced multiyear economic plans and professed to stand for equality and social justice. These efforts had at best mixed results, while clashes between Soviet clients and pro-Western political movements sometimes escalated into real civil wars, for instance, in the former Belgian Congo, a very poor region awash with heavily sought-after raw materials. The Congolese independence leader Patrice Lumumba (1925–1961) was murdered by rebels supported by the United States. At a UN meeting in New York, the discussion about Congo reached such a feverish pitch that Khrushchev took off his shoe and banged it on the table. While colorful, such behavior was deplored among Soviet diplomats as a sign of primitive crudeness. Lumumba was posthumously honored when Moscow's university for foreign students was named after him.

Much of the rest of sub-Saharan Africa was divided into pro-Soviet and pro-Western countries. In order to prevent the spread of Communism, the United States supported colonial and racist regimes in Angola, Mozambique, Rhodesia (Zimbabwe), and South Africa, and corrupt and brutal dictatorships such as that of Mobutu Sese Seko (1930–1997) in Congo (Zaire). The Soviets seemed to gain the upper hand in the 1970s: apart from the informal allegiance to their bloc by socialist regimes such as that of Julius Nyerere (1922–1999) in Tanzania or Leopold Senghor (1906–2001) in Senegal, genuine Marxist states were founded in Ethiopia in 1973 under Haile Mengistu (b. 1937) and in Angola after it received its independence from Portugal in 1975. But the horrible failure of the Mengistu regime in particular caused a sharp decline in the popularity of the Soviet model of economic development in Africa. The Ethiopian famine of 1984–1985, in part the result of an attempt to impose collective farming on an unwilling population, cost about one million people their lives.

In South America, too, Communists gained strength in the first decades after the Second World War, even if extreme economic dependence on the United States prevented most countries' governments from introducing any policies that smacked of Communism or "socialism."[3] Most governments in Latin America felt that they could ill afford to lose U.S. investments. In 1954, the United States made clear that it was implacably hostile to left-wing governments in its own backyard, when it backed a military coup that toppled the democratically elected administration of Jacobo Arbenz (1913–1971) in Guatemala. Later U.S. interventions in the Dominican Republic and Grenada reiterated this point.

But an opportunity for Soviet infiltration arose in 1959, when the corrupt dictatorship of Fulgencio Batista (1901–1973) in Cuba was overthrown by a left-wing guerrilla group. Its leader, Fidel Castro (b. 1926), and his comrades at first hesitated about jeopardizing ties with the United States by nationalizing foreign-owned property. However, egged on by his brother Raúl (b. 1931) and the Argentinian doctor Ernesto "Che" Guevara (1928–1967), both secretly members of the Communist Party of Cuba, Castro took ever more radical steps. This ultimately led the U.S. government to announce that it would no longer buy the Cuban sugar-cane crop in 1961. The boycott was a potentially devastating blow to an economy that was dependent on the sale of this monoculture (its prime cash crop) to the

United States. Khrushchev saw his chance. He offered to buy the entire sugar harvest at a guaranteed price, thus saving Cuba from economic collapse. In addition, the Soviet Union began to deliver arms to Cuba and dispatched "military advisors," especially after the U.S.-sponsored (failed) Bay of Pigs invasion in 1961.

Khrushchev then decided to up the ante. In 1962, with the backing of the Politburo, he ordered the stationing on the island of ballistic missiles capable of carrying nuclear warheads, having convinced Castro that this made Cuba unassailable. Before the first rockets were operational, however, U.S. spy planes photographed the missile launching pads that were under construction. In October 1962, President John F. Kennedy demanded the dismantling of the launching pads and the removal of Soviet missiles from the island. U.S. warships enforced a quarantine, inspecting any ships carrying goods destined for Cuba. After a tense few days, Khrushchev decided to agree to the American demands, without telling Castro first. The Cuban dictator was enraged but nonetheless remained a loyal member of the Soviet Bloc in subsequent years. Khrushchev received a guarantee from the U.S. government that it would no longer threaten to invade Cuba, while U.S. missiles stationed in Turkey were removed. But the Cuban Missile Crisis diminished Khrushchev's stature at home further, especially among the Central Committee membership.

MAO, KHRUSHCHEV, AND BEYOND

The Cuban crisis was not the only foreign policy failure to haunt Khrushchev. Whereas Khrushchev mended the fences with Yugoslavia, the country never became a full member of the Soviet Bloc again. The quarrel that erupted with China, however, was of far greater significance. Perhaps all politics are personal, and Mao Zedong certainly was not impressed with Stalin's successor. Khrushchev, indeed, was no theorist as Marx, Lenin, or even Stalin had been. Mao, a librarian by education, considered the Soviet boss somewhat of an unlettered bumpkin (rumors persist that Khrushchev never properly mastered writing Russian). Far more than under Stalin, however, Khrushchev's Soviet Union sent aid and advisors to China to help it embark on the road to communism. Soviet engineers did not merely build roads, dams, and bridges but also aided the fledgling Chinese arms industry. The Chinese People's Army was further equipped with arms and ordnance made in the Soviet Union or East-Central Europe.

But Mao, still basking in the glow of his 1949 triumph, was chomping at the bit for further victories. He wanted to chase the nationalist government of his rival Chiang Kai-shek (Jiang Jieshi, 1887–1975) from the island of Taiwan, to which it had fled upon its defeat in 1949. There Chiang enjoyed the protection of the United States, which intimated that it would use nuclear arms to stop the People's Republic from ousting him. During a visit by Khrushchev to China, Mao suggested to the Soviet leader that the USSR back a Chinese invasion with Soviet nuclear bombs.

Mao stated that, because of its overwhelming numbers, the Communist world was guaranteed a victory in a nuclear war. Khrushchev was aghast at such cynicism.

Meanwhile, Mao and the zealots who surrounded him in the Chinese leadership became utterly annoyed at Khrushchev's criticism of Stalin in 1956, accusing the Soviets of being "revisionists" and, eventually, "Trotskyites." When Khrushchev engaged in a renewed round of criticism of Stalin in 1961 and particularly attacked the Albanian Communist leader Enver Hoxha (1908–1985) for copying Stalin's megalomania, the Chinese delegation attending the Twenty-Second Party Congress of the Soviet Communist Party walked out and returned home. With a leadership as puritanically Communist as Mao's, Albania remained the single Chinese ally in East-Central Europe. Soon after the Twenty-Second Party Congress, meanwhile, the Soviet Union withdrew its specialists and advisors from Communist China.

Mao oversaw a profound albeit disastrous transformation of his country during a dozen frantic years (1957–1969). He introduced the policies of the Great Leap Forward (1958–1961) and the Cultural Revolution (1966–1969), which resembled that of Stalin's Great Turn, although perhaps yielding even fewer positive results. A famine during the early 1960s cost tens of millions of Chinese their lives. The successful detonation in October 1964 (exactly at the time Khrushchev resigned as Soviet leader) of a Chinese atomic bomb did not compensate for such human suffering. Soviet engineers, before their recall, had provided the blueprint for the nuclear bomb. Mao purged any rivals in the leadership during the Cultural Revolution, which imposed a particularly outdated regimented way of life on his country.

The Chinese dictator eventually provoked Khrushchev's successors into an armed conflict about the exact location of the Chinese-Soviet border along the Ussuri and Amur Rivers. Thus, the centuries-old border dispute between Qings and Romanovs was rekindled in 1969. After some battling, somehow cooler heads prevailed and an all-out war between the erstwhile Communist brethren was avoided. Nevertheless, by the time of Mao's death in 1976, China enjoyed better relations with the United States than with the USSR.

After Mao's death, the thaw that descended on China also allowed for better relations with the Soviet Union. China chose a path other than that of the Soviet Union and its successor states to overcome the worst consequences of the naive and suffocating planning of its economy. Although the Chinese maintained their Communist Party's political dictatorship, they allowed the introduction of a capitalist economy. Unwilling to shoot at its own people as the Chinese bosses had ordered their troops to do at Tiananmen Square in 1989, the Soviet leadership introduced capitalism together with a democratic type of government, guaranteeing human rights and freedoms to its population. Today, Communist China is as important a trading partner of Russia as it is of the United States. Because of the shrinking population of Russia (not in the least in Asian Russia), and the vast mineral wealth of Siberia, some observers predict a renewal of Russian-Chinese hostility as China casts a covetous look on the riches of its northern neighbor.

THE "SECRET" SPEECH AND ITS CONSEQUENCES

After the fall of Beria and the relegation of Malenkov to the second tier, Nikita Khrushchev appeared to be the uncontested first leader of the Soviet Union. But his power was far from unlimited. Although Molotov lost the foreign office in 1955, defense minister Kliment Voroshilov, prime minister Nikolai Bulganin, trade minister Anastas Mikoian, and ideological chief Mikhail Suslov were far from Khrushchev's yes-men. Observers at the time, and historians afterward, have wondered whether or not Khrushchev's proposal to denounce Stalin's crimes before the Twentieth Party Congress was part of a strategy to rid himself of the more recalcitrant types among his fellow leaders.

After "Beria's" initial amnesty of 1953, which had primarily released those accused of minor (and mainly nonpolitical) crimes from the Gulag, Khrushchev and his colleagues ordered a wholesale review of the cases of all of those who lingered in the camps. This led to the release of the great majority of the camp inmates (some of whom had participated in large-scale riots after Stalin's death). The authorities stopped short of full (mainly posthumous) rehabilitation of most who had suffered under Stalin, for two key reasons. First, acquitting so many people from crimes they had not committed might add up to an admission that the regime had terrorized its population in the previous quarter century. And second, the Soviet authorities did not have sufficient means to compensate the victims for the wrongs that they had suffered.

But the review of many dubious judicial cases did lead the Soviet leadership to order an investigation into the extent of Stalin's crimes. The numbers that were conveyed to the Politburo by the judiciary, the Ministry of Internal Affairs (MVD, which had fewer responsibilities than under Stalin), and the new security police, the KGB (formed after Beria's fall), were staggering: more than four million people had been convicted for "counterrevolutionary crimes" between 1920 and 1953, almost all of them after 1929. Millions more had been tried for nonpolitical crimes (usually receiving shorter sentences than political convicts). Such bewildering amounts shook Khrushchev and several of his comrades to their core. The Politburo established an investigative commission to assess the terror in the party's own ranks. It disclosed that tens of thousands of honest Communists had fallen victim to Stalin's meat grinder. The revelation of the magnitude of Stalin's purges seems to have been the catalyst leading to the Secret Speech. Khrushchev suggested to his fellow leaders that an attempt should be made to wipe the slate clean at the first Party Congress after Stalin's death.

It remains curious that Khrushchev was astounded by the scale of the Great Terror. As the city's party boss in 1937, he had been in Moscow a member himself of one of the special judicial trios sentencing thousands of alleged counterrevolutionaries to their death and had been likewise involved in Ukraine in 1938. On the eve of the congress in early 1956, Lazar Kaganovich and Molotov (who recalled perhaps better than Khrushchev the extent of the operations in 1937 and 1938) in particular protested against the idea of admitting to any wrongdoings. They believed that admission of error in even a fraction of the cases might damage the party's reputation at home and abroad. Khrushchev persisted, however.

Khrushchev's Secret Speech concluded the Twentieth Party Congress in February 1956. It was far from comprehensive in sketching the extent of Stalin's tyranny. Nikita Khrushchev tried to perform a balancing act of separating the good Stalin, who had led the country through the successful introduction of a planned economy, industrial modernization, and collectivized agriculture, from the bad Stalin, who in the last fifteen years of his life had become morbidly suspicious, killing some of his most talented military and political collaborators in sudden bouts of paranoia. Khrushchev did not go as far as to call for the rehabilitation of Trotsky, Zinov'ev, or Bukharin, but he did sponsor the posthumous restoration of the good name of Marshal Mikhail Tukhachevskii, Politburo members Robert Eikhe (1890–1940) and Ian Rudzutak (1887–1938), and those who had been executed in the Leningrad Affair.

Khrushchev implied that Stalin had begun his tyranny when at the 1934 Seventeenth Party Congress the Boss learned about an effort to replace him with Sergei Kirov. Kirov's murder later that year was probably carried out on Stalin's orders, Khrushchev suggested. This assassination provided the excuse for the People's Commissariat of Internal Affairs (NKVD) to detect an ever-widening circle of conspiracies against the Soviet leaders, the government, the economy, and society. The NKVD's investigative zeal was halted only in late 1938. In 1956, a commission was organized to investigate the Kirov murder, but it could never find definitive evidence that pointed at Stalin as ordering the death of his onetime close friend.

Khrushchev's balancing act did not really convince independent observers sympathetic to the Soviet cause. Few were willing to believe that Stalin had only in 1934 descended into madness. Indeed, Khrushchev noted Lenin's doubts about Stalin in his speech, which implied that Lenin had already discovered Stalin's evil side in 1922! Meanwhile, Khrushchev deliberately leaked the speech. While this can be interpreted as showing his good faith in trying to come clean, it may have been a ploy to prevent his opponents from removing him and pretending that nothing had ever happened. Everyone in 1956 had dirty hands, but some hands were dirtier, especially those of Khrushchev's rivals Molotov, Malenkov (who was hoping for a comeback), and Kaganovich.

An integral English version already became available in the West in the spring of 1956. But rather than its restoring faith in Communist honesty, in response many Western Communists left the movement altogether. In Poland and Hungary, voices were raised that challenged the Communist dictatorship ruling the countries. In Poland, the former party secretary Wladyslaw Gomulka (1905–1982), who had been jailed, was restored as chief of the Communist Party. His considerable personal authority in the country, his reputation as a Polish patriot, and a variety of economic reforms (by which, among other things, Poland abandoned collective farming) prevented a widespread protest from turning into a revolution. In the fall of 1956, Soviet leaders visited Poland, worried about a repeat of

1830–1831 or 1863. They allowed Gomulka considerable leeway when events in Hungary took an even stronger anti-Soviet turn.

The Hungarian Communist leader Imre Nagy (1896–1958), who like Gomulka was released from prison after Stalin's death, declared his country a neutral country, abandoning the recently created Warsaw Pact. This went too far in Soviet eyes. The Soviet army moved into Hungary, taking control of government offices, radio stations, and the press, and arresting the ringleaders of the plot. The Hungarians fought with rifles, bricks, and sticks against the Soviet tanks but were overcome at the cost of hundreds of lives. Imre Nagy fled to the Yugoslav embassy, only to be given up to the new Hungarian dictators, who had him executed after a perfunctory trial in 1958.

The Western world merely expressed its disapproval of the suppression of the Hungarian revolt. The NATO countries honored the division of Europe into a Soviet and a Western sphere, to which Stalin and Churchill had agreed in October 1944. In addition, the revolt unfolded right at the moment of a serious crisis over the Suez Canal, which threatened the unity of NATO. Khrushchev was thereby given a most opportune lightning rod to divert the world's attention away from the Soviet violence in Hungary. He even went as far as to threaten Britain and France with nuclear bombing, if their soldiers and their Israeli allies did not withdraw from the Suez Canal region.

After the bloody suppression of the Hungarian rebellion, tranquility descended over the Soviet camp. The bloodshed made abundantly clear that the Soviet rulers would not tolerate any serious threat to the Communist dictatorships in their satellites. Whereas a modest version of the Soviet "Thaw" can be noticed across East-Central Europe after 1956, this seldom entailed a direct challenge to Communist rule but for two celebrated cases, those of Czechoslovakia in 1968 and Poland in 1980–1981.

In the Soviet Union, only parts of the Secret Speech were read to selected audiences of party members and others deemed sufficiently loyal to the regime, while the so-called Cult of the Personality of Stalin was more broadly condemned in a rather watered-down version. But those who had cautiously raised their voices immediately after Stalin's death were emboldened by the criticism of Stalin. Between early 1956 and Khrushchev's dismissal in October 1964, a steady current of publications (fiction and nonfiction), films, and other works of art were released that decried the crimes committed by Stalin's regime. Some went too far for even the liberal censors of the age, such as the novel *Life and Fate* by Vasily Grossman. It made a direct comparison between Stalin's Gulag and the Nazi German extermination camps. In 1962, Aleksandr Solzhenitsyn's startling novella *One Day in the Life of Ivan Denisovich* was published in the journal *Novyi Mir* ("New World"), to which hundreds of thousands of Soviet citizens subscribed. It depicted in stark terms one day in the life of a concentration camp inmate in Kazakhstan.

Stalin's name was more or less banned from public life. During the Twenty-Second Party Congress of 1961, his embalmed body was removed from the mausoleum on Red Square, where it had been lying next to Lenin since 1953. Nonetheless, Stalin had been the architect of the Soviet system over which Khrushchev now presided.

Denouncing him could end in denouncing everything that had happened since 1924 in the USSR, for the Gulag and mass killings predated 1934. During the 1960s and 1970s, many "dissidents" (the term used for opponents of the regime) indeed concluded that the system had failed from the beginning. Molotov and Kaganovich had warned of this dangerous consequence, and the Chinese Communists eventually began to see the criticism of Stalin as blasphemy. Mao may have begun to truly despise Khrushchev because the Soviet leader did not even understand the elementary logic that condemning part of Stalin really amounted to criticizing all of Stalin.

KHRUSHCHEV'S DOMESTIC PROGRAM AND FALL

Neither his erratic foreign policy nor his naive denunciation of Stalin caused Khrushchev's fall in 1964, however. At first he seemed to ride a wave of popularity that was generated by the greater liberalization of the regime, the higher incomes given to collective farmers, and a sustained economic growth. Before 1962, Khrushchev's ouster indeed seemed inconceivable.

In June 1957, Khrushchev overcame a last-gasp attack by his political rivals by staging a Central Committee meeting that overrode the Politburo. Instead of Khrushchev resigning because of his decentralization policies, he forced out most of the old guard (Molotov, Kaganovich, Malenkov, Bulganin, and eventually Voroshilov as well).[4] Only Marshal Zhukov, ideological boss Suslov, and trade expert Mikoian supported Khrushchev in the Politburo, but the party's first secretary had the overwhelming support of the provincial and republican party secretaries in the country, whose power had increased in recent months. Since the 1920s, almost all of them were Central Committee members. An impromptu Central Committee meeting was organized after many of them flew into Moscow in military planes (provided by Zhukov's subordinates). The meeting ousted the "Anti-Party Group" from the Politburo. In the end, Khrushchev's moves amounted to a sort of Stalinist strategy, following the recipe used by Stalin in the 1920s against his Politburo rivals.

A few months later, Khrushchev deftly forced out Zhukov, by then defense minister, on accusations of behaving too independently and of organizing a personality cult. Even KGB chairman Ivan Serov (1905–1990) was removed in 1958, an act that made Khrushchev the unrivaled leader of the country. His position seemed unassailable. Nevertheless, he managed to lose this credit within the next five years.

It can be argued that whoever led the Soviet Union in the first five years after Stalin's death would have presided over a gradual improvement of the standard of living and an improvement in the general sense of well-being. The spartan circumstances resulting from the devastation of the war and Stalin's prioritizing of expenditure on defense in the early Cold War had made the "hungry 1940s" resemble the "hungry 1930s." By 1952, the acute capitalist threat perceived by the Soviet leadership, and especially Stalin, lessened. The Soviet detonation of the hydrogen bomb in that year occurred a mere three years after the successful test of a regular atomic bomb.

It seems that around this time, that is, even before Stalin's death, Beria, Malenkov, and Khrushchev all concluded that the heavy burden carried by the long-suffering Soviet population could be lessened. Once Stalin died, they agreed that some radical steps were needed. More consumer goods were being produced, and construction of apartment buildings boomed: most urban Soviet families acquired a separate apartment in the 1950s and 1960s, no longer sharing a kitchen and bathroom with their neighbors. Gradually, households acquired radios, televisions, and refrigerators, even if waiting lists for such goods were long and waiting times sometimes reached a decade. More Soviet citizens began to travel on their vacations, both within their country and sometimes, in groups, within the countries of the Communist Bloc.

Buoyed by these developments, Khrushchev, fondly remembering the titanic labor he had supervised in building the Moscow subway during the 1930s, decided that another leap forward was in the offing. He announced at the Twenty-First Party Congress in early 1959 that the Soviet Union was embarking on the building of communism, having completed its socialist phase. This new society would witness an economy in which everyone could enjoy all the goods that they needed and would be ruled by the people themselves, because the state would "wither away," as Marx and Lenin (in his *State and Revolution* of 1917) had predicted. A new party program was developed and released at the Twenty-Second Party Congress in 1961. It announced that communism, the society of plenty and of social harmony, would become a reality in the Soviet Union by 1980. Although much remained unclear about this plan, the leading role of the Communist Party was for the time being confirmed. In practice, the creation of a society of plenty depended on formidable economic growth rates, which were to remain out of reach. After Khrushchev's fall in 1964, his ambitious program was quietly shelved.

Khrushchev felt it necessary at the same time to tinker with the economic and political system, especially when toward 1960 growth levels did not meet expectations and shortages continued to plague the economy. A plan to outstrip the United States in terms of meat and dairy production by 1961 miserably failed. In 1959, Khrushchev visited the United States and was highly impressed with the vast farms he saw growing corn in Iowa. He decided that Soviet kolkhozes, too, needed to plant maize as a fodder crop, but the plant failed to thrive in the cold climate of much of the Soviet Union. He tried to amalgamate collective farms into large agribusinesses (called "state farms," or "sovkhozes"). In the sovkhozes, farmers were paid a wage instead of being remunerated on the basis of the amount of crops, meat, or dairy delivered to the state. But the wages were low and little incentive was offered to work harder; in addition, the farms were to submit their decisions to local party secretaries, and this proved to be a further break on initiatives toward innovations in the production process or practical measures to increase yields.

Even before he had become the unrivaled leader of the Soviet Union, Khrushchev had organized the cultivation of millions of acres of previously unused land in Kazakhstan and western Siberia. On the regime's invitation, thousands of enthusiastic, overwhelmingly young, people moved there in the middle of the 1950s to work the new farmland. This Virgin Lands project at first seemed a roaring success, dramatically increasing grain production. But the poor soil, dry weather, and incessant wind of the region led to the development of a dustbowl. It destroyed much of the newly sown land in the early 1960s, almost negating the increased crop yields reached in the 1950s. In 1963, the entire Soviet Union was affected by extreme drought, leading to a shortage of grain for bread baking and cattle foddering. Khrushchev, showing his rediscovered humane side once again, ordered the importation of foreign grain to prevent a famine. But this was a blow to his own prestige within the country and to that of the Soviet Union abroad. The country that with Yuri Gagarin (1934–1968) had put the first man into space in 1961 was unable to feed itself two years later.

The straw that broke the camel's back was Khrushchev's effort to improve economic results by splitting the party organizations at regional levels into an industrial and agricultural section. This diminished the power of the provincial party secretaries, who had managed both areas before but now were assigned only one of these sections. Khrushchev thus lost the support of those who had been his greatest allies when he had defeated the Old Guard in 1957 and who had stood by him after that. As the secretaries were members of the party's Central Committee, it was now heavily stacked against him. Returning from a holiday on the Crimea in 1964, Khrushchev was puzzled when he was met at the airport in Moscow by an unusually small delegation. He was driven to the Kremlin, where he was denounced for his "voluntarism" and his attempt to begin his own "cult of the personality." The seventy-one-year-old leader was forced to retire, ironically mainly by his own protégés whom he had promoted to the Politburo from 1957 onward.

Khrushchev, perhaps, had indeed become overconfident and began to believe too much in his own invulnerability, forgetting about the all-important role played by the party secretaries in the Soviet power structure. Their backing had sustained both Stalin and him. With Khrushchev's departure, Soviet Communism likely lost its "last best chance." His successors lacked his energy and possibly even his unwavering faith in the radiant future of communism. Mikhail Gorbachev was to model himself for a while after Khrushchev but was forced to concede that too much time had been wasted in the intervening period that separated his tenure from that of Khrushchev, the last of the true believers. In retirement, Khrushchev was to speak his memoirs into a tape recorder, thus leaving us with the most extensive and invaluable account provided by any Stalin-era leader about his life.

COLLECTIVE LEADERSHIP AND LEONID BREZHNEV

Leonid Brezhnev (1906–1982) had risen through the party's ranks since the 1930s. A Russian speaker, he had been a client of Khrushchev's when the latter was Ukrainian party chief. Brezhnev became the party secretary of the Ukrainian city of Dnipropetrovsk (the former Ekaterinoslav) during the Great Terror, when he was barely thirty years old. He had subsequently been first secretary of the party

organization of the Moldavian Socialist Soviet Republic and was in 1952 promoted to the central leadership. He had joined the Politburo permanently in 1957
and was official head of state from 1960 to 1964. He had also become second party
secretary behind Khrushchev in the last months of the latter's leadership, replacing
the ailing Frol Kozlov (1908–1965). At first, Brezhnev shared power with prime
minister Aleksei Kosygin (1904–1980) and Soviet president Nikolai Podgornyi
(1903–1983), as well as with other Politburo members, among whom Mikhail
Suslov proved to have the most staying power.

After 1964, only through very careful maneuvering did Brezhnev rise to a position
of power that began to resemble that of Stalin or Khrushchev before him. He reached
such status only in the middle of the 1970s. Brezhnev's key support was located once
again in the party apparatus, and he carefully cultivated a patronage network among
the regional party secretaries. He had learned from Khrushchev's demise that these
local bosses preferred to rule their fiefs without too much upheaval. Brezhnev appeared to guarantee quiet stability and full enjoyment of the perquisites as well as the
more unambiguously corrupt practices in which many engaged. Indeed, Brezhnev
set himself as the example for the lavish lifestyle in which the elite indulged (usually in places that were far away from the view of those kept outside of the circle of
power). The general secretary owned dozens of fancy Western-made cars and went
on luxurious hunting trips with his colleagues and friends.[5]

Brezhnev replaced the notion that the Soviet Union had moved toward the final
establishment of communism with that of a country that was at the stage of "developed socialism." What this exactly meant was unclear. The new 1977 constitution
did not make it any clearer. Brezhnev and company seem to have been primarily
concentrating on foreign policy, endeavoring to match the United States in global
influence and military might. They meddled in the Middle East but failed to find
many loyal friends among the Arab countries, despite their hatred of Israel on which
the Soviets played. In the Soviet Union itself, anti-Semitism flared up again when
more and more Soviet Jews began to apply for exit visas. Soviet Jews, traditionally
urban because of the long-term prohibition for Jews to own land in Eastern Europe,
were often highly educated but frequently barred from work at top levels in scholarship and science, the military, economy, and government. Others chafed at the Soviet
antireligious policies. Many therefore tried to move to Israel or via Israel elsewhere
but were often refused an exit visa. In the West they became known as refuseniks.

In other parts of the Third World of developing nations, Soviet success was equally
middling. The Soviet Union became the strongest supporter of North Vietnam and
the Vietcong during the American intervention (1964–1973) in Indochina, but the
North Vietnamese leader Ho Chi Minh nonetheless steered an independent course
in an effort to keep his Chinese neighbors happy. Relations with Cuba remained
close, but of the African countries only Ethiopia after 1973 and perhaps Angola
became close allies.

The most significant Soviet intervention in the Third World under Brezhnev
began in late 1979, when Soviet troops crossed the border into Afghanistan to aid

their client Babrak Karmal (1929–1996) in taking power in Kabul at the expense of a Communist rival. While the Afghan Communists engaged in internecine warfare, much of the rest of the country rose in revolt against their government, rejecting the Communists wholesale. The mujahedin (Islamic guerrilla fighters) proved tenacious, gradually taking control of much of the country outside the few big cities and incessantly harassing Soviet troops. The Afghan resistance performed so well not only because of its knowledge of the terrain and its capacity to sustain great hardship but also because it was better equipped by advanced U.S.-made arms. The Afghan adventure contributed to the growing self-doubt that was to beset the Soviet leadership after Leonid Brezhnev's death in 1982.

Meanwhile, in the Soviet Bloc itself, unrest flared up after a quiet decade following the Polish and Hungarian episodes of 1956. The Romanian leaders Gheorghe Gheorghiu-Dej (1901–1965) and Nicolae Ceausescu (1918–1989) began to follow a more independent line in foreign policy, while imposing severe economic hardships on their own people in an attempt to have their country become economically self-sufficient. In Poland, strikes broke out in Gdansk in 1970 against price increases. But at first the strongest anti-Communist and anti-Soviet movement emerged in Czechoslovakia in the spring of 1968. In this Prague Spring, students and intellectuals ever more boldly questioned the one-party dictatorship in their country, after censorship had been relaxed by the Communist leader Alexander Dubcek. Especially harsh criticism was leveled at Dubcek's Stalinist predecessors and their kowtowing to the Soviet leadership. In August 1968, tanks from the Warsaw Pact states (Romania excepted) moved into Czechoslovakia. Party leader Dubcek was called before the Soviet leaders to explain his liberal policies (he himself had called it "socialism with a human face") and to be told to whittle them down. The Czechs and Slovaks desisted from resisting violently. Dubcek was stripped from his positions in 1969, while many of the intellectual leaders of the Prague Spring either fled abroad or spent years in jail for alleged subversion.

But the greatest challenge to Soviet supremacy in East-Central Europe was issued by the Poles in 1980 and 1981. In 1980, food shortages in shops led to another round of strikes on the Gdansk shipyards. On this occasion, however, the strikers found support across the country and organized an independent trade union, called Solidarity (Solidarnosc). For more than a year, the Polish Communist Party's monopoly on power was challenged by Solidarity. Poland witnessed a degree of open public discussion of the country's social, economic, and political ills unprecedented in Communist states. The Soviet leadership was utterly reluctant to adhere to the principles of the protection of "socialism" in allied countries by way of an armed intervention, as had ended the Prague Spring in 1968. Not only was Poland a larger country than Czechoslovakia, but the Soviet armed forces had their hands full in propping up the "socialist allies" in Afghanistan. Instead, the Soviets encouraged the senior army commander Wojciech Jaruzelski (b. 1923) to execute an armed coup and declare martial law, ostensibly to preempt a Soviet military intervention. Jaruzelski jailed thousands of trade union activists and managed to restore order. But Poland's adherence to Communism seemed utterly wobbly.

And foreign protest to Soviet domination was echoed by opposition at home, even if perhaps only a few hundred people between 1964 and 1985 were bold enough to raise their voices in opposition, for which most suffered heavy retribution. It is actually a mistake to suggest that the suppression of the dissident movement started after the fall of Khrushchev, for the young poet Iosif Brodskii (Joseph Brodsky; 1940–1996) had already been sentenced in 1964 to hard labor for his alleged parasitic life. Although living as a full-time writer, the future Nobel Prize laureate Brodskii had refused to join the Soviet Writers' Union and had preferred to draw his own plan without its patronizing and censorious tutelage. Such artistic freedom was not permitted in the Soviet Union. When Khrushchev's successors tightened censorship rules, more people fell victim to accusations of anti-Soviet activities. Thus, Andrei Siniavskii (1925–1997) and Yuli Daniel (1925–1988) were tried in 1966 for publishing their works abroad without permission from the Soviet authorities. They had already incurred the wrath of the KGB when they had been the pallbearers for Boris Pasternak's coffin. Pasternak had been awarded the Nobel Prize for Literature in 1958 for his novel *Doctor Zhivago*, which had been published abroad without permission from the regime. Pasternak had been denounced in a noisy press campaign but had not been jailed, perhaps an indication that Khrushchev's bark was louder than his bite.

In protest to Daniel and Siniavskii's sentence, demonstrations (by only a few individuals) were organized, leading to further arrests and sentencing. An underground system gained force by distributing subversive literature and information about human rights abuses perpetrated by the regime. Books and pamphlets were copied by way of retyping them and using carbon copy to make two copies of each original (this so-called self-publishing was called *samizdat*). Forbidden literature was smuggled in from abroad, as were vinyl phonograph records and eventually tape recordings with Western pop music. Powerful broadcasting stations in the West beamed Russian-language radio programs across Soviet territory, where they were often jammed by load noises but occasionally received. This further fueled an atmosphere in which a slowly increasing number of people began to question the regime's legitimacy.

Apart from the spread of literature that defied the aesthetics of socialist realism and the return of non-Communist political opposition for the first time since the 1920s, the 1960s and 1970s witnessed as well the rise of religious and nationalist protest against Moscow's Communist dictatorship. Whereas open defiance was practiced by only a very small number of individuals, it is evident that across the Soviet Union the protesters often had sympathizers who preferred to remain silent until the opportunity to voice disagreement offered itself in earnest.

NOTES

1. Russians formed slightly over half the population according to the 1959 census, Ukrainians one-fifth. Eastern Slavs always formed at least 80 percent of the Soviet population, and

more than two-thirds of them were Russian. The Azeri and Central Asian populations in particular grew rapidly during the second half of the twentieth century, with their populations doubling from the 1959 to the 1989 census. The number of Russians, Ukrainians, and Belarusyns grew only by approximately 20 percent over the same period.

2. The Nineteenth Party Congress of October 1952 renamed the Politburo the Presidium, but it reverted to Politburo at the Twenty-Third Party Congress in 1966.

3. In the United States, the terms "socialism" and "communism" were (and often are) conflated, ignoring the clear distinction between social democracy as represented by the British Labour Party, the SPD in Germany, or indeed the Mensheviks (all believing in democratic government and personal liberty) and the Bolshevik Soviet type of Communist rule.

4. Khrushchev had abolished several ministries and delegated decision-making power over industry to regional party organizations and soviets.

5. "General secretary" was a title restored to that of the Politburo at the Twenty-Third Party Congress of 1966.

FURTHER READING

Translated Primary Sources

Abramov, Fyodor. *The New Life: A Day on a Collective Farm*. Translated by George Reavy. New York: Grove Press, 1963.

Amalrik, Andrei. *Will the Soviet Union Survive until 1984?* Edited by Hilary Sternberg. New York: Harper, 1981.

Baranskaia, Natalia. *A Week Like Any Other*. Translated by Pieta Monks. Emeryville, CA: Seal Press, 1990.

Brodsky, Joseph. *Less Than One*. New York: Farrar, Straus, Giroux, 1987.

Chuev, Feliks. *Molotov Remembers: Inside Kremlin Politics*. Edited by Albert Resis. Chicago: Ivan R. Dee, 2007.

Grigorenko, Petro G. *Memoirs*. Translated by Thomas P. Whitney. New York: Norton, 1980.

Khrushchev, Nikita. *Memoirs of Nikita Khrushchev*. Edited by Sergei Khrushchev. Translated by George Shriver and Stephen Shenfield. 3 vols. Philadelphia: Pennsylvania State University Press, 2005–2007.

Kozlov, Vladimir A., et al. *Sedition: Everyday Resistance in the Soviet Union under Khrushchev and Brezhnev*. Translated by Olga Livshin. New Haven, CT: Yale University Press, 2011.

Maximov, Vladimir. *The Seven Days of Creation*. Translation of Sem' dnei tvoreniia. New York: Knopf, 1975.

Reddaway, Peter, ed. and trans. *Uncensored Russia: Protest and Dissent in the Soviet Union*. New York: American Heritage Press, 1972.

Rubinstein, Joshua, and Alexander Gribanov, eds. *The KGB File of Andrei Sakharov*. Translated by Ella Shmulevich, Efrem Yankelevich, and Alla Zeide. New Haven, CT: Yale University Press, 2005.

Sakharov, Andrei. *Memoirs*. Translated by Richard Lourie. New York: Random House, 1995.

Solzhenitsyn, Aleksandr. *The Oak and the Calf: A Memoir*. Translated by Harry Willetts. New York: HarperCollins, 1987.

———. *One Day in the Life of Ivan Denisovich*. Translated by Max Hayward and Ronald Hingley. New York: Bantam, 1984.

Voinovich, Vladimir. *The Life and Extraordinary Adventures of Private Ivan Chonkin*. Translated by Richard Lourie. Chicago: Northwestern University Press, 1995.

Zinoviev, Aleksandr. *The Yawning Heights*. Translated by Gordon Clough. London: Bodley Head, 1979.

Scholarly Literature

Andrews, James T., and Asif A. Siddiqi, eds. *Into the Cosmos: Space Exploration and Soviet Culture*. Pittsburgh: University of Pittsburgh Press, 2011.

Bacon, Edwin, and M. A. Sandle, eds. *Brezhnev Reconsidered*. New York: Palgrave MacMillan, 2002.

Baron, Samuel. *Bloody Saturday in the Soviet Union: Novocherkassk, 1962*. Stanford, CA: Stanford University Press, 2002.

Denisova, Liubov. *Rural Women in the Soviet Union and Post-Soviet Russia*. New York: Routledge, 2010.

Fursenko, Aleksandr, and Timothy Naftali. *One Hell of a Gamble: Khrushchev, Kennedy and Castro, 1958–1964*. New York: Norton, 1998.

Gorbachev, Mikhail Sergeevich. *Memoirs*. New York: Doubleday, 1996.

Heller, Mikhail, and Aleksandr Nekrich. *Utopia in Power: A History of the USSR from 1917 to the Present*. New York: Summit Books, 1988.

Igmen, Ali. *Speaking Soviet with an Accent: Culture and Power in Kyrgyzstan*. Pittsburgh: University of Pittsburgh Press, 2012.

Jenks, Andrew. *The Cosmonaut Who Couldn't Stop Smiling: The Life and Legend of Yuri Gagarin*. DeKalb: Northern Illinois University Press, 2012.

Knight, Amy. *Beria: Stalin's First Lieutenant*. Princeton, NJ: Princeton University Press, 1995.

Medvedev, Roy. *Let History Judge: The Origins and Consequences of Stalinism*. 2nd ed. New York: Columbia University Press, 1989.

Medvedev, Zhores. *Andropov*. New York: Penguin, 1984.

Reddaway, Peter, and Sidney Bloch. *Russia's Political Hospitals: The Abuse of Psychiatry in the Soviet Union*. London: Victor Gollancz, 1977.

Siegelbaum, Lewis. *Borders of Socialism: Private Spheres of Soviet Russia*. New York: Palgrave Macmillan, 2006.

Suny, Ronald Grigor. *The Structure of Soviet History*. New York: Oxford University Press, 2002.

Taubman, William. *Khrushchev: The Man and His Era*. New York: Norton, 2004.

Weiner, Douglas R. *A Little Corner of Freedom: Russian Nature Protection from Stalin to Gorbachev*. Berkeley: University of California Press, 2002.

WEBSITE

Cold War, maps, communism, and its legacy today: http://www.globalsecurity.org/

Cold War: http://www.wilsoncenter.org/program/cold-war-international-history-project

FILMS

Moscow Does Not Believe In Tears. DVD. Directed by Vladimir Menshov. New York: Kino Video, 2004.

Not by Bread Alone. DVD. Directed by Stanislav Govorukhin. Washington, DC: Vox Video, 2006.

Siberiade. DVD. Directed by Andrei Konchalovskii. New York: Kino Video, 2007.

Solaris. DVD. Directed by Andrei Tarkovsky. New York: Criterion, 2002.

Stalker. DVD. Directed by Andrei Tarkovsky. New York: Kino Video, 2006.

10

The Fall of the Soviet Union and Beyond, 1982–2013

The collapse of the Soviet Union was surprisingly swift and relatively peaceful. Nonetheless, its consequences are much harder to assess. In most of the successor states, the 1990s and even sometimes the 2000s were years of great economic hardship for most of the population, even if a few enterprising (and frequently criminal) types made their fortune. Russia may have turned the corner in this respect in the last decade, but wealth remains very unevenly distributed among the population, and doubts remain about the stability of the Russian economy.

Only in the three Baltic countries, lucky enough to be welcomed into the fold of NATO and the European Union, a reasonably stable democracy has emerged in which human rights and freedoms are adequately protected (although the Russian minority in Latvia might disagree). Elsewhere far more governments have become increasingly authoritarian, treating political opponents in a crude and often violent fashion. It is too early to draw up a balance sheet, but the promise of the early post-Soviet days has certainly faded. More serious problems may yet develop as a result of the Soviet legacy, from massive ecological disasters to more intense foreign, civil, or independence wars.

RELIGION AND NATIONALISM

Religious observance in the Soviet Union was actively discouraged. Nevertheless, the Orthodox Church as well as Islam had managed to carve out a precarious existence since Stalin had reached out to religious leaders in the dark days of the Second World War. It is evident that even if many of the Orthodox clerics were expected to inform on their flock to the KGB, priests and monks catered as best as they could to the spiritual needs of the Russian, Ukrainian, or Belarusyn Christians. While the church already stood under close state supervision, under both Nikita Khrushchev and Leonid Brezhnev further antireligious campaigns were organized. KGB types broke up processions and harassed those who tried to attend religious services. The priests Nikolai Eshliman (b. 1929) and Gleb Iakunin (b. 1934) were sent to camp for writing an open letter to the patriarch in 1965 denouncing the Orthodox Church's abject subordination to the authorities.

Religious opposition was smoldering in the Soviet Union, but the extent of religious belief or the adherence to organized religion such as Orthodoxy, Catholicism (prevalent especially in Lithuania and parts of Ukraine), Lutheranism (in Estonia and Latvia), or Islam (Shi'a in Azerbaijan and Sunni in the Caucasus and Central Asia) is impossible to assess. In 1937, a census showed alarming levels of religiosity for the Communist regime, with more than half the population bold enough to state to the census takers that they were religious. One can surmise that many more people feigned atheism. This high proportion of religious believers was a key cause for Stalin to order the census's suppression. It is obvious from post-Soviet developments that in most Islamic areas (perhaps the Tatar regions of the Russian Republic excepted), adherence to the religion remained strong thereafter. But this was an Islam that was accepting of many of the tenets of modern life, rather than calling for a society organized according to Sharia law.

Even some Protestant sectarians survived Stalin, as did some Old Believers; Protestants in particular, though, were mercilessly persecuted for decades. The lack of tolerance of revivalist Protestantism persists in Russian society today. Many Russians consider Southern Baptists or Seventh-Day Adventists as alien to their traditions and culture. In Russia, meanwhile, religious mysticism had and has its adherents (Madame Helena Blavatsky [1831–1891] and G. I. Gurdjieff [ca. 1866–1949] were natives of the tsarist empire, after all). Already in the late Soviet period, rumors persisted that Brezhnev made use of clairvoyants and spiritual healers, echoing President Ronald Reagan's use of astrologers. Certainly, after the fall of the Soviet Union, a short period of bewildering religious experimentation occurred. Hare Krishna believers chanted in the Moscow subway, and American proselytizers spread the gospel according to Joseph Smith (1805–1849) or L. Ron Hubbard (1911–1986) across the former Soviet Empire.

The Orthodox Church has experienced an increase of its power and influence since 1991, but the church often seems to be used by the current Russian rulers in a Voltairian manner. In other words, it functions as a sort of auxiliary to the government in safeguarding the country's stability by advocating loyalty and obedience. This is of course an ancient tradition in Russian history. For the Slavic parts of the Soviet Union (as well as for Armenians and Georgians who adhere to their own versions of Orthodox Christianity), however, modern secularism dominated the collective mind-set, both in the age of Brezhnev and in the post-Soviet period. Religious ceremonies (such as the sacraments of baptism or marriage) sometimes mark the important watershed moments in the life of the individual, but few Russians lead the lives of Christian zealots. Whether or not the result of the activities of Soviet militant atheists, religious fervor is mitigated by a general belief in the capability of human beings to change the circumstances of this life in a rational manner, using the insights of science and modern technology.

Given the sudden nationalist boom of the 1980s, it is remarkable how little the Soviet authorities in the 1960s and 1970s were plagued by nationalist movements. Perhaps Stalin's intimidation had worked in this respect. There lingered the deterrent effect of the vicious antinationalist campaigns and deportations of ethnic groups whose allegiance to the Soviet Union was questionable (at least in Stalin's eyes). After the Second World War, as we saw, Ukrainian partisans fought for almost five years a guerrilla war against detachments of the Red Army and People's Commissariat of Internal Affairs (NKVD) in the western parts of their country (which had not been Soviet before 1939). The retribution was ferocious (as was the treatment of rebellious Baltic nationalists rounded up from 1945 onward), involving mass executions and camp sentences for tens of thousands. It seemed to have done the trick, however, for after Stalin's death, few massive nationalist protests flared up. Oddly, among the exceptions were the Georgians, who demonstrated in 1956 against Khrushchev's criticism of their compatriot Stalin. But among the dissidents of the 1960s and 1970s, only a few isolated individuals who called for autonomy or independence of their Soviet republic could be encountered.

The largest nationalist movement of the Brezhnev era was that of the Crimean Tatars, who, different from the Chechens, Ingushetians, and others, had not been permitted after 1953 to return to the peninsula from their place of exile in Central Asia. This seems to have been primarily a consequence of the fear of conflicts erupting between the Tatars and Slavic settlers who had moved into the premises vacated by the Tatars at the end of the Second World War. Perhaps the strategic location of the Crimea further worried the Soviet leaders. The loyalty of these Tatars to the Soviet state, given their treatment by it, was thought to be dubious. Such fickle allegiance was not desirable among a community that would inhabit a stretch of land harboring a key Soviet naval port and facing the shores of NATO member Turkey (and there were historical and religious ties between Tatars and Turks, of course). Crimean-Tatar protest remained peaceful, even if their most celebrated champion, the Red Army veteran officer Petro Grigorenko (1907–1987), was dispatched to a psychiatric clinic in the 1960s. Like other dissidents under Brezhnev, he was injected with psychotropic drugs to cure him of his alleged delusions.

The first sign of mass demonstrations against Soviet rule occurred only after Brezhnev's death, in December 1986. Kazakh demonstrators reacted to Mikhail Gorbachev's replacement of the thoroughly corrupt Kazakh party leader Dinmukhamed Kunaev (1912–1993) with an ethnic Russian. In the Kazakh capital Almaty and elsewhere, these nationalist protests were met with a heavy hand, costing at least 168 people their lives. While these demonstrations were orchestrated by the local Kazakh bosses, they nonetheless were infused with genuinely felt nationalist passion. From that point onward, nationalism caught fire across the Soviet Union, and nationalist opposition to Soviet rule became a key contributing factor to the collapse of the USSR.

Communists from Marx and Lenin onward had believed that nationalism, as a sort of naive capitalist phenomenon, would be trumped by communism with its universal promise of equality, freedom, and justice. Ironically, Soviet Communism ultimately succumbed to nationalism instead. Different from Mikhail Gorbachev's expectations, emerging nationalist political leaders became his regime's most persistent critics, once he allowed Soviet citizens to express their opinions about the wrongs of the past and present of their country. They began to demand national autonomy and, eventually, independence for their nations, first in East-Central Europe and then in the fifteen Soviet republics themselves. In a last-ditch effort, Gorbachev tried to save his country by shifting much of Moscow's power to the republican capitals in his proposed union treaty of the summer of 1991. This led to an ill-fated coup of an old guard nostalgic for the good old days of the hypercentralized Communist dictatorship. Rather than restoring the one-party state, Gorbachev's efforts triggered the immediate collapse of the Soviet Union.

BREZHNEV'S SUCCESSORS

Many a Western observer dubbed the Soviet regime circa 1980 a gerontocracy, a country led by old men. But Politburo members Mikhail Suslov, Dmitrii Ustinov (1908–1984), Arvid Pelshe (1899–1983), Aleksei Kosygin, and Brezhnev all died in the first half the 1980s, as did Yuri Andropov (1914–1984) and Konstantin Chernenko (1911–1985), Brezhnev's immediate successors. The elderly Soviet leaders themselves concluded toward 1980 that some sort of rejuvenation of the leadership was imperative. Thus, from the late 1970s onward, a group of leaders who had been teenagers in the Second World War—and thus remembered little of the trials and tribulations the Soviet Union underwent from 1929 to 1945—were promoted to the highest ranks of the party and government.

Rivalry between the various old men postponed the inevitable until March 1985, but upon Chernenko's death the fifty-four-year-old Mikhail Sergeevich Gorbachev was elected as the Communist Party's general secretary. He was saddled with a difficult legacy: a military fiasco that was unfolding in Afghanistan; an arms race with the United States that could no longer be financed; a population that was expecting greater material well-being than a life in a small and crowded apartment with little more luxury than the use of electricity, a refrigerator, and a television; plummeting enthusiasm to sacrifice oneself for the ever-postponed goal of the society of plenty, freedom, and justice; unresolved nationalist sentiments; and a festering collective trauma as the legacy of the absurdly tragic first thirty-five years of communism in the USSR, about which the silence had been deafening since 1964.

The Soviet planned economy hit a ceiling by the 1970s, beyond which it could not easily grow. It could no longer sustain the enormous outlay on defense that the Cold War rivalry with the West mandated. The Soviet leadership failed to anticipate the use of the computer beyond its military applications. Whereas the quality of Western goods of mass consumption steadily improved, in the Soviet Union the production of consumer goods from cars and refrigerators to televisions and cutlery was insufficient and the quality of the goods produced often shoddy. Despite an all-pervasive censorship, Soviet citizens became acquainted with what they believed to be Western standards of living that far transcended anything in their own country.

In the West in 1985, very few predicted the rapid demise of the USSR. In the 1960s, a Russian dissident, Andrei Amalrik (1938–1980), who had subsequently been exiled to the West, had written an essay that, in a reference to George Orwell's novel, asked whether the Soviet Union could survive until 1984. By 1985, however, Amalrik's doubts seemed to have been no more than wishful thinking. Among Western academics, only the French social scientist Emmanuel Todd (b. 1951) predicted in 1976 the imminent collapse of the Soviet Empire. Amalrik and Todd were not mainstream experts, and their predictions were ignored. "Sovietologists" were of two minds about the changing of the guard in 1985. Some experts saw it as a positive generational change, bringing to the fore those who had come of age after the Second World War. They might usher in slow, incremental reforms. Others believed that no more than a prolongation of the status quo was in the offing. After all, Gorbachev and those moving up with him (such as Egor Ligachev [b. 1920], Nikolai Ryzhkov [b. 1929], and Boris Yeltsin [1931–2007]) had been carefully groomed for decades within the Communist Party apparatus. Nobody, however, argued that they would oversee within a few years the country's collapse.

Indeed, Gorbachev could not have made such rapid promotion had he not, as regional party boss in Stavropol province (situated just north of the Caucasus), hosted the Moscow chiefs on their holidays in the 1970s. He had catered to every whim of KGB chairman Yuri Andropov or ideological chief Mikhail Suslov when they relaxed in the spas in his region. Apart from his personal affability and readiness to please, Gorbachev had made a name for himself as a doer by some (apparently productive) tinkering with the collective farm system. He appeared to be getting better results from his kolkhozniks than were his fellow provincial party secretaries. But he had also succeeded in convincing the elderly leaders that he was a consummate conformist, dismissive of any radical experiments.

Thus, Gorbachev had been transferred to Moscow in 1978 to replace the deceased Fyodor Kulakov (1918–1978, who had preceded Gorbachev as Stavropol party boss) as Central Committee secretary responsible for agriculture. This was an inauspicious time to be promoted to this position, for Soviet agriculture had just entered a prolonged slump. Harvests were so poor in the late 1970s that the regime no longer published statistics about them. But it proved far more important whom Gorbachev knew than what he knew. In 1980, Gorbachev entered the Politburo. It now became apparent that he was a particular protégé of Andropov's. Andropov was less blind to the social and economic problems of the "stagnation" than were his fellow leaders because he received numerous reports about the growing difficulties in the country from his KGB subordinates.

Once Andropov succeeded Brezhnev in 1982, Gorbachev was moved forward as his key deputy. But Andropov did not live long enough to persuade the other leaders that Gorbachev was the best choice to succeed him. The dithering old men in the Politburo thus chose Konstantin Chernenko, who had been for most of his life Brezhnev's personal assistant, to succeed Andropov, who died of kidney failure in the spring of 1984. This was a mere postponement of the inevitable, however, for Chernenko himself spent his months in power mainly in hospital. Apart from Brezhnev and Andropov, Suslov had died in 1982, Politburo member Pelshe in 1983, and defense minister Ustinov in 1984, and long-term foreign minister Andrei Gromyko (1909–1989) was seventy-six in 1985. A younger generation's turn had come.

GLASNOST' AND PERESTROIKA

The American historian Stephen Kotkin has suggested that the peaceful demise of the Soviet Union amounted to an "Armageddon averted." The birth (1914–1921) and death (1985–1991) of the Soviet Union are almost equally long periods of revolutionary convulsions. The cost in human lives during these epochal transformations was, however, vastly different. Perhaps fifteen million people died in the process that gave birth to the Soviet Empire, representing a virtual apocalypse, but its end was almost painless, with deaths from purely political conflict amounting to, at most, one thousand people.

The human cost of the Soviet Empire's fall is of course only in comparison negligible, and this calculation conveniently ignores what occurred in the successor states after 1991. While the greatest number of those dying in the convulsions of the late Soviet years fell in Kazakhstan in 1986 and the Armenian-Azeri conflict that began in 1988, police brutality in Georgia, Lithuania, and Latvia cost several dozens of

Figure 10.1. Mikhail Gorbachev as first secretary of the Communist Party of the Soviet Union, 1980s (RIA Novosti archive)

people their lives, and violent clashes between Slavs and Moldavians in Moldova (which persisted beyond 1991) took a toll. To the relatively small number of deaths as a result of political conflict in the final years of the USSR, there might be added others who became casualties of a regime that failed to transform itself in a timely fashion. For example, the several thousand soldiers who were killed in the Afghan war before the Soviet withdrawal of 1988 could be counted, or the dozens of people in the immediate aftermath as well as the hundreds and perhaps thousands more in the longer term killed as a result of the Chernobyl meltdown in 1986.

Only future historians will be able to assess the cost of the post-Soviet transition for the successor states more precisely, but there is no doubt that it was almost everywhere far higher if counted in human lives cut short. In the first place, even before the official dissolution of the Union in December 1991, gangland warfare began to take its toll. Eventually, organized crime killed thousands in Russia, Ukraine, and elsewhere. It is moot who bears the most responsibility for the as yet unknown number of deaths caused by the economic meltdown of the Soviet Empire that began in about 1988 and ended only after 2000. Most devastating in terms of Soviet and post-Soviet political violence were the two Chechen Wars of 1994–1996 and 1999–2000, wholly caused by the post-Soviet Russian regime. Therefore, even if a true Armageddon was indeed averted, the collapse of the Soviet Empire was anything but painless.

But when one looks strictly at the victims of political violence, the revolution of 1985–1991 seems an inversion of the massive suffering that accompanied the establishment of Communist Russia. Kotkin's argument that it could have been so much worse appears therefore persuasive. The sudden nature of the disappearance of the Soviet system in August 1991 and Gorbachev's hasty departure that followed undeniably caused widespread havoc. But as leader of his disintegrating empire, Gorbachev behaved like an anti-Lenin in his utter caution to avoid bloodshed. A good amount of the credit for the almost entirely peaceful fall of the Soviet Union belongs to him.

Mikhail Gorbachev started his leadership of the Soviet Empire cautiously, disinclined to ruffle too many feathers. He soon coined two terms as shorthand for the guiding principles of his tenure that became a part of the English language: glasnost' and perestroika. The first stood for openness, which at first was intended as no more than an encouragement to Soviet citizens to report corruption or abuse of power by officials. Perestroika, meaning "restructuring," was even less defined: it referred to the economy, but what the extent of its restructuring was to be remained uncertain for some time.

Initially, indeed, Gorbachev appeared a tinkerer like Khrushchev. He seemed inclined to whittle down the overbearing habit of planning as coordinated by Gosplan rather than challenge the wisdom of the plan system as such. Here he may have been inspired by the limited concessions to small private enterprises that had been set up in Hungary by the regime of Janos Kadar (1912–1989), whom Gorbachev befriended. The collective and state farms, as well as the larger factories, were to remain in public ownership. Gorbachev's cautious beginning may have also been the result of the presence of a number of moderates and conservatives in the

Politburo. Its composition changed fairly quickly, however. In 1986, Aleksandr Nikolaevich Yakovlev (1923–2005) became an alternate Politburo member. In the 1970s, Yakovlev had been made ambassador to Canada after he had tried to halt the creeping "restalinization" of the Brezhnev regime. In Canada in the early 1980s, he had met Gorbachev. Gorbachev had been able to recall Yakovlev to Moscow to head a party think tank on global economic and international affairs in 1983. Yakovlev became the key advisor to Gorbachev in making perestroika and glasnost' mean more than empty words.

The catalyst that set Gorbachev and his advisors on the road to genuine reform, however, was the Chernobyl catastrophe. Due to a series of human errors, a rather unsafely built nuclear power station blew up in Ukraine on 26 April 1986. A massive amount of nuclear radiation escaped before workers (most of whom sacrificed their lives in this effort) managed to close the leak by casting the reactor into concrete. It is not quite clear how much was initially explained to Gorbachev about the scale of the disaster. The Soviet citizenry was not informed until Gorbachev allowed this to happen. After all, in the Soviet Union since Stalin's days, the media did not report on crime, traffic, industrial accidents, or natural disasters. While Gorbachev was assessing the impact of the calamity behind closed doors in Moscow, the world was alerted through the observations of Scandinavian seismic stations to a radioactive cloud moving westward across Europe. Particles of the fallout would eventually force even the shepherds of Wales to destroy their flock.

Whereas many rescue workers died while preventing a further meltdown of the other reactors at Chernobyl, until this day the total number of victims of the disaster is unknown. Soviet authorities evacuated the residents of nearby towns and villages far too late. These people were not made aware of the disaster because of the cult of secrecy surrounding any disasters. The presence and location of nuclear power stations across the country had never been advertised. Gorbachev admitted to the disaster at Chernobyl only in May 1986, after more than a week of hesitation, thereby damaging the health of countless people. It seems that this fumble made him understand the danger of Soviet society's closed nature. If media had operated with the sort of freedom they enjoyed in the West, alarm bells might have rung earlier. An independent press, too, might have warned earlier about the dangerous design of power stations such as Chernobyl's. Fortified by the strong support he had received at a recent party congress, Gorbachev now launched a truly ambitious program to reform his country.

GORBACHEV REFORMS HIS COUNTRY

In the second half of 1986, steps were taken to end the Afghan war, to lift much of the censorship, to release dissidents from exile and camps, and to sign a comprehensive treaty with the United States to reduce nuclear arsenals and end the Cold War's arms race. In the last case, Gorbachev's far-reaching proposals caught President Reagan by surprise in Reykjavík (Iceland) in December 1986. Eventually, the American president and his successor George H. W. Bush concluded that the Soviet leader meant business and acted accordingly in the subsequent years, signing a series of arms' reduction treaties. These paved the way for the effective end of the Cold War in the last months of 1989, when the Soviets stood by, while the local population in East-Central Europe overthrew one after the other of their Communist regimes and the Berlin Wall was torn down.

By early 1987, the dissident Andrei Sakharov (who had been a key scientist in building the Soviet hydrogen bomb in the early 1950s) was allowed to return to Moscow from his place of banishment in Gor'kii (now again Nizhnii Novgorod). Sakharov immediately proceeded to roundly criticize the Soviet leaders for their continuation of the war in Afghanistan and demanded greater guarantees of human rights and freedoms. He called for the abolition of the Communist Party's status as the only political party in the country. Rather than silencing Sakharov, Gorbachev allowed the scientist to speak out. Concomitantly, various newspapers became bolder, and the regime ceased the jamming of Western radio broadcasts. After a hiatus of a quarter century, the crimes of Stalinism were suddenly again discussed. At first, a sort of Khrushchevite version of Soviet history was upheld. It maintained that Stalin also oversaw positive changes (as in the First Five Year Plan) and had led the country to victory in the Second World War. This version was about as far as some of the moderates in the Politburo, such as Ligachev, were willing to accept. It appeared that this faction remained a powerful force when in March 1988 a letter by the Leningrad teacher Nina Andreeva (b. 1938) was published in a widely distributed conservative paper. Andreeva defended Stalin as having been a great leader.

The Andreeva letter, however, presented a final rearguard battle. The conservative forces were about to be overwhelmed by the momentum of glasnost' and perestroika. Gorbachev pressed ahead, even if he tried to curb criticism from the left as well. In October 1987, he thus removed the radical Boris Yeltsin, the Moscow party boss, from his post, subsequently ousting Yeltsin from among the Politburo's alternates. Yeltsin had accused Gorbachev of using dictatorial methods. This was true, of course, given that Gorbachev's power was in principle as vast as Brezhnev's or Khrushchev's had been. Yeltsin called for greater democratization, although his program seemed far from coherent in early 1988.

By May 1988, the first Soviet forces began to withdraw from Afghanistan, a retreat that was complete by February 1989. Responding to the ever bolder reforms imposed from above, Soviet citizens began to criticize virtually everything that ailed their country in the course of 1988, and people began to leave the Communist Party. The works by Aleksandr Solzhenitsyn were published for the first time or, in the case of a few, republished. Rather than the few thousand whose names and reputations had been (mainly posthumously) rehabilitated from the false accusations of Stalin's courts during the 1930s, now the good name of virtually all victims of Stalinism was restored. By 1989, *Novyi Mir* (which had more than one million subscribers) dedicated a series of issues to the full publication of Solzhenitsyn's *Gulag Archipelago*.

By 1988, Gorbachev and his advisors finally recognized that the official or legal economy hardly functioned without the operation of the second or black-market economy, which made up for the vast shortages in goods and services. More and more leeway was given to private entrepreneurs, in an attempt to legalize the second economy and to stimulate renewed economic growth. But steps in this direction remained hesitant. A series of unstable and poorly operating compromises was struck in an attempt to create an economy that balanced the bloated state-owned sector with the fledgling private sector. Before 1991, this did not lead to any tangible positive results; rather than stagnating, the Soviet economy was actually shrinking in the last few years of the country's existence.

Meanwhile, the relaxation of the stultifying control the regime had exerted over the country led to other destabilizing developments. After decades of enforced silence, nationalist sentiments began to be expressed, as we already saw, beginning in Kazakhstan. In 1988, clashes erupted between Azeris and Armenians. They led most Armenian workers to depart Baku, while a tense standoff developed over Nagornyi Karabakh, an Armenian enclave surrounded by Azeri territory. These conflicts were suppressed by deploying the Soviet army but until this day have never been resolved to the satisfaction of all parties involved. In the Baltic countries, nationalist movements were organized that began to clamor for independence in 1988. They called for the publication of the secret clauses to the German-Soviet Non-Aggression Pact of 1939, claiming that those points had provided the grounds for the illegal Soviet occupation of their countries.

In the summer of 1988, Gorbachev convinced the Nineteenth Party *Conference* (the first such meeting since 1941) that multicandidate elections should be held for the soviets, the official legislative bodies of the USSR. In March 1989, elections were held for a replacement for the All-Union Supreme Soviet: candidates not nominated by the Communist Party could stand for this new type of parliament, which was given the name Congress of People's Deputies. When this congress met in March 1989, Gorbachev, elected its speaker, made an irritated impression in the debates that were televised live throughout the USSR. The open debates between party faithful and independents meanwhile brought glasnost' and perestroika to households in the remotest areas of the country.

GORBACHEV EMBATTLED

But Gorbachev and his team of advisors were not thanked for their efforts in creating an open society.[1] By early 1989, Gorbachev himself had become overwhelmed by what he had unleashed. All sorts of pent-up frustrations were now voiced. The population was particularly anxious about the ever-increasing shortages of basic staples, almost every day queuing for hours for their bread and milk that, like many other goods, had been rationed. Ration cards returned in the daily lives of Soviet citizens for the first time in forty years. Soviet citizens witnessed a serious fall in the standard of living toward 1990, and Gorbachev's rule for this reason, too, began to be resented by an ever-growing part of the population. These shortages resulted from the usual poor agricultural yields combined with a faltering official distribution system and the hoarding of consumer goods by middlemen, hucksters, and criminal organizations, which found their origins in the second economy. The last types now often made the transition to legality successfully, with the help of lower-level politicians and government officials who shielded them.

In July 1989, a miners' strike broke out in Siberia; it spread across the entire country and forced the government to major concessions. It also rang the death knell for the official trade unions that had been under the party's control since the Tenth Party Congress in 1921. Workers finally organized themselves again in the Soviet workers' state. While the Congress of People's Deputies was debating on television, ethnic clashes erupted in Uzbekistan's Fergana Valley, the scene of long-term guerrilla war against Russian and Soviet rule in the 1910s and 1920s. It led to the departure of one of Stalin's "Punished Peoples," the Meshketian Turks, who were finally repatriated to Russia. Further ethnic clashes followed in the first half of 1989 in Kazakhstan, Tajikistan, and Kyrgyzstan. In the Caucasus, Abkhazians clashed with Georgians. Meanwhile, the leadership of the various republics began to introduce nationalist policies, privileging the language and culture of the titular nation (i.e., the Tajiks in Tajikistan) over Russian. This followed the example set in 1988 by the Baltic republics. In August 1989, inhabitants of all three western Soviet republics joined hands between Tallinn, the Estonian capital, and Vilnius, the Lithuanian capital. The human chain commemorated the Molotov-Ribbentrop Pact that had been concluded fifty years earlier and had sealed the fate of the three countries.

In hindsight, it seems evident that these developments heralded the beginning of the end. The genie of nationalism was now out of the bottle. As events in Yugoslavia soon proved as well, it could not be put back into it. But in 1989 both Czechoslovakia and Yugoslavia were intact, as was the Soviet Union. Nationalism had historically not been much of a threat to the survival of the Russian Empire or the Soviet Union, primarily being a force in peripheral areas such as Poland or Finland and perhaps Georgia. Of course, nationalist rebels had fought the Soviet army in western Ukraine and the Baltic region after the Second World War, but the revolts had been overcome. Before 1986, it appeared that Soviet nationality policy, with its sensitivity to, and support of, local language and culture, had been a measured success. It was true that in order to make a career in the party, state, economy, or academic world one needed to be fluent in Russian, but most non-Russian Soviet citizens seemed willing to learn Russian as a second language.

But the encouragement of local languages, music, theater, and literature and the study of local history had in fact given rise to a much more defined national identity in the various Soviet republics, autonomous republics, regions, and so on. Resentment to Russian hegemony, as should have been clear to Gorbachev and his comrades from the Kazakh riots in 1986, was strong. Russians (and sometimes Ukrainians) often held the more prestigious jobs in the various territories and seemed a privileged lot to the native population. The Slavs did not always behave delicately toward the non-Slavic populations, lording it over them at times as colonial rulers. In addition, the native elite of the various republics realized that separation from the Soviet Union might remove the Slavs (either those in Moscow or those in the republican capitals) with whom they had had to share power, thus opening up hitherto unheard-of possibilities. Of course, local specificities had an impact on the strength of nationalist movements. The Baltic countries were fortified by the fall of Communism in Eastern Europe in 1989 and clamored for a place among the European states. In Azerbaijan, the local leaders counted on the seemingly endless oil reserves to sustain independence. Still, apart from the Baltic area, the national leaderships of the Soviet republics were not composed of firebrand nationalists, as all had been groomed in the Communist apparatus.

It does seem then that, besides Estonia, Latvia, and Lithuania, the Soviet Union might still have survived had Gorbachev and his comrades realized the danger of resurgent nationalism for their country's survival. As good Marxists, however, and taking into account the lack of ethnic tensions in previous decades, the Communist leaders underestimated nationalism's power. They failed to develop a timely strategy that might keep it within bounds. Meanwhile, the 1989 Eastern European revolutions emboldened Soviet radical oppositionists who challenged the party's dominance in Soviet politics. At the second session of the Congress of People's Deputies that opened in December 1989, opposition members in the parliament called for an end to the monopoly on power of the Communist Party in the Soviet Union by removing article 6 of the 1977 constitution, which enshrined this special position. Although Andrei Sakharov, the most prominent radical deputy, died in the midst of the debates, the party tottered on its pedestal. By March 1990, article 6 was amended in such a way that the Communist Party's hegemony in the USSR was ended. Gorbachev was now elected president of the Soviet Union by the Congress of People's Deputies.

Early 1990 saw renewed ethnic clashes in Azerbaijan and Armenia, killing dozens of people. This was followed by republican and regional elections for the local parliaments, which led to a resounding defeat of the Communist Party's candidates in the Baltic countries and elsewhere. When the Lithuanian parliament proclaimed independence in March, Gorbachev and company at first tried to reimpose Soviet rule by moving in armed forces, as if it was August 1968 in Prague, but then thought better of it. Lithuania was cut off from trade with the rest of the Soviet Union, but when Estonia and Latvia followed suit and declared independence, Gorbachev decided to accept the inevitable. He asked an advisory council to draft a new union treaty, in a last-ditch attempt to keep the Baltic states within the Union, or at least hold the twelve remaining republics together.

At the May Day parade in Moscow in 1990, Gorbachev was booed by the crowd rather than greeted by the usual immaculately marching elite troops. Soon thereafter, the Russian parliament met in Moscow for the first time and elected Boris Yeltsin, the erstwhile Moscow party boss, as president of the Russian Republic. In July, the

Twenty-Eighth and last congress of the Communist Party of the Soviet Union met in Moscow. The rift between Gorbachev and the bulk of party bosses appeared beyond repair. Gorbachev could defy this opposition as the party had become a rapidly declining force, for it no longer had any official position of leadership in Soviet society since the constitutional amendment to article 6. At the end of the congress, no ranking member of Gorbachev's government obtained a place in the party's Politburo, but it did not matter. That more than 10 percent of members left the party in the course of 1990 illustrates the organization's declining power and prestige.

There was a serious backlash by conservative forces opposed to Gorbachev's reforms in the second half of 1990 and the early months of 1991. Different from Communist China, where democratic protesters were massacred on Tiananmen Square in May 1989, even the conservative Soviet leaders never contemplated a massive violent crackdown on the opposition. Indeed, too many among the Soviet leaders themselves, beginning with Gorbachev, sincerely wanted to create a "socialism with a human face." They longed for a country that would finally deliver on the promise of equality and justice, freedom, and harmony, the seemingly utopian ideals of Marx. But what the humane Soviet chief and his shrinking circle of friends did not realize was that the lofty ideals of communism had been too much tainted to become believable again for the Soviet citizens. Cynicism reigned, shortages were rampant, and everywhere the call got louder for national self-determination.

Gorbachev seems to have taken fright at his own boldness in the last year of the existence of his country. But he was not willing to contemplate a retreat toward a Communist dictatorship. That, in any event, would have ended his political career, too, for he would have become the scapegoat for the implosion between 1985 and 1990 of the Communist Party's hegemony. Behind his back, a faction of his appointees, including the KGB chief, the minister of internal affairs, the prime minister, the defense minister, and the vice president hatched a plot to prevent the acceptance of a Union treaty in the summer of 1991. The draft of this agreement made the country into a decentralized state with limited powers for Moscow. The plotters hatched their plans while direct elections returned Boris Yeltsin (who had been elected Russian president by Russia's parliament in the previous year) as president of the Russian Republic in July 1991. Mindful of Khrushchev's ouster in 1964, the conspirators staged their coup when Gorbachev was on vacation on the Crimea.

But the August 1991 coup miserably failed. The Russian parliament and Russian president Yeltsin refused to recognize the plotters' emergency committee. Demonstrators in Moscow and Leningrad faced down tanks that had been ordered out to enforce the rule of the new dictators. Three people died in the scuffle in Moscow, before the tanks' personnel switched allegiance to Yeltsin. Some of the conspirators committed suicide, others tried to flee, and several were arrested. A shocked Gorbachev was received at the airport in Moscow by Yeltsin's allies. Yeltsin prohibited the Communist Party of the Soviet Union and began immediate negotiations with the leaders of Ukraine (Leonid Kravchuk, b. 1934) and Belarus (Stanislau Shushkevich, b. 1934) to break up the Soviet Union into fifteen independent states. The trio signed an agreement on 8 December 1991 that recognized each other's states as independent. The few All-Union posts that remained lost any significance. In late December 1991, Mikhail Gorbachev went on television to announce the dissolution of the Union of Socialist Soviet Republics.

RUSSIA AND ITS FORMER COLONIES

Even more than twenty years after the fall of the empire, it is too early to tell what the most significant consequences have been (or are) of the sudden collapse of the Soviet Bloc between the spring of 1989 and the fall of 1991. Since we do not have the benefit of historical hindsight for the post-Soviet years, the following remarks should by no means be taken as the last word on the period 1991–2011.[2] It is also impossible to do justice to the increasingly varied paths followed by the fifteen successor states in a mere few pages.

The Russian Federation and the other states that succeeded the Soviet republics have developed in a checkered manner since 1991. Their fate has been dramatically different. Some countries have been fortunate enough to join the European Community (Lithuania, Latvia, and Estonia). Several seem to have been forgotten and appear mired in poverty and stagnation (Moldova and Armenia). Ukraine and Georgia are torn apart by domestic strife manipulated by foreign powers (first and foremost by Russia). Other states are ruled by repressive regimes that seem heirs to the Soviet dictatorial model, even if they have developed their own specific iterations of single-party rule (Azerbaijan, Belarus, Kazakhstan, Tajikistan, Uzbekistan, Kyrgyzstan, and Turkmenistan).

The emergence of these authoritarian states during the last two decades underlines how to a considerable degree the Soviet Union (like tsarist Russia before it) was a colonial empire, for they appear to copy the history of the postcolonial states of Asia and Africa. The role of the Russian language as a lingua franca in the "near abroad" (as the Russians call the republics) is not unlike French or English in parts of Africa and Asia (although ethnic Russians reside in most countries in far higher number than French or English do in their former colonies). As in parts of Asia and Africa, a postcolonial elite rules in the same high-handed fashion as its Soviet (colonial) predecessors, suppressing political opposition and lining its own pockets unabashedly. Dictatorships routinely violate human rights, while corruption has been rampant, but of all successor states only the Turkmenbashi Saparmurat Niyazov (1940–2006) in Turkmenistan and the Uzbek dictator Islam Karimov (b. 1938) resembled the Burmese junta, the Central African emperor Jean-Bédel Bokassa's (1921–1996) regime, or Uganda's Idi Amin's (1925–2003) despotism. The dictatorship of the Aliyevs (father Heydar [1923–2003], son Ilham [b. 1961]) in Azerbaijan and of Aliaksandr Lukashenka (b. 1954) in Belarus are more on par with that of father Hafez Assad (1930–2000), rather than his bloodthirsty son Bashar Assad (b. 1965) in Syria.

All successor states are to some degree multinational countries, in which, if we may judge from developments elsewhere in multiethnic or multicultural states, there is potential for serious ethnic conflict. In Russia, ethnic violence has flared up in Chechnya, Ingushetia, and Dagestan, as it has in Georgia in Abkhazia, South Ossetia, and Adzharia. Violent conflict has erupted but usually merely for a short period. No massive bloodletting has occurred, with the exception of the two Russian-Chechen wars.

The Russian meddling in Georgia seems to show that Russia sometimes considers the "near abroad" as its backyard, in which no other powers should have much of a say. On many an occasion, Russian leaders demand a cooperative and friendly attitude from these states, which is often interpreted by the latter as evidence of hegemonic desires. But at other times, the Russian government appears to behave as the United Kingdom in the British Commonwealth or France in the global Francophonie, a benevolent friend who has everyone's best interest in mind.

Although the comparative perspective has only limited value, as, for example, in many respects Ukraine does not resemble India or Nigeria, it can yield some useful insights. Comparison suggests that not just in political terms the postcolonial experience of the Russian Soviet Empire has been better than that of the African or Asian states. Economically, whereas the standard of living of Moldovans, Belarusyns, or Uzbeks has deteriorated and poverty even in Russia is still widespread, famine as plagued African countries has not occurred. At the same time, the three Baltic states have been lucky to enter the European Community, guaranteeing their population a level of material prosperity not far below that of the Western world. Russia and Azerbaijan, as well as some of the Central Asian successor states, benefit from a great amount of oil and gas reserves, which has allowed them to reach growth levels that are impressive. Even so, those resources will eventually run out, and none of the governments of the successor states has been actively trying to develop a diversified economy (only Russia itself may have one sufficiently complex). Indeed, the proceeds from the mining and drilling end up in the bank accounts of a very small group of profiteers in most countries, entrepreneurs who skillfully manipulated the chaotic circumstances of the early 1990s to acquire control over most of the precious assets in the various countries. The rulers lend them a willing ear in exchange for kickbacks. The gap between rich and poor outside the Baltic countries has been vast.

However, it could have been much worse, with desperadoes taking over in Kyiv or Moscow and lobbing nuclear missiles at each other or the West, or a civil war of the Rwandan or Yugoslav kind. None of that came to pass, despite ethnic tensions and high levels of poverty in some areas and other profound problems that have not been addressed by the governments of the successor states in any comprehensive fashion.

Finally, two key phenomena plaguing the post-Soviet countries deserve to be singled out because of their pervasiveness and scope. They are, however, not unique to the successor states, and the rulers of the fifteen republics often handle them as well, or as poorly, as their peers in other countries. In the first place, the debilitating levels of environmental problems rankle at home and abroad. The environment suffers not just from Chernobyl's consequences but also from the fallout from nuclear testing at Semipalatinsk (Kazakhstan) and nuclear accidents elsewhere (as at Cheliabinsk in 1957), chemical pollution in all sorts of industrial regions, the drainage of the Aral Sea, and so on. Second, the common habit of bribing officials sometimes offends foreign investors and limits investment, and corruption seems almost universal at times.

CHANGE AND CONTINUITY IN RUSSIA

Why did the Soviet realm not descend into chaos after 1991? All kinds of explanations have been given. Most convincing is the argument that stability was to a considerable degree maintained because most of the post-Soviet leaders came from the more enlightened sections of the party. They were seasoned political operators with experience in governing a country (or at least part of it). Economically, various observers speak of a Komsomol revolution, indicative of the great number of entrepreneurs who came from the Communist Youth League's leading ranks. In an earlier age, the Komsomol cadres had supplied the future leaders of the party and the KGB. They also furnished the managers of the great industrial enterprises of the Soviet Union. Those may have been part of a state-controlled economy, but a plant with thousands of workers still had to be run with many of the management techniques used in similar ventures across the industrialized world.

Through their networks, expertise, and education, Komsomol, party, or KGB personnel members were often in the most advantageous position to seize the limited opportunities of perestroika and the breathtaking prospects the free-market economy offered after 1991. This economic transformation was ushered in by Yeltsin's economic advisors, chief among whom was Yegor Gaidar (1956–2009), in the first months after the dissolution of the Soviet Union. A select group of oligarchs, as they were called by the second half of the 1990s, thus was in position to buy up most of the vouchers that were distributed during a privatization wave of public enterprises in the mid-1990s. The vouchers gave workers shares in the ownership of the company for which they worked. Since few companies were worth much on paper at that time, most holders sold their share vouchers for hard cash, necessary to make ends meet. Not all those who bought them out (often via straw men) had been bosses in the Youth League, for many a former KGB officer plus President Yeltsin and his plundering entourage hit the jackpot as well, but many of the most successful *businessmeny* had once been Komsomol cadres.

Social protest did erupt, but most of the disaffected followed leaders who had few solutions to offer and were too closely associated with the lost cause of Soviet Communism. Such was the case when President Yeltsin faced down one particularly tenacious group of opponents in bloody clashes in Moscow in October 1993, ultimately having loyal army units storm the Russian parliament (known as the White

House) in which the opposition had ensconced itself. Yeltsin blamed them of stalling far-reaching economic reforms and a desire to turn back the clock. The president believed in turning Russia into some sort of capitalist liberal democracy, while his opponents were unwilling to follow the impulsive president in his radical transformation of Russia. While Yeltsin struggled with "conservative," quasi-Communist opponents, in various other republics similar clashes occurred between those who preferred an authoritarian government and those who clamored for human rights and freedoms. Different from Russia and the Baltic countries, however, throughout the 1990s the authoritarian forces gained the upper hand in most post-Soviet states. And even in Russia, both Yeltsin himself and his successor Vladimir Putin (b. 1952) increasingly ruled in authoritarian fashion.

The Russian Communist Party (newly founded in 1990) failed meanwhile to attract enough of a vote to threaten the president, although Yeltsin was reelected in 1996 as Russian president only with the help of a fear-mongering propaganda campaign in the media (and possibly thanks to widespread voting fraud). His Communist opponent Gennadii Ziuganov (b. 1944) could not muster the same sort of funds, nor did he have a significant media empire available to him. A spectacular offensive on behalf of Yeltsin on the radio and television and in the print media managed to inculcate in the electorate enough fear of a return to the dark days of the Soviet Union if Ziuganov were elected. But it seems that in exchange for their support, the president had to allow a bevy of oligarchs (many of whom had a significant stake in media companies) to do as they pleased. In his second term, Yeltsin's health deteriorated sharply because of heart problems and immoderate drinking. He began to disappear from public view, leaving the shop to his advisors and ministers, who played for time and enriched themselves in league with the tycoons. Once in a while one of the magnates was sacrificed to show the government's efforts at weeding out corruption. But government efforts to show that it lorded it over the billionaires rather than the other way around did not convince most Russians.

President Putin (and his successor and predecessor Dmitrii Medvedev [b. 1965]) has continued to persecute certain moguls for their alleged fraud, tax evasion, insider trading, racketeering, bribing, and so on. But such efforts remain inconsistent and the motivation to prosecute some of the tycoons murky. Whereas Boris Berezovskii (1946–2013) and Vladimir Gusinskii (b. 1952) fled into exile and Mikhail Khodorkovskii (b. 1963) was sent to a Siberian jail, Oleg Deripaska (b. 1968), Roman Abramovich (b. 1966), and Yelena Baturina (b. 1963; wife of former Moscow mayor Yuri Luzhkov [b. 1936]) have been allowed to enrich themselves without restriction.

Often the Yeltsin government announced that prosperity was just around the corner, and most Russians decided to wait rather than take to the streets. It is a matter of speculation whether a social revolution might have broken out once again in Russia, if the economic tide had not quickly turned after a market crash in 1998. But turn it did, and for more than a decade thereafter the Russian economy grew at a fast clip.

Russia's transition from Communism to capitalism was as rocky as it was in the other republics. The early twenty-first century seems to have witnessed a drastic improvement in the standard of living in Russia (as well as in the Baltic countries and a few other successor states), but the 1990s exacted a grim toll on the population. Yeltsin had little idea how to remake his country into a democratic state with a free-market economy. Many of his actions were rash, while he often abandoned policies that were not given sufficient time to assess their effect. Poverty and homelessness became widespread during the 1990s, while alcoholism was rampant. All of the former Soviet Union also saw a massive increase in intravenously administered drug addiction, leading to high levels of HIV infections and drug overdoses.[3] In the prison system, contagious diseases, such as untreatable open tuberculosis, spread.

And whereas a sort of capitalist trickling down of the vast riches acquired by the tycoons has benefited most Russians in recent years, the social problems of the 1990s have persisted. Russians pay fairly low taxes, but many do not pay any taxes at all, and especially the fabulously rich and powerful are guilty of evasion. The resulting meager revenue hampers the government's attempts to maintain a social safety net. In the 1990s, Western pundits wrote of a "Wild East" in an analogy to the U.S. "Wild West" of the nineteenth century. A better comparison is, however, with the America of the Gilded Age, of the robber barons such as Cornelius Vanderbilt (1794–1877) or Andrew Carnegie (1835–1919). Russia perhaps needs a sort of American-style Progressive Era to redistribute some of the wealth and introduce social reform that improves the fate of the elderly, street urchins, sick, and those confined in orphanages and prison camps. But the problem is not merely poor collection of taxes or insufficient taxation levels.

Few countries have succeeded that attempted to introduce the free market and a liberal democratic government overnight, as did most of the former Soviet states. Such efforts were doubly difficult in Russia given its sheer size. Independence meant disruption of former communication and trade links and of an All-Union integrated economy. Radical experiments of wholesale privatization following the Polish recipe were never implemented with the hypothetical fast pace and comprehensiveness advocated by Western economists such as the Harvard economist Jeffrey Sachs (b. 1954). But rather than their implementation being flawed, it stands to reason that Russia, Ukraine, and the other countries needed to find a happy match between their own traditions and economic circumstances and foreign models of capitalist development. Every democracy, like every capitalist economy, is different in the West, too, and the former Soviet countries need (or perhaps needed) to find their version of it.

VLADIMIR PUTIN

After a series of prime ministers with whom Yeltsin grew quickly disaffected, he appointed a relative political neophyte, Vladimir Putin, as prime minister in 1999. By Christmas of that year, Yeltsin announced that he was stepping down. In the absence of a vice president in the Russian political system, Putin, a former KGB officer, was to succeed him. This choice was confirmed by Russian voters in the presidential elections of 2000. Putin's electoral victory was surprisingly easy. It was attributed to his firm hand in suppressing the Chechen government that had existed quasi-independently since the end of the first Chechen war in the spring of 1996. Chechen rebels who stood for a radical Islamist agenda and did not agree with their government in Groznyi had invaded Ingushetia in the summer of 1999. Bombs went off in Moscow, Volgodonsk (near Volgograd), and Dagestan in September that were blamed on Chechen terrorists. Russia accused the Chechen government of involvement. This time the Russian army was sent into Chechnya with orders to destroy everything in its path. At the expense of the utter devastation of Grozny, Chechen independence fighters (moderates and Islamists) were dispersed into the Caucasus. Tens of thousands of Russian soldiers, security troops, Chechen warriors, and civilians died in the conflict.

President Putin managed to sign a peace treaty with a faction of Chechens who were willing to give up their anti-Russian stance in exchange for a free hand in their country. Sporadic violence in the Caucasus flared up throughout the 2000s, and occasionally spilled over, as with the hostage taking of theater spectators in Moscow (October 2002) and of schoolchildren at Beslan in North Ossetia (September 2004). Putin's strategy to fight Chechens with Chechens worked nonetheless: Ramzan Kadyrov's (b. 1976) ruthless regime established law and order of a certain kind in Chechnya after 2004. The Putin government preferred not to be reminded of the massive violations of human rights that this involved. Instead, President Putin was hailed in the media as the peacemaker who had finally brought the conflict in the northern Caucasus to an end. He easily won the presidential elections of March 2000.

The Russian public has given Vladimir Putin much of the credit for solving the Chechen problem. He has also been popular because he has been associated with the economic turnaround and a restoration of law and order after the lawless 1990s. Of course, in economic terms, cynics have observed, Putin merely benefited from Russia's good fortune to be a major supplier of scarce raw materials for a world market on which prices for such resources rose sharply in the 1990s and 2000s. The lawlessness, meanwhile, was ended only by co-opting some of the gangsters, who had terrorized each other and the law-abiding citizenry, into the power structure. A few were held responsible because they managed to antagonize Putin. Finally, the Chechen problem seems to have been countered only by having Kadyrov, himself a former rebel against Russian rule, lord it over Chechnya in brutal fashion, while the Russian authorities look the other way. And that Caucasian terrorism is not quite a thing of the past was proven through the Moscow subway bombings of March 2010.

Ultimately, nonetheless, perhaps there is reason to be optimistic, or at least relieved that no major war or full economic collapse followed the events of 1991.[4] But it all depends on one's perspective: in the 1960s (and certainly Khrushchev and Brezhnev shared that belief at the time), it appeared quite likely that the standard of living in the Second World would soon catch up with that in the First World. Indeed, the apartment flats in the *banlieues* of Paris did not look too different from their Soviet or East-Central European counterparts. The Soviet educational system was excellent,[5] the transportation system worked well and was cheap for consumers, and the Soviet state provided universal health care for all. Perhaps the Soviets enjoyed less of a choice in terms of consumer goods, while durable household items were in short supply, but the growing Soviet economy surely would produce more and better goods in the future. And how many television or automobile brands does one really need? Soviet citizens, too, regularly went on vacations, even if mainly within their own vast country.

One feels forced to compare the current living circumstances in the former Soviet Union favorably to life in the independent African countries that replaced the French and British empires in the 1950s and 1960s. But that such a comparison seems valid means at the same time that the former USSR's standard of living has fallen far behind that of much of the West (except in Estonia, Latvia, and Lithuania). Soviet citizens would have been appalled in the 1960s if someone had told them that in a generation the average age at which men died would be sixty. It can be argued that some of the fall in the standard of living was compensated for by the freedom of expression that was the rule in most of the successor states for a while. In almost all of them, however, human rights and freedoms have been violated and curtailed in the last decade on a regular basis without, in fact, triggering too much protest. In Russia, "democratic" and "democracy" became dirty words, for those who supported these concepts appeared to manipulate them in order to line their own pockets.

Several republics, and particularly Russia itself, may have overcome the economic hardship that accompanied the collapse of the Soviet Union. But the Russian recovery has been uneven. Wealth has not been redistributed in any great measure to provide for the weakest in Russian society, nor has capital been sufficiently diversified into a variety of ventures. The Putin government moved to designate all who were older than twelve (and some younger) during the Second World War as veterans worthy of special treatment, benefits, and pensions. Regardless of the question of how deserved such distinction is for every older Russian, it does translate into somewhat more systematic government support for those who in the 1990s and early 2000s often were forced to beg because their pensions were inadequate.

As argued earlier, Russia, Azerbaijan, and some of the Central Asian states survive on the rather volatile revenue from the winning of oil, gas, or other resources, whose deposits ultimately are finite. Only the production of arms seems to be another genuinely thriving branch of the Russian economy. Meanwhile, life expectancy in Russia and the other successor states remains low, especially for men, and the European successor states suffer from a negative population growth. Although this is in no small measure due to poverty, environmental damage, about which nothing is done, is also a cause. In addition, ethnic-nationalist strife has flared up in various regions, most bloodily in Chechnya, only to be ruthlessly suppressed. It is a sign that the Russian Federation, still a country that harbors some one hundred ethnic groups, may yet further dissolve into smaller components through other violent clashes.

PAST AND PRESENT

Meanwhile, the post-Soviet states themselves have not yet developed a "useful past." The 1990s and 2000s have seen the release of many previously secret documents, which have incomparably enriched historians' understanding of the Soviet past. But there is no consensus about the pros and cons of twentieth-century history among academic historians, whether Russian, Ukrainian, Georgian, or Estonian. Non-Russians in the "near abroad" tend to paint the Soviet Union as a Russian colonial empire and read Lenin's or Stalin's excesses (and even the far less violent policies of their successors) as the outcome of a sort of Russian imperialism. Thus, the famine of 1932–1933 becomes a strictly Ukrainian Holomodor, even if hunger killed hundreds of thousands in southern Russia as well (and about one million Kazakhs). People are accustomed to projecting current sentiments into the past in the former Soviet Union and elsewhere. For instance, Ukrainian historians detect a widespread Ukrainian nationalist movement in 1917–1918, whereas in reality Ukrainian nationalists could almost be found only among the very few members of the native intelligentsia in those days. Certainly, there is an apparent tendency to whitewash one's own sins and blame ills committed in the past on others alien to the dominant population's heritage, whether Russian occupiers, Slavic immigrants, or Uzbek settlers.

Ukrainian, Georgian, Azeri, and Kazakh nationalists ignore the widespread support before 1991 for the Soviet regime among their compatriots and the existence of a Communist Party and government apparatus in the non-Russian territories staffed primarily by the local population. Perhaps one could call people such as the Armenian Anastas Mikoian, the Georgians Sergo Ordzhonikidze and Lavrentii Beria, the Ukrainians Nikolai Podgornyi and Petro Shelest (1908–1996), the Kazakh Dinmukhamed Kunaev, and the Latvian Arvid Pelshe traitors to their own countries, but their willing participation in the Soviet project was similar to that of many (and sometimes most) of their compatriots. It bears repeating that the Soviet regime by its policies galvanized the formation of a national identity in the republics in a way that the tsarist regime never did. And this was not merely because of antinationalistic policies but as much, if not more, because of pronationalistic policies, such as the introduction of universal education in the local language.

As is common in other countries, cruder (or distorted) versions of academic history are popular among politicians and the media. The thinking about Stalin among Russian politicians and the public remains tortured. Although documents published on collectivization and the purges leave no doubt about the bloodthirsty massacre Stalin unleashed on his subjects, a surprising number of people maintain that he was instrumental in winning the Second World War and was responsible for a host of other positive accomplishments, such as the (imagined) eradication of crime. This is astounding since other documents show how Stalin stubbornly ignored all the warnings that came to his desk about an impending Nazi attack. As a result, it caught the

Soviet armed forces unawares and enabled the deep penetration of Nazi forces into Soviet territory in 1941 and 1942.

Ultimately, a sort of post-Franco Spanish or post-Hitler West German scenario appears to unfold. Silence and denial will eventually make way for a more dispassionate view of the past. Until the last of its stalwarts are in their dotage, however, the criminal nature of the Soviet regime will be hotly contested. For example, the death sentence handed down in 1954 to former state security chief—and therefore a wholehearted participant in mass murder—Viktor Abakumov (1894–1954) was posthumously reduced to twenty-five years in the 1990s because he had been innocent of some of the crimes of which he had been accused at his trial. That he was responsible for far worse crimes was ignored. This legal precision was perhaps a milestone on the way to establishing a fair and just legal process but otherwise offended people's sense of justice.

For the time being, admitting that one's life has been dedicated to a futile, wrongheaded, and harmful attempt to change human society is probably too much to ask from the survivors. Instead, one witnesses the somewhat shrill attempts to salvage something from the wreckage. Thus we see the lavish celebrations of the undeniably crucial Soviet contribution to the defeat of the Nazis. At the moment that the last Stalinist generation has passed away, when emotions are no longer visceral, historians and possibly the courts can assess blame (despite the apparent destruction of some crucial incriminating files in archives) and face the terrible truth of a country that wasted three-quarters of a century and tens of millions of people's lives for a failed experiment to create utopia.

NOTES

1. Most prominent among Gorbachev's team of advisors were Yakovlev, prime minister Ryzhkov, and foreign minister Eduard Shevardnadze (b. 1927).

2. In addition, many of the reasons behind political and economic developments have remained opaque without the benefit of candid memoirs or broad access to archives.

3. Still in 2012, HIV was spreading in Ukraine at the fastest pace in Europe and in Central Asia at the fastest rate in the world.

4. There was one scary moment in 1998, when the international community tacitly allowed Russia to default on its loans!

5. After 1991, many Western universities benefited from the influx of highly qualified scientists from the former USSR.

FURTHER READING

Translated Primary Sources

Politkovskaya, Anna. *Putin's Russia: Life in a Failing Democracy.* Translated by Arch Tait. New York: Holt, 2007.

———. *A Russian Diary: A Journalist's Final Account of Life, Corruption and Death in Putin's Russia.* Translated by Arch Tait. New York: Random House, 2009.

Putin, Vladimir. *First Person: An Astonishingly Frank Self-Portrait by Russia's President.* Translated by Catherine A. Fitzpatrick. New York: PublicAffairs, 2000.

Yakovlev, Alexander. *A Century of Violence in Soviet Russia.* Translated by Anthony Austin. New Haven, CT: Yale University Press, 2004.

Scholarly Literature

Alexievich, Svetlana. *Voices from Chernobyl: The Oral History of a Nuclear Disaster.* New York: Picador, 2006.

Arbatov, Georgy. *The System: An Insider's Life in Soviet Politics.* New York: Times Books, 1992.

Borogan, Irina, and Andrei Soldatov. *The New Nobility: The Restoration of Russia's Security State and the Enduring Legacy of the KGB.* New York: PublicAffairs, 2010.

Bullough, Oliver. *Let Our Fame Be Great: Journeys among the Defiant Peoples of the Caucasus.* New York: Basic Books, 2010.

Colton, Timothy. *Yeltsin: A Life.* New York: Basic Books, 2008.

Engerman, David. *Know Your Enemy: The Rise and Fall of America's Soviet Experts.* New York: Oxford University Press, 2011.

Gessen, Masha. *The Man without a Face: The Unlikely Rise of Vladimir Putin.* New York: Riverhead Books, 2012.

Gleason, Abbott. *Totalitarianism: The Inner History of the Cold War.* New York: Oxford University Press, 1997.

Khalid, Adeeb. *Islam after Communism.* Berkeley: University of California Press, 2007.

Kotkin, Stephen. *Armageddon Averted: The Soviet Collapse, 1970–2000.* New York: Oxford University Press, 2000.

Ledeneva, Alena. *How Russia Really Works: The Informal Practices That Shaped Post-Soviet Politics and Business.* Ithaca, NY: Cornell University Press, 2006.

Lucas, Edward. *Deception: Spies, Lies and How Russia Dupes the West.* London: Bloomsbury, 2012.

Raleigh, Donald J. *Soviet Baby Boomers: An Oral History of Russia's Cold War Generation.* New York: Oxford University Press, 2011.

Remnick, David. *Lenin's Tomb: The Last Days of the Soviet Empire.* New York: Vintage, 1994.

Roxburgh, Angus. *The Second Russian Revolution.* London: BBC Books, 1992.

Sakharov, Andrei. *From Gorky to Moscow and Beyond.* New York: Knopf, 1990.

Satter, David. *It Was a Long Time Ago, and It Never Happened Anyway: Russia and the Communist Past.* New Haven, CT: Yale University Press, 2011.

Shevardnadze, Eduard. *The Future Belongs to Freedom.* New York: Free Press, 1991.

Todd, Emmanuel. *The Final Fall: An Essay on the Decomposition of the Soviet Sphere.* New York: Karz, 1979.

Volkogonov, Dmitry. *Autopsy for an Empire: The Seven Leaders Who Built the Soviet Regime.* New York: Free Press, 1998.

Waal, Thomas de. *The Caucasus: An Introduction.* New York: Oxford University Press, 2010.

Zyuganov, Gennady. *My Russia: The Political Autobiography of Gennady Zyuganov.* Armonk, NY: M. E. Sharpe, 1997.

WEBSITES

The Caucasus: http://kavkazcenter.com/
The CIA and the former Soviet states: https://www.cia.gov/library/publications/the-world
   -factbook
Iandeks.ru, leading Russian search engine: http://www.yandex.ru
Interfax, Russian news from government's perspective: http://www.interfax.com/
Itar-Tass, main Russian news agency: http://www.itar-tass.com/
RIANovosti, Russian news from government's perspective: http://en.rian.ru/
Russian archives: http://www.iisg.nl/abb
Russian films with English subtitles: http://stagevu.com/chanvideos/101606/Soviet%20
   and%20Russian%20films%20with%20English%20subtitles
Russiapedia (sire of Russian TV): http://russiapedia.rt.com/
Russia Today, government-sponsored English-language TV channel: http://rt.com/on-air

FILMS

Brother. DVD. Directed by Sergei Bodrov. New York: Kino, 1997.
Little Vera. DVD. Directed by Vasilii Pichul. Los Gatos, CA: Netflix, 1988.
The Return. DVD. Directed by Andrei Zvyangintsev. New York: Kino, 2004.
Russian Ark. DVD. Directed by Aleksandr Sokurov. New York: Fox Lorber, 2004.
The Second Circle. DVD. Directed by Aleksandr Sokurov. New York: Kino, 2006.
Tycoon: A New Russian. DVD. Directed by Pavel Longuine. New York: New Yorker Films, 2004.
The Vanished Empire. Directed by Karen Shakhnazarov. New York: Kino, 2008.

Chronology

Tenth century–1598	The Eastern Slavic states of Kievan Rus' and its successors ruled by descendants of the mythical ninth-century tribal chief Riurik (Riurikid dynasty)
988	Conversion of Eastern Slavs (or at least their leaders, led by their grand prince [or grand duke] St. Vladimir)
1054	Schism of Eastern and Western Christian churches; the Eastern Slavs side with Orthodox side against the Western church and the pope.
1237–1238	Beginning of Mongol rule in Eastern Slavic territories (capital at Sarai, located within Volga estuary)
1240s	Novgorod's military commander St. Aleksandr Nevskii halts Swedish and "Teutonic" attempts to conquer Eastern Slavic realm in northeast Rus' but refuses to challenge Mongols. Russian princes are subject to Mongols, who appoint the most loyal prince as Grand Prince of All Rus'.
Fourteenth century	Rise of Lithuania, which conquers much of today's Belarus and Ukraine. Lithuanian-Polish (since 1385) rule separates the Eastern Slavs and leads to development of three separate languages. The head of the Eastern Slavic Orthodox Church moves his see from Kyiv, via Vladimir, to Moscow (1320s). Besides Lithuania and Moscow, the merchant city-state of Novgorod represents a third Eastern Slavic political entity.
1380	Muscovite prince Dmitrii Donskoi defeats Mongol army at the Battle of Kulikovo; while a significant victory for Muscovite self-confidence, it is another century before a Moscow prince proclaims independence from the Mongols.

Fifteenth century	Mongolian unity collapses. After a lengthy succession war, Moscow's prince emerges as the sole contender for the title of Grand Prince of Rus'.
1462–1505	Ivan III (the Great), Grand Prince of Muscovy. Construction of Moscow Kremlin begins. In 1472, Ivan marries niece of last Byzantine emperor (Zoe or Sophia Paleologos). Novgorod is subjugated. Beginning of long-term conflict with Poland-Lithuania (lasts until 1667). In 1480, after "Standing at the Ugra," Ivan III renounces Mongol rule.
1505–1533	Vasilii III. Growing contacts with Europe: first famous Western account of Muscovy (by Sigismund von Herberstein, Imperial ambassador). Vasilii attempts to conquer Tatar (Mongolian) khanates of Kazan and Astrakhan. Wars with Poland-Lithuania.
1533 (1547)– 1584	Ivan IV the Terrible. After a promising first decade (1547–1557), reign becomes steadily more irrational. Introduces first musketeer corps in army, reforms canonical law in church as well as the state's law code, and conquers Kazan (1553) and Astrakhan (1556). Arrival of English merchants in Moscow (Richard Chancellor, 1555). Livonian War (1558–1583). In 1564, after "resigning," Ivan organizes a blood purge, executed by *oprichnina*, culminating in the firing of Novgorod (1570). Moscow's environs pillaged by Crimean Tatars (1571). Meanwhile, economic crisis (misharvests, plague, and war combined) begins.
ca. 1550– ca. 1700	"Mini Ice Age": cooling off of temperature across Europe and Asia.
1580s–1590s	Decrees are issued prohibiting peasants from leaving their landlords even after acquitting themselves of all labor and rent obligations owed to their lord. Period of blight, poor harvests, and starvation.
1583	Yermak Timofeevich and Cossacks cross Ural Mountains and establish Russian bridgehead in Siberia.
1584–1598	Fyodor I Ivanovich, last of the Riurikids, rules. His main advisor is his brother-in-law Boris Godunov.
1589	Establishment of Russian patriarchy (first patriarch: Iov)
1591	Death of ten-year-old Dmitrii, son of Ivan IV, at Uglich; Prince Vasilii Shuiskii's investigative commission concludes that there was no foul play involved in the boy's death.
1596	Union of Brest, "reuniting" Ukrainian Orthodox Church with Catholicism; pope is recognized as head of this church. This creates Uniates (Ukrainian or Greek Catholics), who are especially encountered in western Ukraine. Many Orthodox believers do not follow their priests and higher clergy in making this switch.

1598	Godunov elected tsar by Assembly of the Land (Zemskii Sobor)
1601–1603	Series of misharvests leads to massive famine.
1603–1613	Time of Troubles (Smuta)
1605	Death of Boris Godunov; the succession of his young son Fyodor II is contested; several high boyars decide to support the first false Dmitrii (likely one Grigorii Otrep'ev), who has led an invasion army into Muscovy from Poland.
1606	Dmitrii is overthrown and succeeded by Vasilii Shuiskii (r. 1606–1610).
1606–1607	Rebellion of downtrodden (slaves and serfs) led by Ivan Bolotnikov
1607	Bolotnikov's forces surrender near Tula. First news about another false Dmitrii ("The Thief of Tushino").
1608	The second false Dmitrii camps out at Tushino with a motley crew of supporters, including Cossacks, Polish nobles, and Russian servitors. Dmitrii is recognized as tsar in many parts of central Russia.
1609	Shuiskii concludes a pact with Sweden to aid his fight against the Tushino Thief. Polish troops invade Muscovy.
1610	Thief of Tushino flees before troops loyal to Shuiskii. Poles move up to Moscow. Boyars depose Shuiskii and invite the Polish crown prince Wladyslaw to become tsar on the condition that he convert to Orthodoxy. Poles enter Moscow on invitation of boyar regents.
1611	Beginning of "liberation movement" at Riazan (headed by Prince Prokofii Liapunov). Its inspiration are letters sent to Orthodox believers from occupied Moscow by Patriarch Germogen. Internal conflict between various factions causes its collapse. At Nizhnii Novgorod, a more successful popular militia is organized by the meat trader Kuz'ma Minin.
1612	Popular militia moves from Nizhnii to Iaroslavl', and then to Moscow. There it manages to beat back a Polish force sent to assist the Polish garrison in Moscow. The Poles surrender. Death of Patriarch Germogen.
1613	Assembly of the Land elects sixteen-year-old Mikhail Romanov tsar (r. 1613–1645).
1617	Peace with Sweden (Treaty of Stolbovo)
1619	Truce of Deulino with Poland; Filaret (F. N. Romanov), the tsar's father, released from Polish captivity and elected patriarch.
1632	Andries Denijszoon Vinius (1605–ca. 1658) founds ironworks at Tula, which will produce cannon and cannonballs as well as other weapons.
1632–1634	Smolensk War with Poland

1637	Don Cossacks capture Azov.
1637 or 1639	Cossacks (led by Semyon Dezhnyov) reach Pacific.
1642	Assembly of the Land refuses Azov.
1645	Death of Mikhail; his successor is Aleksei (b.1629, r. 1645–1676).
1647	First secular book printed in Russia; it is a guide for army drill.
1648	Moscow revolt (provoked by taxation). Khmelnitskii's Cossacks rise against Poles. Semyon Dezhnyov explores Bering Straits.
1649	Assembly of the Land, attended by more than three hundred representatives (no one represents serfs), ratifies law code (Ulozhenie). Serfdom universal. Beheading of English king Charles I causes Aleksei to banish trade with English merchants at Arkhangel'sk.
1650	Revolts in Pskov and Novgorod. Yerofei Khabarov (1603–ca. 1671) navigates the river Amur.
1652	Western Europeans forced to live in segregated suburb near Moscow (*nemetskaia sloboda*).
1652–1658 (–1667)	Nikon, patriarch. Reforms of Russian Orthodox rituals.
1654	Treaty of Pereiaslav, formally making Aleksei ruler of most of Ukraine (instead of the Polish king)
1654–1667	Thirteen Years' War with Poland-Lithuania
1656–1661	War with Sweden (after armistice in 1658, ended by Peace of Kardis in 1661)
1659–1677	The Croat Juraj Krizanic (ca. 1618–1683) active in Russia; he is a sort of forerunner of the Slavophiles.
1662	Copper riot against debased coinage in Moscow
1664	Postal system established, providing fast relay of messages and mail to and from West. The government official Grigorii Kotoshikhin escapes to Sweden and writes a treatise about Russia.
1666–1667	Church synod deposes Patriarch Nikon but accepts his reforms of Russian Orthodox ritual; beginning of church schism (Avvakum and "Old Believers" [*Raskolniki*] separate).
1666–1671	Cossack revolts in Don area and along lower reaches of Volga; in 1670–1671, led by Stepan (Stenka) Razin.
1667	Treaty of Andrusovo with Poland. Eastern Ukraine and Kyiv officially recognized as Russian by Poles. Foreign trade statute increases fees of commodity trade conducted by Westerners with Muscovy. Trade agreement with Iranian Armenians in an attempt to capture more of the silk trade from Iran.
1667–1668	Building of Tsar Aleksei's wooden palace at Kolomenskoe near Moscow
1667–1670	Dutch shipbuilders build ships for the tsar to convoy silk transports across Caspian Sea.

1668–1676	Old Believers of monastery on Solovetskii Island in revolt against tsar
1672	First play performed in Russia before the tsar, directed by Johann Gregory, a German-Lutheran pastor residing in the sloboda.
1672–1681	First war with Ottoman Turkey
1676–1682	Rule of Fyodor III
1682	System of genealogical precedence (*mestnichestvo*) abolished. Avvakum is burned at the stake as heretic. Bloody reckoning in May with Naryshkin faction (supporters of Aleksei's second wife Natalia and her son Peter) by Miloslavskii faction in name of Tsar Ivan V.
1682–1689	Regency of Sofia Alekseevna for her brother Ivan and half brother Peter
1682–1696	Formal co-rule by Ivan V and Peter I (b. 1672)
1683	Beginnings of Slavonic-Greek-Latin Academy, first institution of higher learning in Russia. Turkish siege of Habsburg Vienna.
1686	Polish-Russian alliance
1687	First campaign led by Vasilii Golitsyn toward Crimea
1689	Treaty of Nerchinsk with Qing China. Second campaign commanded by Golitsyn toward Crimea.
1693	Completion of Church of the Intercession at Fili, prime example of architecture of "Moscow Baroque"
1696	Capture of Azov by Peter's army and river fleet
1697–1698	Grand Embassy of Peter to Western Europe; Peter learns to build ships on wharves of Dutch East India Company in Amsterdam. Many Western Europeans are recruited to work in Russia as craftsmen, ship's officers, and military officers.
1697–1718	Rule of Charles XII as king of Sweden
1698	Peter forces his first wife to become a nun.
1700–1721	Great Northern War (primarily, Russia versus Sweden): on Russian side are Saxony, Poland, and Denmark; some Cossacks, Polish magnates, as well as Ottoman Turks, support Charles XII.
1700	Swedes defeat Russians at Narva. Death of last Russian patriarch before 1917.
1703	St. Petersburg is founded on what still is officially Swedish territory.
1703–1709	Building of canal to link Volga with waterways draining into Baltic Sea at St. Petersburg
1706–1707	Cossack rebellion around Volga mouth (led by Fyodor Bulavin)
1709	Battle of Poltava. Peter defeats Charles and his Cossack allies.
1711	Creation of Senate to replace Boyar Duma; this is both a rubber-stamp advisory council and the highest judicial court. Battle of Pruth. Turks defeat Russians, and Peter barely escapes with his life.

1712	Peter marries Catherine (Skavronskaia), his second wedding.
1714	First Russian naval victory over Swedish fleet at Hangö
1717	Peter replaces traditional government departments with ministries (*kollegiia*).
1718	Poll tax introduced to replace household and land taxes. Death under torture of Peter's only son Aleksei in St. Petersburg.
1719	Creation of fifty provinces as territorial administrative divisions (and earlier territorial reform had occurred in 1708)
1720–1721	Municipal reform
1721	Treaty of Nystadt yields Russia large stretch of Baltic coastline, including territory on which St. Petersburg has been built. Abolition of patriarchy; it is replaced by Holy Synod, led by lay Oberprokuror (the first is Peter's "ideologist," Feofan Prokopovich).
1722	Introduction of Table of Ranks for all military and civil servitors of the tsar. Peter abolishes hereditary succession.
1722–1723	Invasion by Peter of Iran (territory relinquished in 1732)
1725	Opening of Academy of Sciences. Russia has approximately thirteen million inhabitants.
1725–1727	Rule of Catherine I, Peter's second wife. Key courtier is Aleksandr Menshikov.
1725–1730	First Kamchatka expedition, led by Vitus Bering
1727–1730	Rule of Peter II, a mere boy, grandson of Peter the Great. Menshikov's influence is replaced by that of the Golitsyn and Dolgorukii families.
1730	Anna Ivanovna, Duchess of Courland, succeeds. She is a daughter of Peter the Great's half brother, Ivan V. By calling on middling nobility, she outmaneuvers attempts by grandees (organized in Supreme Privy Council) to limit her power.
1730–1740	Anna Ivanovna, tsaritsa of Russia
1735–1739	War with Turkey that yields Russia Azov but otherwise preserves status quo; around same time Kazakhs recognize Russia's suzerainty for the first time.
1740–1741	Brief "rule" by Ivan VI
1741–1761(2)	Reign of Elizabeth (Elizaveta Petrovna), daughter of Peter the Great
1755	Moscow University founded (among its founders is "Russia's first scientist," Mikhail Lomonosov)
1756–1763	Seven Years' War: Russia allied with Austria, Sweden, Saxony, and France against Prussia and England
1759	Battle of Kunersdorf: Russo-Austrian victory over Frederick the Great's army
1760	Russian occupation of Berlin

1762	Peter III succeeds and concludes peace with Prussia. Peter issues manifesto on freedom of nobility from obligatory state service. Peter is deposed after half a year in a coup staged by the Imperial Guards; his wife Catherine succeeds.
1762–1796	Catherine II the Great's rule
1767–1768	Meetings of the Legislative Commission, convened to discuss Catherine's Instructions (*Nakaz*). No laws are introduced as a result of its deliberations.
1768–1774	War with Turkey: northern shore of Black Sea and Crimea occupied by Russian armies
1769–1770	First Russian magazine published, edited by Nikolai Novikov
1772	First Polish Partition
1773–1775	Pugachev's rebellion spreads along the Volga.
1775	Provincial (territorial administrative) reform. End of autonomy of Ukrainian Cossacks (and of most of the other Cossacks).
1783	Official annexation of Crimea; (part of) Georgia places itself under Russian protection.
1785	Charter of the Nobility issued
1787–1791	War with Turkey
1789	Outbreak of French Revolution
1790	Aleksandr Radishchev's *Journey from St. Petersburg to Moscow* is finished but before publication confiscated; its author, who condemns serfdom, is sent to Siberia.
1791	Polish rising
1792	Arrest of Novikov
1793	Second Polish Partition
1793–1856	N. Lobachevskii, world-renowned mathematician
1795	Third Polish Partition. Poland-Lithuania disappears altogether.
1796	On Catherine's death, her son Paul succeeds. Russia has thirty-six million inhabitants, 3.5 times as many as in 1678, according to estimates; 53 percent are Russian speakers, 22 percent Ukrainians, 8 percent Belarusyn; most (three-fourths of the population) are Orthodox Christians. Paul succeeds Catherine.
1798–1799	Russian armies (some commanded by Aleksandr Suvorov) campaign against France in Western Europe (Italy, Switzerland, and Holland).
1799	Napoleon First Consul
1799–1837	Aleksandr Pushkin
1801	Paul murdered
1801–1825	Aleksandr I
1803	Decree on Free Cultivators, intended as first step toward serfdom's abolition
1804	Napoleon proclaims himself emperor.

1805	Battle of Trafalgar
1807	Peace of Tilsit
1809	Finland placed under Russian rule
1809–1852	Nikolai Gogol
1812	French invasion; Moscow occupied (Kutuzov commands Russian side); Speranskii dismissed
1813	Battle of Nations at Leipzig
1814	Russians in Paris
1814–1815	Congress of Vienna; Holy Alliance formed
1814–1841	Mikhail Lermontov
1815	Battle of Waterloo
1818–1883	Ivan Turgenev
1820	Beginning of Greek uprising against Ottoman Turks; unrest elsewhere in Europe
1821–1881	Fyodor Dostoyevsky
1825	Decembrist Uprising
1825–1855	Nicholas I
1828–1829	Russo-Turkish War; Greece independent in 1829
1828–1910	Lev N. Tolstoi
1830–1831	Cholera epidemic. Polish Rebellion.
ca. 1830–1861	Caucasian resistance to Russian rule (Imam Shamil)
1832	Speranskii completes law codification.
1834–1907	Dmitrii Mendeleev, creator of periodic table in chemistry
1836	Glinka's opera *A Life for the Tsar* premieres. Publication of Pyotr Chaadaev's letter, which argues that Russia had never contributed anything positive to world civilization.
1838–1848	"Marvelous Decade": birth of intelligentsia (Westernizers and Slavophiles)
1842–1924	Prince Pyotr Kropotkin, anarchist
1846	Founding of Cyril and Methodius Society in Kyiv (first organization of Ukrainian nationalists, who count Taras Shevchenko among their number)
1848	Revolutions across Europe; Marx and Engels publish *Communist Manifesto*.
1849	Russian army suppresses Hungarian revolt on behalf of Habsburg emperor Franz Josef (r. 1848–1916). Arrest of Petrashevtsy Circle (including Dostoyevsky, who is pardoned just before he is to be executed by firing squad).
1849–1936	Ivan Pavlov, physiologist and behavioral psychologist
1851	Opening of railroad between Moscow and St. Petersburg. Russia has approximately sixty million inhabitants.
1853–1856	Crimean War
1855–1881	Aleksandr II

1857	Aleksandr Herzen and Nikolai Ogaryov begin publishing *The Bell* (*Kolokol'*) in London.
1858	Ivan Goncharov (1812–1891) publishes *Oblomov*.
1858–1860	Further Russian expansion in the Far East at the expense of China
1860–1904	Anton Chekhov
1860s–1870s	Wanderers (Il'ia Repin, Vasilii Surikov, et al.) painting society
1861	Serfdom abolished; Russia has about eight hundred thousand industrial workers and a total population of about seventy-three million.
1862	Chernyshevsky publishes *What Is to Be Done?*
1863–1864	Polish Rebellion
1864	*Zemstva* introduced in European Russia. Reform of judicial system.
1865	Tashkent conquered
1866	Karakozov's attempt on Aleksandr II's life
1866–1880	Dostoyevsky publishes his four great novels (*Crime and Punishment, The Idiot, The Brothers Karamazov*, and *The Devils*).
1867	Marx publishes first part of *Capital*. Sale of Russian Alaska to United States.
1869	Tolstoi's *War and Peace* published. Nikolai Danilevskii publishes Pan-Slav manifesto *Russia and Europe*.
1870	Municipal councils introduced
1870–1924	V. I. Ul'ianov (Lenin)
1870s	The Mighty Five in music (Balakirev, Mussorgsky, Cui, Rimsky-Korsakov, and Borodin) as well as heyday of composer Pyotr I. Tchaikovsky.
1871	Paris Commune; proclamation of Imperial Germany at Versailles
1872	The anarchist Mikhail Bakunin (1814–1876) expelled from First International by the Marxists
1874	Army reform, introducing the draft and reducing time spent in active service for recruits. Going to the People movement (*khozhdenie v narod*).
1875	Revolts against Turkish rule erupt in Bosnia.
1876	Bulgaria and Serbia revolt against Turks. Formation of Land and Freedom (Zeml'ia i Vol'ia). Creation of Turkestan province.
1877–1878	Russo-Turkish War
1878	Treaty of San Stefano and Congress of Berlin. Vera Zasulich (1849–1919) wounds St. Petersburg governor Trepov with a gunshot.
1879	People's Will separates from Land and Freedom.
1880s	First Russian Marxist group forms in exile (led by G. V. Plekhanov, Pavel B. Akselrod, and Vera Zasulich).
1881	Aleksandr II assassinated. Pogroms break out in Pale of Settlement to which Jewish residence in Russia is restricted.

1881–1894	Aleksandr III; he imposes from the outset martial law, which will continue until 1917 (but for a brief period in 1905 and 1906).
1887	Execution of Aleksandr Ul'ianov, Lenin's older brother
1891	Massive famine
1891–1892	Franco-Russian military alliance concluded
1891–1903	Construction of Transsiberian Railroad
1892–1903	Sergei Vitte, minister of finance, overseeing wave of industrialization
1894–1895	Sino-Japanese War
1895	Lenin arrested and exiled to Siberia
1897	Census: 125 million inhabitants: 43 percent of population are (Great) Russians, 17 percent Ukrainians, 4 percent Belarusyn, 3 percent Tatars, 3 percent Kazakhs; 21 percent of population is literate, but this percentage is to double over next two decades.
1898	First Congress of (Marxist) Russian Social Democratic Labor (Workers') Party (RSDLP) in Minsk; almost all delegates are arrested. Foundation of Moscow Art Theatre (led by Konstantin Stanislavsky).
1900	Boxer Rebellion in China
1900–1914	Silver Age of Russian art and literature (Blok, Esenin, Akhmatova, Mayakovsky, Mandelshtam, Pasternak, Bely, Bunin, Diaghilev, Skriabin, Nijinskii, Chaliapin, Rachmaninov, Stravinsky, Prokofiev, Chagall, Kandinsky, Malevich, and Stanislavsky)
1901	Formation of Socialist Revolutionary Party (SR): "Peasant Socialists" following the model of *narodniki* of 1870s
1902	Lenin publishes *What Is to be Done?* Beginning of liberal movement in Russia, leading to Kadet (constitutional democratic) party by 1905.
1903	Second Congress of RSDLP leads to split of Marxists into Bolsheviks (following Lenin) and Mensheviks.
1904–1905	Russo-Japanese War
1905	Bloody Sunday; formation of first *sovety* (soviets or workers' councils); October Manifesto; arrest of Petersburg socialists
1906	Basic Laws promulgated; introduction of Duma (parliament); abolition of compensation payments and encouragement of peasants to set up individual farms
1906–1911	Pyotr Stolypin, prime minister
1907	Anglo-Russian Treaty (whereby British, French, and Russians have become allies)
1908	Bosnian Crisis
1909	*Vekhi* published (articles by Nikolai Berdyayev, Pyotr Struve, et al., critical of the revolutionary movement and the intelligentsia)

1910	Premiere of Stravinsky's *Firebird*
1912	Bloody suppression of strikes in gold mines near Lena River.
1912–1913	Balkan Wars
1913	Premiere of Stravinsky's *Sacre du printemps* (*Rites of Spring*) in Paris, staged by Diaghilev's Ballets Russes; riots break out in the audience
1914–1918	Russia participates in the First World War
1916	Brusilov Offensive
1917	**February:** Tsar deposed
	April: Lenin returns to Russia from Switzerland; proclaims April Theses; main points are "All Power to the Soviets!" and immediate unilateral armistice.
	June: Failed offensive against Central Powers. Lenin: "Soldiers voted with their feet"; massive desertion.
	August: Kornilov "putsch" fails
	October: Bolshevik coup staged in St. Petersburg; its program is for land to the peasants, peace, self-determination for non-Russians, and workers' control over factories.
	October–December: Most Russian soviets declare themselves for the Bolsheviks. Ukraine, meanwhile, separates.
	November: Elections for Constituent Assembly, which is fated to meet for only one day in January 1918; more than half of deputies elected by universal adult franchise are SR; Bolsheviks get 25 percent of votes and seats.
November– February 1918	Negotiations at Brest-Litovsk for a peace with Central Powers.
	December: Formation of Extraordinary Commission for Combat of Counterrevolution, Speculation, and Sabotage (Cheka), under Feliks E. Dzerzhinskii
1918	**February:** Unwilling at first to submit to onerous terms imposed by Central Powers, the Council of People's Commissars (PC or Sovnarkom) withdraws from negotiations at Brest-Litovsk. But the Central Powers meet no resistance advancing farther into Russian territory. Capital moved to Moscow.
	March: Peace of Brest-Litovsk; crucial vote to ratify peace treaty in Central Committee of Bolshevik Party: 7 for, 4 against, and 4 abstain. Lenin's point (to preserve the Communist triumph at the cost of huge slices of territory) prevails. Left SR leaves government out of protest to peace treaty. Ukraine and Finland officially independent; Baltic and Poland in German hands; concessions to Turkey in Caucasus region.

June: Assassination of German ambassador Mirbach; Left SR and Bolsheviks fight each other in Moscow. This is usually seen as beginning of Civil War, although already Cossacks in south (Don), led by generals Pyotr Krasnov and Lavr Kornilov, are in revolt against Bolsheviks.

June–1920 Spring: Various anti-Bolshevik movements emerge across Russia. At first, a moderate SR-led government leads them, but gradually former tsarist generals lead the anti-"Red" forces in the Civil War. Red Army ultimately manages to defeat the various White armies in the Baltic (commanded by Iudenich), Siberia (Kol'chak), and on the southern front (Denikin and Vrangel). Massive bloodshed, famine, and epidemics; millions perish.

1919   Formation of Central Committee's Politburo (PB), Orgburo, and Secretariat. Foundation of Comintern.

1920–1921 Polish-Russian war. Polish attempt to annex Ukraine fails, even though a large slice of Belarus and Ukraine became part of Poland by Treaty of Riga in 1921. Red offensive in Caucasus leads to Communist control over Azerbaijan, Armenia, and Georgia. But Baltic countries, Poland, and Finland preserve independence, while Bessarabia (Moldavia) is annexed by Romania.

1920–1924 Communists establish their rule in Turkestan.

1921   Green (peasant) rebellions (in Tambov and elsewhere) at their height (Red Army brutally suppresses them, using poison gas); Kronstadt Revolt. Tenth Party Congress forbids factions within Communist Party (CP); meanwhile, most non-Communist parties are outlawed (SR and Mensheviks survive until 1924). New Economic Policy (NEP) introduced (measure of free market).

1922   Treaty of Rapallo with Germany (secret clause about military cooperation). Lenin falls sick. Stalin elected CP's general secretary.

1922–1924 Formation of Union of Socialist Soviet Republics (USSR), of which main architect is Stalin. Its constituent republics will be "national in form, socialist in content."

1923–1924 Trotsky is sidetracked by Senioren Konvent (rest of PB) in Lenin's absence.

1924   **January:** Death of Lenin

1924–1925 Stalin outmaneuvers Zinov'ev (boss of Leningrad and Comintern) and Kamenev (Moscow party boss).

1926–1927 Futile attempts by "United Opposition" to oust the adherents of Stalin and the "General Line"

1927–1928	Development of concept for a planned economy by economic organizations, including State Planning Bureau Gosplan. Late 1928 is the official date of the beginning of the First Five Year Plan of economic development, but at first hesitation exists about its precise direction and the pace of the transformation envisioned.
1928	Shakhty trial of "wreckers" of industry
1928–1929	Stalin defeats "Right Deviationists," led by Bukharin (head of Comintern after Zinov'ev), Rykov (chairman of Council of PC), Tomskii (chief of trade unions), and Uglanov (Moscow boss after Kamenev). The alleged "Rightists" caution against quick-fire industrialization and collectivization of agriculture.
1929	Trotsky exiled abroad
	Summer: Within a brief period, the Five Year Plan's targets for economic growth suddenly are maximized by a quantum leap, both in terms of industrial and agricultural production.
Fall–March 1930	Stalin's "Great Turn" implemented: In agriculture, collectivization causes utter chaos at first. The Bolshevik antireligious offensive takes on renewed momentum. Kulaks and priests are exiled to remote areas, while their numbers swell quickly in the mushrooming labor camp system in the remote and inhospitable regions of the USSR, creating the Gulag Archipelago. In industry, an enormous wave of building of new factories overtakes the country, but the plans often outstrip industrial capacity.
1930	**March:** Stalin calls for temporary halt to collectivization in *Pravda*, the national newspaper; nevertheless, as a result of the imposition of enormous taxes on individual homesteads, most Soviet peasants join a collective farm by 1935.
	April: Vladimir Mayakovsky, the foremost Soviet poet, commits suicide.
	November–December: Trial of Industrial Party. Problems in industry because of impossibly ambitious construction, and production targets are blamed on sabotage.
1931	**March:** Trial of Mensheviks
1932	**April:** Beginning of move toward the creation of Writers' Union and socialist realism (Central Committee issues resolution to this effect).
	Summer: Illegal circulation in party circles of "Riutin Platform," criticizing Stalin and Great Turn.
	August: Law of 7 August 1932 (draconian penalties for gleaning of grain and other "theft of socialist property")
	November: Suicide of Nadezhda Allilueva, Stalin's wife
	December: Introduction of internal passports

1932–1933	Ukrainian, southern Russian, and Kazakh famine
1933	**January:** Adolf Hitler appointed Chancellor of Germany
	May: Opening of White Sea Canal, built by *zeks* (*zakliuchennye,* or labor camp inmates)
1933–1937	Second Five Year Plan
1934	**January:** Seventeenth Party Congress
	August: First Congress of Soviet writers (They are called "engineers of the human soul.")
	December: Murder of Sergei M. Kirov
1935	"Cleansing" of Moscow and Leningrad of antisocial elements, including sundry counterrevolutionaries, former White Guardists, Trotskyites, Mensheviks, and so forth. Completion of first line of Moscow Metro.
	February: Standard kolkhoz charter introduced
1936	**August:** Show trial against Zinov'ev and Kamenev
	December: Introduction of new constitution, Stalin Constitution, allegedly "most democratic in the world"
1936–1939	Spanish Civil War
1937	**January:** Trial of Piatakov and Radek
	February–March: Central Committee Plenary Session: Bukharin and Rykov arrested; Stalin calls for selection of substitutes for party cadres at all levels.
	June: Alleged plot uncovered in Red Army; ringleaders arrested (Tukhachevskii and Gamarnik; Iakir commits suicide)
	July–August: Arrest quotas of enemies of the people dispatched by People's Commissar Yezhov to local People's Commissariat of Internal Affairs (NKVD) departments in provinces and republics.
(From August)	Deportations of Soviet Koreans from Far East to Inner Asia begin.
1937–1938	Stalin and his closest lieutenants, such as Molotov, Kliment Voroshilov, Andrei Zhdanov, Andrei Andreev, and Lazar Kaganovich, personally sign lists of thousands of names of people to be executed; in 1937–1938, almost 1,700,000 people are arrested, and more than 690,000 are executed, usually by firing squad. Almost all others end up in labor camps.
1938– **June 1941**	Third Five Year Plan
1938	**March:** Trial of Bukharin and Rykov; Anschluss of Austria with Germany
	September: Czechoslovakia dismantled by Hitler, Benito Mussolini, Neville Chamberlain, and Edouard Daladier at Munich.

Fall: Publication of *Short Course*: this Soviet history according to Stalin becomes bible of the Soviet Communist Party and international Communist movement.

November: Stalin and Molotov order end to mass arrests; fall of NKVD commissar Yezhov.

1938–1939 Armed clashes between Japanese and Soviet forces in Far East

1939 **Spring:** Eighteenth Party Congress

August: Soviet-Nazi Non-Aggression Pact (secret clause dividing up East-Central Europe)

1 September: German invasion of Poland begins.

17 September: Soviet forces occupy eastern Poland.

1939–1940 Winter War with Finland

1940 **April:** Massacre by NKVD of interned Polish officers in Katyn forest and elsewhere

May: Hitler begins campaign against Low Countries and France.

June: Beginning of Soviet annexation of Baltic states; after that, Lithuanian Socialist Soviet Republic (SSR), Latvian SSR, and Estonian SSR are officially established.

August: Annexation of Romanian Bessarabia: Moldavian SSR founded

August–September: Battle of Britain

November: PC of foreign affairs Molotov visits Berlin.

1941 **April:** Nazis invade Yugoslavia and Greece; Japanese foreign minister Matsuoka meets Stalin in Moscow.

22 June: Operation Barbarossa: invasion of USSR by German-led coalition

Early July: Stalin makes first public speech on radio, addressing Soviet peoples as "brothers and sisters." Meanwhile, so-called Volga Germans (Soviet citizens living in eastern Ukraine and along Volga) are beginning to be deported; operation is not completed before arrival of Germans in area.

August: Collapse of Soviet Western Front (facing German Center); suicide of its commander Dmitrii Pavlov

September: Kyiv in Nazi hands; murder of Kyiv Jewish community (more than thirty thousand people) at Babi Yar; Leningrad encircled. German SS Einsatzgruppen behind front round up Jews elsewhere, organizing mass executions.

October: In middle of month, panic in Moscow as rumors spread that Germans are poised to take city; much of government and party administration moved to Kuibyshev (Samara) on Volga. Stalin stays in the capital.

November: Beginning of Leningrad famine, perhaps costing one million people their lives

7 November: Stalin commemorates October Revolution by speech in subway station, broadcasted by radio.

December: First successful Soviet counteroffensive, aided by support from Siberian divisions; Germans are forced back from approaches before Moscow; Kalinin (Tver') and Rostov-on-Don recaptured. Pearl Harbor. Hitler declares war on United States.

1942 **January:** Wannsee Conference: in Berlin, Nazi Sicherheitsdienst boss Reinhard Heydrich and others decide on the contours of Final Solution, the execution of all European Jews; key manager of project is Adolf Eichmann.

February: Soviet offensive grinds to halt; gradually Second Shock Army (commanded by Andrei Vlasov) is encircled by German-Finnish forces near Moscow–Leningrad railroad (Volkhov River); Vlasov surrenders and becomes most notorious Russian Nazi collaborator.

Spring: Renewed German offensive, in southeastern direction: Rostov again in German hands; Germans by summer capture northern Caucasus (all the way to Makhachkala in Dagestan).

September: Germans begin maneuver to capture Stalingrad, key city on the Volga.

November: Beginning of Soviet counteroffensive at Stalingrad: Paulus's Sixth Army encircled.

1943 **February:** German surrender at Stalingrad.

1943 **June–Fall 1944:** Deportations of alleged traitor nations: Kalmyks, Chechens, Balkars, Ingush, and Crimean Tatars

1943 **July–August:** German attempt to retake initiative at tank battle at Kursk; Soviet victory

November: Teheran Conference of "Big Three"

1944 **January:** Leningrad's encirclement definitively broken

6 June: D-Day

August: Red Army completes the liberation of Ukraine. Romania switches sides. Finland also leaves war. In Ukraine, partisans continue to fight for independence of Ukraine (Banderaites).

September–October: Warsaw Rising of Polish resistance (Armija Krajowa); Soviets await events on other side of Vistula River.

October: Churchill in Moscow: "percentage agreement"

1945 **January:** Auschwitz liberated by Red Army

February: Yalta Conference of Big Three

April: Hitler commits suicide. Founding of United Nations in San Francisco.

May: Victory in Europe (9 May for Soviets). Prague liberated with help of Russian Liberation Army under Vlasov; Vlasov captured by Soviet troops. Americans end Lend-Lease.

July: Potsdam Conference of Big Three; successful test of A-bomb in United States. Soviet Union begins in earnest development of its own nuclear bomb.

6 August: Atomic bomb dropped on Hiroshima

9 August: Nagasaki bomb; Soviet Union declares war on Japan.

2 September: Surrender of Japan

1945–1946 Nuremberg Trials of Nazi war criminals

1946–1950 Fourth Five Year Plan

1946 **March:** Churchill's speech at Fulton, Missouri ("Iron Curtain has descended on Europe"). People's Commissariats renamed ministries.

Summer: Beginning of cultural campaigns against writers, composers, philosophers, and scientists (sometimes called Zhdanovshchina)

1946 Fall– Famine in the USSR
Winter 1947

1947 **Winter:** Announcement of "Truman Doctrine" ("Containment" of Soviet expansion is U.S. goal.)

June: Marshall Plan announced

September: Formation of Cominform

1948 **February:** Communist takeover in Czechoslovakia; murder of Jewish actor Solomon Mikhoels in Minsk

May: Israel founded; Soviet-Yugoslav rift public

August: Death of Andrei Zhdanov

Fall: Beginning of anti-Semitic campaigns in press (against "rootless cosmopolitans")

1948 June– Berlin Blockade
May 1949

1949–1950 Leningrad Affair

1949 **August:** Successful test of Soviet A-bomb

October: Chinese Communists under Mao in control of Chinese mainland

1950 Beginning of Korean War

1952 **Fall:** Nineteenth Party Congress, first in thirteen years

1953 Announcement of Doctor's Plot, which supposedly has succeeded in eliminating Moscow boss Aleksandr Shcherbakov (d. 1945) and Zhdanov

March: Death of Stalin. First amnesty begins to empty out the Gulag Archipelago.

June: Arrest of Beria

Summer: Increase in prices state pays for collective farm goods

1954 Beginning of Virgin Lands project. Formation of KGB (Committee for State Security) to replace MGB (Ministry of State Security).

1955	Malenkov resigns as prime minister (Bulganin succeeds). Withdrawal of Allies from Austria.
1956	**February:** Twentieth Party Congress; Khrushchev's Secret Speech. Beginning in earnest of "Thaw."
	Fall: Unrest in Poland. Hungarian Uprising. Suez Crisis.
1957	Fall of Anti-Party Group (Malenkov, Molotov, Kaganovich, Pervukhin, Saburov, and Shepilov). Independence of Ghana. Publication abroad of *Doctor Zhivago*; its author, Boris Pasternak, is victim of merciless campaign in press and by the Writers' Union. Launch of *Sputnik* satellite.
1958	Dismissal of Bulganin and Zhukov
1959	Twenty-First Party Congress: it announces that communism will be reached in twenty years. Khrushchev visits United States. Vice president Nixon visits USSR. Castro takes power in Cuba.
1960	Congo Crisis
1961	Twenty-Second Party Congress. Definitive Sino-Soviet split. New round of denunciations of Stalin. Stalin's body removed from mausoleum on Red Square. Yuri Gagarin first man in space. Building of Berlin Wall.
1962	**October:** Cuba Crisis. *Novyi Mir* publishes *One Day in the Life of Ivan Denisovich* by Aleksandr Solzhenitsyn, a former political convict.
1964	**October:** Khrushchev ousted, accused of "voluntarism and subjectivism." Brezhnev becomes the leading figure by 1966.
1965	**September:** Arrest of writers Aleksandr Sinyavsky and Yuli Daniel
	December: Demonstration on Moscow's Pushkin Square against persecution of writers and others critical of Soviet regime
1966	**February:** Trial of Sinyavsky and Daniel
1967	**May:** Yuri Andropov becomes KGB chair, succeeding Aleksandr Shelepin.
1968	**April:** First appearance of *Chronicle of Current Events*, an underground (*samizdat*) magazine
	June: Appearance in *samizdat* of Andrei D. Sakharov's *Reflections on Progress, Peaceful Coexistence and Intellectual Freedom*
	August: Invasion by Warsaw Pact armies of Czechoslovakia
1969	Solzhenitsyn removed from Writers' Union; General Grigorenko, an advocate for the Crimean Tatars, arrested and placed in a psychiatric clinic
	March: Border clashes between Soviet and Chinese armies at Ussuri River in Eastern Siberia

1970	**June:** First Soviet-Jewish emigrants leave for Israel.
	August: Official treaty with Western Germany (recognizing territorial changes in Europe at end of Second World War)
	Fall: Solzhenitsyn receives Nobel Prize in Literature
1971	**September:** Death of Khrushchev
1972	**February:** President Nixon in China
	May: Signing of SALT-1 (arms limitations treaty) with United States (President Nixon in Moscow). Vladimir Bukovskii sentenced for exposing abuse of political prisoners in psychiatric clinics.
1973	**April:** Andropov and Foreign Minister Gromyko enter Politburo
1974	Solzhenitsyn forcibly exiled (flown to West Germany)
1975	**April:** Fall of Saigon to North Vietnam and Vietcong (Soviet allies)
	August: Helsinki Accords signed
	December: Sakharov receives Nobel Peace Prize
1975–1977	Pol Pot's murderous communist regime in Cambodia
1976	**May:** First Helsinki Committees organized by Soviet dissidents to monitor compliance with terms of Helsinki Accords on human rights.
1977	Podgornyi succeeded as president of Soviet Union by Leonid Brezhnev (who remains general secretary, his most important post)
	October: New Soviet Constitution comes into force (replacing 1936 Constitution).
1978	**April:** Communists take power in Afghanistan.
1979	Signing of SALT-2 (never ratified by United States). Gorbachev (Central Committee secretary for agriculture since 1978) candidate member of party's Politburo.
	December: Soviet invasion of Afghanistan
1980	Sakharov banished to city of Gor'kii (Nizhnii Novgorod)
	Summer: Olympic Games in Moscow: Western boycott
	August: Formation of free trade union Solidarity in Poland
1981	**December:** State of emergency declared in Poland (Solidarity prohibited)
1982	**November:** Death of Brezhnev; Yuri Andropov becomes general secretary of Communist Party
1984	**February:** Death of Andropov; Konstantin Chernenko succeeds as general secretary
1985	**March:** Death of Chernenko; Mikhail Gorbachev succeeds as general secretary

1986   **April:** Chernobyl disaster

October: Gorbachev meets President Ronald Reagan at Reykjavík; Reagan fails to take Gorbachev's far-reaching proposals for arms limitations seriously.

November: Limited private economic enterprise permitted

December: Riots in Kazakh capital of Almaty, first stirrings of growing nationalism across USSR.

1987   **October:** Boris Yeltsin, Moscow's party boss, resigns from Politburo.

1988   Early in year, Pasternak's *Doctor Zhivago* and Vasily Grossman's *Life and Fate* published

February: Armenian-Azeri clashes (at Sumgait and in Nagornyi Karabakh)

April: Formation of first "popular front" in Estonia

1989   **February:** Soviet troops complete withdrawal from Afghanistan.

March: Elections staged for new Congress of People's Deputies; a number of non-Communist candidates (including Sakharov) elected; debates in next few months broadcast on television

April: Suppression of nationalist demonstration in Georgia

July: Coal miners' strike begins in Siberian Kuzbass.

August: *Novyi Mir* begins serialized publication of *Gulag Archipelago* by Solzhenitsyn.

September: Formation of non-Communist government in Poland

November: Fall of Berlin Wall

December: Communist Party chief Nicolae Ceausescu ousted and murdered in Romania. Death of Andrei Sakharov.

1990   **March:** Constitutional clause assigning leading role to Communist Party removed from Soviet Constitution. Lithuania officially announces secession from USSR. Islam Karimov (b. 1938) becomes president of the Uzbek Socialist Soviet Republic and remains in office after Uzbekistan becomes independent in late 1991.

June: Abolition of all media censorship

October: Reunification of Germany

1991   **Winter:** Attempt to suppress independence movements in Baltic countries; some bloodshed, but ultimately Moscow retreats.

April: In Kazakhstan, Nursultan Nazarbaev (b. 1940), a Soviet Politburo member, becomes president.

June: In Russian Republic, general elections return Boris Yeltsin as president.

June–July: Warsaw Pact dissolved

July: START (arms reduction treaty) signed by Gorbachev

August: Failed coup by Emergency Committee. Communist Party of the Soviet Union prohibited by Soviet parliament.

	November: Dzhokhar Dudaev (1944–1996) declares Chechnya sovereign.

November: Dzhokhar Dudaev (1944–1996) declares Chechnya sovereign.

December: Dissolution of Soviet Union

1992 **January:** Radical introduction of free-market economy in Russia: enormous rise in prices. Privatization law dismantles state ownership of large parts of economy.

March: Chechnya declares independence.

March–June: Clashes in Moldova between Moldovan government and Russo-Ukrainian government residing in Tiraspol, which proclaims independence from Moldova

1993 **September–October:** Standoff between Russian parliament and Yeltsin; Yeltsin suppresses rising and rules by decree.

December: New constitution introduced in Russia and new parliament (Duma) elected

1994 Aliaksandr Lukashenka (b. 1954) elected president of Belarus. His rule becomes a dictatorship in the course of the following years.

December: Russian army invades Chechnya.

1996 Yeltsin reelected as Russian president

August: Cease-fire in Chechnya; Russian armed forces withdraw.

1998 Russian government defaults on debts.

1999 **October:** New Russian invasion of Chechnya

December: Yeltsin resigns as president; Vladimir Putin, caretaker president.

2000 **March:** Putin elected president of Russia

August: The submarine *Kursk* sinks.

2002 **October:** Nord Ost hostage crisis in Moscow

2003 Ilham Aliyev (b. 1961) succeeds his deceased father as president of Azerbaijan.

2004 Putin reelected as Russian president. Mikheil Saakashvili (b. 1967) elected Georgian president.

September: Beslan school hostage crisis; hundreds of children murdered by Chechen rebels

2005 Viktor Yushchenko (b. 1954) elected Ukrainian president. Height of "Orange Revolution" promising greater democratization.

2006 Murder of the journalist Anna Politkovskaia (1958–2006) in Moscow

2008 Dmitrii Medvedev (b. 1965) elected Russian president; Putin becomes prime minister.

2010 Viktor Yanukovych (b. 1950) elected Ukrainian president

March: Bombs explode in Moscow Metro.

2011 Former Ukrainian prime minister Yulia Timoshenko (b. 1960) sentenced to jail for corruption

2012 Vladimir Putin elected Russian president; Medvedev becomes prime minister again.

Index

money, use of, 12, 15, 23, 110–11, 157, 212. *See also* ration cards
Mongolians (Mongols). *See* Tatars
Mongolia (region/state), 95, 163, 188, 242, 246
monks, 1, 6, 11, 19, *25*, 35, 113, 132, 157, 168, 178, 273
Mons, Anna, 41
Montenegro, 161
Montesquieu, 56
Mordvinians (Mordvi), 102, 165
Moscow occupation (1610–1612), 1, 299
Moscow rising of 1682, 10, 12, 42, 301
Moscow (Show) Trials, 220–22, 309–10
Moscow (State) University (Lomonosov University), 49, 52, 302
Mozambique, 257
mujahedin, 267
Munich Conference, 233–34
municipal duma, 113
Muravyov-Amurskii, Nikolai, 143
Muscovy, 1, 6–7, 9, 11, 18, 20, 27, 41, 44, 48, 187, 298–300. *See also* Russia
musketeers. *See* strel'tsy
Muslims. *See* Islam
Mussolini, Benito, 310
Mussorgsky, Modest, 121, 305
mustard gas. *See* gassing of civilians
muzhik (peasant), 158

Nabokov, Vladimir, 22
Nagasaki, 242
Nagornyi Karabakh, 282, 316
Nagy, Imre, 262
Nakaz. See Instruction
Naples, 79
Napoleon I Bonaparte, Emperor of the French, 60, 73, 75–78, 81, 95, 106, 136, 237, 303
Napoleon III, Emperor of the French, 107–8
Narodnaia vol'ia. See People's Will
Narodniki. See Populists
Naryshkin clan, 10, 36, 301
Naryshkina, Natalia, 10, 18, 301
nationalism, 9, 55, 87, 89, 115–16, 133–34, 139, 143, 161, 163, 167, 170, 188,

196, 198, 273, 275–76, 283–84, 306, 316
Nautilus Pompilius, xi
naval stores, 12
navy, 10, 34, 37, 39, 47, 72, 88, 108, 145, 152, 162–63, 301
Nazarbaev, Nursultan, 316
Nazis, 59, 78, 82, 131, 136, 147, 203, 216–17, 223, 226, 231–32, 234–41, 245, 262, 293–94, 311–13
"near abroad," 286–87, 293
nemetskaia sloboda. See foreigners' suburb
Netherlands, 89. *See also* Dutch
networks. *See* kinship networks; patronage
New Commercial Code (1667), 10, 300
New Economic Policy (NEP), 195, 206, 308
New England, 145
New Russia, 57, 59–61
Newton, Isaac, 37, 39
Nicholas I, Tsar of Russia, 69, 75, 80, 83–85, 87–89, 100, 105–8, 114, 117–18, 121, 133, 151, 170, 304
Nicholas II, Tsar of Russia, 69, 105, 111, 123, 127, 132–33, 135–36, 139, 148, 151–54, 157, 162–63, 176, 178, 191
Nightingale, Florence, 109
Nijinskii, Vachlav, 168, 306
Nikon, Patriarch, 17, 24, 26, 300
1984 (Orwell novel), 228
1905 Revolution, 105, 111, 123, 128, 131–32, 135–36, 139, 147–48, 150–54, 157–59, 163, 165–66, 306
1917 Revolution, x, 20, 22, 39, 70–71, 82, 89, 106, 122, 136, 139, 147–48, 150, 157, 159, 167–68, 178–89, 192–94, 196, 204, 210, 220, 223, 226–27, 242, 245, 256, 293, 301, 307
Nixon, Richard, 314–15
Niyazov, Saparmurat, 286
Nizhnii Novgorod, 18, 214, 281, 315
NKVD. *See* People's Commissariat of Internal Affairs
Nobel brothers, 97
Nobel Prize, 170, 268, 315
nobility, 6, 8–9, 11–13, 18–19, 22–23, 26, 34–37, 42, 47, 49–51, 56–58, 61, 68,

About the Author

Kees Boterbloem is the author of four books and numerous articles on Russian and Soviet history. He has taught Russian and European history at universities in Canada and the United States. Currently, he is professor of history at the University of South Florida in Tampa, where he is the coordinator of Russian, East European, and Eurasian studies. He has been the chief editor of *The Historian* since 2008.